The Plunder of Jewish Property during the Holocaust

The Plunder of Jewish Property during the Holocaust

Confronting European History

Edited by

Avi Beker

with a Foreword by Edgar Bronfman and Israel Singer

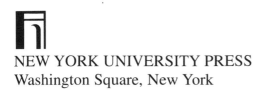

NEW YORK UNIVERSITY PRESS
Washington Square, New York

Editorial matter, selection and Chapters 1 and 8 © Avi Beker 2001
Foreword, Chapters 2–7 and 9–20 © Palgrave Publishers Ltd 2001

First published in the U.S.A. in 2001 by
NEW YORK UNIVERSITY PRESS
Washington Square
New York, N.Y. 10003

This book is printed on paper suitable for recycling and
made from fully managed and sustained forest sources.

Library of Congress Cataloging-in-Publication Data
The plunder of Jewish property during the Holocaust / [edited by] Avi Beker.
p. cm.
Includes bibliographical references (p.) and index.
ISBN 0–8147–9867–5 (alk. paper)
1. World War, 1939–1945—Confiscations and contributions—Europe. 2. Jewish
property—Europe—History—20th century. 3. Banks and banking—Corrupt
practices—Switzerland—History—20th century. 4. Jews—Europe—Claims. 5.
Holocaust, Jewish (1939–1945) 6. Restitution and indemnification claims
(1933–)—Germany. I. Beker, Avi.
D810.C8 .P58 2000
940.53'18—dc21   00–055041

This book is printed on paper suitable for recycling and
made from fully managed and sustained forest sources.

10   9   8   7   6   5   4   3   2   1
10   09   08   07   06   05   04   03   02   01

Printed and bound in Great Britain by
Antony Rowe Ltd, Chippenham, Wiltshire

Contents

List of Plates		vii
Foreword by Edgar M. Bronfman and Israel Singer		viii
List of Abbreviations		ix
Notes on the Contributors		x

1 Introduction: Unmasking National Myths – Europeans
Challenge their History 1
Avi Beker

2 The Inexplicable Behaviour of States 33
Stuart E. Eizenstat

3 Estimating Jewish Wealth 48
Sidney Jay Zabludoff

4 The Holocaust, 'Thefticide' and Restitution:
a Legal Perspective 66
Irwin Cotler

5 Defrosting History: the Restitution of Jewish Property in
Eastern Europe 83
Laurence Weinbaum

6 A Commentary on Europe's Looted Gold, 1938–45 111
Arthur L. Smith Jr

7 German Assets in Switzerland at the End of the
Second World War 125
Sidney Jay Zabludoff

8 Why was Switzerland Singled Out? A Case of Belated Justice 142
Avi Beker

9 The Great Culture Robbery: the Plunder of Jewish-Owned
Art 164
Hector Feliciano

10 France and the Burdens of Vichy 177
Shmuel Trigano

11 Quiet Collusion: Sweden's Financial Links to Nazi
 Germany 193
 Sven Fredrik Hedin and **Göran Elgemyr**

12 'Ex-Enemy Jews': the Fate of the Assets of Holocaust
 Victims and Survivors in Britain 209
 Stephen Ward and **Ian Locke**

13 The Norwegian Moral and Material Statement:
 White Paper No. 82 to the Storting 227
 Norwegian Ministry of Justice

14 Austria: the Evasion of Responsibility 244
 Itamar Levine

15 Franco's Spain: Willing, Unwanted Ally of Nazi Germany 258
 Cesar Vidal

16 Portugal's Double Game: Between the Nazis and the Allies 269
 Antonio Luca

17 The Robbery of Dutch Jews and Postwar Restitution 282
 Gerard Aalders

18 Italy: Aspects of the Unbeautiful Life 297
 Furio Moroni

19 The Vatican and the Shoah: Unanswered Questions of
 Material Complicity 313
 Arieh Doobov

20 Confiscation in Belgium: Diamonds and other Jewish
 Properties 327
 Viviane Teitelbaum-Hirsch

Index 342

List of Plates

1 General Dwight D. Eisenhower inspecting art looted by the Nazis
2 Antisemitic poster protesting at the restitution of Jewish property in Poland
3 A political cartoon targeting Switzerland's dealing with Nazi Germany
4 Newspaper headlines reveal the Swiss story
5 Hitler and Goering examine plundered works of art
6 Goering at the Jeu de Paume in Paris admiring a confiscated painting
7 Egon Schiele's *Portrait of Wally* (1912)
8 Entrance to a Dutch swimming pool which Jews were forbidden to enter
9 Jewellers removing precious stones from gold jewellery discovered in a German cache

Foreword

When the World Jewish Congress prompted the international Jewish community to establish the World Jewish Restitution Organization (WJRO) in 1992, with the support of the Israeli government, we set out to write an overlooked chapter of the Holocaust – to attain the historic justice the Jewish people had been denied for half a century. As a result of international pressure and with the courage of a new generation, numerous countries were forced to confront the dark periods of their history. This painful process of moral and material restitution represents a defining moment in the history of the Holocaust.

The world media has played a central role in generating international pressure on governments and financial institutions. It was clear to the media that at stake were not merely financial claims, but rather a moral struggle for historic justice. The core of that struggle was to uncover the truth about the conduct of those states and nations that had collaborated with the Nazis and stood by while Jews were being killed and plundered.

The Nazis and their accomplices intended to liquidate the Jewish people by a brutal process of de-legitimization and de-humanization. They stripped the Jews of their rights, their assets, and of their very status as human beings. Therefore, the struggle to regain Jewish property is first and foremost a quest to restore human dignity and basic human rights, including the right of repossession, to the Jewish people – to the heirs of the six million Jews who perished in the Holocaust.

Edgar M. Bronfman
President
World Jewish Congress

Israel Singer
Secretary General
World Jewish Congress

List of Abbreviations

AAMD	Association of Art Museum Directors
AIVG	Aide aux Israelites victimes de la Guerre
AJB	Association des Juifs en Belgique
BIS	Bank for International Settlements
CDJ	Comité de Défense des Juifs (Jewish Defence Committee)
CDJC	Contemporary Jewish Documentation Centre
CEDA	Confederacion Espanola Derechos Autonomos
CGQJ	Commissariat Général aux Questions Juives
CRIF	Conseil representatif des israélites français
ERR	Einsatzstab Reichsleiters Rosenberg
IARA	Inter-Allied Reparations Agency
IMT	International Military Tribunal
IRO	International Refugee Organization
LiRo	Lippmann, Rosenthal & Co. (Bank)
MNR	Musées nationaux de la récupération
MV	*Militarverwaltung*
NATO	North Atlantic Treaty Organization
NSDAP	National Sozialistische Deutsche Arbeiter Partei – the Nazi Party
OKH	Oberkommando des Heeres
OSS	Office of Strategic Services
RSI	Italian Socialist Republic
SCAP	Service de Contrôle des Administrateurs Provisoires
SD	Sicherheitsdienst
SEC	Section d'Enquête et de Contrôle
SNB	Swiss National Bank
TGC	Tripartite Gold Commission
UBS	Union Bank of Switzerland
UN	United Nations
VVRA	Vermögensoerwaltung and Rententanstalt
WJC	World Jewish Congress
WJRO	World Jewish Restitution Organization

Notes on the Contributors

Gerard Aalders works in the Institute for War Documentation in Amsterdam, and is preparing two volumes on the looting of Jewish property in the Netherlands during the Second World War. He wrote *The Art of Cloaking Ownership* (with co-author Cees Wiebers) on Swedish neutrality and economic collaboration with Nazi Germany.

Avi Beker is the Director of International Affairs of the World Jewish Congress in Israel, and head of its Research Institute in Jerusalem. He received his PhD in international relations at the Graduate Center of the City University of New York and served on the Israeli delegation to the United Nations. He has written and edited several books and many articles on Jewish affairs and international security, including *The United Nations and Israel*, and (together with Yaacov R'oi) *Jewish Culture and Identity in the Soviet Union*.

Irwin Cotler is a Member of Parliament in Canada and Professor of International Law at McGill University, Montreal, and has been an international human rights activist for many years.

Arieh Doobov is Associate Editor of *Dialogues* (a newsletter on interfaith affairs) and has been a contributing editor for *Jewish Communities of the World* (1996). He holds degrees from the Hebrew University of Jerusalem and Sydney University.

Stuart E. Eizenstat was the US Under-Secretary of State for Economic, Business and Agricultural Affairs. He coordinated two studies of the American Administration on holocaust-era assets and served as a special envoy of President Clinton for the restitution of Holocaust assets (1996–9).

Göran Elgemyr studied history, political science and literature, and has written books on the history of broadcasting and television in Sweden, and on Sweden's domestic and foreign policies during the Second World War. He has produced numerous documentaries and other programmes for the Swedish Broadcasting System, and is a member of the Executive Board on Interdisciplinary Media Research.

Hector Feliciano is Editor-in-Chief of World Media Network and a former cultural writer for the *Washington Post* and the *Los Angeles Times*. He wrote *The Lost Museum: The Nazi Conspiracy to Steal the World's Greatest Works of Art* (1997).

Sven Fredrik Hedin served in the Swedish Diplomatic Service for over forty years. Having entered the Foreign Ministry in 1949, Ambassador Hedin has served as Deputy Permanent Representative to the United Nations, and as Ambassador to Tanzania, Argentina, Portugal and Italy. Ambassador Hedin was Marshal of the Diplomatic Corps in Stockholm between 1990 and 1993.

Itamar Levine has been deputy editor of the Israeli financial daily *Globes* since April 1996. He has covered extensively the process of restitution in Europe and has written *The Last Deposit*, about the theft of Jewish assets by Swiss financial institutions (1998).

Ian Locke is a historian and graduate of Oxford University.

Antonio Luca is a historian at the Institute of Contemporary History of the New University of Lisbon. His book *Nazi Gold and Portugal* was published in 1997.

Furio Moroni is an Italian journalist serving the Italian News Agency in different Middle Eastern posts. He wrote a book on Nazi plunder entitled *Oro di Razza: La grande rapina Nazista Ai danni delle Banche Europee & delle vittime dell Olocausto* (1997).

Arthur L. Smith, Jr is Professor of History at California State University, Los Angeles. He has published *Hitler's Gold: The Story of the Nazi War Loot* (1989).

Viviane Teitelbaum-Hirsch is a journalist and historian from Belgium. She is the author of *Comptes d'une Mort Annoncee* (1997), a book on the despoliation of the Jews of Belgium.

Shmuel Trigano is Professor at the University of Nanterre and Director of the Alliance Israelite Universelle's College of Jewish Studies, a Fellow of the Jerusalem Center for Public Affairs and heads its Paris bureau. Most recently he has edited *La Société juive traverse l'histoire*, a four-volume encyclopaedic work on Jewish society and civilization, and *Letters to a Perplexed Jew: From Exile to Dispersal?* (1996).

Cesar Vidal is Professor of History at the University of Saragosa, Spain. He has published a number of books on Franco's relation to the Nazi regime and the Holocaust.

Stephen Ward is a historian, journalist and Associate Director of the Holocaust Educational Trust, London.

Laurence Weinbaum is Senior Research and Editorial Officer of the Institute of the World Jewish Congress and a history lecturer at the College of Judaea and Samaria. He is the author of a book on relations between the New Zionist Organization (Zionist Revisionists) and the Polish Government in the 1930s, entitled *A Marriage of Convenience*, and the co-author of a forthcoming book about German Jews in Israel.

Sidney Jay Zabludoff is an expert on illicit financial flows and finding hidden assets. He has worked for the Central Intelligence Agency, the Financial Crimes Enforcement Network (FinCen) and the White House.

1
Introduction: Unmasking National Myths – Europeans Challenge their History

Avi Beker

According to all indications, history was to record 1995 as the year which witnessed the final lowering of the curtains on the horrors of the Second World War. Throughout Europe, from East to West, ceremonies were held to commemorate the 50th anniversary of the end of the war and the defeat of Nazi Germany. Leaders of European states made public declarations denouncing antisemitism and Nazi crimes and some also admitted the guilt of their countrymen and took responsibility for their collaboration with the Nazis.[1] In Germany, some intellectuals and politicians stated that the time had come for 'normalization' of the national memory and an end to the confrontation with the past.[2]

History, however, did not adapt itself to this plan. Guilt-filled ghosts from the past emerged to haunt Europe. In Germany, for example, Daniel Goldhagen's book *Hitler's Willing Executioners*, dealing with what he described as the Germans' violent and 'eliminationist' antisemitism, opened a Pandora's box and led to a heated public debate both in the country and abroad.[3] In other European countries, public discussion centred on the issue of responsibility and the obligation to return Jewish property which had been looted or confiscated during the Holocaust. During 1996 and 1997, particularly in democracies of Western Europe, the question of Jewish property unexpectedly surfaced from the past and opened a hitherto almost unknown dimension to the discussion of the Shoah.

It was precisely matters such as real estate ownership and responsibility for exploitation of victims as they were led to the death camps, which touched a raw nerve within European society. As long as the issues at hand were war crimes – the horrors of the Holocaust and the gas chambers – many Europeans reacted with shock, distress and contempt, alluding to human rights, principles and moral lessons to be

1

drawn. To a certain extent, it was convenient to focus the discussion on the guilt of Nazi Germany and of Hitler and his accomplices, who wrought destruction on many nations and a Holocaust on the Jews of Europe. Claims on property highlight the fact that Germany's horrible schemes could not have been realized without the complicity of those who took advantage of the distress of their Jewish neighbours. Each nation created for itself a collective national memory, in which historical facts were mingled with myths, half-truths and self-denial. The Austrians, for example, cultivated the myth of the Anschluss, conveniently portraying themselves as being the first victims of Nazi Germany's expansionism; the French invented an artificial distinction between Vichy – the French regime which collaborated with the German – and the 'authentic' French people and the Republic, whilst the Swiss were even more successful in convincing themselves and others of their honourable model of 'neutrality'.

Restitution and reparations from Germany

During the Second World War, the World Jewish Congress (WJC) began preparing the ground for property claims and restitution to be submitted by the end of the war. During the early 1940s, Dr Nehemiah Robinson of the WJC's Institute for Jewish Affairs commenced research aimed at estimating the extent of Jewish material losses and began to formulate Jewish claims for restitution. Robinson also put forward the idea of establishing the 'Jewish Rehabilitation Agency' for the purpose of presenting these claims in the negotiations with the relevant countries.[4] Even in the context of preparations for the termination of the war, it was difficult to fathom the scope of the tragedy. By the end of the war, it became evident that one-third of the Jewish people – the overwhelming majority of European Jewry – had been destroyed.

Many of the survivors lived in conditions of poverty in displaced persons camps, awaiting emigration to Palestine and elsewhere. At the same time, the major effort of the Jewish people had shifted to the Zionist enterprise, the establishment of the Jewish State in Eretz Israel. The WJC, too, changed its order of priorities. During the war and immediately thereafter, the major effort was gradually focused on the goals of saving Jews and on the struggle to secure Jewish sovereignty.[5] In the realm of restitution, Jewish diplomacy was concentrated on the negotiations for compensation and indemnification from Germany.[6]

With the horrors of the Holocaust still fresh in the individual and national consciousness, contacts with Germany after the war turned out to be a difficult and complicated diplomatic endeavour. Through its research institute, the WJC prepared the Jewish claims. Under the leadership of the WJC President, Dr Nahum Goldmann,, the head of the WJC's European Executive, Dr Noah Baro, commenced talks with the West German government, in close cooperation with the Israeli government. Goldmann, who had established a special relationship with Chancellor Konrad Adenauer, succeeded in breaking though the deadlocks which arose during the negotiations. In October 1951, Goldmann founded the Conference of Material Claims Against Germany to represent Jewish organizations and communities. This umbrella organization symbolized the unity of the Jewish people and their support for Israeli claims. Until the September 1952 signing of the Luxembourg Indemnification Agreement between the Federal Republic of Germany and the State of Israel, Prime Minister David Ben-Gurion faced threats and abuse from within the Knesset and outside. Goldmann, who had acted as a lightning rod, deflecting criticism away from the Israeli government, suffered a barrage of shameful abuse which threatened his public position. The opposition to the agreements, led by the leader of the Herut Party, Menahem Begin, rejected any contact with Germany, decried the transfer of 'blood money' and warned that the agreement would rehabilitate Germany.

From the Israeli perspective, the reparations from Germany were a much-needed form of assistance which helped Israel extricate itself from its very difficult economic circumstances. Hundreds of millions of dollars flowed into the country, greatly alleviating the economic and social burdens of the state, which had barely been able to deal with the task of absorbing hundreds of thousands of new and generally destitute immigrants. German restitution funds were used to develop the Israeli economic infrastructure, particularly in industry, the electrical system and the transportation network. Individual indemnities supplied foreign currency and contributed to the economic well-being of the thousands of survivors and victims of the Nazi regime. As for Ben-Gurion, the process of negotiations with Germany entailed an outstanding partnership with the Diaspora. As head of the executive authority of a sovereign state and as a proud Zionist, he felt that this was a unique challenge. In 1952 Ben-Gurion wrote to Nahum Goldmann:

It is highly significant that representatives of a world Jewish organization took part in securing recognition of the claim to reparation. . . . For the first time in the history of a people that has been persecuted, oppressed, plundered and despoiled for hundreds of years in the countries of 'Europe', a persecutor and despoiler has been obliged to return parts of the spoils . . . This is beyond question the outcome of the re-birth of the State of Israel . . .[7]

The Cold War and containment

When dealing with the issue of Jewish property claims in the 1990s, the question is often raised: why did the Jews wait fifty years to pursue this matter? The answer is complex and multifaceted: postwar Jewish power-lessness, the focus on restitution from Germany; lack of documentation until the opening of archives (some made accessible only after fifty years), the collapse of Communism in Eastern Europe; the rise of a new generation which was ready to reexamine the wrongs and evils perpetrated by their parents; and, finally, the lack of public awareness of the seemingly 'minor' aspects of the Holocaust, which included the despoliation of Jewish property.

Surrounding the issue of property and bank accounts there was a conspiracy of silence, the origins of which were psychological, and a selective national memory. International Cold War strategic considerations affected it and, in the background, sheer greed. It is evident that in the countries of Eastern Europe Jewish claims fell victim to the hostile environment of totalitarian regimes. If it was impossible to discuss the basic human rights of all citizens, then putting forward property claims was obviously out of the question. Moreover, in many places in Eastern Europe returning Holocaust survivors were met with hostility and even pogroms.[8]

In order to understand what occurred in Western Europe, one must examine the overall changes in the international system at the time. Even before the end of the war, the United States, together with Britain, and more gradually with France, began to brace themselves for conflict with the Soviet Union. As early as 1945 British Prime Minister Winston Churchill had coined the phrase 'Iron Curtain' and incorporated it in his famous speech in Fulton, Missouri, after leaving office. In 1947, after the Communist takeover of Eastern Europe, the US announced the Truman Doctrine, which elaborated its policy of containment in order to counter the Soviet threat to Europe and the rest of the world. The Marshall Plan was created to deal with the transfer of assets for the economic rehabilitation of democracies in Europe. It had a critical impact on the nature of the relations which evolved between the US and its allies in Europe. In some measure, this development explains the conciliatory attitude of the Americans, even to the extent of disregarding the European failure to comply with economic commitments laid out in the peace agreements.

According to Adam Ulam, a prominent historian of the Cold War, the Marshall Plan was designed to heal the European economy by providing for its immediate needs and enlarging its industrial foundation and agricultural infrastructure. This plan involved a sacrifice on the part of the American taxpayer, and was seen as an investment in the future well-being of Europe. Thus, Ulam explains, economics and defence were interwoven: on the one hand, an appeal to the generosity of the American public and on the other, the politics of fear. President Truman presented his policy unequivocally: if we do not supply massive economic aid, countries such as France and Italy will fall into Communist hands.[9]

The Marshall Plan was a dramatic shift from the American tradition of isolation and non-interference in Europe (extreme events such as world wars notwithstanding), and therefore necessitated political persuasion, public relations and educational campaigns in order to influence senators and congressmen who were hesitant in supporting the process.

The 1947 Paris Convention on Restitution gave the United States sound legal grounds for retrieving property plundered by the Nazis. However, implementation of this would have run against the basic principle of the Marshall Plan, namely that American philanthropy would strengthen the European democracies. In such an environment, the Americans and, in particular, their defence establishment and intelligence agencies contributed to the conspiracy of silence. As new documents from the Allies' archives have revealed, it is evident that intelligence agencies of both the US and Britain knew of Jewish deposits and other Jewish property, in addition to the plundered gold which was transferred to Switzerland, Sweden and other neutral countries.

The general atmosphere which the Americans cultivated in the battle against Communism served as fertile ground for the development of myths in countries of Western Europe. Many Europeans were reluctant to confront the dark chapters of their collaboration with the Nazis, which also included robbery of Jewish property and even assistance in the killing. France, as defined by American interests, won recognition as a major power with the right of veto in the United Nations Security Council and as a central force in Europe against the danger of a resurgence of Germany. Belgium, the Netherlands (which took over Jewish property), as well as other countries, became partners in the Western defence treaty of NATO, established in 1949 as an American national interest of the highest degree. With regard to Austria, which received independence in 1955, the political irony was even greater, and, under Western inspiration, additional credence to the myth of Austria as Germany's 'first victim' was given. Switzerland too, benefited from the void created by the Cold War and from the international oversight of its debts to the three powers, thus succeeding in covering up the greatest bank robbery in history.

The issue of restitution of Jewish property was addressed by Jewish organizations even before the end of the war. According to Robinson's research, by 1944 the need to carry out a worldwide effort to identify heirs to the plundered property was already being discussed, especially in the face of 'so many deaths of Jews'.[10] Goldmann, too, was obliged to address the issue in November 1944, at the emergency meeting of the WJC held in Atlantic City. He stated then that it was clear that 'most owners of the robbed Jewish property were no longer among the living', and therefore claimed:

> It seems only fair, then, to ask that the Jewish people as a whole should be considered the heir of those of its members who have been murdered. It would be adding mockery to tragedy if non-Jewish individuals, communities and governments would fall heir to property which, if not legally then certainly from a moral point of view, belongs to the Jewish community and must be used to rebuild Jewish life and to provide for the future of the Jewish People.[11]

However, despite the fact that groundwork for proving Jewish claims had already been initiated and discussions held in Jewish circles, the forces of the international system were stronger. In the face of enormous pressure of security interests and *realpolitik*, it was difficult to expect those weak and diminished Jewish communities, which had risen from the ashes of the Holocaust, to stand up and demand their basic rights. At the same time, the organized Jewish world was occupied with the ultimate political effort of creating the State of Israel. After the rebirth of the Jewish state, and its development, in part with the assistance of indemnities from Germany, international diplomacy was required to ensure Israel's economic prosperity, secure its physical safety in the face of a hostile Arab world, and guard its political status in international circles. In the face of the forces of history, the struggle to secure the rights to the stolen Jewish property was postponed.

WJRO activities

It is an historical irony that the battle for the return of Jewish property in Europe focused at first on Eastern Europe, which had broken the chains of Communism. The World Jewish Restitution Organization (WJRO), under the chairmanship of WJC President Edgar Bronfman, was established in 1992 as an umbrella organization encompassing major Jewish bodies, including Holocaust survivors organizations in Israel and around the world, to deal with the restitution of Jewish property.[12] The Communist countries, satellites of Moscow in Europe, had actually frozen history behind the Iron Curtain. Jewish property which had been confiscated by the Nazis, was later turned over to the state authorities which nationalized it in accordance with the Communist ideology. The collapse of Communism signalled a change in East European economies and a desire for a structural and judicial revolution which would create a free market economy. Within this framework, governments began to prepare the necessary legislature adjustments which would clear the path for a gradual transfer of the means of production as well as ownership of capital and property into private hands. The WJRO entered this historic 'window of opportunity' with the mission of clarifying to heads of states and parliaments in Eastern Europe that the Jewish people had claims to part of the property which was now designated for privatization.

According to the charter of the WJRO, the WJC was given the responsibility for contacts with the Jewish communities in Eastern Europe, as well as for conducting negotiations with the governments. In November 1992 a memorandum of understanding was signed between Edgar Bronfman, and the Israel Minister of Finance, Avraham Shochat, in which special emphasis was placed on Israel's role in the process of property restitution. The memorandum stated that 'the State of Israel sees itself as the principle and natural heir to Jewish communal property, as well as heirless private property, together with the local Jewish communities and the Jewish world'.[13] The cooperation and coordination with the Israeli government was reinforced in successive letters by prime ministers Yitzhak Rabin, Shimon Peres and Binyamin Netanyahu.

Eastern Europe

The WJRO, according to its charter, is authorized to deal with communal and heirless private property. However, when negotiating with East European countries, its representatives also strive to secure the rights of individual Jews to restore ownership of private property through customary legal procedures. The WJRO has struggled against discriminative legislation, existent in most countries, in which local citizenship is a prerequisite for privatization claims. The first step in the process involves negotiations with each local Jewish community. Following that, contacts with the state authorities are launched in partnership.

Negotiations on Jewish property in East Europe are difficult and complex. The economic difficulties of the former Communist countries, as well as their political instability, hamper the process. In Poland, for example, five prime ministers have been replaced since the establishment of the WJRO, and this sort of problem quite often necessitates restarting the negotiations from scratch. In addition to the objective problems, governments exploit the natural opposition of the populace to the return of property, which sometimes takes on antisemitic overtones.

From the outset, WJRO leadership was concerned with securing international support for its activities in Eastern Europe. In Washington and in the European capitals, the diplomatic groundwork was laid so that the issue of restitution of Jewish property would be included in the broader realm of the integration of Eastern European countries into various international organizations. These new democracies were eager to create commercial ties (often under privileged conditions) with the West and were interested in joining Western institutions such as the European Union and NATO. On 10 April 1995, the leaders of the Republican majority and the Democratic minority in the US House of Representatives and in the Senate, sent a letter to Secretary of State, Warren Christopher, expressing their support for the claims made by the WJRO. They complained about the discriminatory legislation existing in East Europe pertaining to Jewish property, and insisted that the US make it clear to such countries that their conduct concerning the issue of Jewish property would be seen 'as a test of their respect for basic human rights and the rule of law and could have practical consequences on their relations with our country'. President Bill Clinton, who publicly expressed his support for the activities of WJRO, appointed Ambassador and later Under-Secretary of Commerce, Stuart Eizenstat, as a special emissary for property claims in Eastern and Western Europe. In August 1996, Ambassador Eizenstat testified before the Congress on his mission and contacts on behalf of the American administration to twenty different countries.[14]

Progress in most countries was painfully slow and disappointing. Granted that the economic means of former Communist countries are meagre, very little has been done in the realm of legislation. Heads of the WJRO have made it clear that they do not expect the immediate return of the assets and do not intend to evict present tenants from their apartments, but rather demand the implementation of the moral and judicial principle of recognition of Jewish ownership.

In Hungary there has been a breakthrough in legislation and the Hungarians have acknowledged their obligation according to the Peace Treaty of 1947, to provide reasonable compensation to property owners from the Holocaust period. In July 1996, the Hungarian government reached an agreement with the WJRO concerning the establishment of a joint foundation of $26.5 million, together with the Jewish community, which would oversee the distribution of compensations and restitution of property. This is a limited agreement at present, but the principle of commitment to restitution of property has been recognized.

In the case of Poland, there exists a vast chasm between the declarations and pledges of the government and its deeds. The legislative process is very slow and has been far from satisfactory. In Poland, whole communities were wiped our (about 3 million Jews were murdered by the Nazis); they possessed communal property which is estimated at hundreds of millions of dollars, not to mention private property worth several billions, which only in very rare cases was returned to its owners. In February 1997 the Polish parliament approved a bill on the restitution of property to religious communities. The law, however, is very limited and refers only to active religious communities (tiny remnants numbering some few thousand Jews) and does not deal with private and heirless property or the property of extinct communities. In Romania, Slovakia, the Czech Republic, Ukraine and the Baltic states (the situation in Estonia is somewhat better) only limited progress has been made. The case of Bulgaria is somewhat different, since most Jewish property was returned immediately after the war but then sequestered and returned again after 1989. There are, however, over a hundred buildings in Sofia which were not returned to their Jewish owners.

Efforts made to return property in Eastern Europe have caused a resurgence of antisemitism. In Hungary, Romania and Poland this has found expression in the media and in various publications. Quite often, when meeting with leaders of the WJRO, government representatives have excused the delay in negotiations by claiming that antisemitism could erupt if Jewish property were to be restored. It is interesting to note that certain antisemitic elements in Polish-American circles attempted to hinder the process of property restitution by turning directly to Polish President Alexander Kwasniewski, accusing him of being too 'conciliatory' to the Jewish groups. The Polish President rejected the accusations and argued that there was no place for racial discrimination and hostility towards religious and national minorities.

Fantasy versus reality in the archives

In the course of 1995–7 Western media was flooded with information on stolen Jewish property which had not been returned. The phenomenon itself was amazing: material on confiscation of property, bank deposits and gold transactions, which would usually be suitable for historical journals, found its way onto the front pages of national newspapers, capturing international media interest with extraordinary intensity. It was as if the facts had been revealed for the first time, and material which in the past had been the basis of Hollywood action movies, suddenly appeared to be the historic reality. It became evident, for example, that British author Frederick Forsyth's bestseller, *The Odessa File*, which was also made into a successful movie in the 1970s, contained some authentic material. The plot of *The Odessa File* centres on the postwar secret network of former SS officers using vast sums of gold smuggled out at the end of the war to establish themselves in economic and political positions of power. There were, indeed, persistent rumours about a secret meeting of some industrialists in Strasbourg, then in occupied France, at the end of 1944, when it was clear that Germany's defeat was close. The group met several weeks after the unsuccessful attempt on Hitler's life, to plan the escape of the Nazi elite, to secure their assets and lay the ground for a future 'Fourth Reich'.[15]

Western historians had speculated in the past about whether such an event actually took place but for the most part only Communist historians supported the possibility that it had. Recently uncovered files, in fact, document a meeting in which heads of companies such as Volkswagen and Krupp, as well as an SS general, participated. As a result of the so-called *Odessa* ring in Strasbourg, thousands of Nazis were spirited out of Europe, mostly to Latin America, and hundreds of millions of dollars were transferred to that continent. The Argentinian dictator, Juan Peron, was an enthusiastic partner in this mission and received millions of dollars in profits. According to documents of the American secret service, his wife Evita Person, while on official trips to Europe, secretly travelled to Switzerland in order to make deposits of millions of dollars into her family's private account.

In Sweden, as in Switzerland, there are two categories of property: deposits made by Jews living outside Sweden and transfers of Nazi gold. Documents uncovered reveal that the Swedish government and the heads of the banks knew all through the war that part of the Nazi gold deposits were actually stolen from countries and from individuals, including Jews. The Governor of the Central Bank of Sweden, Ivar Rooth, received information from the Allies concerning the source of the gold, and he conveyed it to ministers in the Swedish government (Dag Hammarskjöld who later became Secretary-General of the UN, served at the time as Director-General of the Swedish Ministry of Finance and was among the addressees). Graver still were the revelations concerning Swedish firms which supplied war materials to the Nazis.[16]

In addition to the myth of Swedish neutrality, which has been put to the test, another fascinating affair involves members of the family of 'Righteous Gentile' Raoul Wallenberg. Once again, the details of this affair had been previously known but little public discussion or investigation was initiated to examine the implications. Raoul Wallenberg, whose mysterious disappearance in a Soviet detention camp has not been solved to this day, saved over 100,000 Jews in Hungary in 1944, endangering himself as well as his diplomatic position. His two uncles, Jacob and Marcus Wallenberg, however, controlled a family business empire which provided vital economic assistance to Nazi Germany. American intelligence files show that the activities of the Wallenberg businesses, which encompassed many areas such as banking, iron mines, communication et cetera, caused great concern in the United States. In February 1945 American Secretary of the Treasury, Henry Morgenthau, wrote that it was imperative to avoid any contact with the Wallenbergs and that they were acting as a cover for sustaining Nazi Germany. Bank Enskilda, owned by the Wallenberg family, dramatically enlarged its capital during the war, raising the question as to whether it also violated the economic and financial boycott which had been imposed on the Nazi regime. An in-depth historic study, conducted by two Dutch researchers, raises the argument that Wallenberg's disappearance was a Soviet reaction to his family's dealings with the Nazis. The book scans the means by which the Wallenberg brothers transferred gold worth millions of dollars, which was taken from Jews and from central banks in occupied Europe.[17]

In Norway, national conscience also awoke after fifty years. Here, too, details were discovered unexpectedly – in this case, by two young Norwegians who had been working quite separately and only later learnt of each other's research. One, Bjarte Bruland, was a student at

Bergen University, who had been greatly influenced by Claude Lanz-man's movie *Shoah* and decided to research this chapter in Norwegian history. He discovered that the physical destruction of 720 Nor-wegian Jews (out of a total of 1800) was accompanied by the expropria-tion of their property. To his surprise, he discovered that this chapter had hardly been studied. As he began his research, delving into recently opened files, Bruland uncovered detailed lists of confiscated property. Bjorn Westlie, a journalist working for the economic paper *Dagens Naer-insliv* also uncovered documents in 1995 pertaining to the economic liquidation of the Jews of Norway and began publishing a series of articles on this issue.

While hundreds of Norwegian Jews were herded to their destruction, the special Board for the Economic Liquidation of the Jews, headed by a Supreme Court Judge and representatives of the pro-Nazi regime of Vidkon Quisling, took control of their property. At the same time that some Norwegians assisted some 1000 Jews in fleeing to neighbouring Sweden, others took over their property. Almost nothing was done to return it to its owners or to their heirs when they returned to their homes after the war. Following revelations made by the WJC to the world media and a special report it published, public pressure on the government in Norway was intensified. Finally, the demands of public opinion and a few members of parliament to 'erase the black blotch' on Norway's past, led to a government decision being taken. In March 1996, the Minister of Justice appointed a committee of experts which included representatives of the Jewish community, among them Bjarte Bruland. In contrast to many countries in Eastern and Western Europe, Norway has moved relatively quickly in dealing with its moral and political commitment to resolve this painful issue.[18]

In Belgium and the Netherlands, too, some Jews were indeed saved, but the majority of them, particularly in Holland, were sent to their death. The story of Anne Frank, the 12-year-old Jewish girl from Amster-dam, who recorded the story of her family hidden in an attic which was transformed into a museum after the war, focused attention on the refuge that the Dutch provided the Jews. Much less wellknown, how-ever, perhaps even deliberately, was the fact that Anne Frank and her family, like the majority of the Dutch Jews, were handed over and sent to the death camps with the active aid of many Dutch people. In the Netherlands, the relative percentage of Jews sent to the death camps was the highest in all Western Europe (almost 90 per cent). They left behind property worth hundreds of millions of dollars which was sequestered and much of which was never returned.[19]

Switzerland's False Neutrality

Early in 1997, a year and a half after the astounding revelations concerning its financial activities during the Second World War, Switzerland has begun to confront its past. The antisemitic language used by former Swiss President Pascal Delamuraz, concerning 'Jewish extortion', at the end of 1996 served to demonstrate all too well the psychological state of mind of the ruling elite in the Swiss establishment. His belated and unconvincing apology initiated, paradoxically, a wave of antisemitism throughout Switzerland. The Jewish community reported a rise in antisemitic incidents and, for the first time, a repelling antisemitic caricature of the *Der Stürmer* type appeared in the Swiss press. Not since the Second World War had such an anti-Jewish expression ('Jewish blackmailers') been made by the leader of a democratic country. French premier Charles de Gaulle's declaration in 1967 about 'arrogant Jews', made in the wake of the Six Day War, was stereotypic and hostile enough, but was made in conjunction with the Arab–Israel conflict.[20]

It took the Swiss judicial system fifty-five years to exonerate Paul Gruninger, the policeman who forged documents in order to assist Jews to enter Switzerland as refugees and thus rescued them from Nazi clutches. Gruninger, who was commander of the border station of the canton of St Gallen, was arrested in 1940 and tried for his 'crimes'. Only in 1995 was his name posthumously cleared. At the beginning of that same year, then Swiss President Kasper Villiger stood before his people and confessed, for the first time, the guilt of the Swiss people in rejecting the Jewish refugees during the war. But, not even in their worst nightmares, did the Swiss imagine that within a few months, a snowball would roll down the Alpine slopes which would trigger an avalanche of criticism on the integrity of the Swiss banking establishment and question the myth of Swiss neutrality. The documents uncovered in the archives, concerning assets belonging to the Jewish victims, as well as the laundering of Nazi loot, will, it is hoped, induce Switzerland and other countries to rewrite their history of the Second World War period and to pay close attention to their subsequent actions.

The thousands of documents which have been unearthed and published in the media shed new light on the course of the war and the strength of Germany. It may be argued, as did the weekly *Newsweek* in an article based on archival material, that were it not for the financial services rendered by Switzerland, the Nazis would have collapsed for lack of funds. According to Swiss historian Jacques Picard, between 1940 and 1945 all production and commerce in Switzerland was enlisted to the German war effort. What the Germans confiscated from banks, shops and private collections of art and jewellery, found its way primarily to Switzerland. According to a Belgium document, for example, all the polished diamonds from some 1200 diamond-cutting firms in Antwerp (most of which were of Jewish ownership), were sold by the Nazis in 1940 to Switzerland and Spain and from there were also exported to the United States. According to documents of the American delegation in Bern, some $160 million worth of gold confiscated in the Netherlands, including 39 tons taken mostly from Jews, was transferred to Switzerland. But, in accordance with the Washington 1946 Agreement, the Swiss paid for only $58 million worth of stolen property, a pittance compared to what was transferred to them, but enough to induce the Allies to sign away any other claims.[21]

In his meticulous historical research, Arthur Smith outlines the tortuous path of the Nazi gold to the central bank of Germany and from there to the vaults of the Swiss banks, despite sharp criticism on the part of the Allies. Part of the gold extracted from the Jewish victims, including bags of tooth-caps labelled 'Lublin' 'Auschwitz'; this gold was smelted in Germany and sent on to Switzerland. After the war, the Allies set up the Tripartite Commission which included the US, Britain and France, and which was empowered to secure the return of assets to the plundered central banks and to other parties, but its mission came to a halt during the Cold War and not all the gold was returned. The Commission still meets sporadically in Brussels and it is clear to Smith that when the Commission's archives are opened a wealth of information concerning stolen property from the Second World War, will be revealed.[22]

The campaign against the Swiss banks, led by the WJC, received remarkable attention and help from the media. As a matter of fact, for two years it was engaged in a barrage of new revelations, cover stories in leading magazines, front-page stories in prominent newspapers and numerous essays, commentaries and editorials – all directed against Switzerland.

In the US, leaders of the WJC – President Edgar Bronfman and Secretary-General Israel Singer – together with Holocaust survivors and heads of Swiss banks, testified before the Senate Banking Committee, chaired by Senator Alfonse D'Amato. Only slowly did the Swiss banks and their government realize the damage done and the future threat to their prestige and actual financial standing. They feared that actions taken in the US Senate and House of Representatives would lead to a withdrawal of funds and even legal restrictions of Swiss banks' licensing in some states. D'Amato became a target of criticism and hostility in the

Swiss press. As a result of this pressure, in May 1996 the Swiss Bankers Association signed an agreement with the WJRO and the WJC. According to the agreement, an International Committee of Eminent Persons was established, headed by Paul Volcker, former chairman of the US Federal Reserve. The task of this committee is to oversee the auditing of dormant Holocaust accounts in the private Swiss banks. After additional application of pressure, the Swiss government, with the cooperation of the banks, announced in February 1997 the establishment of a humanitarian fund for Holocaust survivors. This fund, with capital of 280 million Swiss francs, would not prejudice other Jewish claims for dormant accounts and Nazi gold transfers.

In the face of the barrage of criticism (which also brought about the resignation of the Swiss ambassador to the United States, after publication of his diplomatic dispatch recommending a declaration of war against Jewish organizations) the Swiss Foreign Minister Flavio Cotti made this historic, introspective declaration in January 1997:

> In Switzerland we were in fact rather proud of the overall balance-sheet of our conduct during the Second World War. Many of us were even blinded by the myth of a Switzerland imbued with zeal and uprightness. There were many among us who, looking back, thought that the protective hand of our patron St. Nicholas de flue, had been as it were the supreme guarantee against the extension of the war to our country... (it was) a combination of truth, half truth and also myth, together with insufficient depth of historical knowledge... Today we have to admit that we were wrong... We are now determined to recognize this omission in its entirety...[23]

Re-evaluating history

> ...in the unique circumstances of World War II, neutrality collided with morality; too often being neutral provided a pretext for avoiding moral considerations... (the) neutral countries were slow to recognize and acknowledge that this was not just another war. Most never did... the fact that they pursued vigorous trade with the Third Reich had the clear effect of supporting and prolonging Nazi Germany's capacity to wage war...
>
> (The Eizenstat Report)[24]

The impressive and unprecedented 210-page study, known as the Eizenstat Report, was released on 7 May 1997 after seven months of work by eleven US federal agencies. The work was coordinated by Stuart E. Eizenstat, Under-Secretary of Commerce for International Trade, and prepared by State Department historian, William Slany.

The fact that a government of the world's leading superpower, undertook to review and analyse events which took place more than fifty years ago, is in itself very unusual in international politics. For many months federal agencies, including the Central Intelligence Agency and the Departments of Defense and Justice, scoured the US National Archives in their investigation of American efforts to identify and restore Nazi loot. The study addressed, in its own words, 'a vital but relatively neglected dimension of the history of the Second World War and its aftermath'.

Eizenstat points out in his introduction that the gold issue 'became the focus of intense political, diplomatic and media attention over the last year'. However, the Report does not refrain from self-criticism: while praising American efforts in lending its military, material and moral might to the free world's fight against the Nazis, including the economic front, it also 'raises serious questions about the US role'. It stresses that 'no country, including the United States, did as much as it might have to save innocent victims of Nazi persecution', and it also mentions restrictive immigration policies which kept hundreds of thousands of refugees from finding safety in the United States. The Report also criticizes a lack of American leadership and support in the negotiations after the war with the neutrals on the restitution of assets, and an 'even greater lack of attention to ensuring implementation of negotiated agreements'. Clearly the report specifies how the 'unrelenting opposition from the neutral countries', as well as 'new Cold War imperatives' facing the Soviet threat, caused these 'inadequacies of US postwar policy'. The Report criticizes the Truman administration for unfreezing Swiss assets in the US before Switzerland met its obligations.

The Eizenstat Report assails Switzerland for its role as the Nazis' bankers and financial brokers whose assistance helped prolong the war, from which it emerged 'as one of the wealthiest nations in Europe'. In his report Eizenstat writes that the wartime behaviour of the neutral nations appears "often harsh and unflattering. Many profited handsomely from their economic cooperation with Nazi Germany, while the Allied nations were sacrificing blood and treasure to fight one of the most powerful forces of evil in the annals of history." The Eizenstat Report, the most comprehensive on the subject to date, confirms what was widely suspected for many years. The amazing fact is that the basic charges against Switzerland and other neutrals were in the public domain for many years. In the 1996 edition of his work, Arthur Smith, who wrote his scholarly book *Hitler's Gold* in the 1980s, expressed surprise that his 1989 edition, while presenting 'the full scholarly account for the gold story... received virtually no attention and the Swiss connection has suddenly become headline news with demands from various quarters for the whole truth'.[25]

In September 1996 the British Foreign Office published an official report on Nazi gold and on Allied dealings with Nazi loot after the war.[26] The report, according to an editorial in The *Times* was 'a fascinating account of greed, deception and double-dealing half a century ago'. While it did not admit to a British conspiracy, it pointed out its responsibility 'to an almost unconscionable delay in overcoming the legal and bureaucratic obstacles that stood between the Nazis' victims or their heirs and representatives, and the money plundered from them to fund Hitler's war machine'.[27]

The British report, released by Foreign Secretary Malcolm Rifkind, highlighted the refusal of Switzerland to return more than a fraction of the booty hidden in its banks. It showed that at the end of the war, Britain's Ministry of Economic Warfare knew that Switzerland, and to lesser extent Sweden and Portugal, were vital sources of foreign currency which Berlin bought with gold.

From both reports it became clear that Swiss vaults and gold transfers to other neutrals included also 'non-monetary' gold, meaning not just reserves which were snatched by the Nazis from banks in occupied Europe but also gold that was grabbed from individuals, seized also from Jewish families and businesses and melted down. Part of this gold was literally torn from the victims' teeth in the death camps.

The British Foreign Office called for the convening of an international conference on Nazi gold in London on 2–4 December 1997. Forty governments were invited, as well as a Jewish delegation. According to the official invitation, the aims of the conference were to gather information on the Nazi gold taken 'from both countries and individuals' and to review what was done and what should be done further to compensate 'individual victims and reimbursements of countries'.

The reports in the United States and Britain are only part of the overall trend in many countries in the Western world. Following the media campaign, pressure from Washington and New York and local public opinion in each country, more that forty national and international commissions were established to investigate how each country behaved during the war and how stolen Jewish property was dealt with after the war (see Appendix at end of chapter). In the countries of Eastern Europe, the former Soviet satellites, there was less readiness for straightforward confrontations with this part of the national collective memory. The years of Communist totalitarianism are still fresh in mind, overshadowing the horrors and crimes of the Second World War. These developing democracies, struggling with their new free-market economies and the evolving free press, are not yet ripe for a sincere and thorough look into the antisemitic dimensions of their history. Most of the archives in these countries were opened only selectively, in particular the files of the KGB in the countries of the former Soviet Union and other archives of the secret services.

The case of Norway, the first European country to appoint a commission to deal with the broader context of collaboration with the Nazis during the war, provides a good example of the difficulties for a country faced with reevaluating its own history. In June 1997, because of a lack of agreement within the commission, it was decided to submit two separate reports. The majority took a narrow approach, focusing on settling the accounts of Jewish assets reports. The minority believed that it must take the 'historical and moral perspective', as part of the responsibility of Norway towards the Jews who were to be collectively killed. This internal clash of approaches in the committee demonstrates the difficult challenge of defusing sensitive chapters in national histories. Even from a distance of fifty years, wartime actions can still be a source of embarrassment for governments and society. They can provoke nationalistic feelings as well as bureaucratic reluctance to assist in investigations. In France, for example, the trial of Maurice Papon, which began in October 1997, reopened wounds that some Frenchmen hoped were healed. It created a controversy with an ugly antisemitic backlash. In Norway, however, the government, with the complete support of the media and all political parties, repudiated the majority report, and its Minister of Justice, Grad Liv Vaala, declared:

> The loss of the Jews cannot be limited to economic calculations only. The organized deportation and liquidation was mass murder, murder of a people. We cannot change what happened, but we can set a moral standard to remind everyone of this dark chapter in the history of Europe.[28]

In July 1998 the Norwegian government submitted a $60 million package of compensation to Jewish survivors and to the Jewish community. Norway was the first country to establish a commission and the first to offer a comprehensive settlement, providing a shining example of confrontation with its past and moral decency.

Arnie Ruth, editor-in-chief of *Dagens Nyheter*, Sweden's most influential newspaper, who wrote extensive investigative reports and essays on Sweden's wartime dealings with Nazi Germany, has touched on the need to fill the necessary gaps in Europe's history. Writing on the rifts in the Norwegian commission and its lessons for the rest Europe, Ruth concluded:

> Besides all its other dimensions, the Holocaust was robbery with murder on the grandest scale in history, with a network of victims, murderers, fences and profiteers extending across a whole continent. That part of history still remains to be written.[29]

This task of evaluating national history was clearly confronted by the Americans and some Europeans. The significance of the Eizenstat Report lies precisely in the embarrassment that it created in countries which are mentioned in it and in the standards which it sets in international relations. Nations that cannot confront evils in their past will have difficulties in confronting their future.

Europe on the psychiatrist's couch

Many factors contributed to the 'conspiracy of silence' around the issue of Jewish property in Western Europe. Besides the reasons already mentioned, it is clear that psychological elements and national memory tended to repress traumatic events of the past. But as in the case of a patient suffering from a mental disorder, the suppressed traumas tend to resurface and topple the psychological balance of the collective national memory.

In 1994 a research study was published in France, which proved quite clearly that, in his youth, President François Mitterrand was an enthusiastic supporter of the extreme right and was active in the Vichy regime which collaborated with the German occupation of France.[30] Such rumours had been aired previously but had been suppressed. The revelation caused major shock waves and brought to light Mitterrand's annual custom of laying a wreath on the grave of Marshall Philippe Pétain, which he justified by saying that the wreath was intended to honour the hero of the First World War, not the man who headed the Vichy government.

The conflict in which some French found themselves was made more acute by the fact that among its heads of state were men who had served the Vichy regime. Maurice Papon, for instance, is accused of taking part in the deportation of the 1690 Jews of Bordeaux (including 233 children) to the death camps. After the war Papon was head of the Paris police and later went on to serve as minister of finance under President Valéry Giscard d'Estaing. The legal process against Papon has been dragging on since 1982. Mitterrand confessed in 1994 that he had intervened to delay the investigation against Papon. In this case, Mitterrand was not disturbed by the fact that Papon had served the government of his political rival; the desire to conceal the memory of Vichy overshadowed all other considerations. Mitterrand explained his attitude towards the French collective memory by saying, 'one cannot continue to live on memories and resentment for ever'.[31] His predecessor, Georges Pompidou, when it came to the less glorious aspects of French history such as the Second World War, preferred 'to cast a veil [over what happened] and to forget'.[32]

It was Mitterrand's successor and political rival, President Jacques Chirac, who for the first time publicly confessed to France's guilt in cooperating with the Nazis. Chirac made this statement on 16 July 1995, at a ceremony commemorating the Fiftieth anniversary of the mass deportation of 70,000 Jews of France to the death camps.

President Chirac's admission, however, was but one step in the process of reconciling the French people with their troubled past. A few months later, another affair caused a new uproar – the sale of hundreds of apartments owned by the municipality of Paris (Chirac was a former mayor of Paris) which had been confiscated from Jews sent to the death camps with the willing aid of the French. The sudden disclosure of this theft caused great dismay and in January 1997 the French prime minister declared the appointment of a committee of experts which would examine the seizure of Jewish property by the Nazis and their Vichy French collaborators. This affair involves several hundreds of apartments, property and some 2000 works of art which are presently exhibited in museums throughout France (see Plate 1).

Several days beforehand, the French court of appeal had ruled that 80-year-old Papon would stand trial for crimes against humanity. In contrast to other Vichy functionaries, around whom there had also been public debates and whose cases the legal system had also been reluctant to prosecute, such as Paul Touvier (intelligence chief of the Lyons militia) or Klaus Barbie (Gestapo agent), Maurice Papon had been a high official in the Vichy government. For the first time, France was prosecuting a member of the Vichy regime and, in so doing, placed the collective past of a significant element of French society in the dock. For an entire year the politicians squirmed and the courts evaded the issue, but finally, belatedly and after many reprehensible acts, France is compelled to take a good look at itself and to suffer genuine shame.

The French Jewish philosopher André Glucksman pointed to the link between national memory and the Cold War:

> Prior to the fall of the Berlin Wall, we wrapped ourselves in Western self-righteousness. We blamed the other side and did not look at ourselves. We ignored that niche of neutrality hidden in most men, the neutrality which represents the basic instinct of a man seeking to save his skin.[33]

In Austria the public auction, in October 1996, of 8000 art objects stolen by the Germans and the Austrians from their Jewish owners, once more directed attention to the active participation of the Austrian people in the destructive machinery of the 'Final Solutions'. Art treasures were returned to Austria by the American army in 1955 with explicit instructions to return them to their rightful owners and heirs. The Austrians, however, hastened to store the spoils in the Mauerbach monastery in order to avoid dealing with the terrible truth. Deep in the cellars of the monastery situated near Vienna, the city in which half a million citizens cheered Hitler in 1938, Austria attempted to bury its national memory and foster the myth of the *Anschluss*. Only in 1991 did Austrian Chancellor Franz Vranitsky admit that the Austrians had not been victims but, rather, willing collaborators of the Nazis. On the occasion of the auction he reiterated his remarks and expressed regret for the repression of the truth, stating that the Austrians had been partners in the destruction of the Jews, and calling for a major effort to combat the trends of forgetfulness.

During the international campaign against Kurt Waldheim, President of Austria and former Secretary-General of the United Nations, many Austrians reacted with a surge of antisemitic propaganda and even violence. Kurt Waldheim, in his autobiography, concealed the fact that for three years he had served as a Nazi officer in combat zones and places of atrocities against the Jews. This amnesia symbolized Austria's repression of its enthusiastic collaboration with the Nazis. Austria was reborn after the war in the interests of Western countries, bearing the false birth certificate of a victim of Nazism. According to Austrian psychologist Irvin Rongel, the Austrians' reaction to the Waldheim affair was actually a clinical psychological process. A whole nation was laid down on the psychiatrist's couch and forced to address the past that it had repressed and hidden.

This analogy, in the country of Sigmund Freud, father of modern psychoanalysis, can be applied to what is happening today in Europe and elsewhere. In an age when both survivors and collaborators of Nazi crimes are gradually disappearing, the most incomprehensible horrific images have risen with great force. The common denominator of the various cases presented here illustrates the political and psychological process of repression that has occurred in each country and society, which, once the cannons fell silent, turned to the task of rehabilitation. The horrors of the Holocaust remain beyond human imagination and understanding. The wheels of justice, in particular after the Nuremberg Trials which dealt with only a small number of Nazi criminals, were halted in order not to impair the process of national recovery. Fifty years after the Holocaust, external pressure exerted by Jewish organizations and the media, especially in the US, accelerated an awakening of Europe's conscience. Ceremonies held throughout Europe commemorating the fiftieth anniversary of the end of the Second World War and the Holocaust (a fiftieth anniversary, according to Jewish tradition, is also a time for national – social introspection and pardon) led to a more moral contemplation. The collapse of Communism, the opening of state archives and the readiness of some people to confess wrongdoing are only excuses for a deeper uncontrollable human need. There is a stage in a man's life, as in the life of a nation, when traumatic and hitherto repressed memories of the past burst forth. The sudden recollection and pursuit of suppressed memories, and the moral anguish which it has produced, has led all of Europe, as an historic – cultural collective, to the psychiatrist's couch.

Appendix: Committees of Inquiry and Historical Re-evaluation

Argentina

The 1992 investigation.   A three-person team of investigation was appointed in 1992 by President Carlos Menem. After four years of poring over 22,000 documents in the archives of the Foreign Ministry, the chief investigator, Beatriz Gurevitch, spoke of a 'web of cooperation' between the pro-fascist regime of Juan Peron and Nazis trying to flee Germany. A secret American document from April 1945 estimated that Nazis secretly sent more than $1 billion for investments in Argentina.

In December 1996 the Argentine Central Bank handed vital information on bank accounts to Jewish researchers, detailing funds transfused from banks in

Switzerland, Spain and Portugal between 1939 and 1949. On March 1997, President Carlos Menem ordered the Central Bank archives to be opened for investigation on Nazi funds.

The Commission on Nazi Activities. On 21 May 1997, President Menem, through an executive order, created the 'Commission of Inquiring of Nazi Activities in Argentina'. The commission is composed of three separate bodies: an international panel, including local and foreign historians, an advisory committee, including local and foreign representatives, and an academic committee. A coordinating committee from government agencies in Argentina will be in charge to obtain the material and provide technical support leading to a final report. Ten research units investigate different aspects such as: quantification of war criminals, routes of escape (Italy, Spain), German naval activities in Argentine waters and collaboration with its military, Central Bank transactions with the Nazis and their investments etcetera.

Austria

The Commission on Art Objects (*Ministry of Education and Culture*) began its work on March 1998 and included all relevant federal museums.

The Commission on Jewish Property. In October 1998, the government and the Jewish community agreed to form a commission of inquiry, with broad terms of reference, to examine the fate of Jewish property and to discuss restitution. In March 1999, the International Steering Committee on Restitution presented the Austrian chancellor, Viktor Klima, with a set of principles concerning Austrian Jewish survivors and their heirs. The steering committee is made up of the Committee for Jewish Claims on Austria (Claims Conference), the Federation of Jewish Communities in Austria, the Council for Jews from Austria in Israel and the World Jewish Congress.

Belgium

Commission to Study the Fate of Jewish Property. In October 1997, the government of Belgium appointed an official committee to conduct a study on the property stolen from Jews during the Second World War. The commission is chaired by Baron Jean Godeaux, former governor of the Central Bank. The Godeaux Commission is to study the fate of any form of assets looted during the war, and property, and in particular the fate of gold and diamonds. It includes members from government agencies and the Jewish community. In April 1998 Godeaux resigned and was replaced by Lucien Buysse.

Brazil

The Commission on Nazi Assets. In April 1997 the President of Brazil, Fernando Henrique Cardoso, signed a decree establishing a 'Special Commission to Investigate Nazi Assets'. The commission includes government officials, historians and representatives of the Jewish community. The commission was asked to investigate the entry and the existence in Brazil of assets illicitly confiscated from victims of the Nazi regime.

Croatia

The Commission for Investigation of Historical Facts on the Fate of Property of the Victims of Nazis was established in November 1997. It includes officials from various ministries.

The Czech Republic

The Commission on Restitution started work in March 1999 and is chaired by Deputy Prime Minister Pavel Rychetsky. The commission aims to establish a compensation fund for lost Jewish assets administered by the Federation of Jewish Communities.

Estonia

The International Research Commission of Estonia, Latvia and Lithuania is presently being formed. Its task will be to research crimes against humanity perpetrated in the Baltic countries by the Nazi and Soviet occupation authorities between 1939 and 1991.

France

The Matteoli Commission. In February of 1997 the French prime minister, Alain Juppé, appointed Jean Matteoli as head of a French commission charged with probing the fate of Jewish property stolen in France. Jean Matteoli, a member of a Resistance group during the war, is the head of France's Economic and Social Council. The mandate of the commission was reconfirmed after the elections by Prime Minister Lionel Jospin. The main task of the Matteoli Commission is to determine the fate of missing valuables, investigate who benefited from them, and discover whether any public authorities still possess property seized during the war (either the occupying power or the Vichy regime). The scope of the study includes the disposition of plundered Jewish property, including *objects d'art*. About 2000 works of art seized from Jews were still in the custody of French museums fifty years after the end of the war. French banks will also be investigated to trace the fate of cash and valuables seized from the Jews who were arrested and deported. Some prominent members of the Jewish community in France have been appointed to this commission, including Jean Kahn, Professor Ady Steg and Serge Klarsfeld. The commission employs twenty-one historians and archivists, and is assisted by two additional committees, one on banks and the other on insurance companies.

The Paris Commission. A special commission has been established by the mayor of Paris to evaluate whether Jewish properties in Paris were confiscated and not returned to their rightful owners. The paris Commission is presided over by Noel Chahid Nourai, a senior civil servant.

Lyon Commission. A committee has been established by the city of Lyon to investigate the fate of seized property and valuables in Lyon municipality.

Art Commission. A government body determined early in 1997 that 1995 works of art, possibly seized from Jews, were still 'provisionally' in the custoday of French museums. The minister of culture, Philippe Douste-Blazy, and the director of the French museums system said that the works will be returned to their rightful owners. Later in 1998 Michael Laclotte, former director of the Louvre, was asked to coordinate the research of art objects.

Italy

Commission on Holocaust Assets. The Italian commission was appointed in December 1998 and held its first working session on March 1999. The president of the Commission is Tina Anselmi, a former minister and member of the anti-fascist Resistance in the Second World War. Among its members are senior government officials from various ministries and archives; directors of associations of banks and insurance companies, as well as historians and representatives of the Jewish community.

Latvia

The International Research Commission of Latvia, Estonia and Lithuania is currently being formed. Its task will be to research crimes against humanity perpetrated in the Baltic countries by the Nazi and Soviet occupation authorities in the years 1939–91.

Lithuania

See Latvia.

The Netherlands

The Dutch Gold Commission. In March 1997 the Dutch government established a commission, headed by regional governor Dr Van J. A. Kemenade. The commission is charged with the task of reviewing information on gold stolen by the Nazis from Dutch reserves and from private Dutch citizens. The Finance Ministry turned to the commission to advise the government on possible claims for restitution of stolen gold, particularly in Switzerland.

The Jewish Property Commission. Following a request by the Jewish community of The Netherlands, the government extended the mandate of the Kemenade Commission to include the investigation of confiscated Jewish property. This new commission is headed by Dr W. Scholten, former chairman of the Dutch government's highest advisory board. The commission examined financial losses suffered by victims of war (including bank accounts, insurance policies, shares, fees and receivables).

The Jewish Valuables (LIRO) Commission. This commission, headed by Kordes, is tracing information from Lippmann, Rosenthal & Co. (LIRO) on the sale in 1968 of Jewish assets to employees of the Ministry of Finance.

The Committee on Paintings. In July 1997 the Dutch government announced the establishment of another commission (Ekkart) on Jewish and other ownership of Nazi-plundered art. This investigation, under the Ministry of Culture, will focus on 3700 paintings that were looted by the Nazis during the war. The paintings, including works by Monet, Van Gogh, Rembrandt and Rubens, were returned to The Netherlands after the war.

The Commission of Dutch Museums was announced on March 1998, by sixteen Dutch museums, to inquire into art acquisitions during and after the Second World War.

Norway

The Skarpnes Committee. The Committee of Inquiry on the Confiscation of Jewish Property in Norway during World War II was appointed by the Ministry of Justice in March 1996. The seven-member committee was chaired by Country Governor Oluf Skarpnes and it included two members appointed by the Jewish community. The committee's mandate was to establish the fate of Jewish property during the Second World War. This includes a description of the rules laid down by the Quisling regime concerning the seizure of Jewish property, the procedure for such seizures, and the estimated value of the property seized. The committee was also instructed to determine how and to what extent seized assets were restored after the war, and their value.

The members of the committee did not reach an agreement among its members and decided to submit two separate reports (June 1997). The majority, including the chairman, took the view that their task was limited to settling estates and accounting for assets. The minority believed that the issue could not be addressed without placing it in a 'historical perspective and putting it in a moral framework'. The minority report explains that 'in order to understand the economic losses incurred by the Jewish minority during World War II, the physical and economic liquidation of the Jews must be regarded as two aspects of the same crime...'

The government decided to accept the minority report and in June 1998 submitted to the parliament a 'white paper' granting a $60 million package of economic compensation to Holocaust survivors in Norway, to the Jewish community and to projects for tolerance and Jewish heritage.

Portugal

In June 1997 the **Central Bank of Portugal**, with the cooperation of the government, appointed a special commission to investigate the treatment of the gold which Portugal received from Nazi Germany during the Second World War. The chairman of the commission is former President Mário Soares and its members include a Portuguese academic, Professor Jaime Reis of the European Institute in Florence and Israel Singer, the Secretary-General of the World Jewish Congress. This group will accompany the work of the economic historian Joaquim Costa Leite, who was appointed in December 1996 by the National Bank of Portugal. The Bank of Portugal announced its commitment to make its archives accessible to public consultations in order to make clear 'its transactions relating to the sale and purchase of gold during the period of 1936 to 1946'.

Spain

The Commission on Nazi Gold. In October 1997 the Spanish government named a special commission to study the issue of Nazi gold sent to Spain. The president of the commission is Enrique Mugica, member of parliament and former minister of justice. The committee includes a number of historians who are examining documents from various Spanish archives. The commission is also investigating non-monetary gold sent to Spain and German assets located there.

Sweden

The Commission on Jewish Assets in Sweden at the Time of the Second World War. This government-appointed commission started its work in March 1997. Rolf Wirten, a former country governor, is the chairman. Among its other members are representatives from the foreign and finance ministries, state archives and the Jewish community. The mandate of the commission covers Jewish deposits, Nazi gold, art and other assets. The final report, submitted in March 1999, deplored actions of the Swedish government and various private organizations (including Enskilda Bank) which dealt with Nazi Germany, and condemned their absence of moral scruples in conducting such transactions. The commission left the government to make decisions on conpensation.

The Central Bank inquiry. In 1997 an investigative team was convened to examine the bank's acquisition of gold from Nazi Germany.

The Living History Project, launched in June 1997, is led by Swedish prime minister Groan Person. Together with several other governments (USA, United Kingdom, Israel and Germany), the Swedes established an international project on Holocaust education. This endeavour was discussed at the Washington Conference on Holocaust Era Assets in December 1998, followed by a major international conference in 2000. The Living History Project may be seen as an integral component of Swedish policy towards restitution and historical reevaluation.

Switzerland

The Foreign Ministry Inquiry commissioned by the Swiss government, through its 'Task Force for the Assets of Nazi Victims', met in October 1996 and submitted its report in January 1997. Two historians, Peter Hug and Marc Perrenoud, were asked to clarify 'questions arising in Switzerland from any possible links between assets of victims of war and the Holocaust and compensation agreements with Eastern European states'. Their study proves how reluctant were the Swiss to respect property claims after the war and how 'Switzerland was able to make use of international developments (the Cold War) and adapt its situation accordingly'. The 142-page study also reveals the antisemitic trends in Swiss society and its social elite before, during and after the war.

The Volcker Committee was established by formal agreement between the Swiss Bankers Association, the WJC and the WJRO on May 1996. This 'Independent Committee of Eminent Persons' is composed of three Jewish representatives and three representatives of the Swiss banking establishment, chaired by Paul Volcker, former chairman for the US Federal Reserve. This committee's mandate is to carry out a thorough audit in Swiss banks in order to identify and recover dormant accounts and investigate deposits of Holocaust victims. A large staff from international accounting firms is employed by the committee to achieve this objective.

In October 1997 the Volcker Committee appointed two separate subcommittees: **The Claims Resolution Tribunal** (chaired by Professor Hans Michael

Riemer) and **The Panel of Experts on Interest Fees and Other Charges** (chaired by Henry Kaufman).

The Historic and Legal Research Commission was appointed in December 1996 and is chaired by Professor Jean François Bergier. The mandate of this commission is 'to study the part played by Switzerland and its financial role within the context of World War II'. The commission consists of eight historians from Switzerland and other countries specializing in the Holocaust and the Second World War. The commission mandate covers all kinds of looted property: bank deposits, *objets d'art, gold,* trade and currency transactions during the war and their treatment after the war.

Turkey

In 1998 Turkey established a **Commission on World War II Properties**. The commission is under the direction of state minister Professor Sukrm Sina Gurel, with the assistance of a secretariat comprised of historians, economists and academics.

The United Kingdom

The Foreign Office Report. The British Foreign Office released a report in September 1996 entitled 'Nazi Gold: Information from the British archives 1996'. The official study started earlier that same year, following pressure from the media and the parliament. The report highlights the refusal of Switzerland to return more than a fraction of the booty hidden in its banks. It also provided the first official confirmation by a government on the estimates of gold which were sent from Germany to Switzerland.

The Report on Ex-Enemy Assets. In September 1997 and in April 1998 the government published reports of recent research into British bank accounts, including those which had belonged to Holocaust victims. The President of the Board of Trade, Margaret Beckett, publicly apologized in April 1998 for the 'insensitive handling of the issue after the war'. A special body for repayment was established in June 1998, chaired by Lord Archer of Sandwell.

The International Conference on Nazi Gold. The British government called for the convention and international conference on Nazi gold to be held in London on 2–4 December 1997. Forty governments, three banks and a Jewish delegation were invited to discuss the historical facts and review steps taken for compensation.

The United States

The First Eizenstat Report, coordinated by Stuart E. Eizenetat, Under-Secretary of Commerce for International Trade, and prepared by state department historian William Slany. This study was released in May 1997. Eleven US federal agencies participated in the study, which was based on millions of declassified secret documents. The title of the 210-page study is: 'US and Allied Efforts to Recover and Restore Gold and other Assets Stolen or Hidden by Germany during World War II'.

The Eizenstat Report assails Switzerland for its role as the banker of the Nazis; its behaviour and that of other neutrals prolonged the war. It shows how the neutrals profited from their cooperation with Nazi Germany and it includes a condemnation of US policies towards war refugees and the failure to pressure the neutrals after the war on property restitution.

The Second Eizenstat Report was released in June 1998. This study focused on the activities of other neutral states (Argentina, Portugal, Spain, Sweden, Turkey and the Holy See) and included hundreds of pages of documents and analysis.

The Presidential Commission on Holocaust Assets. Following the decision by the Congress in December 1998, President Clinton appointed Edgar M. Bronfman, President of the World Jewish Congress, to chair the 23-member commission. The commission will conduct original research on the collection and disposition of Nazi victims' assets that came under US military and government control from 1933.

In December 1998 the state department hosted the **International Washington Conference on Holocaust-era Assets.** More than forty states and Jewish organizations attended the conference, which gave special attention to the issues of Nazi-looted art and insurance claims from the Holocaust.

The Museums Task Force. In light of reports of Nazi-looted art in American museums, the American Association of Art Museums Directors established a task force. In June 1998 the task force released its 'Statement of Principles' and guidelines to coordinate information and create a data base, in order to assist efforts to identify looted art.

The International Commission on Insurance

The commission was established in October 1998 in order to resolve all unpaid insurance claims of Holocaust victims. The chairman is former US Secretary of State, Lawrence S. Eagleburger, and among its thirteen members are US and European insurance commissioners, representatives of the State of Israel and the WJRO and six European insurance companies: Allianz, Axa-UAP, Basler Leben, Generali, Wintherthur Leben and Zurich.

Corporations' Commissions of Historians

Facing a mounting wave of Holocaust-related lawsuits, several big corporations hired historians and specialists to examine their records. Among these companies are Ford Motors, General Motors, Deutsche Bank, German publisher Berterlsmann, and the German smelting company, Degussa.

Notes

1   Statements of responsibility and apology were made in Eastern Europe after the collapse of the Soviet Union. In 1994 and 1995 many were made both in East and West; for instance: 'Hungary says "Sorry" to Jews', *East European Report*, 9–15 October 1994; 'The Bishops of Hungary', *Ha'Aretz*, 12 December

1994; and the Vatican: 'Pope and Church must acknowledge previous sins', *Jerusalem Post*, 15 November 1994. In the Knesset several foreign leaders made announcements of this kind: the president of Austria (15 November 1994) and the president of Lithuania (2 March 1995). Also, there was a dramatic statement by the President of the International Committee of the Red Cross (*International Herald Tribune*, 31 May 1995), and a speech by the president of Germany on 8 May 1995.

2   See, for instance, the debate in Germany on the exhibition on the crimes of the Wehrmacht (the German Army) since its opening in 1995.

3   Daniel Jonah Goldhagen, *Hitler's Willing Executioners: Ordinary Germans and the Holocaust* (New York, 1996).

4   Nehemiah Robinson, *Indemnification and Reparations* (New York, 1944).

5   David S. Wyman, *The Abandonment of the Jews: America and the Holocaust, 1941–1945* (New York, 1984), pp. 68, 47, 167, 172.

6   Avi Beker, 'Diplomacy without Sovereignty: the World Jewish Congress Rescue Activities', in S. Ilan Toren and Benjamina Pinkus (eds), *Organizing Rescue: Jewish Solidarity in the Modern Period* (London, 1992).

7   Nahum Goldmann, *Autobiography: Sixty Years of Jewish Life* (New York, 1969).

8   Behind the infamous pogrom of 1 July 1946 in Kielce, Poland, were rumours that the Jews were coming to reclaim their property; see, for instance, 'Kielce' in *Encyclopedia of the Holocaust*, vols 1–2 (New York, 1990); Yaffa Eliach, 'A Pogrom in Postwar Poland', *New York Times*, 6 August 1996.

9   Adam B. Ulam, *The Rivals: America & Russia since World War II* (New York, 1977), p. 127.

10   Robinson, *Indemnification*, p. 260.

11   Nahum Goldmann, *Community of Fate – Jews in the Modern World: Essays, Speeches and Articles* (Jerusalem, 1977), p. 52.

12   For more on the WJRO in Eastern Europe, see Laurence Weinbaum, 'Defrosting History: The Restitution of Jewish Property in Eastern Europe' (see Chapter 5 of this book, pp. 83–110). In the media, see 'Robbing Peter to Pay Paul: Claims of Heirs of Former Property Owners are a Troublesome Holdover from Totalitarian Regimes', *Time*, 29 May 1995. The WJRO is comprised of the WJC, Jewish Agency, B'nai B'rith, International American Jewish Joint Distribution Committee, American Gathering of Jewish Holocaust Survivors, Center of Organizations of Holocaust Survivors in Israel, Conference of Jewish Material Claims Against Germany, World Zionist Organization, and World Agudath Israel.

13   WJC archives, Jerusalem.

14   Report by Ambassador Stuart E. Eizenstat, the Under-Secretary for International Trade, US Department of Commerce. Submitted to the Honorable Benjamin A. Gilman, Chairman, Committee on International Relations, House of Representatives, 1 August 1996.

15   'Don't Cry for Evita: She Made Millions Helping the Nazis', *The Observer*, 3 November 1996; 'Don't Cry for Him: Peron's Nazi Outreach Program', *Newsweek*, 3 February, 1997. The original document on the Odessa File is in a memo from RG84, State Department, Economic section, Box 10, 9 May 1945, or see a letter from London dated 27 November 1994 from the Economic Warfare Division of the State Department (Dispatch No. 19, 498), a classified

document describing the meeting in Strasburg, including list of participants: industrialists, SS officers, etc.

16 See Chapter 11 on Sweden by Sven Hedin and Göran Elgemyr in this volume, and 'Sweden to Probe Alleged Nazi Exports', *Jerusalem Post*, 10 February 1997.

17 According to a Dutch study, the Wallenberg Bank was involved in purchasing stolen Jewish property in Europe. The Wallenberg brothers were playing a double game between the Allies and the Nazis and, though this was known to the secret services of the United States and Britain, this was not investigated after the war. See Gerald Aalders and Cees Wiebes, *The Art of Cloaking Ownership* (1996), pp. 98–100.

18 Bjorn Westlie, 'Coming to Terms with the Past: the Process of Restitution of Jewish Property in Norway', *Policy Forum*, no. 13, Institute of the World Jewish Congress, Jerusalem (November 1996).

19 A. J. Van Schie, 'Restitution of Economic Rights after 1945', in Jozeph Michman and Tirtsah Levie (eds), *Dutch Jewish History*, vol. 1 (Jerusalem, 1984), pp. 401–20.

20 'The Sinister Face of "Neutrality" – the Role of Swiss Financial Institutions in the Plunder of European Jewry', *Policy Forum*, No. 14, Institute of the World Jewish Congress, Jerusalem (November 1996). See also: 'Swiss Envoy Resigns over Strategy Paper', in *Washington Post*, 28 January 1997, and 'How Swiss Strategy on Holocaust Fund Unraveled', *New York Times*, 25 January 1997.

21 'Secret of the Swiss', *Newsweek*, 24 June 1996, pp. 14–20.

22 Arthur L. Smith, Jr, *Hitler's Gold: The Story of the Nazi War Loot* (Oxford, 1996), and 'Closing the Books in Nazis' Gold', *International Herald Tribune*, 10 September 1998.

23 Address by Swiss Foreign Minister and Federal Councillor, Flavio Cotti, to the Swiss People Party, 17 January 1997.

24 'US and Allied Efforts to Restore Gold and Other Assets Stolen or Hidden by Germany during World War II', coordinated by Stuart E. Eizenstat, Under-Secretary of Commerce for International Trade and Special Envoy of the Department of State. With the participation of Central Intelligence Agency, Department of Commerce, Department of Defense, Department of Justice, Department of State, Department of Federal Bureau of Investigation, Federal Reserve Board, National Archives and Records Administration, National Security Agency, US Holocaust Memorial Museum. Released on 7 May 1997 (210 pages).

25 Smith, *Hitler's Gold*, p. xvii.

26 The Foreign Office Report was released by the British government in September 1996. In a similar manner to other governments, the British initially denied any knowledge of the matter. When pressured by the media and a group of MPs, led by Greville Janner – who revealed declassified documents – the official inquiry began. United Kingdom Foreign and Commonwealth Office, *Nazi Gold: Information from the British Archives, 1996*.

27 'Tainted Gold – Switzerland's Behaviour is Unworthy of a Democracy', *The Times*, 11 September 1996.

28 *The Boston Globe*, 24 June 1997.

29 *Dagens Nyheter*, 17 June 1997.

30   Pierre Pean, *Une jeunesse française: François Mitterrand, 1934–1947* (Paris, 1994).
31   *Jewish Chronicle*, 29 April 1994.
32   'The Search Goes On', *The Economist*, 1 February 1997.
33   'The (Not So) Neutrals of World War II', *New York Times*, 26 January 1997.

2

The Inexplicable Behaviour of States*

Stuart E. Eizenstat

This report addresses a vital but relatively neglected dimension of the history of the Second World War and its aftermath, one that has become the focus of intense political, diplomatic and media attention over the last year. It is a study of the past with implications for the future.

The report documents one of the greatest thefts by a government in history: the confiscation by Nazi Germany of an estimated $580 million of central bank gold – around $5.6 billion in today's values – along with indeterminate amounts in other assets during the Second World War. These goods were stolen from governments and civilians in the countries Germany overran and from Jewish and non-Jewish victims of the Nazis alike, including Jews murdered in extermination camps, from whom everything was taken down to the gold fillings of their teeth.

Our mandate from the President in preparing this report was to describe, to the fullest extent possible, US and Allied efforts to recover and restore this gold and other assets stolen by Nazi Germany, and to use other German assets for the reconstruction of postwar Europe. It also touches on the initially valiant, but ultimately inadequate, steps taken by the United States and the Allies to make assets available for assistance to stateless victims of Nazi atrocities.

It is in the context of this mandate that the report catalogues the role of neutral countries, whose acceptance of the stolen gold in exchange for vitally important goods and raw materials helped sustain the Nazi regime and prolong its war effort. This role continued, despite several

* This essay was originally written as the Foreword to the US State Department report by Stuart E. Eizenstat, then Under-Secretary of Commerce for International Trade. The report, entitled 'U.S. and Allied Efforts to Recover Gold and other Assets Stolen or Hidden by Germany during World War II', and its full text and a subsequent report of June 1998, can be found on the internet.

warnings by the Allies, even long past the time when these countries had any legitimate reason to fear German invasion.

Among the neutral countries, Switzerland receives the most attention in the report. We have no desire to single out a country that is a robust democracy, a generous contributor to humanitarian efforts, and a valued partner of the United States today. But Switzerland figures prominently in any history of the fate of Nazi gold and other assets during and after the Second World War because the Swiss were the principal bankers and financial brokers for the Nazis, handling vast sums of gold and hard currency.

Prepared by the chief historian of the State Department, Dr William Slany, the study is the product of an extraordinary seven-month effort on the part of eleven US government agencies, which I coordinated at President Clinton's request. All involved have worked tirelessly in beginning the process of reviewing 15 million pages of documentation in the National Archives. This represents the largest such effort ever undertaken using the Archives' records, and it has required the classification and transfer of more documents at one time 3–4 between 800,000 and one million pages – than ever before in the history of that repository. Those documents are now available to researchers for the first time.

Nevertheless, this study is preliminary and therefore incomplete. Not every US document related to looted Nazi assets could be located and analysed in the very short time we had to conduct and complete the study. As we progressed, additional documents were constantly found. While we were compelled to rely mostly on US documents, we are well aware that not until the documents of other countries are examined can a more complete picture be drawn.

This is a report by historians. It is a search for facts from the past. It seeks neither to defend nor offend any nation; it endeavours to shade no hard realities, obfuscate no issue. It focuses on the role of the US government and touches on the roles of countries who are now among our closest friends and allies, from our wartime Allies to the then-neutral countries of Argentina, Portugal, Spain, Sweden, Switzerland and Turkey (which joined the Allied effort just before the end of the war).

The picture which emerges from these pages, particularly of the neutral nations, is often harsh and unflattering. Many profited handsomely from their economic cooperation with Nazi Germany, while the Allied nations were sacrificing blood and treasure to fight one of the most powerful forces of evil in the annals of history. At the same time, our team knew that if we were going to shine the bright light of history on other nations, we also had to look carefully at America's role, and the study does so.

Why the sudden surge of interest in these tragic events of five decades ago? There are a variety of explanations. The end of the Cold War gave us the chance to examine issues long pushed to the background. Some previously unavailable documents have been declassified, and made publicly available. As Holocaust survivors come to the end of their lives, they have an urgent desire to ensure that long-suppressed facts come to light and to see a greater degree of justice to assuage, however slightly, their sufferings. And a younger generation seeks a deeper understanding of one of the most profound events of the twentieth century as we enter the twenty-first.

But the most compelling reason is the extraordinary leadership and vision of a few people who have put this issue on the world's agenda: the leadership of the World Jewish Congress, Edgar Bronfman, Israel Singer and Elan Steinberg; a bipartisan group in the US Congress, in particular, the early, tenacious and important role of Senator Alfonse D'Amato of New York; and President Bill Clinton, who has insisted on our establishing and publishing the facts. These leaders have stirred our conscience and stiffened our resolve to achieve justice, particularly for the surviving victims of the Holocaust and Nazi oppression.

Major conclusions and policy implications

A number of major conclusions arise from the pages of this preliminary study, some of which have significant implications today. First, the massive and systematic plundering of gold and other assets from conquered nations and Nazi victims was no rogue operation. It was essential to the financing of the German war machine. The Reichsbank itself – the central bank of the German state – was a knowing and integral participant. It was the Reichsbank that knowingly incorporated into its gold reserves looted monetary gold from the governments of countries occupied by the Nazis. Judging by German reserves at the beginning of the war, the majority of the gold was looted from central banks. It is also evident from the documents we have uncovered and reviewed that some amount was confiscated from individual civilians, including victims of Nazi atrocities, and incorporated into Reichsbank gold stocks. It was the Reichsbank that assisted in converting victim gold coins, jewellery and gold fillings into assets for the SS 'Melmer' account. The Reichsbank organized the sale or pawning of this concentration camp loot, and the resmelting of a portion of this gold into gold ingots with their origins often disguised and therefore indistinguishable by appearance from that looted from central banks.

As its trading partners began to refuse to accept the German Reichsmark, Germany increasingly had to turn to making payments in gold in exchange for foreign hard currency and for materials and goods vital to the German war effort. Between January 1939 and 30, June 1945, Germany transferred gold worth around $400 million ($3.9 billion in today's values) to the Swiss National Bank in Bern. Of this amount, the Swiss National Bank bought about three-quarters, worth $276 million ($2.7 billion today), and the remainder went directly to the accounts of other countries in payment for goods and raw materials.

Secondly, in the unique circumstances of the Second World War, neutrality collided with morality; too often, being neutral provided a pretext for avoiding moral considerations. Historically a well-established principle in international law, neutrality served through centuries of European wars as a legitimate means by which smaller nations preserved their political sovereignty and economic viability. But it is painfully clear that Argentina, Portugal, Spain, Sweden, Switzerland, Turkey and other neutral countries were slow to recognize and acknowledge that this was not just another war. Most never did. Nazi Germany was a mortal threat to Western civilization itself and, had it been victorious, to the survival of even the neutral countries themselves.

Of course, we must be cautious in making simplistic moral judgements about the conduct of neutral nations in wartime. None of these nations started the Second World War or caused the Holocaust; that responsibility rested squarely with Nazi Germany. No country, including the United States, did as much as it might have or should have to save innocent victims of Nazi persecution – Jews, Gypsies, political opponents, and others. America itself remained a non-belligerent for over two years following the outbreak of the war in Europe. Restrictive US immigration policies kept hundreds of thousands of refugees from finding safety in the United States, most tragically exemplified by our refusal to allow the St. Louis to dock with its cargo of refugees, many of whom perished when the ship was forced to return to Europe. Nevertheless, the US froze German assets in April 1940 (eighteen months before entering the war), conducted little trade and commerce with Nazi Germany, and generously assisted Britain, the Soviet Union and the anti-Nazi cause (despite fierce domestic opposition) through programmes like Lend-Lease.

Many of the neutrals had a rational fear that their own independence was only a Panzer division away from extinction. But if self-defence and fear were factors in that rationale for neutrality, so too were profit in all neutral countries and outright Nazi sympathy in some. The neutrals ignored repeated Allied entreaties to end their dealings with Nazi Germany. Whatever their motivation, the fact that they pursued vigorous trade with the Third Reich had the clear effect of supporting and prolonging Nazi Germany's capacity to wage war.

In considering the actions of the neutrals, three phases can be identified:

- During the **first phase**, from the outbreak of war in 1939 until the battle of Stalingrad in early 1943, German military prowess was such that there was a legitimate fear of imminent invasion.

- In the **second phase**, the tide of battle shifted in the Allies' favour and culminated in victory. Beginning in mid-1943 with the Allied invasion of Italy, the D-Day invasion in June 1944 and the diversion of German forces to halt the Soviet Army's advance, the Nazi occupation of Europe was rolled back and the threat to the neutrals greatly diminished, although there were still fears of other forms of reprisal. Commerce with Germany, however, continued. German assets in neutral countries were not frozen, despite Allied requests and warnings. The neutrals continued to profit from their trading links with Germany and thus contributed to prolonging one of the bloodiest conflicts in history. During this period, the Allies suffered hundreds of thousands of casualties and millions of innocent civilians were killed.

- In the **third phase**, the immediate postwar period, the neutrals disputed the legality of the Allied request to control German assets; often denied they had any looted Nazi gold; defended their commercial interests; dragged out negotiations with the Allies; and eventually pressed their own claims for restitution against Germany. In contrast to the other wartime neutrals, Sweden was relatively forthcoming in terms of the extent and pace of its cooperation in transferring Nazi gold and other assets to the Allied powers. Spain, Portugal, Switzerland, Turkey and others continued to resist cooperation even though the war was over.

To varying degrees, each of the neutrals cooperated with Nazi Germany for their own economic benefit. Sweden was one of Nazi Germany's largest trading partners, supplying critically-needed iron ore and ball-bearings, among other goods. Portugal supplied a variety of vital mineral resources for the Third Reich's war machine, including the ore for tungsten, a key additive used in the production of weapon-grade steel. Spain maintained an active trade in goods and raw materials. Turkey was Germany's source of very scarce chrome. Argentina's pro-Axis regime failed to control the transfer of German funds from Europe.

Thirdly, of all the neutral nations, the one with the most complex roles in the Second World War, together with the deepest and most crucial economic relationship with Nazi Germany, was Switzerland. Switzerland's role was very mixed. It ended the Second World War as one of the wealthiest nations in Europe. It conducted trade with the Allied countries as well as with the Axis powers. The Swiss National Bank kept gold accounts for and received gold not only from Nazi Germany, but from the United States, Canada and Great Britain as well. Switzerland served as a key base for US intelligence-gathering. It was also a protecting power for the Allies, most critically for our POWs. But as the Swiss government acknowledged as early as 1952 (and reiterated in recent months), there were shortcomings in Switzerland's refugee policies. Switzerland persuaded the Nazis to establish the 'J' stamp which prevented tens of thousands of Jews from entering Switzerland or other potential sanctuaries. Like Canada and the United States, Switzerland tightened its immigration policies, and during the war it virtually closed its borders to Jews fleeing deportation from France and Belgium. As many as about 50,000 Jewish refugees were admitted from 1933 until the end of the war, of whom some 30,000 remained and survived the war in Switzerland. But Switzerland imposed on Jewish communities the burden of sustaining the Jews who were admitted after the outbreak of war (most of whom were interned in labour camps). In August and December 1944, Switzerland admitted an additional 1700 concentration camp inmates from Bergen Belsen, and in February 1945 an additional 1200 from Theresienstadt. Various Jewish communities were required to support these additional survivors. Switzerland also accepted well over 100,000 other refugees after 1940.

As late as the end of 1944, Secretary of State Stettinius and his State Department colleagues concluded that, on balance, Switzerland's neutrality had been more a positive than a negative for the Allies during the war. This relatively benign judgement was not shared by other agencies, from the War Department and Treasury Department to the Office of Strategic Services (OSS) and the Justice Department. These agencies noted that in addition to its critical banking role for the Nazis, Switzerland's industries engaged in direct production for the Axis and helped protect Axis investments; Swiss shipping lines also furnished Germany with a large number of boats for the transport of goods. Switzerland also allowed an unprecedented use of its railways to link Germany and Italy for the transport of coal and other goods. Switzerland provided Germany with arms, ammunition, aluminium, machinery and precision tools, as well as agricultural products. Swiss convoys carried products from Spain across France through Switzerland to Germany. Swiss banks serviced Nazi markets in Latin America. This conduct continued even as the Germans retreated and the threat of invasion evaporated. As late in the war as early 1945, Switzerland vitiated an agreement it had just reached with the United States to freeze German assets and to restrict purchases of gold from Germany.

The amount of Germany's gold reserves before the war was well known. Clearly, the evidence presented in this report is incontrovertible: the Swiss National Bank and private Swiss bankers knew, as the war progressed, that the Reichsbank's own coffers had been depleted, and that the Swiss were handling vast sums of looted gold. The Swiss were aware of the Nazi gold heists from France of Belgian gold as well as from other countries.

Switzerland's 'business as usual', attitude persisted in the postwar negotiations, and it is this period which is most inexplicable. The Swiss team were obdurate negotiators, using legalistic positions to defend their every interest, regardless of the moral issues also at stake. Initially, for instance, they opposed returning any Nazi gold to those from whom it was stolen, and they denied having received any looted gold. The Swiss contended they had purchased it in good faith, that it was part of war booty obtained in accordance with international legal principles by the Third Reich during its victorious campaigns, and that there was no international legal principle which would entitle the Allies to recover and redistribute Nazi assets. Finally, after long, contentious and difficult bargaining, agreement was reached in the form of the 1946 Allied–Swiss Washington Accord. The Accord obligated Switzerland to transfer 250 million Swiss francs ($58.1 million) in gold to the Allies and to liquidate German assets, transferring 50 per cent of the proceeds from the assets to the Allies for the reconstruction of war-torn Europe, of which a portion would be directed to assistance of stateless victims. At the same time, the Swiss made a commitment in a side letter to identify dormant accounts which were heirless and could be used for the benefit of Nazi victims. The $58 million in German-looted gold to be returned to the Allies was far less than the range of $185–$289 million in looted gold the State and Treasury Departments estimated was at the Swiss

National Bank for its own account at the end of the war. An additional $120 million of German-looted gold was also estimated to be on account for other countries at that time. This $58 million in monetary gold was promptly paid to the Tripartite Gold Commission (TGC) for redistribution to the claimant countries.

But the other part of the Accord, the liquidation of hundreds of millions of dollars in German assets, was neither promptly nor ever fully implemented. The Swiss raised one objection after another, arguing over exchange rates, insisting that German debt settlements be included, and demanding that the US unblock assets from German companies seized during the war but which the Bern government claimed were actually Swiss-owned. They refused to make an exemption for the assets of surviving Jews from Germany and heirless German Jewish assets, and continued to make them subject to liquidation. They refused to recognize any moral obligation to return looted Dutch gold when evidence became available after the conclusion of the 1946 negotiations. US negotiators concluded by 1950 that the Swiss had no intention of ever implementing the 1946 Washington Accord. Secretary of State Dean Acheson remarked that if Sweden was an intransigent negotiator, then Switzerland was intransigence 'cubed'.

Over a six-year period, before the final 1952 settlement, the Swiss government had made only a token 20 million Swiss franc advance ($4.7 million then or $31 million today) for resettlement of stateless victims. Finally, in 1952, after a lengthy and frustrating effort, Switzerland and the Allies agreed to a total payment of only $28 million – far less than the agreed 50 percent of the value of German assets in their country. The amount of German assets in Switzerland after the war ranged between press accounts of $750 million, US and Allied estimates of $250 – $500 million, and Swiss estimates of around $250 million.

This 1952 accord, superseding the 1946 obligation, was concluded within days of the initialling of a Swiss–German debt agreement by which the German government satisfied its wartime debt to Switzerland. Clearly, Switzerland's delay was intended to keep German assets under its control as a guarantee for settlement of Swiss claims against the Nazi regime. Effectively, the German payment was used to fund Switzerland's own payment to the Allies.

It was not until 1962 that Switzerland began to comply with its 1946 side letter agreement to the Washington Accord 'to look sympathetically' at using heirless assets for the benefit of Holocaust survivors. After long denying the possession of any heirless assets, some Swiss banks then found over $2 million in bank accounts, most of which was not transferred to Jewish and other relief organizations until the 1970s. In a renewed effort in 1996, they indicated they had located around $32 million in dormant accounts in various banks. Over the years, the inflexibility of the Swiss Bankers' Association and other Swiss banks made it extremely difficult for surviving family members of Nazi victims to successfully file claims to secure bank records and other assets. This overall pattern of Swiss bankers' apparent indifference to the needs of the victims of the Holocaust and their heirs persisted until the current international pressures came to bear and, for instance, the appointment of an Ombudsman in 1996.

The lack of attention to the letter and spirit of this side agreement was also evident in the separate 1949 agreement the Swiss concluded with Poland, under which Switzerland agreed to transfer funds in heirless bank accounts from Polish Holocaust survivors and other Polish nationals to the then-Communist government of Poland. This was coupled with a Polish agreement to satisfy the claims of Swiss businesses for properties expropriated after the war. Although defensible under international law (since the Poles committed themselves to restore these heirless assets to any surviving Polish claimants), there was no Swiss follow-through. Switzerland failed to provide Poland with the names of Polish heirless account holders until almost fifty years later, in 1997. Switzerland also entered into a similar protocol with Hungary.

Negotiations with other neutrals also had mixed results. Sweden was the most cooperative in liquidating the German assets it held, although it was not until 1955 that Sweden resolved final questions on transferring monetary gold. Negotiations with Spain were lengthier and less successful, with many German assets in Spain virtually disappearing into the Spanish economy by the time negotiations were completed in 1948. A small amount of gold was returned and assets liquidated. Negotiations with Portugal were even more protracted, with gold discussions dragging on into the 1950s because of Portuguese resistance. It was not until 1960 that a small amount of cash and gold was turned over to the Allies. Turkey and Argentina paid nothing in gold or assets. Fourthly, the United States lent its military, material and moral might to the free world's fight against Nazi tyranny and led the magnanimous effort to rebuild postwar Europe through the landmark Marshall Plan. It is fair to conclude that on the Nazi gold and assets issues addressed by this report, the role of the US was also positive. The US government took the lead in economic warfare against the Axis by initiating the Safehaven programme with our Allies. The US scored significant successes in blocking German assets from leaving the country and in tracking the flow of Nazi assets, particularly looted gold, to prevent any Nazi resurgence after the war. The US also led the effort, during and after the war, to obtain compensation for the nations and individuals victimized by the Third Reich. Although restrictive immigration policies remained in place until 1948, the US was the most active in addressing the plight of the refugees, initiating the proposal in the Paris Reparation Conference to ensure some share of reparations went to the victims of Nazism, and proposing an early conference on assistance for refugees. The US also provided substantial funds for displaced persons and for the resettlement and rehabilitation of refugees.

Nonetheless, the report raises serious questions about the US role. American leadership at the time, while greater than that of our Allies, was limited. There was a demonstrable lack of senior-level support for a tough US negotiating position with the neutrals. Moreover, there was an even greater lack of attention to ensuring implementation of negotiated agreements. Because, for instance, the US government decided to unblock frozen Swiss assets in the US soon after the signing of the 1946 Accord, and, over the objections of the Treasury Department, decided not to pursue sanctions, most leverage was lost before Switzerland had met its obligations. Finally, neither the US nor the Allies pressed the neutral countries hard enough to fulfill their moral obligation to help Holocaust survivors by redistributing heirless assets for their benefit.

These serious shortcomings in US and Allied policy, coupled with stiff resistance on the part of the neutrals, had two negative consequences:

- With greater support and interest from Allied leadership, it might have been possible to strike a better bargain on the looted gold and other German assets with the neutral countries;

- Allied and interagency disagreements also made it easier for the neutrals to string out negotiations and thereby delay the transfer of needed funds to the Inter-Allied Reparations Agency (IARA) and to the International Refugee Organization (IRO).

The inadequacies of US postwar policy were due to a number of factors which tied the hands of American negotiators, not the least of which was unrelenting opposition from the neutral countries. In addition to interagency disagreements over how tough to be with the neutrals, there were also splits within Allied ranks. The US was the most aggressive in seeking compensation for the refugees, but was met by resistance, for example, from Britain (which, according to the analysis of US officials at the time, feared the policy of providing funds for resettlement of refugees would conflict with its restrictions on the number of Jewish refugees who could enter Palestine).

Most fundamentally, wartime objectives were replaced by the need to rebuild an integrated postwar Europe and then by new Cold War imperatives, including the creation of NATO, in order to contain the Soviet threat so dramatically highlighted by the 1948 Berlin blockade. Putting a democratic West Germany on its feet and strengthening its economy took priority over denying it access to German assets in neutral countries – assets which could be applied to broader European recovery efforts. The Allies knew that German efforts to meet their obligation to the neutral countries would strain their economy. In the case of Portugal, the quest for access to the important Azores air base led negotiators to settle for a token payment. Security interests became paramount with Turkey, a key NATO ally. Switzerland, though neutral, was seen officially in a 1951 decision by President Truman as a democratic deterrent to Soviet expansionism.

Fifthly, the report also deals with the hotly debated issue of whether some victim gold was sent to Switzerland and other neutral countries, and whether it was also included in the TGC gold pool. This was the pool into which looted central bank gold was placed for redistribution by the TGC to the governments from which it was stolen during the war. This study concludes that both occurred. The Reichsbank or its agents smelted gold taken from concentration camp internees, persecutees and other civilians, and turned it into ingots. There is clear evidence that these ingots were incorporated into Germany's official gold reserves, along with the gold confiscated from central banks of the countries the Third Reich occupied. Although there is no evidence that Switzerland or other neutral countries knowingly accepted victim gold, the study provides clear evidence – on the basis of the pattern and practice of Reichsbank gold smelting, the co-mingling of monetary and non-monetary gold, gold transfers and an analysis of a shipment of looted Dutch gold – that at least a small portion of the gold that entered Switzerland and Italy included non-monetary gold from individual civilians in occupied countries and from concentration camp victims or others killed before they even reached the camps.

It is also clear that some victim gold 'tainted' the gold pool. There was great confusion and disagreement between the Allies and within the US government over the definition of 'monetary gold' (destined for the gold pool) and 'non-monetary gold' (to be used for resettlement of stateless victims). In the end, the US decided on a definition that was based on appearance rather than origin. As a result, gold taken by the Nazis from civilians in occupied countries and from individual victims of the Nazis in concentration camps and elsewhere was swept into the gold pool. In addition, the US and Britain agreed that gold bars suspected to be from the Nazi's Terezin concentration camp in Czechoslovakia should be included in the gold pool, although no evidence has been uncovered yet that they were transferred to the TGC. Further research might determine how much was included.

Finally, one aspect of the study deserves immediate attention and action: the plight of those who were victims not only of the war and the Holocaust, but of the sad combination of indifference on the part of the neutrals and inaction by the Allies. The decision by the eighteen nations at the 1946 Paris Reparations Conference to leave assistance and reparations for individual victims to national governments and international relief organizations, while understandable at the time, in hindsight had unfortunate consequences:

- Serious inequities developed in the treatment of victims depending upon where they lived after the war. Those Holocaust victims who met the applicable definitions were assisted in resettlement, and if they emigrated to the West or to Israel, they have received pensions from the German government. But the 'double victims', those trapped behind the Iron Curtain after the war, have essentially received nothing.

- Beyond initial emergency resettlement assistance, most governments did not have a long-term commitment to rehabilitation, to the search for heirs of abandoned assets, nor to the distribution of heirless assets for appropriate causes. This meant that the burden of providing ongoing relief for surviving victims was left largely to private organizations.

For the victims, justice remains elusive. Their grievances must be seen as the appropriate responsibility of the entire international community on behalf of humanity.

Challenges for action

The cumulative facts and conclusions contained in this report should evoke a sense of injustice and a determination to act. Now, half a century later, this generation's challenge is to complete the unfinished business of the Second World War, to do justice while its surviving victims are still alive. To do justice is in part a financial task. But it is also a moral and political task that should compel each nation involved in these tragic events to come to terms with its own history and responsibility.

It is a time for reconciliation as well. A positive, healing process has already begun. Besides the ground-breaking September 1996 British Foreign Office report and this US historical study, a growing number of countries have initiated reviews of their wartime roles, including their relationship to the Third Reich and the theft and disposition of valuables from their Jewish and non-Jewish citizens alike.

Among the neutral countries, Switzerland has taken the lead. It has established two separate commissions: the Volcker Commission to examine assets in dormant bank accounts in Swiss banks; and the Bergier Commission to examine the entire historical relationship of Switzerland to Nazi Germany. Major Swiss banks and companies and the Swiss National Bank have established what is now a $180 million (and growing) fund for needy surviving victims of the Nazis or their heirs. The government of Switzerland has proposed establishing an endowment to generate income for survivors and for other humanitarian causes. Private groups, including churches and high school students, have collected over 500,000 Swiss francs (about $350,000) for Holocaust survivors. The United States welcomes and applauds these significant gestures.

Many other important efforts are beginning. For example, Sweden, Spain, Portugal, France, Norway, the Netherlands, Belgium, Brazil and Argentina have created historical commissions. Poland has published a report of its postwar agreement with Switzerland to settle property claims. The Czech Republic has searched its records and determined that no heirless accounts in Swiss banks were included in Swiss claims settlements. The Austrian Government has established a fund to compensate its Holocaust survivors. Shortly, the government of Hungary will begin paying monthly compensation to over 20,000 Holocaust survivors living in that country. Several other countries in Central and Eastern Europe have also taken steps to restitute communally-owned Jewish and non-Jewish property (such as schools, churches and synagogues) confiscated by the Nazis and/or the Communists, although often at a slow pace. These efforts should be accelerated.

To move this healing process forward, it is vital that all of the facts be made public. The Clinton administration has made an extraordinary effort to declassify documents that may shed further light on these issues. In addition:

- The US favours the immediate declassification of all of the TGC's documents that bear on the origin of the TGC gold pool.

- The US will explore the idea of an international conference of historians and other experts to exchange information, insights and documents about the flow of Nazi assets, relationships with the Third Reich during the war, and measures for finding surviving owners or disposing of heirless property. The US and other concerned governments would then need to assess the results of these efforts. It will be important, for example, to have German Reichsbank records available so that we can all reach a more complete understanding of the origin and flows of looted assets.

The US hopes that other governments continue to build on these hopeful beginnings. We all need to pursue unresolved issues, such as the disposition of heirless assets. We also need to create museums and educational curricula, and to find other ways to teach future generations the truth about the war years and their countries' relationship with Nazi Germany.

Most urgently, these actions should focus on providing justice for Holocaust survivors. That is why we are discussing with Britain and France final disposition of the gold pool. The report concludes that this pool contained at least some individual gold that did not belong to the central banks of governments who have now received it from the TGC. Moreover, there is a moral dimension. The remaining amount, almost $70 million to be divided among the claimant countries, is small, but if a significant portion of this amount could be given to Holocaust survivors, it would help them live out their declining years in dignity. This is particularly important for those 'double victims' in Central and Eastern Europe and the former Soviet Union who survived both Nazism and Communism, and have received little or no compensation from Germany. While we recognize that the final decision will need to be made in consultation with our TGC partners and the claimant countries, we favour a substantial portion of this remaining gold being made available for a fund for the benefit of surviving victims.

There are additional unresolved issues which are only briefly mentioned in this report. One which has arisen recently concerns the disposition of heirless assets in US banks and, indeed, whether there may have been looted Nazi assets in US banks, including the American affiliates of Swiss-owned banks. This is an important matter that requires further investigation by other institutions, including relevant state authorities. It is also important to pursue insurance claims by families of Holocaust victims whose policies were confiscated by the Nazis or whose claims were denied due to a variety of circumstances, including the lack of a death certificate.

Much work remains to be done, but this preliminary study is a major step forward. Ultimately, the United States, our Allies and the neutral nations alike should be judged not so much by the actions or inactions of a previous generation, but more by our generation's willingness to face the past honestly, to help right the wrongs, and to deal with the injustices suffered by the victims of Nazi aggression. Our hope is that this study will advance that broader purpose.

3
Estimating Jewish Wealth

Sidney Jay Zabludoff

Background

The loss of six million Jews in the Holocaust inflicted six million individual tragedies. In the wake of these horrors, less attention has been paid to how a community vanished overnight that for centuries played a key role in the economic, cultural, scientific and artistic development of Europe. This devastating event is unique in modern history. For the Jewish communities of Eastern Europe, conditions deteriorated even further after the war as a result of nearly fifty years of Communist rule. Many Jews left the region to escape oppression, poverty and large doses of antisemitism. The few who remain are surrounded by a vast museum of memorials dedicated to those who perished during the brutal Nazi era.

Thus, within a decade, the long-established and vibrant Jewish community in much of Europe all but disappeared. Although the dimensions of this calamity can never be fully comprehended, this paper helps to put the toll into focus by estimating the pre-Second World War value of Jewish wealth and its composition in the European areas occupied by the Nazis.

The Nazi perpetrators and their collaborators

The Nazis began to confiscate Jewish assets soon after they took power in Germany in 1933. Beginning slowly, the Nazi confiscation of Jewish assets intensified throughout the 1930s. By the end of the decade, they simply took over what remained of Jewish property. When the Nazis invaded other European nations, they moved quickly to seize Jewish assets. Confiscation which took some five years in Germany often took place in months in Nazi-occupied countries. Much of the stolen property was used by the Nazi occupying authorities for their own purposes or turned over to local collaborators. Movable items were often shipped to Germany to help with the war effort or sold at auction. Many of the most valuable collectors' items went to the top Nazi leadership. What remained was taken away when the Jews were forced into ghettos and transported to concentration camps. There most Jews were slaughtered and the last of their possessions collected. This included the infamous gold teeth, spectacles, rings and clothing.

In Italy, and in Nazi satellite countries or regions (Bulgaria, Croatia, Hungary, Romania and Slovakia), the pace of confiscating Jewish assets depended mainly on the country's ability to withstand Nazi pressure. In all these countries, although the local governments instituted anti-Jewish polices which undermined the ability of Jews to earn a living, the total looting of property did not take place until the German military took over the country. Slovakia, Croatia and Romania were the most submissive. After the Nazis took over Hungary in March 1944, all Jewish property was taken away, as Jews were forced into ghettos and then sent to concentration camps. In Italy, some Jewish assets were saved because when the Nazis took over control of the country in 1943, the Allies controlled the southern part.

Jews were able to save a few hundred million dollars from being looted by moving liquid assets before the Nazi takeover. Most of this money came from Germany, where the looting lasted for years. But for most of Europe, the Nazi occupation was swift in cutting off the chance that Jews could escape with even some assets. In Austria and Czechoslovakia the opportunity to remove assets was a few months. In all countries, some Jews were able to place funds in foreign locations before the Nazi invasion, despite strict foreign exchange controls that were prevalent throughout Europe during the 1930s.

Estimating Jewish wealth

Determining the exact value of Jewish wealth lost during the Nazi era is near impossible and impracticable. Considerable records do exist on assets of individuals and businesses, including those meticulously kept by Nazis. The data, however, are far from complete and their accuracy often questionable. To cloud the issue, considerable Jewish possessions were stolen by Nazi collaborators and went unrecorded. Even in the unlikely event that the quality problems of this data could be overcome, the time and money needed to exploit all available records would be enormous.

However, it is certainly feasible to prepare *a reasonable* estimate of the range in which the asset amount probably falls. The heart of this endeavour involves approximating prewar per capita wealth estimates for Jews living in each of twenty countries or regions in Nazi-occupied Europe (see Table 1). These numbers then can be fine-tuned by drawing on available records on Jewish assets and by exploiting the considerable information on the economic characteristics of the Jewish community during the 1920s and 1930s. This approach was pioneered by Nehemiah Robinson, an economist who worked for the World Jewish Congress, starting in the 1940s.

The reasonableness of the Jewish per capita wealth estimates for each country, and the total, can be gauged in a number of ways. The

Table 1 Jewish Assets Seized, 1934–45

	Population (in thousands)	1934		1945	
		Per capita ($)	Value ($ million)	Per capita ($)	Value ($ million)
Germany	575	3500	2000	5200	3000
Hungary	500	1600	800	3200	1600
Czechoslovakia	360	1700	600	2800	1000
Czech Republic	(120)	(3500)	(420)	(5800)	(700)
Slovakia	(130)	(1300)	(160)	(1700)	(200)
Sub-Carpathia	(110)	(500)	(50)	(700)	(75)
Austria	185	2200	400	3300	600
France	270	1500	400	3000	800
The Netherlands	130	2300	300	3900	510
Belgium	65	2100	140	3000	100
Italy	30*	1500	50	3000	100
Romania	850	700	600	1100	900
Yugoslavia	80	1200	100	1500	160
Greece	75	600	40	800	60
Bulgaria	50	700	30	900	50
Poland	3300	700	2000	900	3000
Western USSR	2000	200	400	300	600
Lithuania	145	700	100	900	130
Latvia	90	700	70	900	90
Other**	18	3000	50	3000	50
Total	8700		8080		12850

* In Nazi-occupied Italy as of July 1943.
** Denmark, Estonia, Luxembourg, Norway.

relationship of the numbers must make sense. For example, the average holdings of assets in Poland should be considerably less than those of Germany, which had a wealthier Jewish community. Similar techniques for determining reasonable and feasible estimates are common today. What essentially separates results with a high degree of reliability from those employing educated guesses is the use of procedures to check the consistency of the estimates among themselves and with other data. It should also be noted that well-rounded ranges are used in this endeavour to include all realistic asset values. Finally, the estimating process used here is intended as an analytical structure or baseline that can be used to incorporate and validate new country studies which are likely to appear during the next several years.

Judging per capita wealth estimates

National wealth was an important concept used to compare the economic success of countries and examine the concentration of wealth among the populace, especially from the 1920s to the 1950s. In this study, the emphasis is on private wealth of households and businesses, which excludes assets owned by government entities. US private wealth data are used as a benchmark to judge European country estimates, because it is among the best and most consistent over time. For 1933, the US per capita figure amounts to about $5000 and in 1939 to $5600. These numbers in most instances are roughly double that of the richer countries of Western Europe and four times or more that of the poorer countries of Eastern and Southern Europe. This pattern can be seen in Table 2 which shows GNP per capita numbers. In all countries wealth distribution is highly skewed. In the 1930s, the top 1 per cent of the wealthiest held 40–50 per cent of the assets and the top 5 per cent, some 70–80 per cent.

To be able to compare wealth statistics for twenty countries, local currencies must be converted to a common currency – the US dollar in this study. This necessary step creates a potential inaccuracy, which influences all studies. Exchange rates sometimes do not adequately equate the value of assets because some rates are set artificially by governments and others are distorted by trade and capital controls. Both exchange-rate situations were common throughout Europe during the 1930s. Most notably, German exchange rates were out of kilter. This can be seen in the very high per capita dollar GNP amount for a Western European country. Although part of the distortion reflects the huge arms spending in the late 1930s, Germany's GNP and national

Table 2   Per Capita GNP in the 1930s

	US$
United States	700
Germany	600
United Kingdom	450
The Netherlands	400
Austria	250
Belgium	250
France	250
Italy	200
Czechoslovakia	150
Hungary	150
Bulgaria	100
Poland	100
Greece	75
Yugoslavia	75

wealth expressed in dollars is probably overvalued by at least 25 per cent.

Country population numbers create another source of error in determining per capita wealth. Boundaries of countries were altered considerably during the late 1930s and early 1940s. For consistency's sake, this study uses the total population of a country, and that of its Jewish citizens, that was within the 1937 boundaries.

Issues in determining Jewish wealth

A prime definitional problem in per capita Jewish wealth is: who is a Jew? Does it include just those declaring themselves Jews, and what about the large number of Jews who married outside their faith and their offspring? Counting the Jewish population in European countries often was determined by how many belonged to established religious or other community organizations. This left out some secular Jews. Official census efforts usually were based on those who declared themselves as Jews, or so-called 'confessional Jews'. Some people, however, did not want to indicate their religion to a census official because of the fears created by many years of government antisemitic behaviour. The Nazis used the broad Nuremberg definition which considers all persons Jews if they have one Jewish grandparent. This study uses, when available, the more inclusive Nuremberg Jewish population number, because the Nazis used it to determine those to be sent to concentration camps and which assets to seize.

Another population problem is that a large number of Jews, especially from Germany, Austria and Czechoslovakia, moved to other European countries before the war began in 1939. For this study, these refugees are considered part of their homeland. Thus population numbers are from 1933 for Germany and 1937 for all other countries.

Finally and most important: did the occupational composition of the Jewish community in each country differ markedly from that of non-Jews, thus creating major discrepancies in earning power and wealth? Were there major differences between Jews and non-Jews in the concentration of income and wealth? The answer to the first is a clear yes. There also are differences in wealth distribution but they are not striking.

Throughout Europe, the economic involvement of the Jews was remarkably similar. They were heavily engaged in trade, industry, finance and the liberal professions. Nearly all lived and worked in urban areas; very few followed agricultural pursuits. Most Jews were self-employed. This picture contrasts sharply with the non-Jewish worker. For example:

- Four per cent or less of Jews were gainfully employed in agriculture in Eastern and Southern Europe during the 1930s, while more than half the non-Jewish labour force was in agriculture.

- More than half of employed Jews were in trade and finance; in contrast, the similar share for non-Jews fell between 10 and 20 per cent.

- In the liberal professions, more than half of Polish lawyers and 35 per cent of Polish doctors were Jews in 1937, although the Jews accounted for only 10 per cent of the total population.

- Finally, while most working Jews were self-employed, the percentage among non-Jews normally ran between 10 and 20 per cent.

These differences in average wealth caused by this occupational mix are not as great as they may seem, because most Jews were poor. They were mainly small-scale merchants and Jewish industry consisted largely of craftsman. Most enterprises employed few people beyond family members. Also, Jews were much more adversely affected by the global economic depression of the 1930s than their non-Jewish counterparts. Especially in Eastern and Southern European countries, governments took numerous actions to save jobs for the non-Jews by severely restricting the numbers of Jews in a trade or occupation. As a result, many

Jewish businesses produced little more than a subsistence existence for their owners and many doctors and lawyers were unable to find jobs in their profession. Dependence on community charity or funds from America was common. Even in Berlin, a quarter of the Jewish population was on relief in 1932.

In all, these characteristics meant Jews normally had a somewhat higher average income and wealth than non-Jews and these differences were driven mainly by the much greater involvement of Jews in urban pursuits. According to the studies by Robinson (see Bibliography), average per capita Jewish wealth exceeded non-Jewish wealth by some 25 per cent because of the differences in the occupational mix. That difference is higher in such countries as Italy, which had a very small Jewish population who were mainly in the middle to upper income brackets. With a few exceptions, a uniform 25 per cent higher rate is used to calculate Jewish per capita wealth, because the differences between countries are difficult to estimate and often do not seem to change the wealth estimates significantly.

Jewish per capita wealth is probably somewhat more evenly distributed than that of non-Jews. Although in both cases the wealthiest 5 per cent hold the bulk of all assets, the gap between the remaining individuals and the top 5 per cent group is narrower in the Jewish case, because of its higher urbanization. The numbers are not that much different as to cause a significant difference in the per capita asset numbers. Calculation of Jewish private wealth thus involves multiplying the country's total private wealth by the Jewish share of the population and adding the 25 per cent.

Country data

Information on Jewish assets varies considerably among the European countries occupied by the Nazis. The most comprehensive and detailed data comes from Germany and Austria. Statistics on the distribution of wealth in Western Europe are similar to the rest of Europe. Shown below are estimates of countries with a minimum Jewish wealth exceeding $150 million. Estimates for other countries and more details on those below can be found in publications listed in the Select Bibliography at the end of this chapter.

Germany

The estimate of German Jewish assets is for 1933, the year the Nazis came to power. After that, the asset level began to fall, even though the country's economic activity rose some 70 per cent in real terms by 1938. The increasing restrictions on Jewish participation in German economic activities forced Jews to draw down their assets, especially in the latter part of the 1930s. In addition, about a third of the Jewish population sold what assets they could and left Germany.

Besides using wealth statistics, the level of assets can be estimated by adding together the values for two distinct periods: from 1933 to 1938, when much of the Jewish property was confiscated through the Aryanization process and heavy taxes, especially on those who were lucky enough to emigrate; and after 1938, when the remaining property was simply taken away. The value of assets for the earlier period can be approximated through tax records and the losses in the post-1938 period by a census of Jewish assets that year.

In judging asset value in dollar terms, a realistic rate of exchange must be employed. The Reichsmark (RM) rate after 1933 was that one was worth 40 US cents. Many experts who have looked at the issue feel that the RM was overvalued in comparison to the dollar, especially in the late 1930s, and that 30 cents per Reichsmark is more representative.

The Jewish population in 1933 amounted to 575,000, of which 500,000 were confessional Jews and another 75,000 classified as Jews under the Nuremberg Laws. This meant that, at most, Jews accounted for nearly 1 per cent of the total German population. Using this study's national wealth methodology, Jewish wealth would amount to RM 3.8 billion or $1.5 billion when applying the post-1933 depreciated RM rate of 40 cents per dollar. The resulting per capita Jewish wealth number of $2600 is somewhat more than half of the overall US per capita private wealth.

The second approach, used widely by R. Hilberg and others, starts with the average tax of 25 per cent on assets taken out of the country by Jewish emigrants (165,000) between 1933 and 1938. The RM 940 million in taxes collected (mentioned by many experts) creates an asset value of RM 3.8 billion. Added to this number is the RM 7 billion in remaining assets listed in the 1938 census. Some estimators add RM 1.2 billion or $4.8 billion ($3.6 billion at 30 cents per RM). This reflects Hilberg's estimate of Jewish assets in 1933 of RM 10–12 billion. On a per capita basis that amounts to a range of $5800 to $8300, using both exchange rates.

These numbers are large when compared to the US per capita numbers, which range from $5000 to $5600. The value remaining in 1938 seems especially high. By that time much of the Jewish property had been Aryanized at a low value and the money received was heavily taxed. It is likely that the majority of the Jews still in Germany had to dip into their assets to sustain living conditions. Moreover, a large number of Jews were on relief; for example, 40 per cent in Berlin in March 1937. Finally, the flight tax numbers include the period from 1933 to 1945, with only a third collected between 1933 and 1938. Thus, the remaining two-thirds would duplicate assets in the 1938 census. Several sources at the time indicate the RM 7 billion census figure was too high. A Nazi report indicates the number is closer to RM 6 billion while a 'reliable' source, quoted by Nehemiah Robinson, states the value was approximately half of the census number.

In reality, the flight tax numbers are only modestly useful in gauging assets. At an average 25 per cent tax from 1933 to 1938, the value of the assets per capita amounts to $3000 per capita at most. These earlier very wealthy emigrants probably lost much of their assets through forced sales. After 1938 the RM 600 million paid in exit taxes probably nearly equalled the wealth declared for export, as the tax rate by then approached 100 per cent. The per capita value of these 150,000 emigrants amounted only to $1500. By then most of their assets had been confiscated.

The various estimates produce a range from $1.5 billion to $4.8 billion. Given all the factors discussed above, it is most reasonable to estimate the likely range (well rounded) at $2–$3 billion. The per capita equivalent is $3500–$5200.

Austria

The Austrian situation is much less complex than that of Germany. In March 1938, Austria was absorbed into Germany and within a few months the Nazis began to confiscate Jews' assets. Some 16,000 were able emigrate before that happened, but the remaining 167,000 were not so fortunate. There was a census of Jewish assets in June, which provides some of the most comprehensive country knowledge of property stolen by the Nazis.

Based on wealth data, and Jews accounting for 2.8 per cent of the population, Jewish assets are estimated at 2.1 billion schillings or $400 million. The per capita amount is $2200. The census data, as in the case of Germany, shows a much higher estimate – $600 million or a per capita of $3300. Austrian Jewish wealth probably falls within the two estimates. The per capita numbers are – and should be – lower than those of Germany. Although Vienna produced numerous Jewish intellects, German Jews were richer. They tended to have relatively more very wealthy financiers and industrialists, as well as a proportionally larger middle class. Austria's economy stagnated through most of the interwar years and unemployment remained very high. In Vienna, where most Austrian Jews lived, about one-third of the Jews were dependent on charity in 1935.

Poland

By far, prewar Poland had the largest Jewish population – 3.3 million – within the area dominated by the Nazis. Polish territory at the time included what is today western Belarus, northwestern Ukraine, southeastern Lithuania (including Vilnius), all with sizable Jewish populations. Jews accounted for nearly 10 per cent of the total population and more than 20 per cent of the non-agricultural population. Some one million Jews lived in Warsaw, where they made up one-third of the total.

The calculated Jewish share of national wealth, estimated by Robinson in 1944 and recalculated today, is $2.2 billion, or $700 per capita. A group of Polish Jewish industrialists estimated in 1943 that the wealth stolen by the Nazis from the Jews amounted to $1 billion. The same number was used by the United Nations Information Office in 1944. At $350 per capita, this estimate is considered too low. Robinson, in a 1962 publication, indicated that Jewish wealth in Poland 'must have exceeded $3 billion' or about $900 per capita. He based his new estimate on the fact that this would mean that the Jews in Poland had per capita wealth about one-third of Austrian Jews and two-thirds of Slovak Jews (who were also poor). Thus, a range of $2–$3 billion for Jewish assets is used in Poland with per capita numbers between $700 and $900.

Czechoslovakia

This country was dismembered in 1938 and 1939. As such it is necessary to discuss its three parts separately. They are Bohemia-Moravia (including Sudetenland) which is today the Czech Republic, Slovakia (part of which was in Hungary between 1938 and 1945), and Sub-Carpathia, which during the war was Hungarian and is now part of the Ukraine. In that order, the number of Jews in 1938 were about 120,000 (plus 20,000 refugees, mainly from Germany and Austria), 130,000 and 110,000. The same order starts with the richest and goes to the poorest in terms of wealth. This study looks separately at estimates for Czechoslovakia as a whole and its three major components.

An estimate of Jewish wealth based on national wealth data is available only for Czechoslovakia as it existed between the end of the first

World War and 1937. It amounts to $600 million or $1700 per capita. A British Royal Institute study in 1940 came up with $500 million or $1400 per capita.

For Bohemia-Moravia there are a number of estimates of Jewish wealth, ranging from 12 billion to 20 billion krones. The lower number was published in 1954 and is based on a study by an economist who drew on archival records of Aryanization and the Gestapo. The higher one was prepared in 1939 by the Economic Committee of the Protectorate on the basis of the knowledge of experienced economists and bankers. A 17 billion krones estimate, also published in 1939, is of unknown sourcing. In dollars the three estimates are $420 million ($3500 per capita,) $600 million ($5000 per capita), and $700 million ($5800 per capita). In addition, the Nazis indicated they seized nearly $300 million in Jewish property in the Sudetenland. With 25,000 Jews in this area, this amounts to $12,000 per capita – a number that seems much too high. It was probably announced for propaganda purposes.

Estimates of Slovakian Jewish wealth range from 3 billion to nearly 6 billion krones or $100 million ($800 per capita) to $200 million ($1500 per capita). Another appraisal is based on Nazi seizure records from December 1940. It amounts to 4.2 billion krones ($140 million or $1500 per capita) and covers 89,000 Jews. Some 42,000 Jews, however, were living in the part of Slovakia that was annexed by Hungary in 1938. If the same per capita number is used for the 42,000 Jews, total assets for all of Slovakia (1837 boundaries) would be nearly $200 million. In his 1944 study, Robinson indicated that he preferred the estimate of the Central Committee of Slovakian Jewry of 4.5 billion krones ($160 million or $1200 per capita) No Sub-Carpathia estimates exist. Jews in this region were among the poorest in Europe. Many were farmers and belonged to the mystical Hassidic sect. Sub-Carpathia's per capita wealth numbers are probably less than those of Poland, or from $500 to $700. These per capita estimates produce a range in Jewish wealth from $50 to $75 million for this eastern region of Czechoslovakia.

Combining the three regions roughly provides a range from $600 million to $1 billion. The full range is used in Bohemia-Moravia and Sub-Carpathia, while in Slovakia the more realistic numbers fall between $160 and $200 million. The low end of the full country range about matches the calculated number based on the projected national wealth estimate for all of Czechoslovakia. Overall per capita numbers – from $1700 to $2800 – can be misleading since they hide the significant differences in wealth patterns among the three regions.

Hungary

Hungary's unique situation during the war creates confusion as to the country's Jewish population. These numbers therefore must be clearly defined. As a wartime ally of Germany, Hungary was not taken over by the Nazis until 1944. The Horthy regime did undertake antisemitic actions starting in 1938, in part to appease Hitler and thwart the more hardened local fascists. Although these policies attempted to reduce Jewish economic and cultural influence in the country, mass killings were avoided. The relatively safe position of the Jews until 1944 attracted some 20,000 Jewish refugees from neighbouring countries. They are counted in the statistics of the countries from which they came.

Meanwhile, under various agreements with Germany between 1938 and 1941 Hungary acquired territory from the dismembered Czechoslovakia and Yugoslavia as well as from Romania. These annexed lands contained about 330,000 Jews. In addition, according to the 1941 census, there were some 400,000 Jews living within Hungary's 1937 boundaries. This study uses Hungarian territory as of 1937, thus placing the annexed Jewish population in their original countries. To complicate matters, under the Nuremberg laws there were some additional 100,000 Jews, as a result of decades of high rates of intermarriage and religious conversions. This study thus uses 500,000 (5 per cent of the population) in evaluating the estimates of Hungarian Jewish per capita wealth.

The national wealth estimate yields Jewish wealth of $550 million or $1100 per capita. This number seems low considering Hungarian Jews were among the most advanced economically. They were mainly middle class and accounted for the bulk of Hungarians in commerce, finance and the liberal professions. To accommodate for this apparent problem, Robinson in his 1962 report assumes 10 per cent of all national wealth was in Jewish hands. The use of the 10 per cent factor produces Jewish wealth of $800 million ($1600 per capita).

Three other estimates of Jewish Hungarian wealth are reported. The first two – $6 billion and $4 billion – which came from Nazi sources in 1944, were probably released for propaganda purposes. They are extremely high, accounting for (respectively) more than half and a quarter of total Hungarian wealth, including the annexed territories. The third estimate, prepared by the World Jewish Congress after the war, is $1.2–$1.6 billion for the 1937 Hungarian area. This produces a per capita range of $2400 to $3200. These numbers make more sense when compared with those of Germany, Austria and the Czech Republic. Thus, a range of Hungarian Jewish wealth of $800 million to $1.6 billion is used in this study.

Romania

Among the Jewish wealth numbers available for Romania, some can be disregarded because they are purely Nazi propaganda. These estimates state that the Jews held 65 per cent and 55 per cent of the national wealth while consisting of only 4.2 per cent of the population. The most complete actual accounting of Jewish property was prepared in 1943 and is based on confiscations. It valued assets at about $500 million ($600 per capita), but was not complete. Another government number announced in 1944 is $350 million, which seems too low because the per capita equivalent is only $400. Based on wealth statistics, the Jewish portion amounts to about $900 million ($1100 per capita).

Asset estimates of $600 million to $900 million seem to produce a reasonable range. The low end of the range corresponds to that used in Poland and the upper end is somewhat higher. With few exceptions, the Jewish population suffered economically, even more than the non-Jewish segment during the 1930s. Prior to the 1931 financial crash, the Jews owned many large banks in the country. Bucharest supported the non-Jewish banks during the financial crisis while forcing the Jewish ones into liquidation. During the country's significant economic recovery in 1938–9, Jews hardly benefited because they were restrained by anti-semitic laws.

The Netherlands

The Nazis were extremely effective in confiscating assets of the relatively wealthy Jewish community in Holland, in part as a result of lessons learned in Germany and Austria. A 1933 census indicated there were 130,000 Jews, a number that probably not change much by the late 1930s. In addition, Holland absorbed 25,000–30,000 foreign Jews between 1933 and 1939.

On the basis of national wealth estimates, Jewish wealth amounted to about $280 million ($2200 per capita). A number of estimates of assets looted from Dutch Jews were made, ranging from 500 million guilders ($270 million) to 1.1 billion guilders (nearly $600 million). The lower number was reported by a German newspaper and included 'real estate, enterprises and capital.' This number probably excluded some $20 million in money extorted from Jews in exchange for not deporting them, as well as foreign assets that had to be turned into the Dutch central bank soon after the Nazis took control. With these adjustments the first number exceeds $300 million. The higher estimate comes from a post-war State Department report. Both estimates are reduced 15 per cent to take into account the property confiscated from Jewish refugees. A range of $300 million to $510 million in Dutch Jewish assets seems most reasonable, considering all the above data. This amounts to $2300 and $3900 per capita.

France

The published wealth numbers for France are particularly confusing. In addition, about 15 per cent of the French Jewish population in 1939 were refugees who left Germany, Austria and Czechoslovakia after 1933. When the Nazis invaded, this group amounted to 50,000, while long-time citizens were 270,000.

The French Commissioner of Jewish Affairs in 1943 reported that the value of Jewish property Aryanized was 100 billion francs, which would have been $2.5 billion at prewar exchange rates. This number seems extraordinarily high, being five to ten times more than the proportion of Jews in France. It would yield a Jewish per capita wealth of $7800, even if the refugees are included. Jewish sources indicated that Paris Jews were robbed of property worth 10 billion francs excluding furniture and other household items. Although obviously not the total, it still seems low. Based on this study's national wealth methodology, Jewish wealth is $415 million or $1500 per capita.

In his 1962 study, Robinson suggests that the average value of wealth for French Jews probably equates with that of Austria's $3,000. This seems reasonable. The result would be $810 million in French Jewish wealth. The study uses a rounded range of between $400 million and $800 million.

Soviet-occupied territories

After invading the USSR, the Nazis soon occupied a region including the Ukraine and Belarus, which contained 2 million Jews. Perhaps 40 per cent escaped with the retreating Red Army. Most of those that remained were killed while nearly all lost their possessions. Placing a value on these holdings is very difficult. The Soviets had already nationalized any property holdings and businesses. What was left was essential house-hold items, small savings plus some hidden gold or foreign currency. These might have made up a third of the assets of those in market-oriented countries. Moreover, there were no very rich citizens, who few in number, normally drive up the per capita rate. It thus is hard to conceive that the lost property amounted to more than $200-$300 per capita in the occupied Soviet territories compared with $700-$900 in Poland and the Baltic states. This means total assets of $400 million to $600 million.

Country total

The calculated total amount of assets taken from Jews in all countries of Nazi-occupied Europe ranges from $8 billion to almost $13 billion. The low end essentially reflects estimates made using a national wealth methodology and the higher numbers mainly are based on asset census data. This disparity makes sense because the procedures that are used to calculate wealth data typically underestimate activity and assets of small-scale businesses: for example, the numerous Jewish entrepreneurs throughout Europe at the time. Often this undercounting is in the 10–20 per cent range. The value of household articles also tends to be inadequately counted.

Among countries, the relative per capita levels of Jewish assets seem to fit well with the perceived notions as to the economic characteristics of each. Only major changes in a few countries could appreciably alter total assets. Two countries – Germany and Poland – account for about half the total, and five (the addition of Hungary, Czechoslovakia and Romania) for three-quarters. Although it is unlikely that the Jewish German per capita level would be higher, the Polish estimate might be, because of the difficulty in estimating the assets of its many small-scale traders. But even the influence of this factor on the total has its limits since a very large share of assets are held by a few wealthy individuals. Some asset types also may have been left out. For example, the Austrian data indicate that annuities and unpaid salaries are important categories.

At the same time, it is necessary to subtract from the estimated total several hundreds of millions of dollars in assets the Jews were able to move out of harm's way. In addition, asset values may have been overstated on the forms on which Jewish owners indicated how much their property was worth. Often people feel that their property is worth more than can be obtained in the market, especially during difficult economic times, such as the 1930s. This possibility is indicated by the fact that such asset surveys tend to produce the highest asset value numbers for a country. Given all these considerations, it seems reasonable that the lower end of the range should be $9 billion and the upper bounds, $14 billion.

Asset types

Although the available information compiled on each country's assets by type is minimal, it does reveal some interesting results. The best information comes from the detailed census of Jewish assets in Austria and Germany in 1938 and Slovakia in 1940. In all three countries, Jews were asked to report their assets and liabilities by some ten categories – see Table 3. Real estate was broken down between residential and commercial, with the latter placed under businesses. The most interesting results are:

- Residential real estate consists of some 25–30 per cent of the total.

- Businesses account for nearly 15 per cent to nearly 25 per cent of the total. These amounts are exclusive of debt, while real estate and other categories are not.

- Personal monetary holdings and investments account for at least 40 per cent and probably more than half of Jewish assets. The more detailed Austrian data indicate about 20 per cent of the total assets are liquid.

- The Austrian numbers show an unexpectedly high amount for annuities (20 per cent) and unpaid salaries (10 per cent).

Table 3 Jewish Assets in Austria, Germany and Slovakia in 1938 (percentage of total)

	Austria	Germany	Slovakia	Netherlands
Agricultural/forestry	2	1	11	2
Residential property	23	28	29	20
Businesses	14	14	23	25
Financial				
Securities	12	–	–	30
Capital claims	8	–	–	–
Cash, savings	7	–	–	5
Annuities	20	–	–	–
Unpaid salaries	10	–	–	–
Household items				10
Valuables	2	–	–	3
Insurance, misc.	2	–	–	3
Other		57	37	2

- The average value of enterprise in Germany is $6600, Austria, $3400 and Slovakia, $2400. This is arrived at by dividing the value of businesses by their number.

- About one-third of the Austrian firms had per capita assets of $7000 and the remaining two-thirds had an average value of only $700 each. This shows, as with overall wealth, the high concentration of assets among the larger enterprises.

Based on this information it can be tentatively estimated that about two-thirds of the assets were easily movable. That is arrived at by removing from total assets the amounts for all homes and farms, and half the value of businesses. The Austrian data indicate that about 20 per cent of the total consists of highly liquid assets (securities, currency, gold, etc.). The gold portion probably amounts to 1–2 per cent of Jewish assets. This is derived by assuming roughly half of the $260 million in non-monetary gold looted by the Nazis was taken from Jews.

Select bibliography

General

Don, Yehuda, *A Social and Economic History of Central European Jews* (New Brunswick, NJ: Transaction, 1990).

Hilberg, Raul, *The Destruction of the European Jews* (New York: New Viewpoints, 1973).

Lestchinsky, Jacob, 'Balance Sheet of Extermination – II', *Jewish Affairs*, vol. I, no. 1, 1 February 1946.

Lestchinsky, Jacob, 'Balance Sheet of Extermination – II', *Jewish Affairs*, vol. I, no. 12, 15 November 1946.

Robinson, Nehemiah, *Hitler's Ten-Year War on the Jews* (New York: Institute of Jewish Affairs, World Jewish Congress 1943).

Robinson, Nehemiah, *Indemnification and Reparations, Jewish Aspects* (New York: Institute of Jewish Affairs, World Jewish Congress, 1944).

Robinson, Nehemiah, *Indemnification and Reparations (Fourth Supplement), Jewish Aspects* (New York: Institute of Jewish Affairs, World Jewish Congress, 1949).

Robinson, Nehemiah, *Spoliation and Remedial Action* (New York: Institute of Jewish Affairs, World Jewish Congress, 1962).

Austria

'Report on Jewish Heirless Assets in Austria', US National Archives, RG 59, Department of State, Decimal Files, Box 1080, file 263.0041, 18 May 1953.

Germany

Aly, Gotz and Angress, Ruth K., 'Economics of the Final Solution', in *Simon Wiesenthal Center Annual Report*, vol. 5 (1988).

Barkai, Avraham, *From Boycott to Annihilation: The Economic Struggle of the Jews, 1933–43* (University Press of New England, 1989).

The Netherlands

'History and Present Status of Lippmann, Rosenthal Co.', State Department Voluntary Report of Stanford Sahewel, Vice-Consul, US National Archives, RG 226, entry 133, Box 22.

Poland

Tomaszewski, Jerzy, 'The Role of Jews in Polish Commerce, 1918–39', in *The Jews of Poland between the Two World Wars* (Brandeis University Press, 1989).

4
The Holocaust, 'Thefticide' and Restitution: a Legal Perspective

Irwin Cotler

The question of restitution for Jewish property confiscated or stolen in anticipation, during, and in consequence of the Holocaust finds expression at a historic juncture – the fiftieth anniversary year in 1998 of the *Universal Declaration of Human Rights*, the *Genocide Convention*, and the period of the Nuremberg Trials and Nuremberg Principles. Indeed this historic convergence – as in the case of the Nuremberg Principle – not only codified existing international humanitarian law at the time, but provided the foundation for the contemporary international law of human rights. It included, in particular, state and individual responsibility for criminal violations of human rights, and the correlative right of individuals and groups to protection against these criminal violations, and to redress and reparation for these wrongs.

It is this historic and dramatic development of both international human rights law and international humanitarian law which forms the juridical backdrop and – in the case of the Holocaust – the existential backdrop for the understanding of state responsibility for criminal violations of human rights, including the responsibility for restitution.

Indeed, in the absence of the historiography of 'Nuremberg'[1] or Holocaust law, the notion of 'restitution of property' might well be misleading – if not also a misnomer. For the term restitution, standing alone, ordinarily reflects domestic principles underlying civil and property law – or international law principles respecting state responsibility in matters of expropriation of property or aliens. But restitution for 'Nuremberg crimes' – for genocide, war crimes and crimes against humanity – is something dramatically different in precedent and principle.

Indeed, even the term 'war crimes' is a misnomer; for we are not talking about crimes committed against combatants in the course of the prosecution of a war; rather, we are talking about crimes committed against civilians in the course of the persecution of a race. Indeed, we are talking about crimes committed in anticipation of the Holocaust – or attending the Holocaust – or in consequence of it. In a word, we are talking about 'thefticide' – the greatest mass theft on the occasion of the greatest mass murder in history. As the Norwegian Minister of Justice, Grad Liv Vaala, recently put it, 'The loss of the Jews cannot be limited to economic calculations only. The organized deportation and liquidation was mass murder, murder of a people. We cannot change what happened, but we can set a moral standard to remind everyone of this dark chapter in the history of Europe.'[2]

It is this 'thefticide' which accounts for the *cri de coeur* of Holocaust survivors whose anguish I witness at every conference or seminar on 'the restitution of confiscated and other jewish property in the Second World War'. What they are trying to tell us is that behind every dormant Swiss account, behind every plundered property, behind every gold dental bridge, behind every unrecovered insurance policy, is the narrative and the horror of the Holocaust.

The problem, of course – in this convergence of the existential and the juridical – is that the transcendental horror of the Holocaust – of the liquidation of a people as well as property, or the plunder of property attendant upon the liquidation of people – belies any legal remedy or remedy of restitution; while the civil and international law principles of restitution could not have imagined the Holocaust. In a word, the existential character of the evil overtakes the law's capacity to address it, while the law's capacity to address it requires us to banalize the evil.

It appeared almost as if each of the European countries against whom a claim could be made had its own 'national' myth – which myths were often also overlapping – while all countries asserted a shared generic myth of non-responsibility in juridical terms arising from their respective national myths in historical terms. What follows is, first, an inventory or set of case studies of these national myths; and, second, a corresponding rebuttal to the myths anchored in a restatement – or contextualization – of the principles of the law of restitution.

Myth 1: 'We were victims not perpetrators'

Indeed, in the case of Austria, it cultivated the myth of being the first victim of Nazi Germany, and therefore under no obligation to compensate any claimants; and it anchored this revisionist history in revisionist law – that is, that the *Moscow Declaration* of 1943 recognized Austria as an occupied country – while it ignored that part of the *Moscow Declaration* which speaks to Austria's collaboration with the Nazis during the war.

The fact is that most Austrians greeted the Nazi *Anschluss* in 1938 with great enthusiasm; while one of the first acts undertaken by the Germans in April 1938 – in collaboration with the Austrians immediately after the *Anschluss* – was the appropriation, or Aryanization, of the property of Austrian Jewry.[3]

The postwar restitution process in Austria, then, was founded, and foundered, on the twin myths of historical and legal revisionism. If Austria was the first victim of the Nazis, as the historical myth put it, how, then – as the legal myth then took over – could she be responsible for the crimes of the Nazis. Indeed, recompensating the Jews, so went the myth, would be granting them privileged treatment. In effect, then, Austrian Jews suffered double jeopardy; not only were they not compensated, but they were required to regard their Austrian perpetrators as fellow victims.

Myth 2: 'The crimes were committed by a foreign government, by the German Nazi-occupied regime'

Indeed, in the case of France, for example, it nurtured, and projected, the historical myth that the perpetrators were the Nazi Vichy government and not the French; the French government of today asserts the related legal myth that it cannot be held responsible for the crimes of the 'foreign' Vichy government of the past.

But, as the witness testimony and documentary evidence of, *inter alia*, the trial of French war criminals has revealed – including the trial and conviction of high-ranking Vichy official Maurice Papon of crimes against humanity – the Vichy government was French and not German; the crimes were perpetrated by French nationals, and not just German Nazis; and the plunder of property of French Jewry – 75,000 of whom were deported to the death camps – was carried out by French Vichy and not German officials.

Myth 3: 'We were not only victims,' as the Dutch put it, 'but we were the vanguard of the resistance, while protecting Dutch Jewry'

Indeed, the diary of Anne Frank, the 14-year-old Dutch girl from Amsterdam who recorded the life of her family which was hiding during the war – the house was transformed into a museum after the war – became a metaphor for the refuge the Dutch afforded the Jews. What is not so well known, if it is known at all, was that Anne Frank and her family – as well as the large majority of Dutch Jews – were sent to the death camps with the collaboration of the Dutch themselves.

The destruction of Dutch Jewry and plunder of their property in anticipation – and in consequence – of their murder, was only too familiar. When the Germans invaded The Netherlands in May 1940, approximately 140,000 Jews – including 15,000 refugees from Germany and Austria – were living in the country. The persecution of Jews – and theft of their property – began almost immediately, including an order later in August 1941 instructing the Jews to deposit, in one bank ('Li-Ro'), all cash holdings and cheques, as well as their bank accounts, savings schemes and securities.[4]

Myth 4: 'We were victims, not only of the Nazis, but also the Communists'

Indeed, in the case of Eastern European countries – as reflected in the metaphor of 'captive nations' – the myth has developed into one of 'double jeopardy' – of having twice been victimized – so that claims of restitution are rejected as being as misplaced as they are misguided. And more: the 'double victim' myth sometimes shades into the 'double resistance' one – the Eastern European countries fought both the Nazis and the Communists.

Admittedly, in the case of the former Soviet Union, it did fight the Nazis, but it also confiscated the property of the Jews, whereas, in the case of the 'captive nations' like Lithuania and Latvia, historical revisionism cannot mask the unvarnished truth – that economic liquidation foreshadowed physical liquidation. The only double victims were the Jews – of both the Nazis and their Eastern European collaborators.

Myth 5: 'We were officially neutral', as the Swiss put it

Indeed, the Swiss have maintained not only that neutrality was their policy, but that it was sanctioned by the Swiss domestic and international legal regime of the day. Accordingly, no restitution was to be made, so the legal myth began fifty years ago, since the Swiss were not perpetrators but neutrals, and law sanctioned their neutrality.

Fifty years later, that myth has imploded – both historically and legally – and the Swiss are now confronted by the compelling evidence of their complicity with the Nazis and – worse – that such complicity may even have supported and prolonged the Nazi war effort.

Myth 6: 'The time has come to bury the past'

Indeed, it is perhaps not surprising that the same argument used to immunize Nazi war criminals from justice at the beginning of the Cold War and since, is now being used to immunize the perpetrators of 'thefticide' from making restitution at the end of the Cold War and beyond. In a word, the exculpatory generic myth – of 'non-responsibility' – underpins both. But whereas the Nazi war criminals are being immunized and protected respecting Nuremberg crimes committed fifty years ago, Europess confiscators and looters are participating in a continuing Nuremberg war crime, with the denial of restitution a standing case of unjust enrichment.

Myth 7: Alongside the myth that no restitution is owing is the parallel myth that 'restitution has already been made'

This factual and juridical sleight of hand is accomplished by invoking German restitution to Holocaust survivors, and concluding thereby that reparations have been paid and the victims duly indemnified.

What appears also to be a set of myths – that restitution should not be made because the time has come to bury the past – and that restitution has already been made so that the 'past' has been redressed – are actually anchored in the same moral and legal shibboleth: that no one is responsible. Indeed, by imputing to Germany the assumption of responsibility for restitution, the rest of Europe is saying not only that restitution has been made, but is asserting the myth that 'we didn't commit the crimes'.

Myth 8: 'The remedy of restitution has been prescribed'

Again, the same argument used to immunize Nazi war criminals from justice today is being used to immunize the perpetrators of 'thefticide' today; namely, that the remedy of restitution – if it even existed – has been foreclosed by the passage of time; that a statute of limitations, as it were, has descended across Europe; that, in a word, any claim for restitution has been prescribed, so that survivors have no standing to advance a restitutionary claim. Again, this myth partakes of historical and legal revisionism for it ignores the continuing character of the crime in factual terms, and its imprescriptibility in legal terms.

Myth 9: 'Restitution is Jewish blackmail'

The notion that restitution is nothing other than 'Jewish extortion' – and that it will provoke an antisemitic backlash – is a particularly insidious and Orwellian myth; indeed, the addendum to the myth that the advancing of such claims can only hurt the Jews themselves simply compounds the felony. In a word, this myth is a classic example of 'blaming the victim', where the victims of 'thefticide' are characterized as 'Jewish blackmailers' for seeking justice, while the perpetrators – and continuing beneficiaries – of the murderous robbery are to be rewarded for their antisemitism.

In effect, then, the juridical responsibility of the European governments who participated in the economic liquidation of European Jewry attendant upon their physical liquidation – who partook of 'thefticide' – is criminal rather than civil, involving 'crimes under international law' rather than mere violations of international law, and engaging international rather than just domestic responsibility. 'Restitution', then, is a moral/juridical imperative resulting from such international responsibility for Nuremberg Crimes – for criminal violations of human rights; indeed, it is a responsibility anchored in the following nine basic Principles of State Responsibility for such international crimes – and the corresponding restitution or reparation that is owed to the victims.

Principle 1: Doctrine of State Responsibility for Wrongful Acts

One of the oldest and universally recognized principles of international law is that a state is not only responsible under international law for the injury caused by its wrongful act, but it is also responsible for the reparation and indemnification of such wrongful injury.[5] This principle has been enunciated in a number of leading cases, including the *Cherzow Factory* case,[6] where the Permanent Court of International Justice held that 'it is a principle of international law, and even a general conception of law, that any breach of an engagement involves an obligation to make reparation'.

Moreover, as set forth above, the 'wrong' here is not only a 'mere' violation of international law – involving interstate responsibility – but a criminal violation of international law – engaging international responsibility *erga omnes*. And more: it is not only a criminal violation of international law – which would be bad enough – but the commission of the ultimate 'Nuremberg' evil, of Crimes Against Humanity and acts of Genocide, crimes for which 'restitution' – as it is classically understood – appears as understated a remedy as it is unrevealing of the enormity of the crime.

Principle 2: Doctrine of State Succession

International law is clear, as Principle One above demonstrates, that the state responsible for the wrong is also responsible for the reparation or indemnification of that wrong. But what if the state at issue, for example, Norway or France, is not the one which committed the wrongful acts, that is Crimes Against Humanity, but these crimes were committed under Nazi rule by the Quisling government in Norway, or the Vichy government in France? Why should the present governments in Norway and France be held responsible for the wrongs committed by the Quisling government or Vichy government under the German occupation of Norway and France?

The answer is the Doctrine of State Succession, whereby a successor state, like Norway or France, is responsible for the wrongful acts of its predecessor government. Indeed, we are speaking here more of a successor government than a successor state, since the crimes were committed by a Norwegian or French government in the name of the Norwegian State or French Republic, and not a different state or republic as succeeded by Norway or France respectively. In a word, and by way of example, the Act ordering the confiscation 'of all property of any kind belonging to a Jew' in Norway was enacted on 26 October 1942 by a Norwegian authority; the property confiscated was taken over by the Norwegian state treasury; the liquidation of confiscated property was carried out by a Norwegian agency, the Liquidation Board for Confiscated Jewish Property; the designated 'trustees' for Jewish 'estates' (note: the plundered estates were characterized as 'bankruptcies', the sanitized legal term used to obfuscate the plundering of property attendant upon the genocide of a community) were Norwegian officials (mostly lawyers); the transfer of all silver and gold as well as jewellery to the German *Sicherheitspolizei* was done pursuant to an agreement by the Norwegian government with the German occupation forces; and the arrests and deportations to the death camps were carried out by Norwegian officials.

It should be noted that the successor state assumes the responsibility of its predecessor government even where the state – and government – was not that of the successor one. This principle was laid down as early as *The Lighthous Arbitration* case.[7] In that case, France claimed that Greece was responsible for a breach of state concessions to its citizens by the autonomous State of Crete. The breaches were committed before Greece's sovereignty over Crete. The Tribunal held that Greece was obligated to compensate for Crete's breach of contract because Greece was a successor state.

In summary, then, and as the authorities on this point conclude, 'most recent and persuasive precedents support the recognition of a presumption of successor State responsibility as a customary norm in international law.'[8] These precedents include state practice;[9] decisions of international tribunals;[10] and decisions of domestic courts.[11] In the case of Norway or France, for example, where the state succession does not admit of any doubt, the international legal obligation – and Norwegian or French state responsibility – for reparation for the criminal acts of its predecessor Quisling or Vichy government is as clear as if the present Norwegian or French government had committed the criminal violations itself; while even in cases like the Eastern European states, the successor state, pursuant to the *Lighthouse Arbitration* case, assumes the responsibility of its predecessor government even where, as in the case of Poland, for example, the state and government was not that of the successor one.

Principle 3: Obligations under Treaty Law

If the above principles were not in and of themselves complete and compelling, European countries are parties to a series of international undertakings and agreements that give expression to their 'restitution' obligation, and have 'internationalized'[12] this responsibility.

For example, Norway is a Party to the *Universal Declaration of Human Rights*[13] which speaks in Article 17 of the right to own property and to not be arbitrarily deprived of property, which is the Article most often invoked in the international 'restitution of property' issues; but it speaks, more importantly, of the right to life, liberty and security of the person – the most fundamental of rights – and the corpus of rights most egregiously violated in the Nuremberg Crimes of the Quisling government.

Equally, Norway, to its credit, is a State Party to the *International Covenant on Civil and Political Rights*[14] and the *International Covenant on Economic, Social and Cultural Rights*[15] which, together with the *Universal Declaration* and the United Nations *Charter*,[16] constitute what has come to be known as the *International Bill of Rights*,[17] itself inspired by the horrors of the Holocaust; and it is a State Party to the *International convention on the Elimination of all Forms of Racial Discrimination*,[18] the *Convention on the Prevention and Punishment of Genocide*,[19] and the *Geneva Conventions of 1949*[20] – the specific emanations from the Nuremberg Principles – and which seek to prevent, as well as prohibit, any such criminal violations of international humanitarian law and the international law of human rights as occurred during the Second World War.

Restitution, then, is not only a continuing responsibility for the criminal breaches by Norway of international humanitarian and human rights law as represented by the Nuremberg Judgements; but is a continuing state responsibility for undertakings assumed by Norway – to its credit – under International Treaty Law, – and particularly the corpus of international human rights law obligations represented in the post-Nuremberg Treaties.

Principle 4: Principles of International Tort Liability

In the past, tort law was based on a system that centred on the punishment of the tortfeasor.[21] The focus of tort liability, however, particularly 'international tort liability', has shifted. It now concentrates on the compensation of victims and the historical 'righting of wrongs'.[22] For this reason, in matters of tort liability under domestic law, almost all states now provide for the survivability of actions against deceased tortfeasors in both common law and civil law countries.[23] In international law, this principle of the 'righting of wrongs' – and the indemnification of the victim – now underpins the doctrine of state succession, of state responsibility and 'restitution for wrongful injury'; *a fortiori* when that wrongful injury arises from a criminal,and not just tortious, violation.

Principle 5: The Doctrine of Unjust Enrichment

This doctrine is one of the more compelling ones engaging state responsibility on both moral and juridical grounds. It is organized around the principle that, where a state illegally takes or receives property which does not belong to it, such a state is in the position of a receiver of stolen goods; more particularly, failure to compensate the deprived owner would constitute unjust enrichment by the state. The doctrine is anchored in the foundational principle of every legal system that any 'taking of value' belonging to another is illegal, and which has emerged as a 'general principle for granting restitutionary relief'.[24] Indeed, the American *Restatement of the Law of Restitution*[25] sets the law of restitution squarely within the principle of preventing unjust enrichment as follows: 'A person who has been unjustly enriched at the expense of another is required to make restitution to the other.'

If this is the principle which applies in a civil and domestic law context, then it applies, *a fortiori*, in a criminal and international law context. As Maddaugh and McCamus put it,[26] 'There is well-established authority for the proposition that a murderer shall not be permitted to profit from his unlawful act by acquiring property from his victim.' Or, as the caselaw has concluded.[27] 'The principle . . . is that a man shall not slay his benefactor and thereby take his bounty.'

In a word, the notion that a state might enrich itself from the commission of crimes against humanity – from the ashes of the Holocaust – is as reprehensible as it is unjust – a foundational assault on the very foundations of international law and the international law of human rights – a foundational breach of the Nuremberg Principles.

Indeed, if there were no other principle in international law mandating restitution, this principle alone would suffice; and if there were no other example of unjust enrichment from Nuremberg crimes than the Austrian, Norwegian, Dutch, French or Swiss one – or any of the East European countries – they would be horrific enough. For example, as set forth earlier, at the very moment that Norwegian Jews were being rounded up for deportations to the death camps – the only Norwegian citizens singled out for deportation and murder because of their race – they were being systematically plundered of all their possessions by Norwegian police and Norwegian government officials. Genocide – the intentional physical liquidation of Norwegian Jewry – was the prerequisite for their complete financial liquidation.

Indeed, the principle of 'unjust enrichment', while a foundational principle for restitution, is as understated and inadequate as the principle of 'restitution' itself. For there can never be any 'restitution' for genocide; whatever restitution takes place – and it is as much a moral as its is a juridical imperative – will never compensate for the 'unjust enrichment'. One can seek to provide restitution for property; one can never provide restitution for lives lost for the destruction of a community.

Principle 6: No One Shall Profit from the Commission of an Illegal Act

This principle – a natural corollary to the Principle of Unjust Enrichment – is grounded in the Latin legal maxim of *ex inuria non oritur ius*. It also finds expression in the general principle *nullus commodum capere potest de injuria sua propria*, which prohibits a party who is guilty of some form of wrongdoing from profiting as a result of such conduct.[28] Indeed, it is rooted in the biblical principle, set forth in Kings I, and directly applicable to the case at bar, of 'Will you murder and also inherit?'

In fact, one of the more disturbing manifestations of the physical and financial liquidation of European Jewry – and a rather Orwellian application of this principle of unjust assault in its biblical expression – is that this race-based genocide was actually sanctioned by the laws of the respective European states.

The enormity of this crime Against humanity is beyond vocabulary. Indeed, what is so galling is that this 'unjust enrichment' – or 'profits from the commission of an illegal act', in this case acts of genocide – began even before the deportation and was intimately connected to it. As stated earlier, it was a financial liquidation that not only preceded the genocide but was predicated upon it.

Principle 7: The Principle of Just Compensation

The principle of just compensation is grounded both in the above international law principles as well as in the related principles of 'just compensation' in international law, and may be summarized as follows: that wrongful injury by the state entails state responsibility for such wrongful injury, and engages also the successor regime; that such wrongful injury – and state responsibility – warrants reparation or compensation for the victim; that such reparation or restitution is particularly warranted when the wrongful injury involves criminal violations of human rights and grave breaches of international humanitarian law and the international law of human rights; that such compensation must be just; and that for compensation to be just it must be prompt, fair, effective and non-discriminatory. As set forth as early as the *Cherzow Factory (Indemnity)* case in 1928,[29]

> The essential principle contained in the actual notion of an illegal act – a principle which seems to be established by international practice and in particular by the decision of authoritative tribunals – is that reparation must, as far as possible, wipe out all the consequences of the illegal act and re-establish the situation which would, in all probability, have existed if that act had not been committed.

In a word, the organizing principle of just compensation is restitution or *restitutio in integrum*, the civil law equivalent of 'restoration or restitution to the previous condition'. But what if the 'illegal act committed' was, as in the present case, the act of genocide? How can reparation – or restitution of property – ever 'wipe out all the consequences of the illegal act'? How, in a word, can restitution ever 're-establish the situation which would, in all probability, have existed if that act had not been committed', when that act was genocide, and the lives of European Jewry – let alone its assets – can never be restored?

The General Assembly of the United Nations, in its Resolution 1803, stated that another important element of the compensation requirement is that it be 'appropriate'.[30] 'Resolution 1803 has been accepted in a number of arbitration awards as reflecting customary international law.'[31] Although these arbitration awards have done little to define 'appropriate compensation', the underlying principle of these decisions is that the compensation be made as accessible and equitable as possible.

Finally, the Principle of Just compensation requires that the compensation be non-discriminatory, a restitution criterion that is also founded on 'property law' principles. As the *American Restatement of the Law* put it, 'Formulations of the rules on expropriation generally include a prohibition of discrimination, implying that a program of taking that singles out aliens generally, or aliens of a particular nationality, or particular aliens, would violate international law.'[32]

Similarly, the *Amoco International Finance Corporation* v. *Iran* case[33] states that '[d]iscrimination is widely held as prohibited by customary international law in the field of expropriation'. Further, 'the Consultation Assembly of the Council of Europe approved the work of OECD in preparing a Draft Convention of the Protection of Foreign Property, in which the following principles were incorporated: (i) fair and equitable treatment without discrimination . . . (iii) no expropriations except in the public interest, and under due process of law and subject to just and effective compensation'.[34]

What emerges from all this is that a baseline restitutional requirement in the case of 'illegal [property] takings' requires just compensation – and that for compensation to be just it must be prompt, fair, appropriate and non-discriminatory. clearly, then, the satisfaction of just compensation in the case of Nuremberg crimes would, at a minimum, have to satisfy these requirements. But while 'just compensation' requirements, grounded in civil restitutional principles, provide a foundational base for relief, it is no less clear that just compensation for criminal violations of international law cannot be based on 'property' considerations alone.

In a word, restitution – and just compensation – in the case of the liquidation not only of the property of European Jewry but the liquidation of European Jews themselves, – must compensate for the lives lost as well as the assets plundered; for the destruction of a community as well as the plundering of the assets of its individual members; for the unjust enrichment over time by the successor governments and citizens as well as for the lack of prompt compensation at the time of the 'takings'; for the fact that Jews were the only group singled out for genocide (and not just the plundering of its property) on account of their race, as well as for the prohibition of discriminatory 'takings' of property on account of race; for the contribution that its murdered human beings might have made – individually and communally – as well as for 'property' appreciation over time.

Principle 8: The Non-Applicability of Statutes of Limitations to Nuremberg Crimes

Restitution cannot be effected or be effective if statutes of limitations are applied. Moreover, the notion the restitutive actions for war crimes and crimes against humanity can be prescribed is to misrepresent the action for which restitution is claimed as well as the law under which it is governed. Again, the paradigm here is not that of restitution in a domestic civil action involving principles of civil and property law, or restitution in an international context involving state responsibility in matters of appropriation of property of aliens; rather, the paradigm – if there can be such a 'paradigm' in so abhorrent a crime – is that of restitution for Nuremberg crimes, which is something dramatically different in precedent and principles.

And just as Nuremberg crimes for which restitution is sought are distinguishable from conventional civil and property breaches and related paradigms of restitution, so is the Nuremberg law regarding restitution distinguishable from the paradigmatic civil and international law regimes of compensation. In a word, Nuremberg crimes are imprescribable, for Nuremberg law – or international laws anchored in Nuremberg Principles – does not recognize the applicability of statutes of limitations, as set forth in the *U-N. Convention on the Non-Applicability of Statutory Limitations to War Crimes and Crimes Against Humanity.*[35] Moreover, there is a specific *European Convention on Non-Applicability of Statutory Limitations to Crimes Against Humanity and War Crimes (Inter-European).*[36]

Principle 9: Neutrality, criminality, and international law: the case of Switzerland

The Swiss argument that they were neutral in the Second World War, and that Swiss neutrality was sanctioned under international law, does have a certain initial and surface plausibility. As Detley Vagts puts it, 'the neutrality of Switzerland has a rather special basis in international law. It was not really that the country chose to remain neutral, but rather, there was an international understanding that it should remain so.'[37] Indeed, the international declaration of the Congress of Vienna in 1815 proclaimed that Switzerland should be 'permanently neutral',[38] and 'implied that Switzerland was supposed to refrain from un-neutral activities, nor were other states to invade [Switzerland] or interface with its sovereignty'.[39]

But as the evidence increasingly discloses,[40] Switzerland not only did not refrain from un-neutral activity, *inter alia*, it actually prolonged the Nazi war effort. Indeed, an inquiry into Swiss neutrality – and the international law of neutrality – in the Second World War invites the view that not only did Swiss 'un-neutrality' breach even the prevailing international law of neutrality at the time, but that the law of neutrality must itself be revisited and refined in the light of Swiss behaviour. In a word, neutrality can never be a cover for criminality, nor can criminality be excused or defended on the grounds of a country's neutrality.

Moreover, the very horror of the Holocaust – and the development of United Nations law in its wake – has made neutrality in the face of evil not only the subject of moral apprehension but legal apprehension as well. As Elie Wiesel has put it, 'neutrality always means coming down on the side of the victimizer, never on the side of the victim'.[41] And he adds: 'when human dignity is at stake, neutrality is a sin, not a virtue... therefore, neutrality, which used to be, at one time, a high ideal or ideal of nations is wrong. Reject it! You must side with the victim, even if you both lose.'[42]

Conclusion

For what must be realized here – and again the *cri de coeur* of survivors is there to remind us – is that restitution cannot simply be a discourse in 'property law' terms, or in the 'bottom-line' language of cost-accountants, though clearly there is a 'property' and 'bottom-line' accounting dimension to restitution; rather, we are talking of the value and worth of human life itself, of the value and worth of entire European Jewish communities selected for genocide – of the 'what might have been' as well as the 'what was' in existential as well as in 'property' terms.

In this context – in the 'Nuremberg' context – restitution is not only the redress of a historical wrong of unspeakable dimensions; not only an important and compelling affirmation of precedent and principle; but one that, on the fiftieth anniversary of the Nuremberg Judgements, or the *Genocide Convention*, and the *Universal Declaration of Human Rights*, will give expression to the Nuremberg principles, to Holocaust remembrance, to the International Law of Human Rights, and to international justice.

Restitution, then, is about the inherent dignity and worth of every human being – the inherent dignity and worth of an entire community. While restitution can never restore these lives, it can seek to restore their dignity.

Notes

1   Article 6 of the Charter of the International Military Tribunal (IMT) at Nuremberg set forth crimes within the Tribunal's jurisdiction for which there was to be individual responsibility – crimes against peace, war crimes, and crimes against humanity. In the words of the Charter of the IMT, the following acts, or any of them, are crimes coming within the jurisdiction of the Tribunal for which there shall be individual responsibility:

   (a)   Crimes against Peace: namely, planning, preparation, initiation or waging of a war of aggression, or a war in violation of international treaties, agreements or assurances, or participation in a common plan or conspiracy for the accomplishment of any of the foregoing;

   (b)   War Crimes: namely, violations of the laws or customs of war. Such violations include, but not be limited to, murder, ill-treatment or deportation to slave labor or for any other purpose of civilian population of or in occupied territory, murder or ill-treatment of prisoners of war or persons on the seas, killing of hostages, plunder of public or private property, wanton destruction of cities, towns or villages, or devastation not justified by military necessity;

   (c)   Crimes against Humanity: namely, murder, extermination, enslavement, deportation, and other inhumane acts committed against any civilian population, before or during the war, or persecutions on political, racial or religious grounds in execution of or in connection with any crime within the jurisdiction of the Tribunal, whether or not in violation of the domestic law of the country where perpetrated.

2   In 1996, Norway became the first European country to appoint a Commission to deal with the question of 'thefticide' and restitution. In June 1997, because of a lack of agreement within the commission, it was decided to submit two separate reports. The majority took a narrow approach focusing on settling the accounts of Jewish assets, while the minority believed that it must take the 'historical and moral perspective' as part of the responsibility of Norway towards the jews who were to be collectively killed. The Norwegian government, with the complete support of the media and all political parties, repudiated the majority report, and its Minister of Justice, Grad Live Vaala, issued this compelling statement.

3   I. Levine, 'The Fate of Stolen Jewish Properties: the Cases of Austria and the Netherlands', Institute of World Jewish Congress (1997) at p. 5.

4   See Chapter 17 in this volume by Gerard Aalders.

5   See, for example, W. Czaplinski, 'State Successsion and State Responsibility' (1990), *Canadian Yearbook of International Law*, 339, where he states: 'State responsibility is a legal relationship created through the violation of an international legal obligation by a state; that violation gives rise to the duty to compensate for any resulting damage, one of the oldest principles of international law and universally recognized in international practice', and M. N. Shaw, *International Law*, 3rd edn (Cambridge, 1995), at p. 483: 'A breach of an international obligation gives rise to a requirement for reparation'.

6 Permanent Court of International Justice (hereafter PCIJ) LCTR [Claims Tribunal Reports] Series A, no. 17, 1928, p. 29; 4, International Law Reports (hereafter ILR), p. 258. See also the *Corfu Channel* case, ICJ Reports, pp. 4, 23; 16 ILR, p. 155; and the *Spanish Zone of Morocco* claims 2 RIAA, p. 615 (1923); 2 ILR, p. 157.
7 *The Lighthouse Arbitration (France v. Greece)*, (1956), 12 RIAA 155;23 ILR. p. 659.
8 See, for example, M. J. Volkovitsch, *'Righting Wrongs: Toward a New Theory of State Succession to Responsibility for International Delicts'* [1992] *Columbia Law Review*, 2162 at 2168.
9 For example, Indonesia, under its devolution agreement, was considered liable for the delictual obligations of the Dutch colonial authorities in *Van der Have v. The Netherlands*, 1953 NJ No. 133, 20 ILR 80,81.
10 E.g., *The Lighthouse Arbitration*, as cited by Volkovitsch, *'Righting Wrongs'*, Note 14 at 2190.
11 'International law imposes upon a successor State the duty to assume the liabilities of the predecessor State both towards other States and private persons of foreign nationality', see *Rainoldi v. Ministero della Guerra* (1946) 70 Foro It. I., 151, 13 Ann. Dig. 6 at 6; *'Righting Wrongs'*, Note 14 at 2194.
12 T. Buergenthal, *International Human Rights*, 2nd edn (West Publishing, 1995) at p. 20.
13 *Universal Declaration of Human Rights*, 10 December 1948, UNGA (United Nations General Assembly), 217 A (III), UN GAOR, 3rd Sess. Supp. No. 13 at p. 71.
14 *International Covenant on Civil and Political Rights* (1966) 999 UNTS [United Nations Treaty Series] 171, 1976 Can. TS [Canada Treaty Series] No. 47.
15 *International Covenant on Economic, Social and Cultural Rights* (1966) 993 UNTS 3, 1976 Can. TS no. 46.
16 *United Nations Charter* (1945).
17 *The International Bill of Rights* includes also the *Optional Protocol* to the *International Covenant on Civil and Political Rights*.
18 *International Convention on the Elimination of All Forms of Racial Discrimination* (1965).
19 *Convention on the Prevention and Punishment of Genocide* (1948).
20 *Geneva Conventions of 1949*.
21 See Volkovitsch,*'Righting Wrongs'*, Note 4 at 2211 for a list of sources.
22 Ibid. See also *Cherzow Factory (Indemnity)* case, *supra*, Note 12.
23 Volkovitsch, *'Righting Wrongs'*.
24 P. D. Maddaugh and J. D. McCamus, *The Law of Restitution*, 1990, Canada Law Book, p. 11.
25 American Law Institute, *Restatement of the Law of Restitution: Quasi-Contracts and Constructive Trusts* (St. Paul: American Law Institute Publishers, 1937) Part I 20 S.1.
26 Maddaugh and McCamus, *Law of Restitution*, Note 30, p. 484.
27 Re *Hall; Hall v. Knight* [1914] p. 1. CA [Count of Appeals], at p. 7 per Lord Justice Hamilton.
28 Maddaugh and McCamus, *Law of Restitution*, Note 30, p. 483.
29 Ibid., Note 3.
30 *Resolution on Permanent Sovereignty over Natural Resources*, General Assembly Resolution 1803 (XVII) UN GAOR, 17th Sess. Supp. No. 17, UN Doc. A/S217

(1962) 15, at Preamble Section 4. See also the *Charter of Economic Rights and Duties of States*, GA Resolution 3281 (XXIX), UN GAOR, 29th Sess. Supp. No. 31, UN Doc. A/9631 (1974), 50 at ARt. 2(2)(c).

31 Shaw, *International Law*, 525. See especially: *Texaco Overseas Petroleum Co. and California Asiatic Oil Co. v. Libya*, (1977) 53 I.L.R. 389, 17 ILM, 1: *Aminoil Arbitration (Kuwait v. American Independent Oil Co.)*, (1982) 21 ILM, 976; *Sedco Inc. and National Oil Company and Iran*, (1986) 25 ILM, 629.

32 *American Restatement of the Law, supra* p. 712 (Comment section (f)). Other conventions in international law also recognize that discrimination is not permitted, see the *International Covenant on Civil and Political Rights*, (1966) 999 UN TS 171, 1976 Can. TS No. 47, Art. 2; and the *International Covenant on Economic, Social and Cultural Rights* (1966) 993 UN TS, 3 (1976) Can. TS No. 46, Art. 2(2).

33 *(US v. Iran)*, (1987) 15 Iran–US 189 at para. 140.

34 Ibid.

35 *Convention on the Non-Applicability of Statutory Limitations to War Crimes and Crimes Against Humanity, opened for signature at* New York, Nov. 26, 1968, GA Res. 2391, UN GAOR, 23rd Sess., Supp. No. 18, at 40, UN Doc. A/RES/2391 (1968), 754 UN TS 73, 8 ILM, 68, *entered into force* Nov. 1970.

36 *European Convention on the Non-Applicability of Statutory Limitations to Crimes Against Humanity and War Crimes (Inter-European), signed at* Strasbourg, Jan. 25, 1974, Europe. TS No. 82, 14 ILM, 540, *not yet entered into force.*

37 D. Vagts, 'Switzerland, International Law and World War II', *American Journal of International Law*, July 1996 p. 467.

38 Cited in Ibid.

39 Ibid.

40 See, for example, 'The Sinister Face of Neutrality', Policy Forum No. 13, *Institute of the World Jewish Congress*, 1996.

41 E. Wiesel, 'Witness', in I. Cotler (ed.), *Nuremberg Forty Years Later: The Struggle Against Injustice in Our Time* (Montreal: McGill-Queen's Press, 1995), p. 20.

42 Ibid.

5
Defrosting History: the Restitution of Jewish Property in Eastern Europe

Laurence Weinbaum

'Hast thou murdered and also taken possession?'
(Kings 1, 21:19)

The Holocaust was the worst tragedy ever to befall the Jewish people in its long and gloomy history in exile. In East Europe the Germans and Austrians and their local henchmen destroyed the age-old communities that were the cradle of Jewish spirituality and scholarship, the influence of which spread far beyond its borders. The wholesale slaughter of millions of Jews in communities great and small was accompanied by the systematic plunder of the victims' property, movable and immovable, communal and individual, public and private. Innumerable synagogues, houses, apartments, schools, hospitals, factories, workshops, warehouses, books, pictures, clothing, livestock, vehicles, furniture, jewellery and religious articles were seized – the wealth of an entire people accumulated over the course of centuries of toil. The robbery was not limited to the possessions of the Jews. The murderers and their accessories harvested vast quantities of hair, gold, teeth and bones – at once giving new and unspeakably diabolical meaning to the biblical 'Hast thou murdered and also taken possession?' Indeed, the extent of the robbery was such that the poet Henryk Grynberg wrote of the Jews in Poland: 'There is more bread from their ashes than they had ever eaten.'

A new form of plunder-expedition

During the war certain states of East Europe retained at least nominal independence and allied themselves with Germany. These included Bulgaria, Hungary, Romania and secessionist portions of Czechoslovakia and Yugoslavia. The balance of Eastern Europe was directly annexed or occupied by Germany and its allies. This situation determined whether property was seized by occupation authorities or by the autochthonous government and populations of the countries in question. In addition to spontaneous looting, which took place when Jews were deported and killed and booty carted off, a new form of plunder-expedition was devised. The robbery of Jewish assets was enmeshed in a web of bureaucracy in which ostensibly legal means of defrauding the Jews were devised and seemingly permanent administrative transfers of immovable property were implemented. A German term was even coined to describe this activity – *Entjudung* – which is best translated as de-Jewification – the despoliation of Jews.

The fact is that the prospect of both the 'legal – permanent' and 'unofficial – spontaneous' plunder of Jewish property was often a tempting incentive for the local population to actively assist in, or even orchestrate, the murder of Jewish neighbours – and was often exploited as such by the German and Axis authorities. In a chilling diary written during the Holocaust that was to claim its author, Calel Perechodnik described the attitude of his non-Jewish neighbours in the small town of Otwock, near Warsaw. 'Not all are against the persecution of Jews' he wrote, 'there are some among them who assist in it for the price of inheriting the remaining Jewish property.'[1] Before his death in the Bialystok Ghetto uprising, Mordechai Tenenbaum-Tamaroff reported figuratively: 'Today every peasant woman has Jewish jewelry, a Jewish piano and furniture from Jewish salons.'[2] The Dresdener Bank noted: 'Our intensive efforts in the *Entjudung* division have brought a number of valuable accounts and expansion of our credit business. In addition, the specialized activity in the field was highly beneficial to general promotion of business.'[3]

Irrespective of who was responsible for the actual seizure, in almost every instance Jewish property eventually devolved to the state or local authorities, or to the persons or entities occupying it, or in whose possession it was found.

The dormant struggle

By the war's end the Jewish communities of East Central Europe were irreparably scarred. While there was talk of restoring some of the property to the remnant that had survived, and some action taken in this direction, the violence perpetrated by those who had personally enriched themselves and the concomitant imposition of Communist rule ended these feeble attempts. Jews who sought to repossess property – movable and immovable – from those who had taken it were sometimes even murdered. 'Happy' cases were those in which Jews were merely threatened and managed to flee with their lives, if not the property that they had come to claim. This was especially so in Poland, but also in Hungary, Slovakia, in Romania and parts of the Soviet Union, where the individual murders of Jewish survivors was not uncommon. Meantime, those who sought to regain their holdings through legal measures floundered in a sea of Kafkaesque bureaucracy. In most instances, the private properties of those that did succeed in securing restitution was expropriated shortly after it had been recovered, in accordance with the nationalization of the economy.

Only a tiny fraction of prewar Jewish communal holdings was handed over to the reconstituted Jewish communities. In some instances legislation and decrees for the restoration of Jewish property were enacted immediately after the end of the war. However, such laws were often ignored by local authorities. In Poland, for example, an order from the Ministry of Public Administration to local authorities to restore Jewish communal property to the reconstituted local Jewish communities was largely ignored.[4]

By the early 1950s, the Iron Curtain had divided Europe and the restitution issue, at least where Eastern Europe was concerned, disappeared from the international Jewish agenda. Attention was now focused on German *wiedergutmachung*, and on property in Austria and Greece.

For close to fifty years East Central Europe was ruled by Communist regimes inimical to the principle of restitution of private property in general, and of Jewish property in particular. The fact that Jewish property had often been seized by the German occupation authorities was actually convenient for those bent on carrying out a thorough nationalization. In dealing with non-Jews it was necessary to seize property, with all the social unrest that accompanies such operations. In the case of the Jews it merely involved the administrative transfer of property which had already been sequestered – in other words, preservation of the status quo.

During this time, in the absence of strong Jewish communities, hundreds of Jewish cemeteries were laid waste and in some instances built upon; Jewish communal buildings, large and small, were put to use as schools, libraries, discotheques, cinemas, stables, art galleries, restaurants, garages, warehouses, and for countless other purposes generally, without any regard to Jewish sensitivities, let alone the intrinsic historic value of many of these sites. Jewish burial grounds were often ploughed up and buildings erected on them. Moreover, the contents of countless Jewish homes and institutions continued to enrich those who plundered them. In her diary, 13-year-old Eva Heyman of Nagyvarad (Oradea), doomed to die in Auschwitz in October 1944, described the plunder perpetrated by Hungarian gendarmes:

> Everyday they keep issuing new laws against the Jews. Today, for example, they took all our appliances away from us, the sewing machine, the radio, the telephone, the vacuum cleaner, the electric fryer and my camera. I don't care about my camera even though they didn't leave a receipt for it, like when they took the bicycle. They also took Uncle Bela's typewriter, but he didn't care either. When the war ends we'll get everything back . . .[5]

The defrosting of history

The collapse of Communism in East Central Europe and the eventual disintegration of the Soviet Union were followed by a reordering of the socioeconomic structure and the 'defrosting' of history. For the first time, public pressure forced the contemplation of a restoration of nationalized property. In some of those countries, for the first time, there was also open discussion on their own responsibility for the plight of their Jewish neighbours and countrymen. Heads of state and other national leaders, and even certain members of the clergy, have in some instances contributed to the positive atmosphere by issuing declarations of apology for their country's wartime role. Speaking before the World Jewish Congress in New York in 1994, then Hungarian Foreign Minister Laszlo Kovacs apologized for his nation's participation in the murder of Hungarian Jews. Recalling the time in Hungary in which Jews were attacked, banned from certain professions and had their property confiscated, he said: 'It is self-deception if anyone shifts responsibility for the genocide in Hungary solely and exclusively to Nazi Germany.'[6] These expressions of contrition, however sincere, were generally not accompanied by legislation which would restore to Jewish owners, both private and communal, their properties.

Generally speaking, a similar pattern evolved in most of the states of Central and East Europe. The restitution of property was limited to that seized during the period of Communist rule (rather than during the German occupation or the rule by native fascists), and even then its restoration was confined to citizens of the country permanently domiciled there. What lay behind this policy was readily evident. The lion's share of nationalized Jewish property would remain in state or municipal hands, or in the hands of the people or entities occupying it. Most Jewish holdings were seized during the Holocaust, well before the Communists swept to power. The great majority of Jews in East Europe perished in the Holocaust. Of those who did emerge from the inferno only a small number elected to remain in their countries of origin and retain their original citizenship. Linking domicile and citizenship to restoration of property would effectively wipe out the vast majority of Jewish claims.

Those countries with large prewar ethnic German communities or other national minorities which were expatriated, or those which benefited from the realignment of borders at the expense of Germany or other neighbours, ironically justified this policy as the only means of preventing the Germans and other expellees from staking claims. In many instances legislation providing for the restoration of property to various Christian churches and religious communities was quickly enacted. But in the case of Jewish communities – greatly reduced in size through both murder and emigration – such legislation was slow in coming or when enacted insufficient – penalizing the Jews for the fact that they had been murdered.

Such discrimination, of course, violated the most basic rules of international law and obligations under international conventions to which the parties were signatories. In the period of Communist rule, such violations of human rights were the order of the day. Now, however, having thrown off the shackles of Communism, these countries have pledged to restore or institute human rights, and after fifty years a new Jewish generation – represented by the World Jewish Restitution Organization (WJRO) – clamours for justice.

The issue of heirless and unclaimed properties is particularly sensitive. Vast numbers of properties have not (and will not be) claimed by individuals. The owners and heirs were murdered or they emigrated, and in many instances their heirs do not know that they left behind properties. The magnitude of the problem of heirless property is evident when one considers that in Poland and Czechoslovakia some 85 per cent of the Jewish population was annihilated; in Lithuania well over 90 per cent.

Only in former Axis states Hungary and Romania was legal provision made to transfer heirless and unclaimed Jewish property to Jewish entities dedicated to the rehabilitation of survivors. Even before the end of the war, the World Jewish Congress had advanced the demand that the peace treaties with Hungary and Romania include a clear provision that heirless Jewish properties escheat to representative Jewish organizations for the benefit of survivors. Over the objection of these countries a clause was inserted which bound Hungary and Romania to convey heirless Jewish property to Jewish organizations:

> All property, rights and interests in Hungary/Romania of persons, organizations or communities which individually or as members of groups, were the object of racial, religious or other Fascist measures of persecutions, and remaining heirless or unclaimed for six months after the coming into force of the present Treaty, shall be transferred by the Hungarian/Romanian Government to organizations in Hungary/Romania representative of such persons, organizations or communities. The property transferred shall be used by such organizations for purposes of relief and rehabilitation of surviving members of such groups, organizations and communities in Hungary/Romania. Such transfer shall be effected within twelve months from the coming into force of the Treaty, and shall include property rights and interests required to be restored under paragraph 1 of this Article.[7]

However, the imposition of Communist rule in those countries blocked the implementation of this principle and it was thoroughly disregarded. Czechoslovakia and Yugoslavia were treated as Allied powers, even though secessionist portions of these countries had tied themselves to the Axis and taken an active role in the murder and despoliation of their Jewish populations – and thus escaped the onerous provisions of a peace treaty. In Poland, the question of heirless property was dealt with in draconian fashion. A 1946 law on abandoned property provided for the transfer to the state of the assets of most of those who perished in the Shoah. A similar scenario was played out in the other countries of Eastern Europe.

To block private persons from claiming property, the laws of inheritance were often changed so as to restrict the categories of persons entitled to claim properties of those killed. It must also be noted that German compensation laws do not provide for the payment of compensation in respect of property confiscated by Germany in the countries occupied, annexed or under its sphere of influence during the war. Sometimes it is suggested that only Germany is responsible for Jewish material losses. However, as far back as 1944 Dr Nehemiah Robinson of the World Jewish Congress noted:

...responsibility for... indemnification falls upon those who have directly acquired the property of which someone else was illegally deprived, and also upon the subsequent acquirers of these goods. . . According to the common rules of law, the persons who directed the despoliation and helped carry it out bear equal and sometimes even greater responsibility than the illegal possessor, although restitution cannot be carried out by them...[8]

The solutions proposed by the various countries of the region were by no means homogeneous. For the most part, however, they did have certain common characteristics. Israeli judge, Eli Nathan, pointed out in a lecture delivered to the World Council meeting of the International Association of Jewish Lawyers and Jurists on 28 June 1994 in Rome:

Now, almost five years after the advent to power of the new regimes, none of these countries has so far enacted a program of comprehensive and satisfactory restitution legislation. Where such legislation has been enacted it has been found largely to be deficient and inadequate. Where these countries enacted legislation for the privatization of nationalized property they failed to take into account the basic fact that Jewish property was already confiscated during the Holocaust many years before the Communist measures of large-scale nationalization of private property were actually enacted.[9]

This observation remains true today, more than five years after Judge Nathan made it.

From its inception, it has been the policy of the WJRO to seek agreements with local Jewish communities in order to jointly pursue claims for communal property, and to establish foundations to jointly manage it. The WJRO has sought to utilize properties for the benefit of the rehabilitation of Jewish communities (especially survivors), but also to work to safeguard the Jewish legacy in these countries. To date it has reached agreements on the establishment of foundations with Jewish communities in a number of countries. However, the cooperation between the Jewish communities in some of these countries and the WJRO has not always been as smooth as one would have hoped. In some instances those relations have been marked by mutual distrust which has not served the purpose of restitution. The WJRO has consistently maintained that the Jewish communities of Eastern Europe represent but a remnant of the prewar communities. As such, they cannot claim exclusive rights over Jewish property that once belonged to these communities. Local Jews have not always been willing to allow those who have left any say in the disposition of what could amount to a windfall. Moreover, they resent what they see as the high-handed treatment to which they have been subjected by international Jewish organizations and charge that they were left out of the decision-making process. Due to the greatly reduced size of these communities, they have displayed far more modest claims than those of the WJRO, which has been a further source of tension. In a speech before the B'nai B'rith in Jerusalem in 1997, Naftali Lavi, vice-chairman of the WJRO, declared:

> [I]t is much easier for the government to negotiate and deal with the local communities which have very low expectations – hardly any, in fact – and can be satisfied with nearly nothing. The Jews of Romania number today 12,000 to 14,000 out of a community that, until a few years ago, numbered 400,000. Nearly all of those who left immigrated to Israel and have been absorbed in the country as good Israelis. Nearly all of them left private properties in Romania which they cannot claim because of the existing laws and procedures. But they are very much interested that at least the communal properties should revert to the Jewish community, to be used for those who still live in Romania and those who live abroad. They will be satisfied with nothing. We will not.[10]

On a number of occasions, local community leaders have often publicly disassociated themselves and their communities from the more belligerent pronouncements of the WJRO and other international Jewish organizations. When, for example, the WJRO threatened to influence the United States to reject the admission of Poland, the Czech Republic and Romania to NATO, Jewish leaders in those countries distanced themselves from this measure and some even compared it with the behaviour of Soviet 'advisers' sent to these countries after to Second World War.[11]

For the most part, the future solvency of most of the communities in this region is largely dependent on the recovery of communal property and its commercial use. Moreover, the immediate amelioration of the Jewish indigent and elderly -who in some instances subsist on meager pensions distributed by the Joint – is also tied to the swift recovery of these assets. Zeno Dostal, then chairman of the Prague Jewish community and president of the B'nai B'rith in the Czech Republic declared that if the Czech government would not see to it that the Jewish community could retrieve its property in order to carry on its activities: 'We might as well close down the Jewish community in Prague and have only an attraction for tourists, just as Hitler intended.'[12]

From the outset the WJRO has been fully cognizant of the uncertain economic and political situation prevailing in the post-Communist successor states. It has respected the fact that properties currently being used for appropriate non-Jewish social functions (in other words those that do not desecrate the object) can in certain cases continue to be rented out to the present tenants. It also accepts in principle the concept of exchange properties in instances when the exploitation of the property by the entity occupying it is crucial. What the WJRO has sought, however, is to reestablish legal title to properties – even when there is every intention of allowing the present occupants to remain where they are. It is also not oblivious to the fact that over the course of fifty years properties often changed hands and underwent various processes of merger and division, further complicating the issue. Not surprisingly, the issue of the restitution of property has exacerbated existing antisemitic sentiments. The prospect that vast properties – and especially 'our house' – could be returned to the Jews from whom they were seized has been a source of fear.

Antisemites have seized upon the issue of restitution with gusto and in some cases have resorted to violence (see Plate 2). There have been several reports from the Jewish community in Lodz, for example, which has claims for vast properties, of attacks on the synagogue, threatening telephone calls and other hostile behaviour.[13] Corneliu Vadim Tudor, the leader of the antisemitic Romania Mare party, for example, has been particularly outspoken. Himself a close collaborator of Ceaucescu, Tudor recently declared: 'The thousands who died in December 1989 did not sacrifice their lives so that the International Jewish Mafia could steal 400,000 of our properties.'[14] Even liberal politicians in Eastern Europe, who may have believed in the justice of the Jewish cause, have been forced to confront the fact that a forceful stand in favour of Jewish restitution is not likely to win support from the electorate. Consequently, they are forced to achieve a balance between the external pressure from the United States, the European Union and Diaspora Jewry on the one hand, and the constituency at home. Since 1995, however, attention has been focused on looted property secreted in Switzerland, and on dormant accounts of Holocaust victims. This has provided a welcome, if transitory, reprieve for the States of Central and Eastern Europe.

Washington as an advocate

The question of restitution in Eastern Europe has found broad support in Washington. On 7 February 1994, addressing a gathering of the governing board of the World Jewish Congress, attended by several hundred WJC leaders from around the world, then US Secretary of State Warren Christopher pledged support for efforts to recover Jewish property in east Central Europe. In a letter of 10 April 1995, Congressional leaders urged the Secretary of State to take action to advance the cause of restitution:

> It should be made clear to the countries involved...that their response on this matter will be seen as a test of their respect for basic human rights and the rule of law, and could have practical consequences on their relations with our country. It is the clear policy of the United States that each should expeditiously enact appropriate legislation providing for the prompt restitution and/or compensation for property and assets seized by the former Nazi and/or Communist regimes. We believe it to be a matter of both law and justice.[15]

This action was followed by the dispatch of American ambassador to the European Union, Stuart Eizenstat, to the region. Ambassador Eizenstat met with many senior state and government officials and expressed US interest in a just and speedy resolution of the issue. However, the response to Washington's intervention has been mixed and a number of leaders reacted angrily to the Congressional initiative and to Ambassador Eizenstat's *démarche*. The American intervention and initiative was followed by pronouncements in a similar vein by the European Union.

Here it should be noted that in the last few years considerable media attention has been devoted to the fact that vast properties – movable and immovable – in Western Europe were also plundered from Jewish families, and in many instances scant restitution was made after the war. It seems clear that in the coming years settlements with some of these countries, or various enterprises or institutions in them, have already been effected. While this may be seen as a proper precedent for the new democracies of Eastern Europe, no one can ignore the fact that the sums involved (especially in comparison with the size of their economies) are minute. Moreover, such settlements in Western Europe are not likely to produce the social disruption of those in the East.

Country-by-country survey

Bulgaria

On the eve of the Holocaust there were some 60,000 Jews in Bulgaria, constituting about 1 per cent of the total population of Bulgaria. Bulgarian Jewry was the only Jewish community in East Central Europe to survive the war intact. However, Jews in the parts of Yugoslavia (Macedonia) and Greece (Thrace) occupied by the Bulgarians enjoyed no such good fortune. Virtually the entire population of these ancient Jewish communities was deported to German death camps in occupied Poland, and very few survived.

In Bulgaria proper, restrictions on Jewish property were initiated in 1941 with registration of Jewish movable and immovable assets. Jews were expelled from certain branches of the economy and their property so heavily taxed that most were forced to sell assets at a fraction of their real value. In 1943, some 20,000 Jews were expelled from the capital and their assets sold at public auctions. However, the two governments that ruled between September 1943 and the Communist takeover a year later abrogated anti-Jewish measures and initiated the partial return of Jewish property. In March 1945 a law of restitution was enacted, providing for the restitution of Jewish holdings. In cases in which restitution *in natura* was impossible, compensation of up to $100 in Bulgarian currency was paid in cash, with the balance to be paid in bonds over a six-year period. Compensation estimates were based on appraisals made at the time property was confiscated. On account of the fact that the Jewish community of Bulgaria was spared, the World Jewish Congress did not insist upon the insertion into the Peace Treaty with Bulgaria on heirless Jewish property of a clause similar to that involving Hungary and Romania.[16] The subsequent nationalization of private enterprise and other properties affected all Bulgarian citizens irrespective of their religious affiliation or national origin. Schools, hospitals and other social institutions under religious auspices were also nationalized but some indemnification was paid to the communities involved. Later legislation led to the closure of all but three synagogues and their transformation into museums, or their exploitation for other secular uses.

The issue of restitution in Bulgaria was resolved by a series of three laws enacted between December 1991 and February 1992. Under Bulgarian law foreign citizens were able to retrieve property. A 1992 regulation abrogated the nationalization of property belonging to religious communities during the period 1944–89, under which such assets had been taken over by local authorities. As a result the Jewish community has reclaimed several synagogues, cemeteries, schools and community buildings. Although implementation has been slow, Bulgaria is one of the few countries that has enacted thorough legislation on the restoration of private and public property.

The Czech Republic

About 85 per cent of the roughly 110,000 Jews in the Czech land (Bohemia, Moravia and Silesia) on the eve of the Munich Agreement perished in the Holocaust. Most Jewish property was 'Aryanized' immediately following the German seizure of the Sudetenland in September 1938, and the subsequent occupation of the rest of the Czech lands in March 1939. In the period between the liberation of Czechoslovakia and the Communist *putsch*, President Eduard Benes implemented decrees according to which the Sudeten German population was expelled and its assets seized as 'enemy property'. Moreover, a land reform was carried out which deprived the Roman Catholic Church of much of its holdings. Although some provision was made for the restoration of property (law of 16 May 1946) seized during the occupation (so-called Aryanization transactions were declared null and void), only a small fraction was actually returned to its original owners or their heirs. In the case of communal property, often only administration, instead of actual ownership, was restored. All activities aimed at restitution ceased with the Communist *putsch* on 25 February 1948 and all property not restored to its original owners or their heirs devolved to the state.

As a result, the Jewish communities only succeeded in receiving a few decaying burial grounds and synagogues and the seat of the Council of Jewish Communities in Prague – the celebrated sixteenth-century Jewish Town Hall in the Jozefov district. Thus the state wound up with the bulk of Jewish communal property and utilized it for a variety of purposes. Many of these holdings were conveyed to local and municipal authorities to whose discretion was left their ultimate disposal.

After the 1989 'Velvet Revolution' which swept the Communists from power, legislation for reprivatization was immediately proposed. Restitution of property was to apply to natural persons whose holdings were sequestered *after* 25 February 1948. This cut-off date effectively barred the retrieval of property by Sudeten Germans and by the Church (which had been seized between the liberation and the Communist coup) – and also by the Jewish community and the remnant of Czech Jewry, whose properties for the most part, had never even been returned.

Understandably, once the issue of restitution arose, Jewish communal leaders pressed for special legislation to deal with the restoration of

Jewish property, which would take into account the fact that the lion's share of Jewish holdings, sequestered by the Germans, had never been returned. The government was unmoved. Prague feared that any deviation from the February 1948 cut-off date would open a Pandora's box of claims from the period between the liberation and the Communist takeover. Consequently, the 1991 law on restitution was passed without any consideration for its blatant discrimination against Czech Jews. Initial attempts to amend the law to include a special clause on Jewish property ended in failure. An amendment to the original law on extrajudicial rehabilitation explicitly allowed the public prosecutor to revise administrative decisions made after 1948, but not court rulings. This was tantamount to a legalization of the confiscation of Jewish assets implemented on court orders based on Communist amendments to the decree of President Benes.

At the end of November 1993, a WJRO delegation met with President Václav Havel, Prime Minister Václav Klaus, and other members of the cabinet to raise this issue. It was pointed out that the Benes decree calling for the cancellation of all Aryanization moves had never been fully implemented in the first place. No concrete steps to rectify this situation, however, were immediately forthcoming.

The Roman Catholic Church in the Czech Republic backed Jewish communal claims. The Church issued a declaration clearly stating that legislation allowing for Jewish claims dating back to 1938 would not serve as a precedent for the Church in seeking revision of the law where Catholic holdings were concerned. Jewish claims also enjoy the backing of President Vaclav Havel, who has repeatedly declared that the delay in returning property and the constant haggling had brought shame upon the Czech nation and was 'insulting'.[17]

Meanwhile, the WJRO compiled a list of over 1000 items of communal property. However, the community decided to submit a far more modest claim. A list of 202 properties was submitted by the Jewish community, together with a draft regulating the return of private holdings. The list represented only a small part of the community's prewar properties and did not include items which the government or local authorities had sold to third parties or had put up for auction – or items in which such proceedings were pending. In April 1994 the draft of the law was defeated, but at a meeting with the prime minister it was agreed that the communal property would be returned on the basis of an executive decision (decision of the government or appropriate municipal authorities). On that occasion it was also decided that the question of private property would be determined by legislation. To date, however, only about half of the properties have actually been transferred to Jewish communities. Significantly, the items that have been returned are primarily burial grounds and synagogues, rather than income-producing properties that could finance communal activities.

The fact that properties owned by the state constituted only a quarter of the 202 items on the community's list has been an obstacle. The state has actually returned only the items that the community has requested; the local authorities, however, have been far less compliant and the state has not shown any willingness to compel them to hand over the looted items.[18] To date only about half of the properties on the communal list have been restituted.

Not surprisingly, local authorities had displayed no great desire to transfer valuable properties to Jewish hands, and have stubbornly resisted doing so. Moreover, in flagrant violation of the law which had been adopted by the Czechoslovak parliament, some local authorities have continued to dispose of items on the community's approved list, and attached various 'conditions' to the return of others.

In 1999 a new draft bill was submitted to parliament which would restitute Jewish property. Moreover, the Czech Government created a joint commission, under the chairmanship of Deputy Prime Minister Pavel Rychetsky, which will serve as an advisory board to the government in solving the issue of looted Holocaust-era assets. It remains to be seen if these measures will succeed in advancing the cause of those working towards the restoration of the legacy of Czech Jewry. Critics, note, however, that the proposed legislation also enables the state to retain items of property at its discretion.

An amendment (on 29 April 1994) to the 1991 property restitution law enabled Jews to claim individual property originally seized by the German authorities. The 1991 law only provided for restitution of property seized after the Communists had seized power. In July 1994 the constitutional court ruled that Czech citizens who do not permanently live in the Czech Republic are entitled to submit claims for restitution under the law. Czech citizenship laws provide for dual nationality for those already possessing former Czech citizenship who acquired another citizenship before the passage of the law. The law provides for the return of property *in natura*. When that is impossible, monetary compensation may be substituted. Local authorities holding formerly Jewish property are obligated to restore it to the original owners or their heirs. The deadline for filing claims was 30 April 1995.

Despite the seeming equity of this arrangement, there has been a disconcerting attempts to stifle the attempts made by claimants. In the first place, the laws of succession restrict restitution to the direct next of kin. In many cases, where Jewish property is involved, the next of kin perished together with the owner of the property, or died of natural causes in the more than fifty years that have elapsed since the end of the war. Those who are in possession of disputed properties have sometimes succeeded in tangling the claims in the notoriously bureaucratic – and even Kafkaesque – Czech judicial system. In many instances the advanced age of the claimants and the high cost of legal counsel have forced them to abandon their efforts. Moreover, the public has been barred from archival documents with direct bearing on the outcome of property claims. Many of these documents are destined for the shredder.[19] During this time, those who occupied the property were able to continue to derive material benefit from it. Consequently there are still a number of cases in which properties have not been restituted to their rightful owners.

Hungary

As early as 1938, with the imposition of the first anti-Jewish legislation, the Hungarian authorities acted to restrict the economic activities of the Jewish minority. During the course of the next seven years Jews were gradually deprived of their property, movable and immovable, public and private. An estimated 300,000 immovable properties belonging to Jews or Jewish institutions were seized. During the German occupation of the country, which commenced on 19 March 1944, all Jewish assets were seized, including jewellery, precious metals and stones, art objects, automobiles, bicycles, radios and telephones. All Jewish bank accounts were blocked. At the end of the war huge quantities of confiscated Jewish valuables were sent out of the country on the infamous 'gold train'. Most, stripped of all identification of the owners, was returned to Hungary and promptly seized by the state.

The number of Jews under Hungarian rule vastly increased during the period 1938–40, owing to the transfer to Hungary of parts of south Slovakia, Sub-Carpathian Ruthenia and of northern Transylvania. The Hungarian authorities, as co-conspirators of the Germans, played an active role in the despoliation, deportation and murder of some 600,000 Jews under Hungarian jurisdiction. According to a Hungarian government estimate, the assets of Hungarian Jews who perished without direct heirs is estimated at some $3 billion.[20]

After the defeat of Hungary, the new government restored Jewish communal property to the Central Council of Hungarian Jews. That body, representing a numerically much reduced community, elected to dispose of a number of parcels. However, after the Communist seizure of power, Jewish communal properties, like those of other ecclesiastical organizations, were expropriated. This move was undertaken with 'legal' window-dressing. Formal agreements were concluded between the state and the religious communities, according to which the state would contribute to the maintenance of religious institutions and to the clergy. After the Communists were swept from power, a law on freedom of conscience and religious worship was enacted, which repeated the agreements that the religious communities had been coerced into signing.

On 10 July 1991 a law on the ownership status of ecclesiastical property was passed by the Hungarian parliament. That law applies to buildings but not the land (the Church had vast holdings) expropriated after 1 January 1948. The objective of the law is to restore to the religious communities properties needed for the resumption of their traditional ecclesiastical and social role. The implications for the Jewish community were not difficult to discern. Hungarian Jewry, which was severely depleted in the Holocaust, would not be able to claim buildings in which the Jewish presence is negligible or non-existent. The law stands in clear violation of article 27.2 of the peace treaty, in which Hungary pledges to transfer heirless and unclaimed properties of persecutees – including the property of persecuted associations or communities – to organizations in Hungary representative of such persecutees. Law XXV of 1946 provided for the establishment of a Jewish rehabilitation fund. This law only applied to the collection and disposal of unclaimed and heirless assets of individual Jewish persecutees. The constitutional court of Hungary ruled in decisions 15/93 and 16/93 that in failing to transfer the properties under Law XXV/46, Hungary was in breach of its peace treaty obligations.

Between 1991 and 1992 two laws were passed providing compensation for those whose property was expropriated by the Communist and Fascist regime respectively, and in May 1991 the Hungarian Constitutional Court annulled certain legislation on the expropriation of certain residential properties, industrial and commercial enterprises and pharmacies. This was followed by the first compensation law, which applied to property expropriated or nationalized after 8 June 1949 (the date of the first parliamentary session following the Communist takeover), and which became valid as of 24 August 1991. Some 4 million hectares of agricultural land are affected; more than 400,000 residential and business premises; and 3840 commercial and industrial enterprises employing 100 persons or less.

This law affected Jews only to the extent that certain properties were restored to them between the end of the war and the imposition of Communist rule, or otherwise during that time. Clearly the lion's share of Jewish property could only be restored by legislation affecting expropriations dating back to the imposition of anti-Jewish laws by the Horthy regime. The law provided for partial compensation, not restitution or full indemnification, calculated on a regressive scale. Payment was made in the form of compensation vouchers or property bills, a security which can be freely circulated and used for the acquisition of property in the course of the sale of state and agricultural cooperative assets. They could be exchanged for a fraction of their nominal value. Those over the age of 65 have the option of converting the voucher into an annuity. Those who exchanged their vouchers for agricultural land and pledged to work the property for at least five years received the best package. People who opted for this option may ultimately receive an additional subsidy of up to 800,000 forints. The amounts of compensation provided for the law cannot be regarded as 'fair compensation' for property confiscated on 'account of racial origin or religion' but which cannot be restored, of which article 27.1 of the 1947 Peace Treaty speaks. However, the Hungarian constitutional court ruled in its decisions enumerated above that the compensation provided did not violate Article 27.1 and that the payments could be reconciled with provision of 'fair compensation'

The deadline for claims of compensation under the first law was 16 December 1991. But processing of claims is proceeding slowly due to an inadequate number of officials. The second law came into effect on 7 June 1992. It is almost identical to the first, except that it also takes into account confiscations of precious metals, stones, jewellery and art works, for which a lump-sum payment in vouchers is made. The law made no provision for losses of property suffered outside what is present-day Hungary (Hungary within the borders demarcated by the Treaty of Trianon). Thus Hungarian citizens who suffered material losses in northern Transylvania are covered by Article 25 of the Romanian Peace Treaty even though Hungarian authorities were responsible for the despoliation. Those who suffered losses in south Slovakia or Sub-Carpathian Ruthenia are not covered by any treaty and are thus ineligible for compensation.

In 1995, after a series of negotiations with representatives of the WJRO, including Edgar Bronfman and Israel Singer, the Hungarian government agreed to establish a foundation to administer heirless Jewish property. That foundation is administered with the participation of local Jewish communities and the WJRO. The objective of the foundation is to serve as a repository of items of Jewish communal property as well as art works looted from Jewish collection. The income generated from this activity is directed towards a fund which provides assistance to needy Holocaust survivors in Hungary. It also finances facilities for Hungarian Jews dispersed in other countries. However, it remains to be seen whether the fund will energetically pursue claims for communal and heirless property.

It should be noted that the Hungarian government made an initial payment of $24 million to this fund, which is being paid out in annuities to needy survivors. This cannot therefore be regarded as restitution for stolen property, but rather as a form of reparations for the sufferings inflicted upon Hungarian Jews. In fact, this sum actually represents but a fraction of the real value of Jewish assets looted by fascist regime – the great majority of which was never returned to its rightful owners or their heirs. In October 1998 the Hungarian government signed an agreement with the Jewish community to settle certain claims for sequestered property. In exchange for waiving its rights to 151 items of community property valued at $60 million the community is to receive an annual payment of $3, million to finance communal activities. There are still outstanding claims for approximately 3000 items of community property.

Poland

The question of the restitution of Jewish property in Poland is charged with particular emotion. Jews constituted some 10 per cent of the population of interwar Poland – and there were more Jews in Poland than the other countries of Central and Eastern Europe combined (excluding the Soviet Union). In fact, the Jewish population of Poland (nearly 3,500,000) was greater than the entire population of many of the countries of Europe (Ireland, Norway and the Baltic States, for example). On the eve of the Second World War there were some 1415 Jewish communities of more than 100 individuals.

In the larger cities Jews often accounted for one-third of the inhabitants and were often overrepresented in the ownership of urban property. In Warsaw, for example, Jews owned upwards of 40 per cent of all residential property. In many smaller, provincial towns Jews accounted for over 50 per cent of the population and upwards of 90 per cent of the property owners. Moreover, Jews owned a significant part of Polish industry, particularly textiles, chemicals, rubber, food, building materials and paper, and were active in other branches. In 1938 Jewish-owned firms employed more than 40 per cent of the total industrial labour force.[21]

About 85 per cent of Polish Jewry perished in the Holocaust. In the immediate postwar period vast quantities of Jewish property were unclaimed – in part due to the fact that owners or their heirs were often murdered when seeking to retrieve their property, and that many others fled the country. It is difficult to fix the number of Jews murdered in Poland in the period between the liberation and the summer of 1947 but general estimates place the number at 1500.[22] The murder of survivors intimidated many of those who might have sought redress and most made no attempt to retrieve their assets.

According to a decree of 8 March 1946 on abandoned property, all items not claimed by 31 December 1947 (and later extended to 31 December 1948) devolved to the state. Many of the Polish Jews who had survived in the Soviet Union were only repatriated to Poland after the claims deadline had already passed. Others in DP (displaced persons) camps in Germany feared returning to Poland. Moreover, except for individual cases, the Polish authorities blocked the return of Jews from DP camps.

The enactment of a new law of succession on 8 October 1947 further frustrated potential claimants. Intestate succession was restricted to father, mother, descendants and the surviving spouse. Given the magnitude of Jewish losses in Poland (more than 85 per cent) in which often whole immediate families were wiped out, this clearly deprived more distant surviving relatives, and even lateral family members, of the opportunity to claim property. No provision whatsoever was ever made for the transfer of heirless and unclaimed property to appropriate Jewish successor organizations for the relief, rehabilitation and resettlement of survivors.

After the Communist regime was swept from power in 1989, the question of restitution and reprivatization was immediately raised. A special office of ownership transformation, later awarded ministerial status, was created to deal with such matters. Yet those who thought the question would be resolved speedily were quickly relieved of such illusions.

In fact the first large-scale restoration of private property provided for the dominant Roman Catholic Church to retrieve property it had lost. As a part of the first law on the relation of the state to the Roman Catholic Church, vast holdings were transferred to the control of the Church. Despite the Polish population's well-known fidelity to the Catholic Church, this move aroused a considerable degree of anti-Church sentiment. The fact that Church property was restored before the enactment of legislation affecting private property was seen as unfair, and some questioned whether social institutions would be displaced as a consequence. Within the framework of laws relating to the state and various ecclesiastical bodies, property has also been restored to a number of other churches, including the Orthodox, Evangelical Augsburg and Polish Autocephalous Churches.[23]

However, the Polish government was reluctant to conclude such an arrangement with the Jewish community. For one thing, potential Jewish claims, compared to the actual number of Jews in Poland, were enormous. Moreover, large numbers of Polish Jews living outside Poland (who outnumber Jews in Poland by a factor of several hundred to one) maintained that they had a claim to these properties and that Jews living in Poland could not rightly claim to be the exclusive heirs of Polish Jewry. The matter was further complicated by the fact that several Polish governments rose and fell during the negotiations between the Jewish community and the WJRO on one hand and the Polish authorities on the other.

In April 1997 the government finally enacted a law on the relations of the state to the Jewish community. This provided for the restitution of some property to existing Jewish communities. A regulatory commission was set up, the two co-chairman and membership of which was equally divided between those appointed by the Ministry of the Interior and those by the Board of the Union of Communities,

However, it readily became apparent that while the Jewish leadership in Poland was, with some reservations, satisfied by the law, representatives of Polish Jewry outside Poland were not. The remnant of Polish Jewry today living in Poland has no right to claim the legacy of Polish Jewry, they maintained. Moreover, the Polish Jews from abroad claimed that the settlement itself was niggardly – and that the Polish Jews in Poland have settled for less than they could have actually pressed for. Even before the enactment of the law, Polish Jews in Israel sharply condemned it at a stormy meeting with then prime minister Cimoszewicz in Tel Aviv on 17 January 1997. But the protests of the WJRO and other organizations came to naught and the bill was accepted by the Polish parliament. Significantly, the leaders of Polish Jewry in Poland hailed the legislation as a significant step forward. The WJRO, however, was considerably more circumspect. Its vice-chairman, Naftali Lavi, declared:

> In defiance of overwhelming international opinion and support, the Polish Government unilaterally suspended its negotiations with the

WJRO and instead negotiated directly with the local, minuscule Polish Jewish Community to circumvent the WJRO and thus 'settle' the claims at the lowest conceivable cost... The WJRO and the World Federation of Polish Jews protested to the Polish President and to the Minister of the Interior, pointing out the grossly unfair and discriminatory character of the law, which seeks to 'settle' the restitution claims of the world's most vibrant Jewish community by negotiating with the token, vestige Polish Jewish Communities for the transfer of a negligible number of buildings. Such a 'settlement' would render the claims of the pre-World War II Jewish community a mockery and a travesty.[24]

Attempts to establish a joint foundation for the preservation of the heritage of Poland in which the WJRO and the local community would cooperate, have yet to yield fruit and relations between the two groups are characterized by mutual distrust.

The community and the WJRO did in fact reach an agreement which provides for the establishment of a special fund which will retain responsibility for properties restored to the community. To date claims have been submitted for less than 100 properties, including synagogues and other buildings as well as burial grounds. The latter pose the greatest problem, for these are often located in areas in which there are few if any Jews and they require considerable maintenance.

At the same time, the question of restitution of private property – by no means an exclusively Jewish issue – was no less problematic. Since the issue of privatization was first raised, several draft proposals were submitted to the Sejm (the Polish parliament) by parliamentarians and the government, each envisaging various formulae. Regrettably all of these were inimical to certain Jewish concerns. Most of the proposals – which provided for three types of restitution: *in natura*, substitute property and reprivatization bills – included a restrictive eligibility clause which confined restitution to natural persons who held Polish citizenship at the time the property was confiscated, or to their heirs – Polish citizens at the time the law would come into force.

Such legislation would be discriminatory against former owners of Jewish property, in that it deals solely with property taken in the course of nationalizations during the years 1944–60 and it does not take into account that Jewish property was seized during the German occupation. Obviously by 1944 the great majority of Polish Jewry had already been murdered and all of them had been despoiled. This clause clearly violated the most basic rules of international law and obligations undertaken by Poland under a number of international conventions of which it is a signatory. Such a stance actually legitimizes the plunder of Jewish property by German occupation authorities – in effect it recognizes the 'legality' of decrees grounded in the Nuremburg laws.

The issue of property in Warsaw poses special problems in view of the fact that so much of the city was devastated and rebuilt, and also because a decree of 26 October 1945 nationalized all land in the capital (including over 14,000 buildings). While that decree provided for the payment of compensation, none was ever paid. Former property owners have consistently pressed for legislation that would regulate their claims. To date, they have done so with no success.

There have been sporadic instances of the restoration of private property to Polish Jews living abroad but these have largely been determined at the whim of local authorities. In the absence of privatization legislation, this issue will remain high on the agenda. Some sources speculate that the government is deliberately putting the whole question on the back burner in the hope that it will slowly die down. Meantime, the latest draft legislation for the restitution of private property has aroused the indignation of Jewish circles in Israel and the United States, who charge that it is discriminatory.

An entirely different, and perhaps even more sensitive, issue is that of Jewish-owned property in the territories Poland recovered as a part of wartime agreements between the Allied powers. These properties are in bureaucratic limbo with neither Germany nor Poland willing to discuss the matter.

Romania

Forty-three per cent of the Jews under Romanian jurisdiction perished in the Holocaust, many at the hands of the Romanian army, gendarmerie and the Iron Guard. In 1941, under the dictatorship of Marshal Ion Antonescu, all urban Jewish property was declared state property, and a further decree barred Jews from occupying state property. As a result, Jews were dispossessed of tens of thousands of properties throughout the country. All told, some 40,758 buildings were taken (in Bucharest 5236 buildings and 14,492 apartments); 42,320 hectares of farmland were seized, 68,644 hectares of woodlands, and 2062 hectares of vineyards. The Jews also lost 265 mills and 115 sawmills.[25]

After the armistice, the Jewish community proposed an immediate restitution, according to which those occupying Jewish property could move to the rented flats vacated by the Jews. The Romanian government rejected this idea. A law of 19 December 1944 issued by Communist minister of Justice, Lucretiu Patrascanu, ruled that Jews could only reacquire their holdings by bringing suits. A foreign correspondent noted that in Bucharest alone, out of the nearly 20,000 properties, only 3560 had been brought to court, and of those 21 per cent remained unsettled after fourteen months of litigation.[26] Here it should be noted that these properties represent those seized from Jews under Romanian jurisdiction – in other words, it does not take into account the properties of Jews in parts of Romania that later came under Hungarian, Bulgarian or Soviet jurisdiction.

The 1947 Peace Treaty concluded between Romania and the Allied and Associate Powers, as well as the general principles of law and elementary justice, demanded the redress of the material wrongs committed against Romanian Jewry between 1938 and 1944. Article 25 of the Peace Treaty imposed a clear and unambiguous obligation upon Romania to restore Jewish property to survivors. These obligations are identical with Article 27 of the Hungarian Peace Treaty, and include the obligation to transfer heirless and unclaimed property to representative organizations in Romania or to pay fair compensation where restoration is impossible. A report issued by the World Jewish Congress in 1948 noted:

> In Romania most of the masterless properties are situated in Transylvania. Preliminary action on a local basis was taken to comply with the provisions of the Peace Treaty, but no final solution has so far been found. The Bucharest Office of the Congress has prepared bills providing for the limitation of inheritance in Transylvania (to divert property from distant relatives to the Fund) which became Law 50, promulgated on February 27, 1948, and for the mode of administration of heirless assets.[27]

Romania's compliance with the treaty was incomplete. With the intensification of Communist rule the notion of restoration of Jewish heirless property was abandoned and the government set its sights on property which was still in the hands of the Jewish community. In 1949, in order to cloak the theft of communal properties, the Communist-dominated Federation of Jewish Communities 'voluntarily' relinquished control over some 256 communal institutions. Before he was forced into exile, the anti-Communist chief rabbi, Dr Alexandre Safran, had refused to acquiesce to this nationalization.[28]

Under its constitution of 21 November 1991, enacted after the revolution that deposed Ceaucescu, a new constitution was enacted. That document provided for the recognition of the right to own property and the right not to be 'dispossessed except for reasons of public interest specified by law, with just and fair compensation.' In December 1993 an agreement was signed between the Jewish community and the WJRO, in which both sides pledged to act in tandem in pursuing Jewish claims. Together with the late Chief Rabbi, Dr Moses Rosen, talks were held with the Foreign Minister Teodor Meiescanu, to discuss restitution. The foreign minister expressed the government's commitment to the principle of restitution and called for the creation of a Romania—WJRO committee to deal with the matter. Additional meetings took place, notably in April 1994, but little progress was recorded. Meanwhile, the WJRO compiled a list of some 3000 items of community property that the community could claim. According to one community official, communal property includes the site of 295 demolished synagogues.

The 1996 elections, which swept the post-Communist *canaille* from power and brought a new government to office, heralded a change. A small number of confiscated properties were restored and promises were made to transfer others. A fund was established, jointly administered by the WJRO and by the Jewish community, to reclaim other properties. In 1998 that fund was registered in Bucharest. Comprehensive legislation providing for the satisfaction of claims for restitution of private property has yet to be enacted, but the Romanian authorities have pledged to work in this direction. In August 1998, on an official visit to Israel, the Romanian Prime Minister Radu Vasilie pledged to submit legislation in parliament to facilitate the return of property and work towards comprehensive legislation aimed at the restitution of nationalized property.[29]

Slovakia

In 1939, under the leadership of the Slovak nationalist leader, the Roman Catholic priest Josef Tiso, Slovakia seceded from the rump Czecho-Slovakia and became a German satellite. On its own initiative the Slovak government orchestrated proceedings for the despoliation, deportation and extermination of its Jewish minority. The atmosphere surrounding the seizure of Jewish property in Slovakia prior to the deportation is captured in Slovak-Jewish writer Ladislav Grossman's poignant novel *The Shop on Main Street*. Of the nearly 90,000 Jews in Slovak-ruled territory at the start of the war, more than 60,000 perished.

Until the dissolution of Czechoslovakia in 1991, claims in Slovakia were considered no differently than those in the Czech lands. Since that time, however, Slovakia has enacted its own legislation dealing with

Jewish property, and today satisfaction of Jewish claims in Slovakia is more advanced than in most other countries. After considerable negotiation between the Slovak authorities and the WJRO, a law was passed on 27 October 1993 which provides for the partial recovery of property seized from religious communities. In the case of the Jewish community the law provides for recovery of property seized since 2 November 1938. The Slovak law sets an important precedent for other states in the region, insofar as it covers communal properties of both existing and defunct Jewish communities. The Slovak Jewish community, in cooperation with the WJRO, has already drawn up an inventory of close to 1000 properties (including some thirty synagogues) which it has submitted under the provisions of the law. Many of the claims are being processed by local courts with the work facilitated by documents furnished by the WJRO. As of the spring of 1998, some 360 pieces of property had been restored, the great majority of them burial grounds. However, progress has been slow and in Jewish quarters the suggestion has been made that local officials are acting very slowly.

In a related development, both the Czech and Slovak National Banks agreed to pay a total of $950,000 to the Jewish Foundation in Slovakia as compensation for gold and jewels plundered from Slovak Jews and later secreted in the Czechoslovak National Bank.[30]

Post-Soviet countries

In both Latvia and Estonia, following negotiations with the WJRO, certain items of Jewish communal property have been restored to the Jewish community and restitution of private property has not been hampered by questionable regulations regarding citizenship and domicile. In Lithuania, however, the situation is less encouraging and, while individual pieces of communal property have been restituted, the bulk of Jewish property remains in state hands. The WJRO has not given up on improving this situation and sporadic negotiations have taken place.

In Russia, Ukraine, Belarus and Moldova, the bulk of Jewish communal property was sequestered after the Bolshevik revolution. In parts of Ukraine and Belarus, once under Polish, Czechoslovak, Hungarian or Romanian control, and later seized by the Soviet Union in 1939 and 1940, properties were also nationalized. Where this process was incomplete, the German invasion led to the total despoliation of communal and private property. In Russia and the post-Soviet successor states, there has only been sporadic restitution of Jewish communal property. Very often the issue has been left in the hands of local authorities. The

WJRO, aided by local communities, has collected an impressive number of documents in which the magnitude of the Jewish claim is clear. Only time will tell, however, if this issue will be satisfied with proper respect both to basic human rights and to the tragedy that befell the Jewish populations of these countries.

Conclusion

In assessing the restitution record of Eastern Europe, a rather disturbing pattern can be observed. In meetings with the WJRO and other Jewish officials, heads of state and government leaders have expressed encouragement and support for the satisfaction of Jewish claims. But they have taken little action to achieve a comprehensive and equitable solution of this problem. It sometimes seems that in paying lip service to the WJRO representatives it is attempting to assuage world Jewry and to eventually achieve modest arrangements with the local communities. There is also a belief that the longer these countries can prevaricate, the less likely it is that claims will be pursued. To date this tactic has borne some success. One cannot fail to observe the fact that in some instances East European governments have succeeded in cutting deals with local Jewish communities which provided considerably less than the comprehensive (one might even say 'maximalist') demands of the WJRO. Because of the somewhat precarious socioeconomic situation of the new democracies, and their need to balance the demands of their domestic political constituency with the desire for international legitimacy and correct relations with the Jewish world, clearly only a fraction of the vast properties looted from the Jewish people will ever be restored to their rightful heirs (both individual and collective). But to secure even this imperfect settlement, the Jewish world will have to struggle mightily.

Notes

1 Calel Perechodnik, *Czy Ja Jestem Morderca?* (Warsaw, 1994), p. 18.
2 Mordechai Tenenbaum-Tamaroff, *Dapim min HaDeleka* (Jerusalem, undated), p. 55.
3 Joseph Tenenbaum, *Race and Reich* (New York, 1956), p. 139.
4 Jozef Adelson, 'W Polsce tak zwanej Ludowa', in Jerzy Tomaszewski (ed.), *Najnowsze Dzieje Zydow w Polsce* (Warsaw, 1993), p. 431.
5 Eva Heyman, *The Diary of Eva Heyman* (Jerusalem, 1974), p. 80.

6 *The Wall Street Journal*, 7 October 1994. Of course, not all states expressed such contrition. At the Stockholm International Holocaust Forum held in January 2000, the President of Latvia, Vaira Vike-Freiberga, claimed that 'Latvia as a country having ceased to exist at the time, the Nazi German occupying powers bear the ultimate responsibility for the crimes they committed or instigated on Latvian soil.' This sentiment was echoed by the Prime Minister of Lithuania (speaking of a time when nearly the entire Jewish population was wiped out, in large measure due to the enthusiastic participation of ethnic Lithuanian collaborators), Andrews Kubilius, who declared: 'I am hurt and ashamed to hear that sometimes Lithuania is mentioned in the foreign press in relation to the tragedy of the Jewish people during World War II. At that time Lithuania was nothing more than a geographical unit.'

7 Institute of Jewish Affairs, *Unity in Dispersion* (New York, 1948), pp. 277–8.

8 Nehemiah Robinson, *Indemnification and Reparations* (New York, 1944), p. 8.

9 Eli Nathan, address to the International Association of Jewish Lawyers and Jurists, 28 June 1994 (typescript furnished by Judge Nathan).

10 Typescript of speech furnished by the WJRO.

11 *Jerusalem Post*, 12 June 1998.

12 Tom Warner, 'Making Amends in Prague', *B'nai Brith International Monthy*, March 1994.

13 Jacek Mojkowski and Marian Turski, 'Majatek z popiolow', *Polityka*, 8 February 1998.

14 Victor Eskenasy, 'Romania', in Jean-Yves Camus (ed.), *Extremism in Europe* (Paris, 1997), p. 281.

15 Typescript of speech furnished by the US State Department.

16 As explained in an official WJC history: 'Jewish concern with the peace treaties was an outgrowth of a number of factors. First of all, in four out of the five ex-enemy countries (the exception being Finland), the Jewish population had been subjected to the Nazi-devised policy of extermination.... Bulgaria's record... was a decent one. There had been no anti-Jewish persecutions in Bulgaria before Germany's pressure began to be exerted, and the Bulgarian people strenuously opposed the anti-Jewish measures which were introduced under foreign prompting. The situation in Rumania and Hungary was quite different' (Institute of Jewish Affairs, *Unity in Dispersion*, pp. 248–9).

17 *Jewish Chronicle*, 3 February 1995; *Balkan International News and EER*, 3 April 1994.

18 *Respekt*, 12 January 1995, and 23 August 1993.

19 Adrian Levy and Cathy Scott-Clark, 'The Guilt that Dare Not Speak of Shame', *The Sunday Times Magazine*, 30 November 1997.

20 Information on Actual Issues in Hungary, 'Restitution for Jewish Community', Ministry of Foreign Affairs of the Republic of Hungary Press and International Information Department, 11 April 1997.

21 Joseph Marcus, *Social and Political History of the Jews in Poland* (Berlin, 1987), p. 120.

22 Lucjan Dobroszycki, 'Restoring Jewish Life in Post-War Poland', *Soviet Jewish Affairs*, No. 2 (1973) p. 66.

23 Beata Gorowska and Grzegorz Rydlewski, *Regulacje Prawne Stosunkow Wyzna-niowych w Polsce* (Warsaw, 1992).

24   Report by Naftali Lau-Lavi at Cardozo School of Law, New York, 9 February 1998. Typescript furnished by WJRO.

25   World Jewish Congress – Romanian Section, *Populatia Evreeasca in Cifre – Memento: Statistic* (Bucharest, 1945), pp. 118–19.

26   Hal Lehrmann, 'Rumania: Equality with Reservations', *Commentary*, March 1946.

27   *Unity in Dispersion*, op. cit., p. 281.

28   Alexandre Safran, *Resisting the Storm: Romania, 1940–1947 – Memoirs* (Jerusalem, 1987) pp. 283–5.

29   Associated Press, 4 August 1998.

30   *Jerusalem Post*, 27 July 1998.

6

A Commentary on Europe's Looted Gold, 1938–45

Arthur L. Smith, Jr

I

Gold, whether taken from nations or individuals, proved to be an important weapon of war for Nazi Germany. The story of its seizure, disposition and restitution is one of intrigue among nations and insatiable greed.

The first chapter in the Nazi acquisition of plundered monetary gold[1] began with Austria. However, the transfer of over $100 million (1938 value) worth of gold to Germany after the March 1938 annexation (*Anschluss*), was not described at the time as 'plundered'.[2] Austria was absorbed into the German Reich without force, and the world both of politics and banking accepted its disappearance with little or no protest. Only later would the Allies of the Second World War regard the taking of Austria's gold as the beginning of Germany's looting of the banks of Europe.

The second victim was Czechoslovakia. This proved slightly more complicated than Austria, for a large portion of Czech gold on deposit required a release from the Bank for International Settlements (BIS) in Basle, and the Bank of England in London. But in view of the Munich Agreement and the subsequent division of Czechoslovakia, both banks quietly complied with the German Reichsbank's request to transfer $26 million in gold into German hands. Together with what had been secured by Reichsbank officials in Prague, Germany added $44 million in gold to its 1939 reserves.[3]

As the threat of further German expansion loomed over Europe in 1939, concerned nations began the search for a safe haven for their gold. Poland succeeded in moving $64 million of their gold reserve out of the country before the German invasion in September. Entrusted into the care of the French government in the firm belief that the defence system of that nation, the much publicized Maginot Line, would prove invulnerable, the Polish gold made a long and circuitous journey that eventually ended in the French West African port city of Dakar. There it was to remain until after the Allied invasion of North Africa permitted its removal to the United States.[4]

Ironically, the real reason the Polish gold escaped German seizure was not its removal to Africa, but because the Bank of France and German Reichsbank got into endless arguments over the procedure for transferring the gold. The Bank of France maintained that the gold had initially been entrusted to the French government, and therefore was not the bank's responsibility. This meant the matter had to be settled with the Vichy government, but before this could be arranged, the Allies had landed in North Africa and the path back to Europe was blocked.[5] Germany had to be satisfied with the $4 million in Polish gold which had been in the Bank of Danzig.[6]

Unfortunately, both Luxembourg and Belgium followed the Polish example in believing France would never fall. They dutifully delivered their gold reserves over to the Bank of France for safekeeping before their surrender to Germany. Luxembourg's gold, $4,857,823 worth, was still in Marseilles awaiting shipment to Dakar, when France collapsed and the gold was turned over to representatives of the German Reichsbank.[7]

It was Belgium's $223,200,000 worth of gold that became the largest single monetary gold seizure the Germans made. It seemed at first that this huge cache would escape the German grasp, for it had left France for Dakar before the French agreed to armistice terms. The Germans were not to be denied, however, for the terms of the Franco-German armistice dictated full Vichy cooperation. It did not take long for Germany to demand a complete accounting from the Bank of France, and total disclosure of the whereabouts of all gold bullion and coin in the bank's possession.[8]

Vichy complied, but this did not provide any quick resolution, for the gold was in Africa (see Map 1), over 240 tons of it in almost 5000 large crates. This might not have presented such a problem if there had been no war, but Germany had not defeated England, and was already planning the invasion of the Soviet Union. For the Reichsbank to secure the gold, it had to be transported from French West Africa to Berlin, a task that required extensive manpower, security forces and aircraft, all resources that were needed by Germany's war economy. To keep the gold out of the hands of the Allies, it had to travel eastward on the Niger River, north from Gao over the Sahara Desert to Algiers, by air across the

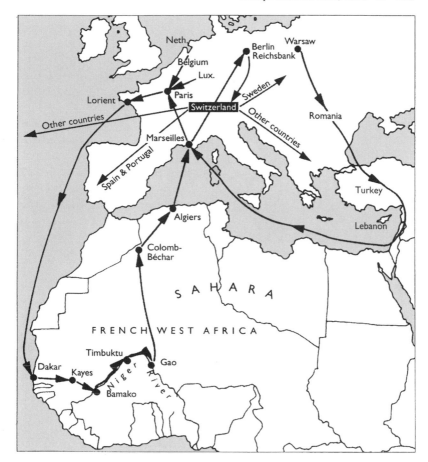

Map 1 The trail of gold looted by the Nazis

Mediterranean to Marseilles, and then on to Berlin. The first shipment left West Africa in October 1940, and the last shipment arrived in Berlin in May 1942.[9]

By this time the Germans had acquired over $540 million worth of looted gold from the banks of Europe. This was supplemented by an additional $80 million in gold from the Bank of Italy in September 1943. Germany called it Italy's 'contribution' to the war that was raging on the eastern front.[10] This brought the grand total to over $621 million in looted gold at Germany's disposal.

One of the unanswered questions in the looted gold story concerns the non-monetary gold that came into the Reichsbank's possession. Officials of the bank later acknowledged receiving deliveries of non-monetary gold from the SS, beginning in 1942. The containers delivered sometimes bore the names 'Lublin' or 'Auschwitz', and, according to Albert Thomas, head of the bank's precious metals department, the shipments were large quantities of gold jewellery, rings, eyeglass frames, dental gold, and a variety of objects made from gold. Before the war ended, the Reichsbank had received seventy-six shipments from the SS, estimated at $14.5 million in value.[11] Just how much of this loot taken from victims sent to concentration camps, or from raids in occupied Eastern areas, was smelted into gold bars and added to the Reichsbank gold reserve is difficult to calculate. There is no doubt that some of the SS-looted gold went into the Reichsbank coffers as monetary gold and assumed negotiable value. As such, its source then became indistinguishable from the general Reichsbank gold pool and was, therefore, used in bank transactions.

The details involving looted gold, whether from nations or individuals, never presented any liquidity problem for the Reichsbank. Even if bankers from neutral nations accepted the subterfuge of resmelting identifiable gold bars and replacing the markings, it only required elementary calculations to determine that much of the gold was looted gold that came out of the Reichsbank after 1941. Officially, Germany's prewar gold reserve was about $70 million worth, and a hidden gold reserve may have doubled that figure, but by mid-war the Nazis had poured over $500 million into their war economy.[12] At that point, any banker in the gold business knew full well that the Germans were dealing in looted gold.

The number of neutral nations during the Second World War that accepted German gold was mostly in Europe. These were Sweden, Spain, Portugal and Switzerland. Turkey was of geographic importance to Nazi Germany, but did not figure prominently in the gold trade. Switzerland was the nation that was Germany's most important partner among the neutrals in helping to dispose of the looted gold. Between March 1940 and the end of the European war in May 1945, Germany transferred over $378 million in gold to Switzerland, an amount far in excess of that sent to any other source.[13]

A vital part of German success in disposing of looted gold was the close relationship its bankers had developed with leading banks abroad. Emil Puhl, the Reichsbank vice-president, was a key figure in the gold transactions, and had enjoyed long and cordial relations with the BIS and the Swiss National Bank (SNB).

The BIS had been created in 1930 to deal with the lingering problems associated with First World War reparations. Its charter was international in character and had been subscribed to by the world's leading banking nations, including the United States and Switzerland. As a banking institution, the BIS occupied a unique position in the world banking community. It had virtual immunity from Swiss banking laws, and a directorship drawn from Germany, Japan, Great Britain, Italy, Ireland, Belgium, the United States and Switzerland. Its primary function, before the war, was to prop up the gold standard, increase cooperation among subscriber banks and establish an internationally accepted gold clearing system in which the BIS acted as the primary bookkeeper.[14]

Even before the war began in 1939, the BIS had played a central role in assisting the German Reichsbank to acquire Czechoslovakian gold. The Czechs had transferred a large portion of their gold reserves, through a BIS account, to the Bank of England before the Munich Agreement in 1938, but with the total absorption of that state by Germany in 1939, the two banks readily cooperated with the German demand for the release of gold.[15] Later, when the secret transaction became public, it would contribute to the rising tide of public anger against policies of France and England.

A most disturbing fact, to the anti-Hitler forces in the United States, was the role an American was playing in the BIS. Thomas H. McKittrick, a prominent banker from New York, was the managing director of the BIS during the war. He headed an institution that furthered the gold policies of the German Reichsbank, and was elected for a second term in 1942, receiving both the Italian and German representatives' votes. While conducting BIS business, McKittrick travelled throughout German-occupied Europe, and even to the United States during the war.[16]

Among the banks in Switzerland, the Swiss National Bank was involved most extensively in the gold trade with Germany. A secret United States report on SNB activities, based on recovered Reichsbank files after the war, revealed that about 70 per cent of all German gold sent abroad during the war went to its gold depot at the SNB. The report also revealed that more than half of the looted Belgium gold ($126 million worth) ended up at the SNB. Prophetically, it was noted in the secret report that haste was important in the 'investigation before Swiss have any excuse for destroying records as obsolete'.[17]

Actually, American investigators had uncovered much of the story when interrogating former Reichsbank officials straight after the war. Albert Thoms, who had headed the Reichsbank's precious metals department, told the Americans about the SNB depot: 'Each month in the last 5 to 6 years', he said, 'perhaps around 3000 to 4000 kilos in gold were sent to Switzerland. All shipments to Switzerland were sent first to the depot at the Swiss National Bank and later maybe sold'.[18]

In 1943, a record year for German gold transactions with Switzerland, the SNB began accepting gold that was identifiable as having belonged to Belgium, and paid the Reichsbank in Swiss francs for it.[19] Recovered Reichsbank records also showed that the SNB had purchased over $31 million worth of gold from Germany that belonged to the Bank of Amsterdam. The recorded smelt numbers in the Reichsbank ledgers were from gold bars made from Dutch guilders, matched perfectly with the shipments of gold sent to the SNB.[20] Of course, the Allies did not have to wait until the war was over to know many of the details of Germany's trade in looted gold to Switzerland, and elsewhere. There was sufficient evidence by 1942 to prompt an Allied declaration in January 1943. It was a formal warning to all neutrals about dealing in loot and plunder, but it had little effect upon the continuing gold shipments from the Reichsbank to Switzerland. Subsequent Allied gold declarations met the same indifference from most of the neutrals, and concern and frustration continued to mount in Washington and London. It was feared that Germany was busily transferring assets abroad in order to build an economic base in the event of defeat.

Incredibly, the Allies were not able to halt the German gold flow into Switzerland until the very last month of the war. Despite the warning of dire consequences ahead, the Swiss continued to refuse to fully cooperate with the Allies. In March of 1945, an Allied delegation, the so-called 'Currie Mission' (Lauchlin Currie headed the mission) travelled to Switzerland intent upon securing an agreement on the disposition of German assets in that country. Although Switzerland generally agreed to Currie's demands, any acknowledgement that the gold from Germany was looted gold and should be returned was absolutely out of the question from Switzerland's standpoint. Without Swiss cooperation, there was no action that the Allies could take to verify their allegations of looted gold being deposited in Switzerland.[21]

While some quarters in Washington hailed the Currie Mission as a success, there remained a number of sceptics. These were people who had been struggling with the question of postwar economic planning, and were generally opposed to permitting Switzerland, most specifically the BIS and Swiss banks, from occupying an important role in that process. Serious deliberations on the matter had taken shape at the international monetary conference in New Hampshire in July 1944. There, at Bretton Woods, the International Monetary Fund and the International Bank for Reconstruction were created as new financial institutions, and there was some opinion expressed that the BIS should be completely eliminated because of its wartime conduct.[22]

The strongest opposition to permitting the BIS to continue business as usual came from the American Secretary of the Treasury, Henry Morgenthau, who wanted immediate elimination of the bank. This was countered somewhat by the US State Department representative at the conference, Dean Acheson, who suggested that no action be taken until the war was over. Support for the continuation of the BIS came from Leon Fraser, head of the First National Bank of Manhattan, and a former BIS president. Claiming the support of leading American bankers, Fraser argued that not only should the BIS not be eliminated, but should be allowed to take the lead in providing financial services in postwar European reconstruction. His argument obviously failed to convince the delegates at Bretton Woods, for a resolution to liquidate the BIS was passed; however, it contained a fatal flaw for it did not stipulate just how and when the liquidation was to take place.[23]

Additionally, Fraser's argument gained some weight from such powerful voices as Britain's wartime leader, Winston Churchill, who cautioned that Switzerland was not to be judged too quickly, for its record during the war was better than that of most neutrals. He stated that the actions taken by Switzerland were necessary at times simply '. . . to keep herself alive.'[24] Churchill's view may have been motivated by a concern that the United States was not ready to assume the leadership in postwar reconstruction, and it would be left to Britain. The BIS and the Bank of England had a close working relationship, and, in such a case, the Basle bank could prove extremely valuable.

When the war ended, however, an investigation of the BIS was undertaken by the United States. An American lawyer involved in the process wrote that there were many unanswered questions about the bank's operations and connections to looted gold. It was pointed out that the American banker McKittrick had never revealed any information about the shipments of looted gold to Switzerland, nor about the close relationship the BIS maintained to the German Reichsbank throughout the entire period.[25]

The investigation was too late, however, because for European leaders struggling with the massive problems of reconstruction, the BIS was an institution with experience and connections to the world of banking. It also offered to assist in tracing any gold suspected of being looted, and make any settlements for which the bank had been responsible. Ultimately, the BIS did contribute a sum of gold (3700 kilograms) to the postwar restitution pool.[26]

The looted gold story did not end with the close of the war, for the complex task of returning all gold that the Allies had recovered in

Germany and elsewhere to the rightful owners had to be undertaken. The first step was to sort out the twisted details of the looted gold trail, determine how much actually constituted looted gold, establish a gold pool, and then create a commission of Allied leaders to oversee the restitution. In an implementation of the Paris Agreement on Reparations in 1945, a Tripartite Commission for the Restitution of Monetary Gold was established with a membership of representatives from Great Britain, France and the United States.[27]

Considering the basic facts that the Gold Commission had to work with, the members faced an interesting challenge: Hitler had stolen over $621 million worth of gold from occupied Europe; the Allies had recovered approximately $338 million in gold (although records indicated that about $378 million in gold had gone from Germany to Switzerland); and, claims from nations that had lost gold to the Nazis came to over $800 million in gold.[28] Before any gold could be restituted to any of the claimant nations, these differences had to be reconciled, and in the process procedures established to determine not only the legitimacy of each claim, but exactly what percentage would be returned.

By early 1947, the Gold Commission had worked its way through the complexities of laying all the ground rules for restitution, and was preparing to distribute the recovered gold. Much had changed in those short two years, however, and decisions that may have seemed simple in 1945 or 1946, were no longer so easy to make. Relations between the Western nations and the Soviet Union had deteriorated dramatically, and the great coalition that fought to defeat Hitler no longer had any common goals. A number of the nations that had lost gold to the Germans had now become Communist states, a fact that definitely was taken into consideration by the Gold Commission in its deliberations.

It could not be denied that Czechoslovakia, Poland, Yugoslavia and Albania had been plundered by Germany, while Austria and Italy had been allied with the Germans. In considering restitution claims, however, the Gold Commission included Austria and Italy in the ten nations to receive a gold share, and indefinitely delayed payment to the Communist states. As for the Gold Commission, a body intended to be temporary, its life has continued into the 1990s.

II

If all of this information on the history of the gold Germany looted from occupied Europe has been available for at least several decades, the obvious question is why has it grabbed world attention only now?

Any reader of the daily news who lived in England or the United States (or Switzerland), was informed of Allied concern over Germany's disposal of looted gold as early as 1942. A United Nations Declaration in early 1943, signed by seventeen nations, warned neutral states about taking gold from the Germans.[29] Again, in February 1944, an even more forcefully worded 'Gold Declaration' was issued when US Treasury Secretary Morgenthau stated: 'The United States Government formally declares that it does not and will not recognize the transference of title to the looted gold which the Axis . . . has disposed of in the world markets.'[30]

In addition to such widely publicized announcements, there was newspaper coverage of the Allied concern with the actions of the BIS at the Bretton Woods Conference in 1944. In 1945, the proceedings of the trial of the war criminals at Nuremberg, through testimony from Reichsbank personnel, revealed the trade in looted gold to Switzerland.[31] All of this information was in the public domain by 1947.

If one wished to go behind the headlines and public documents, a wealth of material was also becoming available in book form as both history studies and memoirs during the 1940s and 1950s. For example: Martin Domke, *Trading with the Enemy in World War II* (New York: Central Book Co., 1943); Thomas Reville, *The Spoil of Europe, The Nazi Technique in Political and Economic Conquest* (New York: W.W. Norton, 1941); Ralph G. Hawtrey, *Bretton Woods, For Better or Worse* (London: Longmans, Green Co., 1946); Roger Aubion, *The Bank for International Settlements, 1930–1955* (Princeton, N.J.: Princeton University Press, 1955); Charles Codman, *Drive* (Boston: Little, Brown & Co., 1957); Stanley Moss, *Gold is Where You Hide It: What Happened to the Reichsbank Treasures?* (London: André Deutsch, 1956).

By the 1970s and 1980s, virtually full accounts of the history of Europe's looted gold by the Nazis and the trade with Switzerland were appearing in print but, unfortunately for those individuals who were still searching for wealth lost to the Nazis, the works received little attention. In fact, the astonishing thing is that even when the looted gold saga first began to make the newspapers in 1996, the story was presented as a new discovery with little or no mention of these early studies. Three of these worth noting are: Willi Boelcke, 'Zur internationalen Goldpolitik des NS-Staates', in M. Funke (ed.), *Hitler's Deutschland und die Machte* (Düsseldorf: Droste Verlag, 1977); Werner Rings, *Raubgold aus Deutschland* (1985); and Arthur L. Smith, Jr, *Hitler's Gold* (Berg: Oxford, 1989, 2nd edn 1996).

Why, with such an abundance of available published information, was there such a long delay before any attention was focused upon the story of the looted gold? It is difficult to provide a satisfactory answer to this question, for there seems to be no single reason why half a century had to pass before any public outrage was registered.

A partial explanation is found in the historical events that occurred following the Second World War. Between the years 1945 and 1948, the leaders of the Western world were fully engaged in European economic reconstruction, and anything that may have delayed or hindered that goal was pushed aside. By 1948, the Cold War was in the open, and engulfed foreign policies completely for the next fifty years. Again, any lingering problem left from the war that threatened to reveal a crack in the anti-Communism campaign of the Western powers (like, who had dealt in looted gold?) was simply ignored. When such things are ignored long enough, they are generally forgotten. It is only when a concerned group is capable of bringing the event into public consciousness through wide media exposure, that the truth is uncovered. When carefully examining the looted gold story, it is important to distinguish between monetary gold taken from nations and non-monetary gold robbed from individuals. The facts surrounding looted monetary gold are largely clear and indisputable concerning the role of Nazi Germany. There is solid evidence of the trail of gold out of Germany, but more information is needed from Switzerland (the SNB), the BIS and the Allied Gold Commission about certain aspects of receiving and disposing of the gold. In this case, the sources that can supply the few remaining details that surround the looted monetary gold story are known. The situation is not the same with the looted non-monetary gold.

The trail of non-monetary looted gold is, by contrast, murky, buried in convoluted byways, and generally lacking in any verifiable documentation. While an interested person could have traced the story of the looted monetary gold years ago, the looted non-monetary gold is another story. The very fact that it has often been the struggle of an individual searching for lost valuables or gold that had belonged to a family many years ago, usually meant a story of little consequence to anyone else. It had to await the aroused interest of powerful public figures and organizations before the world took notice. This began to occur in 1996. As sometimes happens with the reporting of complex historical events, the full story is not presented. The news media accounts of the looted gold often failed to inform the reader of the exact difference between monetary and non-monetary gold, as determined by the Gold Commission. The confusion was intensified by the numerous revelations that began appearing about European Jews who had deposited funds (gold and currency) into Swiss banks, usually through an intermediary, and had subsequently perished without receiving an accounting. When the facts became known that Switzerland had been the major receiver of German looted gold, the question of these unreconciled accounts, or dormant accounts, as the Swiss called them, became an added dimension to the looted gold story. In fact, the real story became the wealth lost by individuals to banks in Switzerland. As it continued to unfold, it was obvious that these claimants, or their rightful descendants, now aided by such groups as the World Jewish Congress, were the driving force behind the growing demand that Switzerland open its banks for inspection.

Although many of the original claimants or their heirs had pursued their demands for a settlement for many years, they had never been able to penetrate the wall of secrecy and bureaucracy that surrounded the Swiss banking community. Of course, the question remains, why have these walls begun to crumble? One reason may relate to the Swiss announcement in 1996 that banks were closing out some old dormant accounts. This item caught the attention of a number of interested observers, for it was something that could be connected to possible deposits made by victims of Nazism who had died in the Holocaust. The challenge was soon taken up by such figures as Britain's Foreign Minister Malcolm Rifkind, Edgar Bronfman of the World Jewish Congress, and American Senator Alfonse D'Amato. Once the story began to gather momentum, almost every news story announced new discoveries, more details, promises of further investigations, and hints of vast amounts of looted gold still in Swiss possession. It is at this point that the looted monetary gold, non-monetary gold and claimants' deposits all blended together as one huge fortune still stored in Swiss bank vaults. International committees were formed, giant accounting and law firms were engaged, and numerous studies were launched.[32]

It is interesting that in the tumult of publicity surrounding the release of news about the looted gold, there was virtually no acknowledgment of the existence of previously published work on the subject. Quite the contrary, for at times information that had already long since been published, would be announced with much fanfare as something just found. Usually it was described as having languished for decades among secret files recently declassified and secured only after aggressive efforts. The plethora of articles and books that began appearing were also generally neglectful of earlier works that had already told the story, but the writers were not ashamed to borrow without acknowledgement.

In addition to unravelling the disposition of deposits of current claimants, a task that may well occupy years, there is still some unfinished business. The Bank for International Settlements has succeeded in remaining relatively aloof from the fray that has engulfed the Swiss banks and government. It has been able to continue its functions as before without fully revealing its part in the looted gold saga. It would appear at this point that the BIS may escape scrutiny and never have to open its archives to any investigative committee.

Equally successful – so far – in avoiding demands to see its records is the Tripartite Commission for the Restitution of Monetary Gold. The very fact that it continues in existence (after more than fifty years) and conducts its business in private in dealing with the whole looted gold question, leaves the distinct impression of secrets that the public deserves to know. The biggest secret could be that the Gold Commission played favourites with gold restitution, depending upon whether or not the nation in question had a Communist government.[33]

It is quite probable that certain aspects of the looted gold story will never be resolved. Some archival material will remain classified indefinitely, some of the vital documentation has already disappeared forever, and people who could have shed the most important light on the entire proceedings have passed on. Fortunately, the search is not yet over, and it is very possible, despite efforts at obstruction, that before it is ended, everything that can be known about the gold that Germany looted from occupied Europe during the Second World War, will come into the public domain.

Notes

1   Monetary gold was later defined as that gold in a nation's reserve at the time of its transfer to the German Reichsbank. Non-monetary gold was defined as gold objects of a wide variety, such as rare coins, reading-glass frames, tooth fillings, jewellery, etc.
2   United States, National Archives, Record Group 260, Office of Military Government United States (OMGUS), Finance and Administration (FINAD), Albert Thomas Report, 'Gold of Austrian National Bank', pp. 1–3.
3   Ibid., OMGUS AG, 1945–46; OMGUS AG to CAD, 3 January 1946.
4   United States, *Foreign Relations of the United States, 1943* (Washington, DC: US Government Printing Office [USGPO]), pp. 443–4, 495–96.
5   Germany, Bundesarchiv, R2, 14552, 25175, Hemmen–deBoisanger correspondence.
6   US, NA, RG 43, Records of International Conferences Commissions and Expositions, World War II Conference Files, Fletcher to Reinstein, 19 April

1948, 'Polish Claims for Restitution of Gold Looted by Germany', p. 1. The Polish claim was not settled until 1976 by the Gold Commission, at which time the original $4 million in gold had become $10 million in gold value.

7 Ibid., RG 332, ETO, SGS, 123/2, Bernstein to Clay, 'Report on the Gold of Sparkasse Luxembourg', 21 October 1945, p. 1. Wisely, Denmark and Norway had dispatched most of their gold reserves ($51 million and $88 million respectively) off to the United States and England before the Nazi invasion in April 1940.

8 US, NA, German records microfilmed at Alexandria, VA, Microcopy T-501, roll 121, frames 616–17.

9 Arthur L. Smith Jr, *Hitler's Gold: The Story of the Nazi War Loot* (Oxford, 1989), pp. 20–4. A variety of problems prevented a rapid return of the gold to Europe. With Germany's widening war fronts, aircraft shortages were common, and the small planes that were available could only transport 2 tons at a time. Since the Mediterranean was a war theatre it was also risky.

10 US, NA, RG 260, OMGUS FINAD, R. A. Nixon to Clay, 11 December 1945.

11 *Trial of the Major War Criminals before the International Military Tribunal* (Nuremberg, 1947), vol. 13, pp. 602, 615–16.

12 Ibid., p. 168; and US, NA, RG 260, OMGUS FINAD, 'Overall Gold Report', 20 November 1946, p. 2.

13 Ibid.

14 Henry H. Schloss, *The Bank for International Settlements* (Amsterdam, 1958), pp. 86–7.

15 Johan W. Beyen, *Money in a Maelstrom* (New York, 1949), p. 137.

16 Charles Higham, *Trading with the Enemy* (New York 1983), p. 11; Schloss, *The Bank for International Settlements*, p. 116; and Smith, *Hitler's Gold*, pp. 55ff.

17 US, NA, RG 260, OMGUS FINAD, R. A. Nixon to Berstein, 11 August 1945, and Nixon to Schmidt, 28 August 1945.

18 Ibid., 'Secret Interrogation of Albert Thomas', 18 April 1945', p. 3.

19 Werner Rings, *Raubgold aus Deutschland: Die 'Golddrehscheibe' Schweiz im Zweiten Weltkrieg* (Zurich, 1985), pp. 8–9, 145.

20 US, NA, RG 260, OMGUS FINAD, General Papers on Gold Study, November 1946, 'Looted Netherlands Guilders Resmelted by the Prussian Mint during 1942', p. 1.

21 Smith, *Hitler's Gold*, pp. 68–72.

22 *Proceedings and Documents of the United Nations Monetary and Financial Conference, Bretton Woods, New Hampshire, July 1–22, 1944* (Washington, DC: USGPO, 1948).

23 Ibid., pp. 404ff.; and, *Morgenthau Diary*, vol. 1 (Washington, DC: USGPO, 1967), pp. 399–402.

24 Winston S. Churchill, *Triumph and Tragedy* (Boston, 1953), p. 712.

25 James S. Martin, *All Honorable Men* (Boston, 1950), p. 281.

26 US, NA, RG 43, WW II Conf. Files, Am. Embassy London to Washington, DC, 5 March 1948, Subject 'Arrangements for Monetary Gold of Illegal Issuance Held by BIS'; and, Great Britain, Parliamentary Command Paper 7456, Treaty Series No. 38 (1948), 13 May 1948, p. 1.

27 Fortunately for the three Western Allies, virtually all of the gold remaining in Germany in 1945, over $252 million worth, came into American possession when it was discovered in a mine in Thuringia.

28   Smith, *Hitler's Gold*, pp. 132ff. The Americans had recovered about $252 million in gold remaining in Germany, and an additional $78 million worth from various sources, including $58 million in gold from Switzerland, as a result of the Washington Agreement in 1946.

29   US, NA, WW II Conf. Files, 'Inter-Allied Declaration Against Acts of Dispossession Committed in Territories under Enemy Occupation of Control', 5 January 1943.

30   US, *Elimination of German Resources for War: Hearings Before a Sub-Committee of the Committee on Military Affairs*, US Senate: Pt 2: Testimony of State Dept., 25 June 1945 (Washington, DC: USGPO, 1945), pp. 134–35.

31   *Trial of the Major War Criminals*, vol.13, pp. 564ff.

32   Former US Federal Reserve Chairman, Paul Volcker, was appointed to head a committee presently investigating certain aspects of the gold that passed into Switzerland. An extensive study, not yet complete, has been undertaken by the US State Department ('U.S. and Allied Efforts to Recover and Restore Gold and Other Assets Stolen or Hidden by Germany During World War II', May 1997). In December 1996, the US House of Representatives Committee on Banking and Financial Services conducted an extensive hearing, and produced a lengthy report on their findings: *The Disposition of Assets Deposited in Swiss Banks by Missing Nazi Victims* (Washington, DC: USGPO, 1997).

33   When this writer suggested as much to a US State Department representative, he was told that the idea was 'nonsense'. Smith, *Hitler's Gold*, n.35, pp.161–2.

7

German Assets in Switzerland at the End of the Second World War

Sidney Jay Zabludoff

Introduction

As the Second World War in Europe was ending, the Allies insisted that all German external assets be turned over to them. This action reflected the considerable evidence that the Nazis were going to use these assets, much of them hidden, to finance a Third World War. Halting another war seemed essential since twice within a quarter century Germany had aggressively attacked other nations. In addition, the Allies wanted to raise money to help repair the enormous destruction the Nazis had inflicted throughout Europe. German external assets were to be pledged to assist Jews and other persecuted individuals who had survived the devastating Holocaust. Such usage made eminent sense, since much of the assets held by Germans in foreign countries were forcibly taken from those who were persecuted. As a result, the Big Four Allied leaders decided at the Potsdam Conference in the summer of 1945 '...to assume control of all German assets abroad and to divest the said assets of their German ownership'.

More than 70 per cent of German external assets in European neutral counties were in Switzerland. In 1945, US officials estimated that amount to be as much as $1 billion. Under Allied prodding, the Swiss Government blocked German assets on 17 February 1945 and took a census of them. By the year's end, Bern released a summary of the results, which indicated an asset level of $230 million. The Allies acceded to the Swiss figure as part of the overall accord reached in May 1946, signed at the Washington Conference. After protracted negotiations (lasting six years after the matter presumably was settled in 1946), the US and Swiss governments finally agreed to an asset level of

$56 million. Half that amount ($28 million) was paid to the Allies in 1953, as stipulated in the 1946 accord. The Allies acquiesced to this small amount from weariness and because other concerns took centre stage, mainly the threat from the USSR.

This report estimates the value of German assets held in Switzerland in February 1945. Although determining an exact amount is highly impractical, a reasonably sound approximation of the total amount of assets can be made. Such estimates are common practice. They are based on the analysis of available and analogous information that helps bound the likely amount, so that it can be said with reasonable confidence that the number falls within a range. In the case of German assets in Switzerland, a number of approaches are available to approximate the number and test its plausibility. This report analyses the nature of capital flows between Germany and Switzerland, examines prewar and postwar estimates of the stock of assets, and appraises the values of major components.

Movement of German assets to Switzerland

The Weimar Republic years

Much of the German investment in Switzerland at the end of the Second World War was placed there from 1924 to 1931. Besides acting as a safe haven, these large money flows into Switzerland reflected German enterprises, use of Swiss financial institutions to hide the ownership of their foreign subsidiaries. They wanted to avoid a repeat of the losses suffered during and after World War, the First when their foreign assets were seized, and conceal their investments in foreign countries that were suspicious of German investment in them. Capital flight from Germany during those years roughly amounted to $4 billion, and about half that went to Switzerland. Given that some of this money was repatriated and some went on to other destinations, a conservative estimate is that there would be $500 million of German assets in Switzerland in the early 1930s. A 'rough census' by the Swiss National Bank in 1931 indicates a range of $500–750 million. The latter figure also includes German investments in Switzerland prior to 1924.

The Nazi connection

During the 1930s, global investment flows and levels were highly influenced by two significant occurrences: the Nazi takeover in

Germany and the global financial upheavals of the early 1930s which led to a worldwide economic depression. After the 1931 financial crises, most nations imposed severe trade and capital controls. The objective was to conserve rapidly depleting gold reserves. For example, Germany saw its gold holding plummet from a respectable $1 billion in 1930 to $55 million in 1934.

While many nations attempted to halt capital outflows, the Nazi regime employed harsh measures only available to a totalitarian government. The maximum penalty for non-compliance was death and, to ensure that nothing escaped, a the Gestapo and other police units were sent to Switzerland to uncover unreported assets. Although these measures contained capital outflows, individuals and corporations always found ways to hurdle the capital barriers. Such methods included the simple transporting of hidden gold or foreign exchange across the border, to more sophisticated money-laundering schemes such as undervaluing exports. Bribes were often paid to Nazi officials. The strict Nazi foreign capital regulations were relaxed in the case of large companies. IG Farben, for example, always seemed to have sufficient foreign exchange in Switzerland.

German holdings in Switzerland also rose, due to interest payments and other income received from investments. Finally, as the Second World War approached in 1939, there was a sizable inflow of additional foreign private and corporate funds into Switzerland. The US Consul in Basle reported an increase in the nominal share value of international corporations at $60 million alone. German capital movements into Switzerland between 1932 and 1939 probably amounted to at least several hundred million dollars or 10–20 per cent of the previous seven years. Partially offsetting the flow of German assets into Switzerland was a reduced value of the German assets already in Switzerland, caused by the worldwide economic depression.

In all, the value of German assets in Switzerland probably changed little during the 1930s. An estimate, based on a 1949 Bundestag study, indicates that the Germans had $450 million in assets in Switzerland in 1939. That number, however, is very conservative, as it leaves out intangible assets such as patents. It is thus not unreasonable to estimate the Swiss portion of German external assets at between $500 million and $1 billion on the eve of the war.

The war years

During the Second World War much of the asset build-up resulted from capital flight. A surge occurred immediately after the war began in 1939, and after 1943, when the tide of battle favoured the Allies. Foreign holdings of the Swiss franc were estimated to have jumped more than $100 million in the early war years. Switzerland clearly was the prime destination for highly liquid assets such as currency, stocks, bonds and valuable art objects, much of them looted by the Nazis throughout Europe. The country was easily accessible and the only one with sophisticated markets open to Germany. This can be seen from the fact that 85 per cent of the gold looted by the Nazis moved into or through Switzerland. Rudolf Hess, commandant of the Auschwitz concentration camp, said that Adolf Eichmann had told him 'that the jewellery and currency were sold in Switzerland and that the entire Swiss jewellery market was dominated by these sales.'

Albert Nussbaumer of the Swiss Banking Corporation estimated that the Germans added between $250 and $375 million to their holdings during the war. This expansion of the investment stock fits well with a statement of an official of the German Foreign Exchange Office that flows of currency and other movable property to Switzerland, for capital flight purposes, amounted to approximately $500 million since 1940. Thus, at least half of these assets remained in Switzerland. In addition, retained earnings from its long-established asset pool probably exceeded more than $100 million during the war. Again, this increase in holdings was partially offset by a decline in the value of some assets already in Switzerland. This time it was caused by fear that the assets would be confiscated. As a result, the 1945 level probably increased somewhat but remained in the $500 million to $1 billion range. Even the Swiss Compensation Office's 1945 census indicated a $100 million rise in German assets in Switzerland between 1 September, 1939 and 1945.

Asset estimates

No serious effort to estimate German assets in Switzerland took place until early 1945 as the war was ending. The last known approximation was the 1931 'rough census' by the Swiss National Bank. Although extremely important to the Swiss economy, no records were kept of the movement of foreign capital in and out of the country, either in total or by source country. Undoubtedly the Swiss financial elite felt that recording and publishing capital flow statistics would hurt business. They would alert other governments that they were losing considerable capital to the Swiss in order to escape taxes and preserve wealth, and that their capital controls were inadequate.

The Allies through their Safehaven programme wanted to pinpoint Nazi assets abroad to prevent their use in prolonging the war and in preparing for a new war. Considerable fervour existed on the second point in that reliable intelligence had indicated a major meeting of leading Nazi industrialists in Strasbourg in August 1944 to achieve that end. In response to the issue, Walter Sholes, the American Consul General in Basle, provided the first information in January 1945. He mentioned his 1942 estimate which indicated that German bank accounts in Switzerland amounted to $115 million. Later in January 1945, Sholes raised his estimate to $250 million to include net German deposits since 1942, and added $50–75 million for direct German investments in Switzerland. In March, the Swiss newspaper *Die Tat* indicated German deposits at $375 million.

Realizing the fragmented reporting on the subject of foreign German assets, the State Department sent a circular telegram to all neutral posts requesting a detailed breakdown of all such assets by categories. The US Legation in Bern prepared the first full estimate – $915 million – with breakdowns in early May and refined these categories during the next few weeks. In a cable to Washington, dated 31 May 1945, it presented its official response with a range of $450 million to $810 million. The post hedged its estimate by indicating it was a 'refined guess' for a number of reasons, including traditional Swiss concealment of assets and the Swiss government's lack of adequate records.

A number of other estimates appeared through 1945 and early 1946, few of which seemed to be based on a detailed analysis. By year end 1945, the Swiss indicated that their census of assets totalled $230 million. At the same time, O. F. Fletcher at the State Department prepared a 'revised approximate estimate' of $600 million, which excludes 'assets secreted in Switzerland or redeposited through Swiss banks in US, and foreign companies controlled through Swiss dummies.' The Swiss stuck to their figure during the March 1946 Allied–Swiss Conference in Washington. The US briefing book for the conference included the US Bern Legation's estimate of May 1945 with slight variations.

Key differences in estimates

Three key interrelated factors are largely responsible for differences in estimates. The most important is the ease by which the German assets were hidden in the Swiss financial system. The investment base also eroded over time, mainly as a result of actions taken by Swiss creditors to recoup likely losses. Finally, major differences existed in which assets were counted.

Hidden assets

Undoubtedly, the majority of German assets placed in Switzerland from the mid-1920s to the mid-1940s were disguised to hide the true owners, whether they were an individual or a corporation. The motivations for secrecy are clear, as already indicated In addition, the Swiss political and financial communities worked closely together to ensure the utmost secrecy, arguing that it was in the best interests of the Swiss economy. Given this circumstance, it was only natural that even the most conscientious operators in the financial community would stretch the possibilities of secrecy. These professionals could do almost anything, since they were protected by Swiss laws penalizing the divulging of client information. Those who were more unscrupulous became involved in illicit money-laundering activities with little fear of sanctions.

Thus, concealing assets in prewar and wartime Switzerland was particularly easy and probably involved the bulk of foreign assets placed there. The numerous concealment means included:

- *Placement of money via third parties and commingled accounts.* Rather than place money directly into a bank account, even a numbered one, the common practice of persons depositing significant sums was to work through third parties. These depositors, who normally were Swiss citizens, placed the funds under their name in a local bank, often commingling the money of several investors. The banks receiving the money thereby did not know the names of the beneficial owners.

  Actions taken by Kurt Kagi, a Zurich lawyer, provide an example of third-party possibilities. In 1938, he was contracted by Heinrich Blattman-Hollweg, the owner of a German-Jewish publishing house, and an acquaintance he had met in law school. The Jewish businessman asked – for a fee – to place some one million Swiss francs in income-generating bank accounts. As Kagi did not want to raise any suspicions he placed the money in some dozen banks throughout Switzerland, with each account under his name. Blattman-Hollweg and his family were sent to a concentration camp, where they all perished. Inquires made by Kagi after the war failed to locate even death records. By 1950, Kagi was using the sizable funds entrusted to him to meet his spending objectives.

• *Money held outside financial institutions.* During the Second World War era, as today, it was common practice to move and hold illicitly acquired or hidden assets in the form of financial assets that can not be traced easily, can be transferred readily and that are perceived to hold their value. In the war period, that mainly meant gold, other precious metals, bearer stocks and bonds, US dollars and Swiss francs. Most of these assets were held in safekeeping devices outside the banking system for Germans by Swiss citizens who were fiduciaries, lawyers, etc.

Among currencies held outside financial institutions, the Swiss franc understandably played an important role in Switzerland and other European countries during the war. The amount of Swiss currency in circulation rose by more than 50 per cent between 1938 and 1945 (after taking out inflation), at a time when the Swiss economy was declining. This substantial increase clearly points to the use of this money as a means to move and store earnings from illicit transactions, such as the selling of goods looted by the Nazis.

• *Falsification of the origin of securities.* Preparing and using falsified affidavits of ownership of foreign securities confiscated by the Nazis throughout Europe was a pervasive practice in Switzerland. Swiss authorities did investigate these practices but presumably the banking community wielded its powerful political clout to prevent a trial. At a pre-trial hearing, Director Hoch and Vice-Director Faust of the Swiss Banking Corporation recognized this practice as common. They did not consider their action as a 'swindle', and declared that the issue should have been submitted to a higher authority; and, if this had been done, the request would have been complied with.

• *Falsification of residence status.* German citizens, along with all foreigners living in Switzerland, had to secure a domicile permit annually. Part of this procedure involved renewing German passports with the German Consul. The Consul, in agreement with the individual, refused to renew the passport under the pretext that the bearer was not a dedicated Nazi. A refusal letter was prepared by the Consul and given by the individual to the Swiss authorities. As a result, a domicile permit was issued, placing the person in the 'without nationality' status. Assets of these new 'political refugees' thus were no longer considered as owned by a German.

- *Under-invoicing exports and over-invoicing imports.* For example, a German exporter charges its Swiss subsidiary or a Swiss company for goods shipped an amount that is much less than the actual value. The Swiss importer pays the German exporter the amount stipulated in the invoice in foreign exchange and places the undervalued amount into the exporter's account in Switzerland, after subtracting out a commission for undertaking the false transaction. On the import side, the German firm places an order for Swiss goods and is billed an amount in excess of the real value. In secret arrangements entered into between the German importer and the Swiss manufacturer it is established what part of these German payments are to be kept for the German importer.

Erosion of assets

The Swiss government, in conjunction with the country's business and financial communities, aggressively pursued efforts to use German assets to pay off Swiss monetary claims against German citizens and corporations. The Swiss clearly held much greater German assets (claims) than the other way around. Their assets topped $1 billion. Although significantly profiting from the war, the fear of losses among Swiss businessmen and bankers grew after the tide of battle favoured the Allies after 1943.

Germans with blocked assets in Switzerland were also trying to free them, fearing their confiscation by the Allies. Although many German firms, anticipating such actions, had already hidden their assets in a variety of dummy companies ostensibly owned by Swiss citizens, information was being received from Allied embassies in Bern and elsewhere of new attempts to rig records and sbecretly dispose of cash and securities held in Swiss companies in which Germans had a large interest.

Thousands of instances in which assets and liabilities were offset probably took place. In most cases, they went undetected as offsets were easily accomplished via company and bank books. The US and its allies learned of some, including:

- The Union Bank of Switzerland, acting on behalf of the defunct Eidgenoessische Bank in Zurich, agreed with Commerzbank AG in Berlin in August 1946 (with an effective date of December 1945) to offset German balances against Swiss claims in Switzerland. The transaction and funds relate to a loan of 750,000 Swiss francs provided to Gewerkschaft Zeche (mining company) Heinrich of Essen-Kupferdreh in 1941.

• Arrangements agreed to between Emil Puhl of the Reichsbank and officials of the Swiss National Bank in April 1945 created considerable loopholes to drain German assets in Switzerland. Germans were allowed to use the Reichsbank account at the Swiss National Bank to pay for interest, dividends, rents accruing from credit balances and property investments, and full insurance and reinsurance payments from mid 1944 (predated) to 30 April 1945.

The US Legation in Bern clearly understood what the Swiss were doing and, in a message to the Office of Military Government for Germany, the United States (OMGUS) in October 1945 stated,

As this Legation has pointed out on numerous recent occasions the Swiss Government is encouraging and sanctioning the disposal of German property in Switzerland without notice to or consent of the Allies. These actions ostensibly are done to protect Swiss interests but clearly are contrary to Allied interests under these circumstances. Legation questions propriety of according special treatment to Swiss property in Germany.

In Washington, the Treasury Department also clearly recognized what was happening. In a letter of 13 September 1945 to the Secretary of State from Secretary of the Treasury, Secretary Vinson states, 'I believe that unless we seize and liquidate German assets in the neutrals within a relatively short time, the probability of achieving our objectives is slight. Delay will afford the neutrals an opportunity to dissipate the German assets and greatly increase the prospect of cloaking by the Germans themselves.'

Conceptual difficulties

Conceptual differences in estimating the value of assets abound. To start with, few estimates were sufficiently comprehensive, for the simple reason that determining the value of hidden assets would have been an horrendous task. The Swiss authorities did not adequately pursue the task and the Allies failed to make them do so. Items such as holdings outside the banking system, patents and insurance were largely ignored by the Swiss in their efforts to list German assets. The value of German-held companies was another thorny issue. For example, large differences existed depending on whether the companies' worth was determined by book value, net worth, market value or the assets it controlled.

Who is considered German was another major coverage issue. Those living in Switzerland and elsewhere who were not repatriated after the war ended (those not considered to be Nazis or Nazi collaborators) seemed to be excluded under the 1946 Washington Accord. The Swiss also did not count those Germans who acquired 'without nationality' status (often falsely as indicated earlier), German citizens who changed nationality between the beginning of the Second World War and the February 1945 blocking decree, and individuals with dual German – Swiss citizenship.

As Linus von Castelmur of the Bergier Historical Commission stated in his 1991 dissertation, 'Paradoxically the true history of the implementation of the Washington Accord is foremost the history of its non-implementation. Only a portion of the regulations envisioned were implemented as planned ... '.[1]

Asset categories

This study looks at eleven categories of German investments in Switzerland. An estimate is made for each category, which involves examining key differences in terms of coverage, concealment and dissipation. Most emphasis is placed on the first three categories as, together, they account for at least two-thirds of all investments, according to both Allied and Swiss government estimates.

Deposits in financial institutions

During the Second World War era, as today, deposits in Swiss banks took a number of forms. All types are included in this study. They include cheque and savings accounts, demand deposits as well as deposits which are invested at the discretion of customers or bank officials. By this broad definition total deposits in Swiss financial institutions in 1945 topped $5 billion, including those held by the numerous private banks.

Estimates of German deposits in Swiss financial institutions ranged from $75 million to $250 million. The lower figure was compiled by the Swiss Compensation Office, based on its 1945 census. As mentioned earlier, this calculation has a downward bias because it excludes some categories of German investors, third-party Swiss depositors and dissipation of assets throughout 1945. The $250 million estimate seems much more reasonable. It would certainly match the Swiss census figure when third-party accounts are included. The conservative nature of the $250 million figure also can be seen by comparing it to the $5 billion in total Swiss deposits. It amounted to 5 per cent of total deposits in Switzerland, a relatively small percentage considering the large volume of foreign deposits and that Germany was the second largest investor, after France. German bank deposits in Switzerland could be as high as $450 million.

Private monetary holdings

This category includes German holdings in Switzerland of precious metals and easily transferable financial instruments (currency, bonds and stocks) that are not included under deposits in financial institutions. All these valuables were either held by their owners or in safe-keeping devices, or placed in the safes of banks, fiduciaries, lawyers or friends. When bank safety deposit boxes were used, often they were under the name of Swiss citizens. Most of these private monetary holdings would have been hidden from view of government census takers.

The Bern Legation's estimate of private holdings was between $95 million and $160 million. This range looks feasible. In 1945, a Swiss banker estimated about one-third ($250 million) of Swiss francs in circulation was in foreign hands. Such an estimate may be conservative considering that today roughly two-thirds of US paper currency is circulating abroad, in part because of illicit undertakings such as narcotics sales. At a minimum, it seems reasonable that 25 per cent of the Swiss francs held by foreigners was in the hands of Germans or Swiss citizens on behalf of Germans – that is more than $60 million. To that amount, it is necessary to add the value of other forms of easily negotiable monetary and financial instruments held outside the banking system. In all, the amount of financial assets held by Germans outside the banks easily would have topped $100 million.

Capital participation in Swiss enterprises

This is a major but highly contentious category of assets because of valuation problems and the tortuous techniques used by German owners to hide their ownership. German control of companies incorporated in Switzerland mainly involved three types of structures: subsidiaries and branches, holding companies and finance companies. The latter was used to raise funds to meet the parent German company needs, and most were established between 1924 and 1931. German control over Swiss enterprises also existed via numerous other means. This includes partial ownership of shares, management contracts, loans, patent usage agreements and informal arrangements that were sometimes oral rather than written. Unquestionably, German companies were the world leaders in employing indirect control devices during the interwar and war years, an era when international cartel arrangements were common. Switzerland was the leading foreign hub through which this control was maintained.

Once the war began the urgency to conceal corporate assets was further encouraged by the Nazi regime. In a letter of September 1939 (dated only three days after the Second World War began), from the Reichsbank to a German multinational, the latter directed was to camouflage its ownership of foreign subsidiaries to '. . . protect the German economy against losses resulting from the seizure by third parties and make sure such seizures are ineffective as far as possible.'

Examples of hidden German investments include:

- *Repurchase assets.* IG Farben, for example, set up the Swiss holding company IG Chemie, which in turn owned the shares of the US company General Aniline. In a memo found by the Allies after the war, Albert Gadow, director of IG Chemie and a German who became a Swiss citizen, agreed that IG Farben, through Hermann Schmitz, a company director (also Gadow's brother-in-law), had the 'option' to buy back General Aniline at any time. Gadow also agreed never to sell these shares to anyone but IG Farben. The IG Farben – IG Chemie linkage was also indicated by a 1940 letter from Schmitz, a secret director of IG Chemie, requesting that the Swiss-based company pay him a promised pension of 18,000 Swiss francs a year. IG Chemie replied that until he was retired from IG Farben, which kept its hidden control through him, he was not retired from IG Chemie.

- *Using a front.* In November 1939, Metallgesellschaft transferred its holdings in several US firms to the Swiss company, Rotopulsor. The concealment was strengthened because Rotopulsor was owned by a Dutch company, which in turn was controlled by Metallgesellschaft. At the time of the transfer, the Rotopulsor board consisted of three Swiss and two Germans. To emphasize that German interest no longer existed, the two German members resigned in 1940 and were replaced by Swiss. In a letter written by Metallgesellschaft to the German foreign exchange office in 1943, the company stated, 'The future existence of Rotopulsor is of paramount interest to us as well as to the German foreign currency economy because of the manipulations – of which you are cognizant – for the camouflage of our American holdings. And we wish furthermore to preserve for the postwar period this valuable instrument for the accomplishment of foreign tasks.'[2]

• *Loan arrangements.* Two officials of the Reichsbank obtained loans from Swiss banks, which were used to reduce the net worth of German corporations in Switzerland. The loan ostensibly was to be made by the Swiss subsidiary of a German company for legitimate purposes but it was soon paid off from funds from the subsidiary. The original loan funds were deposited in Switzerland via a third-party Swiss citizen and hidden away for postwar use.

As a result of these and other concealment techniques, assets controlled by German companies in Switzerland certainly were much greater than any financial measure such as equity ownership and net worth. But, unable to quantify the value of assets controlled, the US Legation in Bern calculated the German ownership of equity interest. It found more than 250 enterprises in Switzerland with combined German ownership valued at about $125 million. More than $80 million were shares in holding and finance companies.

Swiss statistics in 1942 indicated that the country had 17,312 companies with a total capitalization of $1.7 billion. If the latter number is compared to the Legation's German data, 7 per cent of Swiss capitalization would be German-owned. The same relationship for holding and finance companies would be nearly 20 per cent and for other enterprises less than 3 per cent. Such proportions tend to make the Legation's estimates conservative, considering the very close economic and financial ties between the two countries and substantial use of holding and financial companies by the Germans in Switzerland.

A 1939 Swiss survey shows registered foreign firms in Switzerland were worth about $900 million. Using the 1945 estimate, it would mean that the German share would be about 15 per cent. Again, these relationships make the Legation's estimate seem reasonable, if not cautious. Using its calculation, the US Legation in Bern estimated in May 1945 that German assets ranged between $110 million and $180 million. It felt the actual number was near the high end of the range because of the use of book value rather than net worth and because data was lacking on ninety-five enterprises. A January 1945 estimate valued enterprises other than holding and finance companies at $50 million to $75 million. The October 1945 Federal Reserve Board assessment uses the low end of that range.

Nicholas Milroy, in a 1946 State Department study, found 444 firms with a value of $220 million to $280 million, which, using a broad definition, were German-controlled or -influenced firms. Finally, the Swiss in 1948 report a figure of $34 million for equity investment or

40 per cent of the total of German assets. If that percentage is applied against the Swiss total estimate of $230 million in December 1945, the equity proportion would amount to $90 million. But that estimate misses much of the concealed investments. To be extremely conservative, this study uses a minimal estimate of $100 million.

Total assets

When all categories are added together, German assets in Switzerland, as of February 1945, certainly exceeded $500 million. The actual minimum estimate is $585 million. Of that, the three major categories – deposits, private monetary holdings and capital participation – alone account for $450 million or about three-quarters of the total. Even if all the remaining categories, of which some are the result of educated guesses, have a combined total of only $100 million, the overall total would still readily breach $500 million.

As all these estimates are considered conservative, there is a definite possibility that the actual total asset number is higher. Given the various unknowns, the figure calculated by adding up categories plausibly could be some 25 per cent higher, or about $750 million. The three major categories could easily account for another $200 million, and insurance and patents for $50 million.

When this estimate is compared to the various other procedures used in this study, the $500 million to $750 million range holds up well.

Converting the estimated value from the prices of the time to today's prices requires applying two factors – the growth in the value of the assets due mainly to interest/income payments and the change in the value of the Swiss franc. The annual return on assets for the past fifty-three years conservatively would be 4 per cent. The value of the Swiss franc has increased from 24 cents per dollar to 67 cents in 1998. When these two factors are considered, the $500 million to $750 million range in February 1945 becomes $11 billion to $16 billion in February 1998.

Lessons learned

Currently, the world spotlight is focused on two issues regarding Swiss economic behaviour during and after the Second World War: the huge amounts of Nazi looted gold handled by the Swiss; and the onerous roadblocks Swiss banks imposed on Holocaust victims and heirs seeking to recover bank accounts. Another story, however, remains largely untold: the Swiss prevented assistance worth hundreds of millions of dollars from reaching the many refugees left in the wake of Nazi atrocities.

Swiss government officials clearly allowed narrow economic interests to dominate over any moral obligation to help overcome the devastating events of the Second World War. They were able to do so mainly because they turned a blind eye towards the hiding of assets in their country. Concealing assets in Switzerland was effortless for the Germans, while locating them was extraordinarily difficult. Moreover, the large profits earned in hiding property attracted many into the field, thereby greatly enhancing and enlarging the laundering system. Indeed, Swiss money launderers at that time faced far fewer criminal penalties and social stigma than do today's launderers who handle vast amounts of drug money.

Although the Swiss are the main culprit, fault also lies with the inaction of Allies. Despite their clear resolutions with regard to German assets in neutral countries, the Allies took no action when they could. For example, the US government could have used its mighty economic weapons at the end of the war, placing sanctions on Swiss foreign trade and continuing the blockage of Swiss assets in the United States. Although these possibilities were discussed, the Allies allowed the negotiations to drag on for nearly a decade, in part because other concerns took centre stage, mainly the threat from the Soviet Union.

What lessons are to be learned from this and similar situations? The answer is clear. Settlements should be quick and driven by pressing needs and morality rather than by endless legal manoeuvering based on narrow self-interests. In the case of Second World War German assets, the Swiss should have put forward a reasonable amount immediately. They should have recognized that the Nazi horrors were a unique historic event and that meeting the immediate needs of the refugees was compelling. The actual liquidation of German assets then could have been accomplished over time.

Today, governments worldwide still have difficulty in balancing their countries' economic interests and morality. In many cases, the issues are not as clear cut and the circumstances are not as devastating or time-sensitive as during and after the Second World War. There is an exception, especially in regard to timing. The need to immediately assist Holocaust survivors is crucial, given the biological clock. It is also important to help rebuild Jewish institutions in Central and Eastern Europe that were destroyed by Nazi malice and Communist dictators. The most favourable time to achieve that end is now, when new social arrangements are being forged in these countries. An overall settlement, for example, could be made now to restore or replace confiscated community property rather then wait to resolve the endless arguments over ownership rights and the precise amounts due.

Notes

1 Linus von Castelmur, 'Schweizerisch – allerte Finanzbeziehungem in Ubergang bom Zweiter Krig', PhD Dissertation, Basel (1991).
2 Airgram from Leland Harrison, American Minister in Bern to Secretary of State, 27 February 1947 (USNA [US National Archives] RG 84 Entry 3221 Box, German Government Archives and public property in Switzerland).

Select bibliography

Abbreviations:
USNA: United States National Archives, College Park, Maryland
RG: Record Group

Introduction

Fehrenbach, T.R., *The Gnomes of Zurich* (London: Anchor Press, 1966) pp. 98–101.
'Negotiations on German Holdings in Switzerland', Department of State Bulletin, vol. XIV, 30 June 1946.
'US and Allied Efforts to Recover and Restore Gold and Other Assets Stolen or Hidden by Germany during World War II', Preliminary Study, State Department, May 1997.

Movement of German assets to Switzerland

German Property in Switzerland: British Yearbook of International Law (1946) pp. 354–8.
Milory, Nicholas R., 'German Economic Penetration of Switzerland', State Department, no date (probably 1946), USNA RG 239, entry 10, box 24.
Zabludoff, Sidney, 'Movements of Nazi Gold: Uncovering the Trail', Institute of World Jewish Congress, Jerusalem (1997).

Asset estimates

Bell, James C., American Vice Consul, Lugano, 25 May 1945, to Leeland Harrison, American Minister, Bern, 18 May 1945, USNA RG 84, entry 3222, Box 4, file 850.SH.
Sholes, Walter H., American Consul General, Basle to Secretary of State, 18 January 1945, USNA, RG 84, Basel, entry 3228, Box 10, file 851.6. Based on writer's report to the American Legation, Bern, 7 December 1942, USNA RG 84, Basel, entry 3228, Box 3, file 851.7/820.02.

'Estimate of Total German Assets in Switzerland', prepared for use in conversation with Mr G. May 1945, USNA RG 84, entry 3222, Box 4, file 851.6.

Safehaven Department, British Legation, Bern to Economic Warfare Department, UK Foreign Office, 20, January 1948, USNA RG 84, entry 3221, Box 3, file 501.8 SH-Q.

Key differences in estimates

Preliminary List of German Cloaks in Switzerland, USNA RG 169, entry 170, Box 991, file Safehaven exhibits.

Safehaven Report no. 392, London, 6 September 1945, Safehaven Report no. 481, London, 15 October 1945. 2945.

Asset categories

Aalders, Gerard and Wiebes Cees, *The Art of Cloaking* (Amsterdam University Press, 1996).

Faith, Nicholas, *Safety in Numbers* (New York: Viking Press, 1982).

'Looted Art in Occupied Territories, Neutral Countries and Latin America', Foreign Economic Administration, Enemy Branch, External Economic Security Staff, August 1945, USNA RG 84, entry 3221, Box 8, file looted art.

8
Why was Switzerland Singled Out? A Case of Belated Justice

Avi Beker

Prolonging the war

The most popular talk show on German language television in Switzerland is *The Tuesday Club* [*Der Zyschtigsclub*]. On 14 January 1997 the participants of the programme's panel reacted to international accusations and discussed Switzerland's refugee policy during the Second World War. The interviewer felt quite uneasy when somebody made reference to some terrible events which took place at the border of Switzerland. 'I know our refugee policy was antisemitic,' he broke in, 'but wasn't it a *moderate* form of antisemitism?'

This comment was typical of the belated confrontation of the Swiss with their behaviour during the Second World War. After two generations of denial and suppression, they are grudgingly coming to terms with their wartime dealings with the Nazis. Still, despite the stunning revelations about their intimate and critical support of the Axis war effort as the financiers of Nazi Germany, one could hear the same reaction: 'We made mistakes, but we weren't downright criminals, like others.' This was the Swiss line of defence, both in 1944–7 and again in 1996–8. In between, by shrewd and manipulative negotiating tactics after the war, coupled with the drastic changes in the international climate, the Swiss succeeded in containing the Allies' threats and Holocaust survivors' claims, and to hold by a self-righteous, self-serving narrative of their experience of the war based on the deception and suppression of memories (see Plate 3).

The Swiss were outraged when American Under-Secretary of State Stuart Eizenstat suggested in his May 1997 report that the Swiss role in buying and laundering Nazi-looted gold made them guilty of having prolonged the war by months.[1] They immediately reacted with accusations against other European nations and the United States. The Swiss foreign minister cynically commented, 'We could ask the United States why they did not enter the war until later'. Thomas Borer, the head of the foreign ministry's special task force on Holocaust issues, asked, 'What happened to Dutch Jews, French Jews? It isn't discussed.'[2] The statement and judgement about prolonging the war may sound too simplistic, too far-fetched and unconventional in contemporary historical analysis, but, on second thoughts, this is largely the way historians deal with any kind of historical analysis. Can we make these kinds of judgements – including moral ones – in evaluating history? It can be argued that new insights will be regarded as critically significant in future historical analysis of the Second World War. Books on ancient, medieval and even modern history frequently incorporate moral considerations along with historical facts when providing sophisticated and circumstantial evidence about armed conflicts.

Against the half century of Swiss denial there are a few, like Jean Ziegler, a scholar and a member of the Swiss parliament, who stood up and confronted the past in an attempt to reevaluate moral decisions. In his book *The Swiss, the Gold and the Dead*, Ziegler states clearly: 'The awesome, world encompassing financial power wielded today by the major Swiss banks is founded on wartime profits.' He brings documents and facts to sustain his major argument that the

> Swiss bankers were substantially responsible for prolonging World War II, and thus, for the death of unknown numbers of serviceman and civilians our. . . present state of knowledge confirms Switzerland's complicity in prolonging World War II. But for the effective gold-laundering services provided by the Swiss National Bank, and but for Swiss arms deliveries and loans to Berlin, the war would have ended earlier – probably in 1944. Swiss bankers, in particular, were responsible for millions of deaths.[3]

No Jewish leader or Jewish organization went as far as Jean Ziegler in spelling out the ramifications of the Swiss support of Germany during the Holocaust. The economic aspects of the Second World War were not studied sufficiently before the issues of looted Jewish property, Swiss trade in Nazi gold and the dormant accounts in the banks reached the public consciousness. Though it was clear that Hitler, even at the peak of his military achievements, could not secure Germany's economic independence, very few went further to investigate how the Nazi war effort was sustained. Even with his Axis partners, Hitler could not obtain the necessary components of his munitions industry (magnesium, tungsten, iron ore, etc.).[4] The German invasion of several countries from 1939 saved Hitler from complete material distress. Without the Swiss financial services that allowed him to launder what he was looting in the occupied countries, Hitler could not have fuelled his war machine.

In 1943 the Swiss role became even more crucial for the German killing operation. Hitler's triumphant conquest had been contained in the battle of Stalingrad; Germany was losing in North Africa as it would later on in Western Europe. The pressure on Switzerland and the other neutrals from the Allies was growing and was clearer than before: do not accept Nazi gold, do not launder Nazi loot, do not trade war-related commodities. Switzerland, not necessarily a pro-Nazi country, was ready to buy looted gold and supply Germany with disposable foreign exchange, strategic raw materials (also through other neutrals) and even weapons. The Swiss were motivated by greed without any sense of guilt or bad conscience.

Without this irresistible drive for profits, even when the Nazi defeat was seeming inevitable, the war might have ended earlier, perhaps in 1944. Historical speculation is certainly not an exact science, but from a Jewish viewpoint there is no escaping consideration of the awesome, terrible consequences of the economic services provided by Switzerland to Germany at this stage of the war. What comes to mind, for instance, is the destruction of Hungarian Jews on the eve of the Allied victory and Germany's total surrender. The last large Jewish community in Nazi-dominated Europe was liquidated in a swift ruthless campaign while the Soviet forces, in March and April of 1944, were about to cross the Dniester into neighbouring Romania. Almost 600,000 Jews in Hungary, as well as hundreds of thousands of Jews from other countries, were killed at a period during which the war was 'prolonged' or 'sustained' through the help of Switzerland and other neutrals.

Settlement without assuming responsibility

On 12 August 1998 Switzerland's largest commercial banks finally agreed to pay fair compensation to Jewish Holocaust survivors, although even then many bankers described the agreement as 'rough justice'. The $1.25 billion settlement (in addition to the $200 million 1997 humanitarian fund for needy victims of the war) relates to money that was held in the banks from dormant Jewish accounts, profits made from the Nazi gold transactions and money loaned to German companies employing

Jewish slave labour. The settlement was reached only under the hanging sword of financial sanctions by American state and local governments – which control vast pension and other funds – that threatened to discontinue business with the Swiss from 1 September 1998. In the past three years the Swiss have moved from flat denial of responsibility to any Jewish claim, to paying out $1.45 billion, and investing an estimated $200 million more in fees to thousands of lawyers, accountants, public relations agencies in different countries, staff of the different commissions of bankers, historians and others, all engaged to inquire into different aspects of Swiss behaviour during and after the war.

But the Swiss, as reflected in their media and in the attitude of the government, were not ready, even in late 1998, to recognize full responsibility. Neither the Swiss government nor the Swiss National Bank (SNB) took part in negotiating the $1.25 billion settlement. Following the settlement, the Minister of Economics of Switzerland, Pascal Couchepin, said that 'there is no reason for the Swiss government to pay anything'. He then added the cynical and nasty stereotypical remark: 'Many people have the feeling that it was not the search for truth, but more a search for money... we were not accustomed to this exploration of our history'. This attitude was reflected in an antisemitic cartoon in a Swiss newspaper, showing a reproduction of a Swiss bank payment slip of $1.25 billion to be paid to 'The World Jewish Congress', adding in the payment details: 'Ah, yes: pardon, from the Jewish people.'[5]

This response is alarming in light of the clear evidence that the SNB processed most of the gold looted from Jews by the Nazis, and the revelations regarding the intensive and ongoing involvement of many Swiss officials in trade relations and strategic assistance to Germany during the war. The Swiss government also bears responsibility for its obstructionist behaviour after the war, in the negotiations with the Allies regarding Nazi gold and in its role in the covering-up of banks' dormant accounts.

The Swiss government and the SNB failed to act on the recommendations of their own commission. When the WJC published its report on Nazi gold, and when the American administration issued the Eizenstat report, the Swiss rejected their findings and said that they were waiting for their own commission findings. This commission, headed by Professor Jean François Bergier, consisted of eight historians from Switzerland and other countries. In December 1996, it was assigned to look into 'the part played by Switzerland and its financial role within the context of World War II', covering a variety of looted property. The commission, in its first interim report in December 1997, confirmed that more than

$2.5 billion of Nazi gold, by today's value, had been purchased by Switzerland. Only a fraction of this was returned in 1946 and the Swiss had refused to return any more. In May 1998 the Bergier Commission shocked the Swiss public again when it reported that the SNB purchases of gold from the German Reichsbank included 119.5 kilograms of fine gold (worth about $1.2 million at today's prices) that could be identified as having been melted down by the Nazi bankers into gold bars from teeth fillings and wedding rings, torn away from victims in the Nazi concentration camps.

This was the first study sanctioned by the Swiss government that stated clearly what was always denied by Swiss officials: that the SNB wartime managers knew they were buying stolen gold from Hitler's central bank. In the words of the Bergier commission:

> There is no longer any doubt. The governing board of the National Bank was informed at an early point in time that gold from the central banks of occupied nations was being held by the Reichsbank, and the SNB was also aware of other methods used by the Germans to confiscate gold from private individuals before and after the outbreak of the war.... Although it was plain for all to see that Germany was acquiring gold by illegal means, the SNB authorities appear to have remained wedded to 'business as usual'.

Professor Bergier criticized wartime officials of the SNB for following an 'ethic of the least effort' to trace the sources of the gold, even though, starting in 1941, they 'became increasingly aware that Jews and other persecuted groups were being robbed'. The report states that 'in 1943, at the latest, the SNB had knowledge of the systematic extermination of victims of the Nazi regime' but its officials none the less 'neglected taking measures to distinguish looted gold from other gold holdings of the Reichsbank'.[6]

Documents released by the World Jewish Congress, which were part of the American administration's research, demonstrated to what extent officials from the SNB were active in retrieving money from Nazi Germany early in 1944. After informing and clearing it with the Swiss government, SNB officials pressed Nazi authorities to transfer a repayment of commercial debt worth 150 million Swiss francs from fascist Italy. It is clear from the US Treasury document that the transfer of the Italian gold was possible only with Nazi 'authorization and assistance'. This was done by the Germans as a 'considerable concession to Switzerland', as part of their aim to 'influence the Swiss government' to maintain its banking, trade and credit relations with Germany.[7] The significance of this document lies in the fact that it reveals how freely, without pressure or any security need, the Swiss bankers and their government, motivated only by greed and, violating the sanctions against Germany, acted on a regular 'business as usual' basis.

The Swiss government is also implicated in another document, based on the testimony of Emil Puhl, the vice-president of the Reichsbank, from his interrogation before United States prosecutors (17 November 1945). Puhl refers to negotiations between the SNB and the Reichsbank in March–April 1945, in which the two governments 'participated in the actual meetings'. Puhl persuaded the Swiss officials to loosen a freeze on German accounts imposed six weeks earlier under United States pressure. The Swiss government and its bankers, fully aware of horrible Nazi atrocities and knowing the origins of their looted gold, were negotiating the sale of Nazi gold through a special account, to be established in the SNB, and intended to augment German gold stocks in Switzerland. At this point, three weeks before the surrender of Germany, the Swiss could not argue that they feared a German invasion. The Swiss, without any security justification, were therefore violating their agreement with the Allies. For the sake of an expedient economic advantage, they were ready to maintain and secure their ties with the forces of evil, the executioners of crimes against humanity. Puhl testified that he was impressed that the major motive of the Swiss was to maintain a 'friendly relationship with the Reichsbank, not merely at the time, but for the future, regardless of what would happen to Germany at the end of the war'. The Swiss wish was to keep 'good economic relations with Germany after the war'.[8]

Recycling sanctions

Among others, there were two particular aspects in the 1996–8 campaign that were received in Switzerland with outrage. The Swiss media and its officials were angered, as shown before, by the argument that they 'prolonged' the war, and they strongly attacked the threat of using sanctions in order to bring them into a negotiated settlement. It is astonishing to see, from a historic perspective, how the same counter-arguments were already formulated and employed in 1944–5. It is clear that, more than fifty years ago, not only were the facts on the Swiss robbery known, but the same charges and methods of punishment were also seriously considered by the Allies. Sanctions against Switzerland were contemplated and planned at the end of and after the Second

World War because of the widespread belief among the Allies that Switzerland's actions helped to prolong the war. The Allies were outraged by Swiss illegal trade with Nazi Germany which had continued after Germany's defeat at Stalingrad in December 1942, and the Allies' public warning on 5 January 1943 specifying that Switzerland's ownership of looted property supplied by Germany would not be recognized. The Swiss had reacted in complete disregard and had gone on to explore even more opportunities to satisfy their greed.

In 1997–8, as in 1943, Swiss spokespersons and media used the misleading comparison that the United States was also neutral until the Japanese attack on Pearl Harbor, on 7 December 1941. There is no doubt that both the United States and Great Britain made serious mistakes in their assessment of the Nazi threat and in their delayed reaction. It is also clear that both the United States and Great Britain made serious mistakes, immoral decisions and omissions when the news of the killing of Jews reached their capitals.[9] However, ultimately, whereas the Allies joined the war against Germany and sacrificed their soldiers, Swiss diplomacy was engaged in efforts to expand its economic profits at the expense of the Allied war effort. After the expiration of the Swiss – German trade agreements on 15 January 1943, Swiss negotiators went to Berlin to negotiate a revised agreement, offering even more loans so that Germany would be able to buy more Swiss munitions and war supplies. When British diplomats were convinced that Switzerland 'had gone further than was necessary in meeting German demands', Foreign Secretary Anthony Eden decided to intervene personally. Eden told the Swiss ambassador, Walther Thurnten, that 'Switzerland should do all it can not to prolong the war'. Realizing that the Swiss did not understand that the issue was really how to destroy the evil called Nazi Germany, Eden had to add an explicit threat: if the new Swiss–German agreement damaged British interests, 'our action is likely to be unwelcoming to you'. Within a few days of the British request, Washington strengthened the British appeal by raising 'its most forceful objections' that the Swiss negotiations with Berlin would cause a 'substantial rise in Swiss exports to Germany, strengthening the Nazis' military potential and *prolonging the war* [my italics]'.[10]

A further look into the archives shows that the Swiss, in 1997–8, only reiterated the same clichés and distortions expressed in 1943–7. The wartime Swiss foreign minister, Marcel Pilet-Golaz, himself a Nazi sympathizer, irritated and angered Western officials when he compared his country's neutrality to that of the United States until the attack on Pearl Harbor. Neutrality, according to Pilet-Golaz, gave Switzerland the right to 'make agreements with both sides and keep them loyally'.[11] This was just another misleading comparison, since the United States, before Pearl Harbor, provided decisive support to Britain. Washington's 1944–5 requests to stop accepting gold from Germany met with Swiss defiance.

The failure of Switzerland to understand the moral dimensions of foreign and economic policies during and after the war explains their failure in 1996–8 to understand why they were singled out. Nazi gold, lines of credit, money laundering and – even worse – Switzerland's moral disregard for the heirs of dormant accounts, highlighted the Swiss failure to draw a distinction between good and evil, and to comprehend the tragic result of the close economic partnership with Nazi Germany.

It is clear that the Swiss government and its banks knew much about the Nazi death camps and gas chambers. Swiss doctors who accompanied the German military on the eastern front, to help with medical work, were widely aware of Jewish mass murders already in the autumn of 1941. They reported back to the Red Cross and the Swiss government (since the reports came in the name of the Swiss Army).[12] The historic cable from Gerhart Riegner, the WJC representative in Geneva, on the execution of the 'Final Solution' against the Jews reached the West in August 1942, and was later reported in the media. Because of its neutrality and its continuing relations with Germany, Switzerland was therefore a major centre of information-gathering on the Nazis. Jacques Picard elaborates in his book on the information received in Switzerland of the Nazi atrocities against the Jews in the Warsaw ghetto in the spring of 1942. At the same time, the Swiss consul in cologne sent a series of photographs from the eastern front to Roger Mason, the director of Swiss intelligence, showing gassed Jewish bodies.[13]

As shown here, the idea of sanctions against Switzerland and its banks was not invented in 1996–8. Contrary to the antisemitic tones aired in Switzerland, the idea of sanctions did not originate in the campaign of the 1990s in the American Jewish lobby. In addition to some antisemitic articles and cartoons, the Swiss press largely camouflaged its attitudes by directing its most vicious attacks against the non-Jewish senator Alfonse D'Amato, the chairman of the Senate Banking Committee, but emphasized that he was from New York and therefore needed the Jewish vote for his reelection.

Sanctions are rightly regarded as an evil necessity in international relations, and are rarely practised among friendly countries sharing common interests. It is understandable why both in 1945–7 and in 1997–8 the State Department was unwilling to take this course of action against Switzerland. The role of different actors in different historic contexts is interesting. In 1944–7 it was the Treasury Department and also the US military who pushed for sanctions against the Swiss. In 1996–8 local governments in American states and cities organized the mechanism for monitoring Swiss behaviour and facilitated possible economic sanctions. Changes in the international environment, the moral force of Jewish organizations and the highly public awareness of the crimes of the Holocaust provided the critical difference in 1998.

The banks and the government of Switzerland well understood by 1942–3 that their dealings with Nazi Germany were against the will and interests of the Allies. A report of the SNB from 1984 provides a cornucopia of information on Swiss motives and knowledge of the Nazi atrocities as well as the origins of the looted gold at that time. The report explains that the role of Swiss francs, transferred to the Germans for their gold, was 'to pay countries unwilling to accept German gold' as a 'transit point'. Swiss bankers knew about the Allied declaration of January 1943 that all transfers of property from occupied countries were invalid. They were reminded in a *Financial Times* article in June 1943 of the meaning of this declaration:

> This means that neutral central banks will be called upon to restore to their rightful owners the gold acquired from Germany during the war. As the Reichsbank's own gold reserve was very small at the outbreak of the war, and is now about the same, the assumption is that any gold acquired by neutral central banks since September 1939 is looted gold.[14]

This report and others in the media created a flurry of activity in Switzerland, including active involvement of the Swiss Federal Council in the consultations with the SNB. The Swiss Federal Council, the SNB and the entire Swiss banking system continued to ignore warnings from Washington. As a matter of fact, the Swiss government actually encouraged the SNB to continue its deals with Nazi looted gold. They would explain immediately after the war and again in 1996–8 that they acted in good faith.

In 1943, Walther Funk, the Minister of Economics in Nazi Germany and the President of the Reichsbank, admitted that Germany could not do without Swiss transfers for foreign exchange for even two months.[15] The Nazi military drive could not proceed without the economic backing of the Reichsbank, and the Reichsbank could not function without Swiss bankers laundering the proceeds of its genocide and looting. For funding the Nazi genocide, Walter Funk was put on trial at Nuremberg, convicted of war crimes and sentenced to life imprisonment. At this critical juncture in 1943, Swiss bankers, encouraged by their government, intensified their working relations with Nazi Germany. The Swiss ignored the Allies' threats of sanctions (supplies of food and fodder were banned for three months, from May 1943, but were later relaxed) and, in October 1943, signed a new trade agreement in Berlin. At the time, the deputy president of the SNB, Dr Alfred Hirs, refused to meet Americans or Britons, but always welcomed his counterparts from the Reichsbank. Together with his boss, Ernst Weber, the SNB president, and with the backing of the government, they agreed to receive looted gold from Germany. Unlike every other neutral country, Switzerland accepted this unconditionally. Despite the Allied warnings, the Swiss government and its bankers became 'an accomplice and beneficiary of the plunder of Europe'.[16] Along with the bankers, Swiss traders accepted diamonds seized by the SS from Belgian Jews, and art dealers in Zurich and Basle welcomed German officials and SS officers, who bought looted paintings and artefacts.

Swiss historian Hans Ulrich Jost, writing on the military–industrial dimension of the Swiss collaboration with Germany, pointed out that in 1941–2 'about 60 percent of the Swiss ammunitions industry, 50 percent of the optical industry, and 40 percent of the engineering industry were working for the Reich'.[17] A large part of these industrial exports were facilitated by Swiss loans to Germany.

How did the Swiss escape sanctions?

Against this background, it is clear that the Allies were looking for ways and means to stop or at least contain the Swiss–German collaboration. The call for sanctions against Switzerland before the end of the war was not a spontaneous impulse but part of a careful plan which was extensively debated and organized, beginning in 1943. The failure of the threat of sanctions in 1943 led to a more comprehensive set of policies in 1944–5. It was clear to the Americans that declarations of goodwill would not force the Swiss to cooperate, and even tough and binding resolutions in a treaty would require a monitoring organ with a strong intelligence-gathering network. The international legal instrument was provided by the Bretton Woods Resolution VI adopted at the UN Monetary and Financial Conference of July–August 1944. The resolution called for the neutral countries to prevent any disposition or transfer of looted assets and to prevent their concealment. Towards the same aims, the Safehaven programme was formulated in spring 1944 to secure Allied control of Nazi loot, to prevent the transfer of German assets to neutral countries, and to ensure that German wealth would be accessible for war reparations and for the rehabilitation of Europe. It also provided for the return of looted properties to their legal owners. Swiss policies since 1944, pursued in an orchestrated fashion by the government and the business sector, can be described as brilliantly successful in obstructing the Safehaven programme and draining it of both its letter and spirit.

The Swiss role as the chief launderer of Nazi looted gold is highlighted by its actions in concealing the looted gold as well as by the offer of triangular transactions to the other neutral states. Unlike the other neutrals, Switzerland distinguished itself in its readiness to organize sophisticated laundry routes. When the Spanish dictator Francisco Franco, a fascist who overtly allied with Hitler, refused to launder German gold, the Swiss came to the rescue and provided their good offices. When the neighbouring Portuguese dictator Salazar also refused to accept German gold directly, fearing Allied countermeasures, the Swiss again entered the scene.[18]

The system appears simple, but, in the pre-computer age it required thousands of Swiss bankers, clerks, legal advisers, truck drivers, carriers and other workers to implement the laundering deception scam.[19] The Germans delivered the looted gold to Switzerland and were reimbursed in Swiss francs. (The last truckload of looted gold from Germany arrived on 6 April 1945, three weeks before Hitler committed suicide.) With these Swiss francs, the Germans went to Turkey, Portugal, Sweden, Spain and elsewhere to buy strategic raw materials and numerous other goods. Then, these exporting countries' central banks approached the SNB and used Swiss francs received from Germany to buy the very same Nazi-looted gold. This terrifying sideshow of the Second World War and the Holocaust furnished many countries with the pretext that they were engaged in good-faith economic transactions. The Swiss, running and orchestrating the glittering gold triangle, did not care even for the pretext. They felt that the Allies would succumb to their own internal divisions and lack of determination to enforce the sanctions. The Swiss were correct.

In the last stages of the war, from late 1944, frustration with the Swiss among US Treasury and State Department officials was turning into anger. The Swiss were not ready to reduce their trade with Germany and they continued to allow Germany to transport military cargo by rail to Italy, to be used against Allied soldiers. They granted Germany loans, knowing that they would not be repaid, and helped German firms to accumulate money in Swiss banks for use after the war.

Safehaven reports included full details of the money and securities convoys from Germany to Swiss banks and of meetings between Swiss politicians and Nazi officials such as Goering and Himmler. This cooperation continued extensively until a few days before the Nazi defeat. President Roosevelt tried to appeal to the Swiss conscience in writing to Federal President von Steiger:

> It would indeed be a matter of conscience to every peace-loving Swiss to have to live with the knowledge that he had in some way obstructed the efforts of the other peace-loving peoples to liberate the world from a ruthless tyrant... I express myself thus firmly because every day's prolongation of the war costs the lives of a number of my fellow countrymen.[20]

However, it was clear to American officials that an appeal to Swiss conscience was not an effective policy method. The assistant secretary to the Treasury, Harry Dexter White, was among the toughest crusaders against Switzerland, believing that it was 'futile' to expect the Swiss to reveal and control German assets, and therefore concluded that 'sanctions were the only language the Swiss would understand.'[21] Sanctions against Switzerland were considered at length in 1944–5, in particular a proposal to cut Swiss supplies of coal and push the country toward bankruptcy by permanently freezing their $1.9 billion assets in the United States. The State Department, however, with British encouragement, opposed the strong measures of Safehaven raised by the Treasury.

The Swiss, always well informed about the differences and deep disagreements, knew how to exploit these differences to their advantage. At this stage of the war, while Americans and Europeans were counting their dead in the final series of battles against Germany, the Swiss continued, in their typical tranquillity, to trade and extend credit to the killers of the Allies. At General Eisenhower's headquarters in Versailles, the military staff was furious that Switzerland 'was still resisting the Allies' request to reduce its supplies to the Nazis and was thus prolonging the war'. The military suggested sanctions: 'An urgent recommendation had been sent to Washington that Switzerland be frozen into submission by enforcing a complete blockade.' The Swiss tactics, both at this stage and later on, were to prolong, delay, manipulate and mislead, in the hope that the differences between France, Britain and the US would grow and that the Allies' lack of determination would ruin any attempt to punish them. In the meantime, the Swiss leaked the news to the press 'that all the gold shipped by the Germans had been spent'.[22]

At the request of Treasury Secretary Henry Morgenthau, President Roosevelt dispatched his assistant, Lauchlin Currie, to Bern. Currie told Walter Stuckey, the Swiss chief negotiator on German assets, that 'every hour the war is prolonged means more lives, and the lives of our young men are very precious to us.' He blamed Switzerland for continuing to furnish 'great assistance' to Germany. Curry attacked the Swiss notion of neutrality directly: 'It is inconceivable in our view... to maintain an attitude of Olympian aloofness or indifference as to the outcome' of the war. At this stage, the Americans, worried about the Nazis' postwar plans, warned the Swiss that their collaboration with the Nazis to protect their loot would enable them 'to preserve the power of the Nazi party and plan again for world domination'.[23]

The Swiss reaction was another mix of delay and deception. While, in February 1945, they announced a freeze on all German property in Switzerland, they already coordinated with their German clients the transfer of German-owned assets into false accounts under English and other names with addresses in China or South America. But at the same time, the Swiss, again testing the paralysed Western alliance, explained that Switzerland was neutral and since they were dependent upon 'vital imports', they could not stop the trade with Germany.

In this context there are once again interesting similarities between 1944–6 and 1996–8: the accusations that other financial centres want to cripple Switzerland, the antisemitic overtones, the urge to improve the Swiss image, and the strong belief that with perseverance, determination and delay tactics Switzerland will get its way. Stuckey understood that Switzerland was facing a wide front of criticism and was the object of hatred the world over. Stuckey also thought that, basically, the problem was neither a moral one nor a matter of justice, but rather one of public relations. He therefore strove to improve Switzerland's image abroad. When the US was threatening, ineffectually, to freeze Swiss assets, Stuckey blamed Washington for trying to undermine Switzerland's secretive and powerful banks, and, as a result, the whole country.[24]

Antisemitic remarks were made by the Swiss negotiating team in 1945–6, despite the fresh memories of the Holocaust. Swiss resentment against the large Jewish presence in the American delegation was reflected in their reports. Stuckey, referring to Seymour Rubin, exclaimed: 'Why do I have to negotiate with a Jewboy?'[25] The chairman of the Swiss delegation in the Washington talks in 1946, William Rappard, was trying to impress his colleagues in Bern that there was a Jewish conspiracy when he wrote about the visit of a Colonel Bernard Bernstein who, 'in the name of a Jewish organization' asked for 'Jewish funds to be unfrozen' and for payment 'of funds left by Jews deceased without heirs to Jewish organizations'. In March 1946 Rappard wrote to Bern that 'since Morgenthau left the Treasury, all my friends here believe we are now experiencing a gradual demobilization of the Jewish lobby which has had the upper hand for some time under President Roosevelt's influence'. Three years later, in June 1949, after successful Swiss delays, the Swiss could report back home from Washington that they found a new atmosphere: 'Not a single member of the big US delegation of 1946 was in attendance. We were dealing with an entirely new set of people altogether, and they were not under so much Jewish influence or imbued with Morgenthau's spirit.'[26] It took a while, but the Swiss were doomed to confront the Jewish lobby fifty years later, as well as international public opinion imbued with Morgenthau's anger.

Fifty years later, in December, 1996, the Swiss President, Jean-Pascal Delamuraz, spoke as Stuckey had, accusing the West of a conspiracy to destroy Switzerland as a world financial centre because it threatened the larger markets in New York and London. He went on to blame Jewish groups for using declassified documents to 'blackmail Switzerland'. Delamuraz reiterated what can only be described as an attitude commonly expressed in the Swiss media during the campaign. A few days later, after leaving the office of the presidency, Delamuraz publicly apologized. According to a study commissioned by the Swiss government, Delamuraz's remarks 'helped make Jewish stereotypes acceptable and antisemitic sentiment burst into public view'. In 1998 – as in 1946 – the Swiss regarded the pressure from Washington as unjustified and accused the Jewish lobby of manipulating it. Even Under-Secretary Eizenstat, who had serious differences with the Jewish organizations on matters of sanctions and style, was profiled in Switzerland as 'radioactive', due to his Jewish background, and many Swiss identified his views with those of Israel Singer of the World Jewish Congress.[27]

The two historians working for the Swiss Foreign Ministry, Peter Hug and Marck Perrenoud, explain how the Swiss escaped the sanctions in 1946. Immediately after the war, they explain, the Swiss could not ignore their responsibility to the victims of the atrocities committed by the Nazis. That was why they signed the Washington agreement, committing to return half of the non-gold German assets to war victims.

But a few months later, they emphasize, 'Switzerland was able to make use of international developments (the Cold War) and adapt its own situation accordingly. It monitored every perceptive change that took place in the countries with which it was in negotiations (particularly the United States)...the more bitter the conflict between the US and the USSR became, the more the memories of World War II were wiped out.' Switzerland succeeded in putting past criticism behind it, and it never made good its commitments in the Washington talks. This point is included in an interesting political confession by the American administration in 1998:

> The postwar negotiations that the United States, Britain and France conducted with the wartime neutrals were protracted and failed to meet fully their original goals: restitution of the looted gold and the liquidation of German external assets to fund the reconstruction of postwar occupied Europe and to provide relief for Jewish and other non-repatriable refugees. This resulted from the intransigence of the neutrals after the War, dissension within Allied ranks, and competing priorities stemming from the onset of the Cold War.[28]

Rewriting history

Some historians, and many Swiss observers, have claimed in the last few years that indeed few of the revelations in the declassified documents or media stories were new.[29] As shown here, most of the facts as well as the tremendous anger and frustration towards Switzerland were evident in 1945–6. In 1997, an official report by the State Department declared that what President Harry Truman did a half century ago was an enormous blunder, in giving up the measures suggested by the Treasury to force Switzerland to disgorge millions of dollars' worth of Nazi plunder.[30] The unwillingness to impose its will on its war allies and future European allies, the task of rebuilding Europe and the threat of Communism, all led to a lip-service settlement with Switzerland. Part of that settlement was not implemented and only a small token was given to the victims of Nazism.

The more surprising aspect in this retrospective study of history lies in the lack of attention and apprehension of the significance of the Swiss role in financing the war and its extensive dealings with Nazi looted gold. Some books were written on the subject but generally the subject went almost unnoticed in the leading and comprehensive works on the war and on the Holocaust.

Two monumental works, which deal directly with historical retrospectives on the Holocaust in different countries, highlight this continuing error of omission. One book, edited by David S. Wyman, who contributed enormously to the study of what he termed the American 'abandonment of the Jews', demonstrates how in the early 1990s these issues were still not in the academic consciousness. His book, *The World Reacts to the Holocaust*, in over 900 pages covers reactions in about twenty countries in Europe and outside, to the Holocaust, over time.[31] The book does not touch on Norway (with its Quisling regime), nor Switzerland and other neutrals, including Sweden, Spain and Portugal. The real confrontation with the past, and the public debate on these aspects in these countries, started only after the material for Wyman's book was prepared. Another book, published in association with the United States Holocaust Memorial Museum, seems very promising in its title, *The Holocaust and History, the Known, the Unknown, the Disputed, and the Reexamined*.[32] This 1998 book is very disappointing for those looking for analysis of the 1996–8 discussions on Jewish property, Nazi gold, economic collaboration with Germany, and so forth. More than fifty scholars in over 800 pages cover many important subjects (as assigned to them at a conference on the subject). Even in chapter 8, which includes several essays on *'The Axis, the Allies, and the Neutrals'*, there is nothing on Switzerland, Jewish property or the economic collaboration with Germany. In the article on Sweden there is nothing on the trade and supply of material to Nazi Germany but only on Swedish diplomacy in Budapest and its rescue efforts.

The books, which are in and of themselves important contributions to the understanding of the Holocaust, fail to provide the new dimension which was exposed in the late 1990s, particularly in Switzerland. While some aspects of their past were suppressed, most European nations were confronting their past. The case of Switzerland was different. Living under the myth of neutrality, successive Swiss generations wrote off the ambiguities of the war and regarded them as their best times. No one was questioning how Switzerland had become so rich after the war, and other 'unpleasant' questions about missing accounts of Holocaust victims were suppressed. As put by Jean Ziegler: 'No Swiss banker to the Nazis, nor railroad executive or officer responsible for turning away Jews at the frontier has ever acknowledged his guilt.'[33] Most of the facts were known. Even the moral judgement against Switzerland was made in 1945–6, but the failure in Washington to implement the decisions helped the Swiss to return to their self-denial, illusionary myths and suppressed history.

The significance of the campaign against Switzerland lies exactly in this process of demystification. It was not a matter of a special historical context, as Swiss officials continued to explain in 1998. It is clear that the leaders of Switzerland and their economic elite in the banks and industry were able to make moral judgements during the war. It was not just a matter of simply yielding to German pressure. Swiss claims that Jewish accounts could not be identified after the war are proven today to be falsehood. At some point, in July 1997, the President of the Swiss Bankers Association, Georg F. Krayer, admitted:

> I have found no fig leaf big enough to cover the negligence of my colleagues in the postwar era. With a bit of effort we could have achieved more results.[34]

The lessons of the postwar diplomatic process are clear: without a real threat of sanctions the Swiss would not move towards confronting their past. While still complaining about being singled out, the Swiss, at the same time, were 'coming to acknowledge that even in the postwar era, there was a legalistic obstructionism – some would call it greed and duplicity – that shielded German assets from Allied expropriation and blocked survivors' access to the bank deposits of Holocaust victims'.[35]

Itamar Levin, an Israeli journalist who helped to expose the Swiss behaviour, explains that the global settlement with Swiss banks was a necessity because there was no chance of identifying the dormant accounts. The banks of Switzerland destroyed most of the records a long time ago, hiding behind a legalistic shield of banking routine and exploiting legal loopholes created during mergers or between different cantons.[36] In sum, it is clear that many account records are no longer traceable. Swiss profits from Nazi gold and Jewish victims are not simply lying in their vaults. These vanished funds have been invested and reinvested, laundered and relaundered (and the Swiss government earned their taxes in the process), and they appear today under new names, spread in investment portfolios, property holdings, or otherwise.

The Swiss confrontation with its past reflected the psychological constraints and limits of a society which grew up on certain myths and collective memories. The president of the Swiss Confederation, Flavio Cotti, in his speech to the Israel Council on Foreign Relations (May 1998) tried to impress his audience with openness and expressions of regret. He confessed that Switzerland had made many shameful mistakes, 'such as the notorius "J" ', and turning back the refugees 'with the pretext that "the boat is full" '. At the same time, President Cotti took pride in the courageous acts of Carl Lutz, the Swiss consul in Budapest, and Paul Gruninger, the police officer in St Gallen who saved thousands of Jews.[37] Gruninger and Lutz were recognized as 'Righteous Among the Nations' by Yad Vashem Holocaust Memorial. The Swiss President, however, was not courageous enough to express regret over the shameful treatment by successive Swiss governments of these two heroes. The diplomat Carl Lutz was severely reprimanded by his Foreign Ministry superiors three years after the war. Police Superintendent Paul Gruninger suffered demotion, criminal prosecution, and social ostracism, and died a poverty-stricken and forgotten man in 1972. It took many efforts by his family, and even an unpleasant intervention by the American ambassador, before the Swiss system of justice fully rehabilitated him in 1995.[38]

Two years later, under the heat of international criticism, the Swiss political and justice systems blundered again. When Christopher Meili, a security guard in the Zurich offices of the Union Bank of Switzerland, found two containers with books and papers in the shredding room, his curiosity was aroused. The papers dealt with Aryanized properties in Berlin and their acquisition by the Swiss. According to a Swiss Federal Act of December 1996, the destruction of such records was prohibited. Meili, who took the documents to the Jewish community, acted in a just and moral way that people should appreciate and admire. The citizens and bankers of Switzerland thought otherwise in 1997. Meili was promptly dismissed by UBS and was investigated by the police for charges of 'stealing documents and breaching bank secrecy'. Like Paul Gruninger in 1941, Meili lost his job, received threats to his life and was completely ostracized. The *New York Times* commented sarcastically, 'no one espouses the theory that Swiss bankers robbed the accounts of Jewish Holocaust victims better than the bankers themselves.'[39] Meili fled to the United States with his wife and two small children, where, following hearings in the Congress, President Clinton granted him a resident's permit, as required for persecuted refugees.

The Meili case proved better than many other pieces of evidence how the Swiss banks, violating their own laws, destroyed important documents testifying to their complicity with the Nazis, such as their role in Aryanizing Jewish property. It also showed, along with the existence of personal heroes, how the majority of its public and particularly the political system, were not yet ready to draw the lessons and to face justice. In October 1998, after the global settlement with the banks, a group of conservatives submitted to the Swiss court a law suit against Jean Ziegler, charging him with treason for his book *The Swiss, the Gold and the Dead* and for his testimony before the US Senate Banking Committee. The group included leading businessmen and academics, and specifically mentioned Ziegler's contacts with then Senator Alfonse D'Amato – who is described as 'an agent of Jewish organizations'.[40] In trying to define the limits of acceptable behaviour in a democratic society, the plaintiffs equate Ziegler's stance with 'activities against the security of the state by foreign organizations or their agents'. In bringing such a case against freedom of expression and a critical confrontation with the past, this group of angry Swiss bankers and public figures are resorting to political terror with an antisemitic tenor.

Switzerland is not a conventional nation-state. It is a confederation of largely autonomous peoples, each of which possesses its own language, culture, religion and history. Swiss multiculturalism is a fiction, according to Jean Ziegler, and its xenophobia is an inherent necessity for reinforcing its alliance from within.[41] It is this delicate structure and unique history which helped the Swiss to escape the wars of Europe and, at the same time, to build its identity on myths describing Swiss steadfastness against outside pressures (see Plate 4).

The Swiss were not Nazis. Most of them were anti-Nazis during the war, although they may continue to express 'moderate antisemitism', as some Swiss define it. Of course, while one cannot judge today's generation of Swiss by the actions of their ancestors fifty years ago, over the past few years many of today's Swiss have failed to confront their past and take historic responsibility for what happened during and after the war. The same national myths which sustain the Swiss confederation created a smokescreen which did not let the brutal facts stand up in public debate. But even the shredding of documents could not shred a confrontation with history. The real meaning of this confrontation was not about sanctions and threats but the terrible challenge of admitting moral bankruptcy. The gaping differences between contemporary responses in Norway or even neutral Sweden are striking at all levels. The historic contexts are different but the behaviour testifies to the different national character. In those two countries, media, public opinion, parliament, government and even business sectors became actively engaged in a process of reexamining their histories; as a result, policies which compensate victims, provide cultural reinvigoration and teach moral lessons from the war were enacted. It is to be hoped that the state-appointed commission of historians will help the Swiss to learn more about their government, and about banks profiting from their economic relations with the Nazis even in the face of Allied threats of sanctions. Perhaps they will read more about how their banks, with the knowledge of the government and many citizens, shamelessly betrayed the trust of doomed Jews and kept the money left behind by depositors who perished in the Holocaust. Switzerland was singled out by its own distorted collective memory and historical myths.

Notes

1 See Under-secretary of State Stuart Eizenstat's remarks in my essay in Chapter 1 to this volume. In his 'Preliminary Study' (US Department of State: May 1997), Eizenstat emphasizes that even in 1943–44, when the German threat to the neutrals greatly diminished, the Swiss and other neutrals 'continued to profit from their trading links with Germany and thus contributed to prolonging one of the bloodiest conflicts in history. During this period, the Allies suffered hundreds of thousands of casualties and millions of innocent civilians were killed.' In his second report (June 1988), Eizenstat was more restrained and considerate to the Swiss complaints and used a more indirect and diplomatic style: 'This report makes clear that whatever their motivations, and however acceptable by the standards of the time for neutrals, the cumulative trade of the World War II European neutral countries helped *to sustain the Nazi war effort* by supplying key materials to Germany essential to their conduct of the War – in many cases well past the point where, from the Allied perspective at the time, there was a genuine threat of German attack (the same language was used in the preface by William Slany, the Department of State's historian). Foreword by Stuart E. Eizenstat, Under-secretary of State for Economic, Business and Agricultural Affairs, coordinator of the study prepared by William Slany, 'U.S. and Allied Wartime and Postwar Relations and Negotiations with Argentina, Portugal, Spain, Sweden, and Turkey on Looted Gold and German External Assets and U.S. Concerns About the Fate of the Wartime Ustasha Treasury' (supplement to the above preliminary study), June 1998.
2 'Swiss, Irked by Critics, Ask "Why Single Us Out?"' *New York Times*, 6 June 1997.
3 Jean Ziegler, *The Swiss, the Gold, and the Dead* (New York: Harcourt Brace, 1998), pp. 45, 48.
4 See, for instance, B. W. N. Medlicott, *The Economic Blockade* (London, 1978).
5 'Swiss Relief and Report over Settlement of Holocaust Claims', in *International Herald Tribune*, 17 August 1998. On the role of sanctions, the *Financial Times* explained: 'Payment to the Holocaust survivors would only be won at the cost of a severe bruising to Switzerland's international reputation, causing a crisis in the country's self-confidence. A settlement would only come after unprecedented interventions had taken place: class action against the banks, a threat from the largest public pension funds in the US to divest their shares in all Swiss companies, and a threat to block the largest-ever merger in the European banking industry (between UBS and SBC).' 'Banks pay a High Price for Putting the Past Behind Them', *Financial Times*, 9 September 1998.

6   See the text in *Reuters* and *New York Times*, 26 May 1998, for the full reports.

7   'Switzerland Said to Have Backed Nazi Trade', *New York Times*, 23 May 1998.

8   Ibid.

9   For examples, see David S. Wyman, *The Abandonment of the Jews: America and the Holocaust, 1941–1945* (New York, 1984).

10   Tom Bower, *Nazi Gold – The Full Story of the Fifty Year Swiss–Nazi Conspiracy to Steal Billions from Europe's Jews and Holocaust Survivors* (New York: HarperCollins, 1997), pp. 47–48.

11   Ibid., pp.48–49.

12   Adam Lebor, *Hitler's Secret Bankers: The Myth of Swiss Neutrality During the Holocaust* (New Jersey: Birch Lane Press, 1997), p. 28.

13   See Israel Gutman (ed.), *Encyclopedia of the Holocaust* (New York: Macmillan, 1990), p. 1275. For discussion of Nazis and German industrialists' routine connections in Switzerland, see Walter Laqueur and Richard Breitman, *Breaking the Silence* (New York, 1986); and Jacques Picard, *Die Schewiz und die Juden 1933–1945* (Zurich: Chrones, 1994), p. 407.

14   Lebor, *Hitler's Secret Bankers*, p. 52.

15   Ibid., p. 63.

16   Bower, *Nazi Gold*, p.54.

17   Hans Ulrich Jost, 'Menace et repliement', in *Nouvelle histoire de la Suisse et les Suisses*, vol. 3 (Lausanne, 1983), p. 90. After publishing this, Jost was subjected to police harassment, his phone was tapped, and he was publicly attacked. See Ziegler, *The Swiss, the Gold and the Dead*, pp. 13–15.

18   See more on Spain and Portugal in other chapters in this volume.

19   One OSS (Office of Strategic Services – US) agent stationed in Bern counted 280 trucks, all owned by private Swiss firms, identified by a large Swiss flag, riding in convoys, from 1944 to March 1945, from the SNB vaults across France and Spain to Lisbon. The document was released by the WJC on 11 January 1997.

20   The Swiss financial newspaper, *Tash*, on 17 January 1997, mentioned in Ziegler, *The Swiss, the Gold and the Dead*, p. 150

21   Bower, *Nazi Gold*, p. 7.

22   Ibid., p. 74.

23   Ibid., p. 77. On another occasion, in May 1945, among many others, in a meeting of twenty-six American and British officials, the Swiss were blamed for sabotaging US policy and 'making it easy for the Nazi industrialists and other war criminals to conceal their assets'. Orvis Schmidt, from the US Treasury, proposed to threaten the Swiss 'with sanctions, ban supplies of coal and other essential commodities and impose a complete freeze on all Swiss bank accounts in the US' (ibid., p. 96).

24   Peter Hug and Marck Perrenoud, 'Assets in Switzerland of Victims of Nazism and the Compensation Agreements with East Bloc Countries', historical clarification prepared for the Swiss Confederation, Federal Department for Foreign Affairs Task Force, 29 October 1996, Bern (17 January 1997) p. 190

25   Bower, *Nazi Gold*, p. 143.

26   Hug and Perrenoud, 'Assets in Switzerland'.

27   'Inward Look Finds Swiss More Openly Antisemitic', *International Herald Tribune*, 7–8 November 1998, and on Eizenstat see 'Banks Pay a High Price for Putting the Past Behind Them', in *Financial Times*, 9 September 1998.

28 Eizenstat Report II, June 1998, foreword.
29 See reactions in the Swiss press to the new books published on the subject or to other revelations. In particular, the editorials of leading newspapers such as the *Newe Zurcher Zeitung*. This newspaper, which represents the thinking of the Swiss elite, reflected its own inability to confront the facts. See Ziegler, *The Swiss, the Gold and the Dead*, pp. 76, 87–88.
30 Eizenstat Report I, May 1997, foreword.
31 David S. Wyman (ed.), *The World Reacts to the Holocaust* (Baltimore: Johns Hopkins University Press, 1996).
32 Michael Berenbaum and Abraham J. Peck (eds), *The Holocaust and History: The Known, the Unknown, the Disputed, and the Re-examined* (published in association with the US Holocaust Memorial Museum and Indiana University Press, Bloomington, 1998).
33 Ziegler, *The Swiss, the Gold and the Dead*, p. 278.
34 'For Many, Swiss Bank Account Lists Arrive Too Late', *Washington Times*, 24 July 1997.
35 *New York Times*, 6 June 1997.
36 Itamar Levin, 'Swiss Banks – How Jewish Accounts Disappeared', *New Republic*, 27 april 1998.
37 'Switzerland and Israel: 50 Years of Friendship', Speech by the President of the Swiss Confederation, Flavio Cotti to the Israel Council on Foreign Relations, Jerusalem, 17 May 1998.
38 Lebor, *Hitter's Secret Bankers*, p. 139.
39 *New York Times*, 10 January 1997.
40 'Swiss Conservatives Sue Critic who Testified on Jewish Accounts', *International Herald Tribune*, 15 October 1998.
41 Ziegler, *The Swiss, the Gold and the Dead*, p. 17.

9

The Great Culture Robbery: the Plunder of Jewish-Owned Art

Hector Feliciano

Background

The plunder of art is a practice which dates back to antiquity. The Romans began to loot more than twenty centuries ago. They were preceded historically by the Greeks, the Persians, the Babylonians and the Israelites, to name but a few. Throughout history, the plunder of art has been an essential aspect or by-product of war and conquest. One of the most important instances of cultural plunder in recent history is that carried out by Napoleon and his invading armies in Italy, Northern Europe, Egypt and the Middle East. Victors have often tried to annihilate their enemies, not only physically but also morally. The plunder of art and the wilful destruction of cultural heritage has been used by the victors as a supplementary means of conquering and humiliating the enemy. We witnessed this most recently during the war in the former Yugoslavia and the turmoil in the republics of the former Soviet Union. Today, we can observe how many art objects from those regions are being put up for sale – without clear provenance – at art markets in Europe and the United States.

The Second World War was, of course, no exception to this long-standing and, of course, terribly human, tradition. The historian Raoul Hilberg, in his now classic *The Destruction of the European Jews*, states that the confiscation of the extensive art collections and libraries owned by Jews was a part of the entire process that led to the Final Solution and the Holocaust.

From 1939 to 1945, Hitler, the Nazis and their allies collected hundreds of thousands of works of art and millions of books and manuscripts. These were confiscated, forcibly purchased or willingly sold from museums, private collections and libraries throughout occupied Europe.

From an historical perspective, the looting of art by the Nazis was unique. It differed from preceding instances because, not only was it carried out in a methodical and systematic manner, but it was also directed towards specific individuals within the overall population. Besides physically exterminating millions of people and eradicating their long-established culture in large areas of Europe, Hitler's policies for dealing with Germany's enemies included the organized confiscation of the private art collections and libraries of Jews, Freemasons, Poles and political opponents in the occupied countries.

Germans wanted, whenever possible, to destroy their enemies' souls, personalities and memories. Art reflects the soul and personality of its owner. One's art works are usually a projection of one's personality and constitute a part of one's dreams, values and family memory. Thus, a piece of art has much more than a monetary value to its original owners and their heirs. These are the reasons why many families devote a part of their lives to trying to find a missing family painting and, possibly, why public opinion is so moved by their quests.

'Usurpers of Western aesthetic values'

The Nazis considered many Jewish art collectors, such as the Rothschilds, the Rosenbergs, the David-Weills, as pretentious and rapacious usurpers of the highest aesthetic values in Western culture. They had no right to live, let alone to possess great treasures of European civilization.

This unprecedented opportunity for the plunder of art acquired a central and unexpected dimension under Nazism, mainly because of Hitler's own personal interest in painting. A mediocre painter and an unskilled art collector, Hitler had also, as a young student, twice tried and failed the entrance examination to the School of Fine Arts in Vienna. In spite of his incoherent and unsophisticated personal tastes, Hitler favoured the old masters of Northern Europe (Germany, Holland and Flanders) which portrayed figures that confirmed and enhanced his own political views on the superiority of the Germanic race and culture. This view also found expression in the art works commissioned by the Nazi regime.

Hitler despised modern art. In *Mein Kampf* he ferociously attacked modern 'degenerate' art such as cubism, futurism, Dadaism, all of which he considered the product of decadent twentieth-century society. When, in 1933, Hitler rose to power, he sold or destroyed all the modern paintings found in Germany's state museums.

The Führer's objective in gathering together thousands of plundered old masters and realist paintings was the eventual establishment of a museum of European art, to be built in the Austrian city of Linz on the Danube, where he had spent his childhood years. Other Nazi dignitaries, such as Reichsmarschall Hermann Goering and Foreign Affairs Minister von Ribbentrop, were also intent on taking advantage of recent German conquests to increase their private art collections. The extent to which Hitler was obsessed by the project can be seen in the fact that in his last will and testament, penned on the eve of his suicide in Berlin, he wrote: 'The paintings in my collections, which I purchased over the course of years, were not assembled for any personal gain, but for the creation of a museum in my native city of Linz on the Danube. It is my sincere wish that this legacy be duly executed.'

Among the wealthy occupied countries of Western Europe, France was subjected to the greatest degree of plunder, not only because it was probably the richest in art, but also because French Jews were among the best and most important art dealers and collectors at the time. At the end of the war, French officials estimated that one-third of all art in French private hands had been confiscated – plunder of a truly astronomical magnitude. In the years of Nazi rule as many works of art were displaced, transported and stolen as during the entire Thirty Years War or all the Napoleonic wars.

Paris

Until the outbreak of the war, Paris was the world's largest and most important art market. Paris was the place where wealthy European and American collectors bought their old masters and modern painting. Since the beginning of the century, Jewish *marchands d'art* had established themselves as some of the best French art dealers and experts, shaping and influencing taste. The Wildensteins had turned their antique shop into a prestigious art gallery, dealing in old masters and nineteenth-century art. The Bernheim-Jeunes specialized in impressionist and post-impressionist painters. In 1901 they had opened the first important van Gogh exhibition. Paul Rosenberg, the dealer of Picasso and Braque in the 1920s and 1930s held modern art shows in his gallery, which attracted hundreds of visitors every day.

After the occupation of Paris in 1940, the Einsatzstab Reichsleiters Rosenberg (ERR), the official Nazi confiscation service, was created. Headed by Nazi party ideologue Alfred Rosenberg, it was actually controlled by Goering, who planned (in his own words), to build the largest private art collection in Europe. One of its first tasks was to find the various art galleries and confiscate their contents, inventories and the private collections of Jewish art dealers. The Nazis also seized the world-renowned art collections and private libraries of the Rothschild family, banking magnate David David-Weill, financier Alphonse Kann, and wholesale entrepreneur Adolphe Schloss, among many others. The gallery of Paul Rosenberg on Rue de La Boetie was seized and occupied by the 'Institute for the Study of the Jewish Question'.

These cultural treasures were captured through persistent and well-prepared intelligence work, provided by German secret police and by Nazi art historians, as well as by a close network of French informers and collaborationist art dealers. This meticulous scheme achieved impressive results.

The valuable collection of the French branch of the Rothschild banking dynasty was, of course, one of the Nazis' most important targets. The presence of several masterpieces by Northern European painters made this collection a priority for Hitler, who coveted it even before the war started. Consequently, immediately after the occupation began, the Nazis commandeered the family's Paris mansions and seized their property. The three elegant town houses in the exclusive Place de la Concorde neighbourhood (two of which today belong to the American Embassy in Paris) were emptied bare. The Rothschilds' country manors and *palais* were also requisitioned.

The precise inventory compiled by the Nazis describes 5003 objects from the Rothschild collection. Among the priceless masterpieces of incalculable value found there were Vermeer's *The Astronomer*, Rembrandt's *The Standard Bearer*, Frans Hals's *Portrait of Isabel Coymans*, Gainsborough's *Portrait of Lady Alston*, Boucher's *Portrait of Madame de Pompadour* and portraits by Goya. These works and the other objects from the collection were loaded on German military trucks and taken to the Jeu de Paume Museum on the Tuileries Gardens, the official Nazi depot for confiscated art. There, far from intruding eyes, a staff of German art historians, experts, photographers, and maintenance and administrative personnel appraised, filed, photographed and packed the Rothschilds' 'ownerless cultural goods', readying them for immediate transport to the Reich.

Hitler and Goering divided the collection (see Plate 5). Goering was so excited about the catch that he ordered the ERR staff to organize a private show for him of the best pieces. A few days later, he arrived in Paris and visited the Jeu de Paume to spend a moment looking at the masterpieces. Yet he knew that in the case of this particular collection, he would have to defer to Hitler's first choice. The first shipment started in November 1941. On the train to Germany those crates intended for

Hitler were marked with an 'H' and numbered from 1 to 19, while those intended for Goering were marked with a 'G' and numbered from 1 to 23 (see Plate 6). As Goering expected, Hitler took the lion's share of the collection; crate 'H5' contained the portrait by Gainsborough, crate 'H6' the Frans Hals, and crate 'H13' the two portraits by Goya and the major prize of the collection, Vermeer's *The Astronomer*. When Alfred Rosenberg, head of the ERR, learned of the seizure and transport to Germany of the Rothschilds' collection, he wrote a short and self-serving note to Martin Bormann, Hitler's secretary: 'In a rush. Enclosed you will find a report [on art confiscation] for the Führer which will make him, I believe, happy... I also want to inform the Führer that the painting by Vermeer from Delft he had spoken about was found among the artworks confiscated from the Rothschilds.'

These masterpieces then started a five-year journey, waiting for the end of the war. The crates were first sent to Ludwig II's Bavarian castle at Neuschwanstein, the central, confiscated-art warehouse in Germany. Then, when Allied bombing made that region unsafe, the main Rothschild objects were transferred to an underground salt mine near Salzburg in Austria. It was there that they were found at the end of the war by the advancing US Army, still packed in their original marked crates. Ironically, in spite of their haste to confiscate the collection in France, the Nazis had not yet been able to unpack these masterpieces, unwittingly saving them from dispersal. At the end of the war, the collection, minus a few losses, was restored to the Rothschilds.

The fate of confiscated modern or 'degenerate' art, however, was quite different from that of the traditional masters coveted by the Nazis. Those art collections were sold, bartered and broken up. This, of course, would later complicate postwar restitution efforts. The 300 paintings seized from the gallery and private collection of art dealer Paul Rosenberg included works by painters despised by Hitler and other Nazi leaders: Picasso, Matisse, Braque, and Léger, as well as van Gogh, Monet, Renoir, Manet, Degas and Delacroix. Those paintings were confiscated in southern France and transferred and stored in the backroom of the Jeu de Paume museum.

The French Underground curators, who had access to this backroom where Nazis kept 'degenerate' art, called it the Martyrs' Room, in reference to the trials and tribulations awaiting these magnificent works. In fact, since 'degenerate' art was not allowed to enter Germany, a few art dealers close to the ERR came to the museum to choose some of these works that they could easily sell in the French or Swiss markets. The sale or barter of hundreds of these paintings was performed for the personal material benefit of Goering who, in this manner, was able to increase his own art collection. Paul Rosenberg's collection was scattered across Europe during the war, and some seventy of his paintings are missing to this very day. Among those, a large watercolour by Picasso, *Naked Woman on the Beach*, painted in Provence in 1923, seven works by Matisse, and the magnificent *Portrait of Gabrielle Diot* by Degas.

The German foreign minister, von Ribbentrop, brought to the German embassy in Paris a small team of art experts and gave them the rank of commercial attachés; they were to devote themselves exclusively to buying art in France. This was probably the first time in history that a government had appointed diplomats to research, evaluate and purchase works of art fulltime – all for the greater glory of the Third Reich.

The Deutsche Reichsbank, Germany's central bank, had an even more insatiable appetite for looted art. The Reichsbank spent at least 40 million francs on art and antiques in France. Each week, one or two deliveries, by truck or train, each one valued at somewhere around one million francs, left Paris for Berlin. The transport lists were reminiscent of Ali Baba. In addition to the Aubusson tapestries and the Louis XV chairs were mirrors, rugs, mantelpieces, dozens of armchairs and furniture, hundreds of napkins, ten tablecloths designed for tables that could accommodate one hundred people, cases of alcohol, wool blankets, silk throws, hundreds of yards of tulle for curtains, books, and luxury items from the best couturiers and finest shoemakers in Paris. They also sent an astounding variety of canned goods: pheasants, turkey, duck, and – for the really discerning palates – tripe braised in Madeira.

Throughout the war, the Reichsbank's upper management continued to traffic in goods that catered to their fantasies about royal opulence, such as the Sèvres setting for seventy that had once belonged to Louis Philippe, and which had required twenty craftsmen working three full years to complete; or the exquisite examples of mahogany furniture made by the king's cabinet-makers Riesener and Beneman in the eighteenth century; and the four rose hors-d'oeuvre serving dishes that Napoleon had made for Bernadotte, the future Charles XIV of Sweden and Norway. The bankers' obsession with royalty was such that they even purchased a fountain ornament from the Versaillles gardens: a monkey astride a dolphin.

Business as usual

However, the Germans were not alone in benefiting from this plunder. Plenty of ordinary, opportunistic French citizens also managed to tap its treasures. For example, two ERR workers, Amical Leprael and Valentin Breton, took what they knew about the Nazi stockpile to a dealer named Charles Collet. Collet acted on what they told him and ended up buying an enormous quantity from ERR. By the war's end enough works to fill 52 trucks were found in his home. Some French dealers, such as Martin Fabianai and Roger Dequoy, profited handsomely from German confiscations.

The celebrated Parisian decorating firm, Jansen, collaborated with the Germans, particularly with the Reichsbank, which commissioned it to redecorate its headquarters in Berlin. The House of Jansen also sent decorators to Poland to assist Nazi gauleiter Hans Frank spruce up his surroundings. Frank and his henchmen ordered over 1.5 million francs' worth of furnishings, including Louis XV chandeliers and Louis XVI armchairs. These complemented the art collection Frank amassed from confiscations in Poland, which included a Leonardo da Vinci and a Rembrandt. These purchases also furnished a number of Nazi officials and merchants with paintings and carpets. All told, the House of Jansen earned some 42 million francs from its German commissions.

During the occupation, the Parisian art market was inundated with stolen art put up for sale. Matisse, who had stayed in France, found many of his own plundered works offered for sale. The fact is that the French art market flourished during the war. The war was actually a godsend for the Parisian art market. It brought an end to the crisis of the 1930s, when art prices declined by as much as 70 per cent from where they had been earlier, forcing a third of the galleries in Paris to close their doors.

New collectors, and speculators eager to get rid of paper money, (the value of which was unstable), started buying paintings, antiques and rare books. These they saw as solid investments in a troubled time. Significant liquidation sales occurred and the market was flooded with French painting and sculpture from the eighteenth and nineteenth centuries, confiscated from Jewish dealers. The uncertainties of war stimulated both supply and demand. 'People had plenty of cash,' recalled art dealer Alfred Daber, 'but there were no pretty clothes, no new cars, no vacations and no restaurants and cabarets on which to spend money. All you could do was buy butter on the black market. That was why everyone was investing in the art market.'

Moreover, the international clientele that had kept French galleries and dealers afloat before the war had ceded its place to the German conquerors. The sudden arrival of large numbers of German buyers with deep pockets changed the French art market. By the end of the occupation, these Germans and Austrians had established complex commercial relations with French dealers. Representatives from the German museums and galleries, diplomats, civil servants, bankers and industrialists, Nazi party officials, and wealthy private citizens streamed into Paris. They profited from the disadvantageous exchange rate imposed upon the French franc by the armistice (twenty francs to each Reishmark) and from all the commercial and psychological advantages that came with being conquerors. Belgians and Dutch also came, followed by the Swiss who, for all their vaunted neutrality, were to be found everywhere.

Switzerland was the most convenient venue for the disposal of looted art work beyond the borders of the Reich. In the first place, Swiss collectors had more cash than they knew what to do with. Secondly, the fact that they enjoyed complete freedom of movement meant that they represented the only truly international clientele in wartime Europe. Often the Swiss found themselves exchanging German works for those of French impressionists. Swiss museums, such as the Kunstmuseum in Basle, also bolstered their collections by purchasing plundered art fenced in Switzerland. Many of the works that went to Switzerland have remained in the collections of its citizens. Others can be found in Swiss museums – there for everyone to see, though still untouchable. Others have yet to surface. Special mention should be made of the German-born Swiss munitions magnate Emil G. Buhrle. His company, Oerlikon-Buhrle, made vast sums during the war dealing with the German military. During this period he amassed a collection of world-class paintings, which remains in the collection of the Buhrle Foundation in Zurich.

German museums also took full advantage of this situation and enhanced their collection of arts. Among the most eager buyers were the Rheinisches Landesmuseum and the Provinzialdenkmalamt in Bonn, the Stadtische Kunstsammlungen in Düsseldorf, the Folwang Museum in Essen, the Kaiser Wilhelm Museum in Drefeld, the Stadisches Museum für Kunst und Kunstggewerbe in Wuppertal-Eberfeld. These five museums paid at least 31 million francs for at least 204 paintings, drawings, engravings and sculptures, as well as other antiques. The Kunsthistorisches Museum, which since the *Anschluss* had been part of the Reich's museums – but whose curators did not wait until 1938 to collaborate with the Gestapo and confiscate the Rothschilds' collection in Vienna – distinguished itself in November 1942 by acquiring a clavichord constructed by Pascal Tiskin for 127,500 francs from the Parisian manufacturer, Pianos Labrousse.

Specialists in classical and Near Eastern art from Berlin institutes also realized that an opportunity was at hand. The departments of Islamic and Egyptian art thus acquired stone sculptures, stelae, bas-reliefs, marble plaques and vases.

Although museums were generally rather conservative in their selection of paintings, some German dealers and collectors were bold enough to ignore Hitler's directives and even bought works of artists classified as Jewish.

Throughout the war, German curators proudly announced in their local press the arrival of each new acquisition, providing details about the paintings they had bought and where they would go. The museums were little concerned with the provenance of their purchases and acquired many works of suspicious origins. If stolen works were acquired by German museums, part of the blame lies with the French brokers who sold the paintings to them. Some of them were actually in cahoots with the German and French officials responsible for the confiscations of Jewish art. The merciless competition among German clients actually enriched many French dealers.

Shipments of confiscated art to Germany continued until the summer of 1944. The final ERR report, written in July 1944 in Berlin, reveals the extent of the plunder. Between April 1941 and July 1944 no fewer than twenty-nine major shipments of works into Germany from Paris took place. In all, 120 railway cars filled with 4170 crates of art crossed the French border into Germany. From France alone – leaving aside Belgium and The Netherlands – 21,000 objects from 203 collections were confiscated. Some 10,000 of these were paintings, drawings and engravings – all of which were shipped to one of six Nazi warehouses, including Neuschwanstein. Some of the paintings and sculptures from the David-Weill, Rothschild and Rosenberg collections were taken to a warehouse located in the Nikolsburg castle in the Sudetenland.

Many of the works stolen by the Nazis disappeared for many years, went into complex art market circuits, and then, unexpectedly, surfaced again, entering the world's art market without their potential buyers suspecting their troubled histories.

Conclusion

In December 1987, Elaine Rosenberg, Paul Rosenberg's daughter-in-law, was leafing through an art magazine at the Frick Reference Library in New York. Her eyes suddenly came across an advertisement announcing the auction sale of important old masters and modern paintings at the

Mathias F. Hans Gallery in Hamburg, Germany. Rembrandt and Tiepolo drawings, as well as Braques, were to be auctioned. However, what truly attracted her attention was the full-page reproduction of the main work of the sale – the *Portrait of Gabrielle Diot* by Degas. The advertisement explained that the painting had last belonged to the Paul Rosenberg collection in Paris, adding no more details concerning its origin. A stunned Rosenberg quickly recognized the lost painting confiscated by the Nazis in France from her family more than forty years before. She immediately phoned the German art dealer, telling him the real story of the Degas and sparing none of the facts. The dealer explained to her that the owner of the painting put it on consignment at his gallery, hoping to sell it. He added that according to confidentiality rules he could not disclose the owner's name but promised to let him know this very important piece of information. When, a few days later, Elaine Rosenberg phoned back, the Hamburg dealer told her that the 'owner' of the painting had taken back the Degas from his gallery and disappeared without leaving any traces. The painting has not been seen since.

For many lost art works confiscated by the Nazis during the Second World War, that is as close as they will ever come to the world's art market. Aware of the troubled and shady history that surrounds their paintings, the present owners of these art works will try to keep them out of the general art market, away from public scrutiny.

Since the mid 1990s, the issue of looted art has been catapulted into the headlines. Claims over two paintings by the Austrian Expressionist painter Egon Schiele, exhibited at the Museum of Modern Art in New York, are the latest pieces found from the enormous puzzle created by the Nazi plunder of European art. The two paintings, *Portrait of Wally* (see Plate 7) and *Dead City*, were part of a travelling exhibition of Schiele pictures. When the exhibition reached New York, two separate claims were put forward by parties who claimed to be the heirs to the paintings. They argued that the paintings were seized by the Nazis from their Jewish owners in 1938 immediately after the *Anschluss*. After the war, both works were acquired by Dr Rudolf Leopold, whose collection is now a government-financed foundation, which organized the travelling exhibitions.

The two families asked the Museum of Modern Art to hold on to the paintings after the exhibition closed, until their provenances could be rightly identified. But the museum, citing a contractual obligation to return the pictures, and federal and state laws that forbid the seizure of cultural properties on loan in New York, said it had to ship the pictures to the show's next destination, the Picasso Museum in Barcelona. At the families' insistence, a last-minute court subpoena issued by the Manhattan district attorney stopped the paintings from leaving the country until an investigation could be completed. In May 1998 a state supreme court justice ruled that the paintings could be returned to Austria despite the continuing criminal investigation into their provenance. The heirs of Fritz and Louise Gutmann, Dutch Jews murdered in the Holocaust, have spent decades attempting to recover some of their family's art collection, which includes works by Degas, Renoir, Dossi and Botticelli. Following the death of the Gutmanns' son Bernard Goodman (he anglicized his name) in 1994, their grandsons continued the quest. A painting by Degas, *Landscapes with Smokestacks*, turned up in the collection of pharmaceutical industrialist Daniel Searle, and has been the object of litigation. The Dutch government has convened a special commission to deal with issue of art works plundered in The Netherlands.

An important step in the restitution efforts was made by the Association of Art Museum Directors (AAMD), which convened a task force on the spoliation of art during the Nazi era. The report of that task force was clear in stating that the AAMD

> recognizes and deplores the unlawful confiscation of art that constituted one of the many horrors of the Holocaust and World War II. . . and urges the prompt creation of a mechanism to coordinate full access to all documentation concerning this spoliation of art, especially newly available information. To this end the AAMD encourages the creation of data bases by third parties, essential to research in this area, which will aid in the identification of any works of art which were unlawfully confiscated and which of these items were restituted.

The AAMD called upon its members to make public information on works of art which it determines were confiscated during the war, and that it should handle claims promptly and thoroughly; and should it determine that the work in question was illegally confiscated, the museum should 'offer to resolve the matter in an equitable, appropriate and mutually agreeable manner'.

Not a few looted paintings (including items from the collection of Baron Herzog in Budapest) wound up in collections in Russia – having been brought there by Soviet troops who discovered them in Germany, Czechoslovakia, Hungary and elsewhere in Europe. The Duma (Russian parliament) recently passed legislation to the effect that all booty carted off to Russia be considered war reparations and declared as state property. The irony of this is readily evident. It means that art confiscated by the Nazis from Jewish collectors and dealers in France and other parts of Europe can be counted as part of Nazi Germany's reparations to Russia. President Yeltsin vetoed this move, but all international negotiations on the subject are at a standstill.

In the meantime, some two thousand unclaimed works of art remain under the protection of France's national museums. Among them are nearly one thousand paintings, including works by Cezanne, Degas, Manet, Picasso, Matisse and many others. A complete inventory of unclaimed works has never been commissioned. However, at least 500 of these works can be found in the Louvre, at least 110 at the Musée d'Orsay, 38 in the Pompidou Centre, 13 at the Rodin Museum and the rest scattered throughout France in other museums and institutions, in whose de facto possession they are. Many are used to decorate official residences and government offices. All told, some 15,000 works of art were unclaimed. Very little has been done to find the owners or their heirs. Several ministries have known for years about the looted assets in French museums and made virtually no effort to rectify this situation. However, French law clearly states that there can be no statute of limitations on claims to these works. The promise by Prime Minister Alain Juppé to create an independent commission to search for and evaluate Jewish assets is only part of the solution. A concerted effort has to be made to reunite these works with those who can claim them. Justice demands no less.

It may take decades for missing art works to reappear, but they will surface one day. In doing so, their reappearance will be the final frustration of the attempts by Nazi Germany to impose a homogeneous and limited cultural view on the world. Returning looted art is, fundamentally, a matter of moral justice and memory, our chance to do today that which we will not be able to do even a few years from now – to gather all the pieces of the puzzle.

The story of the Nazi art plunder and the puzzle that came out of it cannot be told from the point of view of the looters, nor from the point of view of the unknowing and unwitting museums or current owners. It can only be told from one point of view: that of the victims.

Bibliography

Cassou, Jean (ed.), *Le Pillage par les Allemands des oeuvres d'art et de bibliothèques appartenant a des Juifs en France* (Paris, 1947).

Flanner, Janet, 'Annals of Paris: the Beautiful Spoils', *New Yorker*, 1 February and 8 March 1947.

Hilberg, Raoul, *The Destruction of European Jews* (New York, 1961).

Marrus, Michael R. and Paxton, Robert O., *Vichy France and the Jews* (New York, 1981).

Nicholas, Lynn, *The Rape of Europa* (New York, 1994).

Paxton, Robert O., *Vichy France: Old Guard and New Order, 1940–1944* (New York, 1972)

Rorimer, James J. and Rabin, Gilbert, *Survival: The Salvage and Protection of Art in War* (New York, 1950).

Smyth, Craig Hugh, *Repatriation of Art from the Collecting Point in Munich after World War II* (The Hague, 1988).

Speer, Albert, *Inside the Third Reich: Memoirs* (New York, 1981).

Valland, Rose, *Le Front de l'Art* (Paris, 1961).

10
France and the Burdens of Vichy

Shmuel Trigano

I The Shoah's status in the public arena

Since the mid-1970s, the Holocaust and the history of Vichy have come to occupy a major place in the national debate in France. However, only in the late 1990s, following the first public apology by a French president and the growing international awareness, did the French begin to investigate their behaviour in more systematic fashion. An understanding of the sources of French society's interest in these subjects is a prerequisite for understanding the ramifications of the present debate on the spoliation of French Jewry and, more broadly, of the strategic position of the Jews in this debate, a debate with effects which go far beyond the limits of the question of Jewish property. The situation can be discussed at three different levels: party politics, the macrosociological reality of French society, and developments in the Jewish community. The study of these three factors provides the context in which the current debate about the fate of stolen Jewish property occurs.

The political agenda

The 1980s constituted a turning-point in French political life. For many reasons, the accession to power of the Socialist Party coincided with the end of the postwar period. The fall of Charles de Gaulle's party and the ascent to power of a party which had long been kept from government led to the removal of the Gaullist obstacle which had weighed on this period. This situation coincided with the collapse of the framework in which intellectual and ideological debate had been conducted in France since the Second World War. Its swan-song had been heard in the 1970s with the great flowering of outstanding thinkers. The objective distancing from Marxism, one of the axes of this debate, could explain the turning-point felt from this period, well before the spread of the human rights dialectic inspired by the work of Solzhenitsyn, who quickly became its mythical hero.

France entered a new age, manifest in François Mitterrand's accession to power, with a government which included Communist ministers. The historical baggage that had been suppressed by Gaullist France, which had placed France in the wartime victory camp and had been shielded by the mythicized Resistance, now returned to the scene of history, while the American television productions on the Holocaust (the serial of that name, for instance) invaded European screens. The Socialist Party heritage could not effectively hold back the return of the suppressed facts. As history was later to show, François Mitterrand's wartime past was not as 'pure' as that of General de Gaulle: the new president had compromised himself with Vichy.

In developing his human rights ideology and campaigning against the extreme Right party of Le Pen, President François Mitterrand used the Holocaust and Auschwitz as absolute references. Mitterrand also made extensive use of the numerous Jews in his entourage and of the Jewish community. In fact, it was vital for him that the Jews corroborate the credibility of the fascist threat, which was then quite fanciful (although this is no longer the case today). The president received overwhelming Jewish support, with the representative institutions of the community following the lead of the publishers and intellectuals. The media was flooded with articles on the Holocaust, the Jewish victims, the Jews in general. Very often the 'cover story' was more important for the coverage than for the analysis. In this period war criminals Barbie, Bousquet and Touvier were brought to trial (1987, 1991 and 1994, respectively), with the dual aims of attaining justice and 'transmitting the memory' to the younger generations.

Alongside such a trend, a far greater readiness to confront the heritage of the war should also mentioned: the trials held for crimes against humanity, President Jacques Chirac's declaration (July 1995) assuming eternal French responsibility for the Vichy period (even though it abandoned the republican system of government), the penitence of Catholic bishops (autumn 1997), and Cardinal Jean-Marie Lustiger's publishing of a text on the unique character of the Holocaust (December 1997), are all positive manifestations. It is not generally known, but it is none the less recognized by the ecclesiastical hierarchy, that the *Declaration of Repentance* issued by the Catholic episcopate was followed by a campaign of protest letters from simple believers to their bishops, stigmatizing their Church's unwarranted action, and denying any Church responsibility for the fate of the Jews. Even Jacques Chirac's actions cannot be totally separated from their French political context and the need to distinguish the liberal Right from any connection with Le Pen.

The broad social perspective

This phenomenon must be placed in the perspective of the wide context of French society, since the current conception is not solely the result of political manoeuvres. These manoeuvres in fact are tied to a very real social change, described in the press the 'immigration problem'. Since the 1970s several million immigrants have arrived in France, which required the manpower in order to guarantee its economic development. The problem of their integration into French society was posed once it became apparent that these temporary workers, now settled in France with their families, did not wish to return to their countries of origin. The gravity of this question became more acute with the economic crisis that set in after the oil shock of the 1970s. This was the first time that France had been confronted with a Muslim immigration, and at a time when its national identity had been weakened by the consequences of industrialization and the opening to the large trends of international exchanges inherent in the internationalization process. This was the most concrete problem of French society, with the development of endemic unemployment among its population, the revolt of the suburbs, the forming of urban pockets which the police could not control, and the spread of racism. This immigration in fact constituted a threat to its national identity, such as it had been moulded during the Third Republic. It was in this fertile ground that the National Front developed, combining the new social fractures with the economic crisis, and the concurrent integration of French society into a united Europe in which the individual countries dilute national identities.

A new development in the Holocaust debate, which existed already in the New Left, was recently added to all these controversies: the comparison of Auschwitz and the Gulag. This debate, which is very specific to France, is in fact part of a long-standing purely French debate, opposing liberalism to socialism. A recently published book (Stéphane Courtois, ed., *Le livre noir du communisme* [The Black Book of Communism], 1997), which attributes the responsibility of 80 million dead to the Communists, suggests that the insistence on the uniqueness of the Holocaust shields genocides perpetrated by the other great totalitarianism, Communism. Communist regimes have been responsible for far more deaths than Nazism. This debate stirred up a huge scandal in the media and lasted several months. The Jews found themselves generally accused of insensitiveness to the sufferings of other peoples, and the Holocaust was denounced as an ideological screen hiding the murderous nature of Communism. This criticism of the unique nature of the Holocaust is thus voiced both by the Left and the Right. The critique also targets the historical responsibility of the Left at large, and thus of the French Socialist-Communist coalition government.

The Papon trial

Without a doubt the Papon trial marked the end of a period of turmoil in French public opinion, which was forced to face the memory of the collaboration and the Vichy regime, from the mid-1980s. This was the last trial for 'crimes against humanity' to be held in France and it embraced all the tensions inherent in the debate. This may well explain the divergence between public expectations and the reality of the court proceedings, and of the verdict delivered. All the ambiguity of this trial was derived from the desire to put on trial the Vichy administration in the person of a man who actually occupied only a junior post (unlike Barbie and Touvier). Through Papon, thus, implicitly, judgement was also passed on Bousquet and Leguay, who were already dead. . .

'In Bordeaux, stress was placed on judging the crime against humanity as if it were an ordinary common law crime . . . This was discussed as an "administrative crime", to coin Hannah Arendt's expression,' declared Michel Zaoui, who represented the civil parties (*Le Monde*, 3 July 1998). Accordingly, the verdict did not recognize Maurice Papon as an accessory to murder, even while condemning him as an accessory to a crime against humanity.

The dual intention manifested in this trial (both as a commemorative act and a settling of accounts with the national past on one hand, and an act of justice and punishment on the other) explains the mitigated impact that it had on public opinion. This was all the more so since Papon did not appear as an important figure who could answer for the crimes of Vichy. Certain analysis cast doubt on whether any fresh light had actually been shed on the period of collaboration. Too often, for example, the defendant was asked whether he knew about the Final Solution when he arrested Jews and deported them in sealed cattle cars.

The defendant took advantage of the tribunal offered to him to proclaim his innocence and his loyalty to the state which he continued to serve after the war (Papon had gone on to become minister in several Gaullist governments). Resistance figures testified in his favour and confirmed that he had been a Resistance fighter. This explains the audacity of Papon's lawyer, who several weeks after the verdict, actually

1 General Dwight D. Eisenhower, accompanied by General Omar Bradley, inspecting art looted by the Nazis. The paintings were discovered in a German mine liberated by American forces.

2 This poster on a Krakow street is an example of anti-semitic agitation against the restitution of Jewish property. It reads 'The New Rulers of Poland!!! The privatization of the national wealth of Poland is only for them!!!' (photograph courtesy of L. Weinbaum).

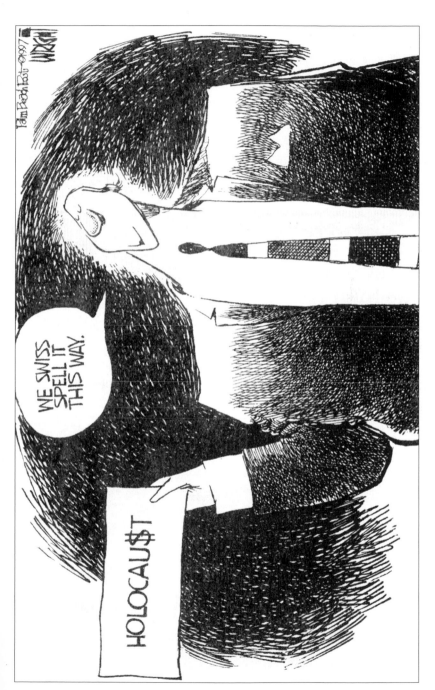

3 An example of one of the powerful political cartoons targeting Switzerland's dealing with Nazi Germany and its subsequent behaviour when pressed to account for its deeds (courtesy of *Palm Beach Post*, 1997).

4 The international press played an active role in revealing the Swiss story.

5 Hitler and Goering examine plundered works of art (courtesy of Yad Vashem).

6 Hermann Goering, during one of his visits to the Jeu de Paume during the German Occupation of France, admiring a confiscated painting (courtesy of Musée d'Orsay, Galeries Jeu de Paume).

7 Egon Schiele's *Portrait of Wally* (1912), currently the object of litigation (courtesy the Museum of Modern Art, New York).

8 Entrance to a swimming pool in occupied Holland. The small sign to the right reads: 'Jews not allowed'.

asked the French Internal Affairs Ministry, upon which his client was dependent, to cover the damages which the court had sentenced him to pay to the families of the victims and survivors. Moreover, public opinion sometimes found the divisions between the civil parties incomprehensible. In view of all the above facts, the aim of holding an 'exemplary' trial may have failed. At the same time, the trial halted (at least for the foreseeable future) the debate on French collaboration and on Vichy.

It is against this background that the French government and public began to investigate its behaviour in the Vichy period. From this point, it is helpful to briefly review the historical facts.

II   The stages of extermination of French Jewry

Very early in its existence, the Vichy regime instituted a policy of legal exclusion of the Jews, which was to lead to their extermination (see Box 1). In its eagerness to forestall the desires of the Germans, it competed zealously, pathetically endeavouring to preserve the external signs of French autonomy under the German occupying forces. The Law on the status of the Jews (of 3 October 1940) banned Jews from the civil service and the liberal professions, basing this discrimination on the criterion of 'Jewish race'. The Law of 4 October 1940 made possible the internment of 'foreigners of Jewish race' in special camps. In order to implement its Jewish policy, on 29 March 1941 Vichy created a kind of ministry for Jewish affairs, the Commissariat Général aux Questions Juives (CGQJ). The Commissariat had a special police force, the PQJ, later the Section d'Enquête et de Contrôle (SEC).

Massive arrests of Jews by the French police began on 14 May 1941 in the Paris region. Mainly they affected foreign Jews, who were taken for internment in the camps of Pithiviers and Baume la Rolande. The second round-up began on 20 August 1941. Among the Jews arrested by the police were 1000 French citizens. The Drancy internment camp was opened. On 12 December 1941, 700 French Jews including many dignitaries, were arrested and interned at Compiègne. The Nazis executed fifty-three Jews from Drancy.

The first deportation to the east took place on 27 March 1942, involving 1112 Jewish men; about half were French Jews interned at Compiègne and half were stateless Jews. After the Germans decided, in June 1942, to deport all of Western European Jewry, the Germans and the French consulted with each other in preparation for the massive arrest of Jewish families. The Gestapo demanded that 40 per cent of the Jews

Box 1   The Vichy Laws

Of the fifty-five laws defining the status of Jews, the following should be noted:

Law of 3 October 1940 on the status of Jews
'To be considered Jewish . . . any person with three grandparents of Jewish race or with two grandparents of that race, if his/her husband/wife is him/herself Jewish' (Article 1).

Articles 2 and 3 exclude Jews from public functions. 'Access to and exercise of the liberal professions . . . are allowed for the Jews, unless civil service regulations have fixed a specific quota for them. In this case the same regulations will determine the conditions in which the excess Jews will be eliminated' (Article 4).

Article 5 bans Jews from cultural professions (press, information, cinema, theatre, radio):
'This law is applicable to Algeria, to the colonies, protectorates and mandatory territories' (Article 9).

Law of 4 October 1940 on foreign nationals of Jewish race
Its first article indicates that foreign nationals of Jewish race can, from the date of promulgation of this law, be interned in special camps by decision of the prefect of the department where they reside.

Law of 2 June 1941, replacing the law of 3 October 1940
Article 1: 'Is considered Jewish:

(1)   Anyone belonging or not to any religion who has at least three grandparents of Jewish race or only two if his/her husband/wife also has two grandparents of Jewish race.
      Is considered as being of Jewish race the grandparent who belonged to the Jewish religion.
(2)   Anyone belonging to the Jewish religion or who belonged to it on 25, June 1940 and who has two grandparents of Jewish race.

The fact of not belonging to the Jewish religion is established by proof of adhering to one of the other religions recognized by the State prior to the law of 9, December 1905. The denial or cancellation of the recognition of a child considered as Jewish are ineffective as regards the preceding provisions.'

Law of 2 June 1941 stipulating the census of the Jews.

Law of 29 May 1942 imposing a distinctive sign: 'the Jewish badge'.

be of French nationality and that the arrests be made by the French police alone. Chief of Police Bousquet decided to accept these conditions on 2 July 1942, the only concession being that the French Jews be momentarily spared. Prime Minister Pierre Laval tried to go one better by proposing that children under the age of 16 also be deported, even though this had not been demanded by the Nazis. The signal for deportation of the Jewish children was thus given to the SS. On 16 July 1942, the Vélodrome d'Hiver round-up took place: 3031 men, 5802 women and 4051 children were arrested by 4500 French policemen. From this round-up and for eleven weeks, three convoys of 1000 Jews left for the east each week.

Protests against the deportations were publicly voiced. Cardinals and archbishops of France sent a letter to the head of state, Marshall Pétain, on 22 July 1942, saying 'we cannot suppress the cry of our conscience'. With the great round-up of the unoccupied zone, the Vichy regime was able to deliver another 6500 Jews to the SS, but this led to widespread protests. The most resounding declaration was that of Monsignor Salièges, Archbishop of Toulouse, and the most efficacious was that of Cardinal Gerlier, Archbishop of Lyons and Primate of the Gauls. These acts of defiance had some positive effect, but the Gestapo finally sent to Auschwitz the 40,000 deportees just as planned in the June 1942 agreement.

In all, out of 300,000–330,000 Jews (divided by half into the two zones – occupied and unoccupied), including about 50 per cent of foreign Jews, 75,721 were deported. This figure included 2.7 per cent children under 6 years of age (2044) and 11.6 per cent children between the ages 6 and 17 (8780), a total of nearly 11,000 children. Over 9700 of the deported Jews were aged over 60. Nearly 43,000 of the deportees were gassed to death immediately. In 1945, there were 2566 survivors, that is, about 3 per cent of those deported, of which fewer than 1000 are alive today. With 3000 who died in the camps before deportation and the thousands of executions, there were a total of 80,000 victims. At least 85 per cent of the Jews deported from France were arrested by the French police (including 24,000 French citizens of whom 7000 where children born in France of foreign parents). The rest of the Jews were spared, and they owe this certainly to the presence of the Resistance movements, but also to the aid offered by certain sectors of civilian society who, on this point, dissociated themselves from the policy of Vichy and the occupying power.

The 'Aryanization' of the economy

As early as 23 October 1940, the French authorities took an inventory of the companies and enterprises owned by Jews of the Paris region in order to transmit the information to the German authorities. One of the functions of the CGQJ was identifying and confiscating Jewish property. The German edict of 18, October 1940 defined a 'Jewish enterprise' and provided for the appointment of provisional adminis- trators to 'Aryanize' the enterprise, that is, to sell it to non-Jews and liquidate its assets at very low prices. These provisions were made more severe by the Edict of 26, April 1941 which deprived the beneficiaries of the income from the sale or liquidation of the enterprise ('only abso- lutely indispensable subsidies' were paid), and then by the Edict of 28 May 1941 which forbade Jews from negotiating the fate of their assets or from trying to protect their property by sale or voluntary transfer instead of Aryanization.

The Vichy Law of 22, July 1941 allowed the seizure of 'enterprises, goods and securities belonging to the Jews', 'with a view to eliminating all Jewish influence in the national economy'. This measure was aimed at all the Jews, and they were removed from management of their affairs and were replaced by provisional administrators. Art collections and bank accounts were confiscated. The law also affected the very numerous small craftsmen and businessmen, who found themselves destitute from one day to the next. These sums of money and the sale of these proper- ties were usually paid into special accounts in a public establishment: the Deposit and Consignment Office. The shares were delivered to the Lands Administration. Jewels and precious objects confiscated from the arrested jews were either stolen or deposited in the Bank of France.

Until June–July 1941, the French government applied the German edicts regarding confiscation but did not take the initiative of promoting the 'Aryanization'. It endeavoured to conserve a certain control through the Service de Contrôle des Administrateurs Provisoires (SCAP), created on 9 December 1940 for the occupied zone, and by ensuring that the administrators be appointed by the prefects. Initially technocrats man- aged this service. However, when Darquier de Pellepoix took charge and

Box 2
German Edicts in the Occupied Zone

27 September 1940: 'Are recognized as Jewish those belonging or who belonged to the Jewish religion or who have more than two...Jewish grandparents. Are considered as Jewish the grandparents who belong or belonged to the Jewish religion. The Jews who have fled from the occupied zone are prohibited from returning there.' Every Jew 'must appear, until 20 October 1940, before the sub-prefect of the *arrondissement* where he is domiciled...in order to be entered in a special register.'

'Any business whose owner or holder is Jewish will be designated as "Jewish Enterprises" by a special sign drawn up in German and in French.'

18 October 1940: The law defines the 'economic enterprise' and what enterprise should be considered as a 'Jewish enterprise'.

28 May 1941: Jewish capital cannot circulate without special authorization.

28 September 1941: The income of the enterprises, of the capital or shares held by Jews, must be deposited in the name of the beneficiaries at the Deposit and Consignment Office which may transfer 10 percent to the *Commissaire général aux affaires juives*. 'The absolutely indispensable amounts can then be paid to the beneficiaries.'

the CGQJ was created, undesirables took over. Gradually the French government came to realize that the French economy was in the process of losing its national assets. The law of 22 July 1941 expresses this concern and corresponds to the desires of the occupying power that required a French legal infrastructure in order to implement its edicts.

On 17 December 1941, the Germans demanded a fine of 1 billion francs from the French Jews, and this amount was taken from the Aryanization income deposited in the Deposit and Consignment Office.

According to historian Joseph Billig, 42,227 enterprises were controlled by a provisional administrator in April 1944, 9680 having been Aryanized. Of these 76 per cent were liquidated at a very low price (less than 200,000 francs). The despoiled economic sectors were textiles, leather and furs, then property, banking and insurance. Who benefited from the spoliation? The very fact that a law existed officially meant that the beneficiaries were not acting illegally. However, many indulged in veritable looting for their own profit. There were about 10,000 to 20,000 provisional administrators who sometimes accrued responsibility for several dozen enterprises. Some helped the former Jewish owners, serving as front men; most were motivated by the lure of profit or by the interests of financial groups or Germans whom they served by buying for them, and at low prices, the enterprises that were being liquidated. However, there were also responsible institutions such as the economic ministries, the Ministry of Production and the Ministry of Finance, and professional committees which took advantage of the spoliation to settle old resentments of competitors. The Deposit and Consignment Office played a major role in the management of the spoliation. Not to be forgotten in all these responsibilities are the legal structures (commercial courts and the Council of State) which gave these spoliations a judicial legality and which designed and supported the official and bureaucratic procedures for stripping Jewish properties. What happened to the funds seized and the balance of the one billion franc fine paid to the CGQJ? The Deposit and Consignment Office itself took from these funds an operating credit (500 million francs before the end of the war). Banks also took amounts from these funds belonging to the Jews. What happened to this money if it was not handed over to the Germans in its entirety?

A special mention should be made of works of art looted and sent to Germany for Nazi dignitaries or for the future 'Museum of the Vanished Race' planned by Albert Rosenberg, to be constructed once the Jewish people were totally annihilated (and to contain 10,000 paintings, 500 sculptures, 2000 items of furniture, etc.).

The problem of the despoiled art works

According to an investigative report of 7 December 1995, as demanded by the third Revenue Court Chamber, it was established that 61,000 works of arts were seized by the Nazis during the war (in particular from Jews). Of these 46,000 were restored to their owners and 1955 were still held by the national museums. These works were stolen or purchased, mostly from Jewish collectors, many of whom were swallowed up by the inferno.

After the war, in 1949, the recovered works were entrusted to the National Recovery Nuseums (MNR – Musées nationaux de la récupération) for return to their legitimate owners. An exhibition was held at Compiègne, to ensure the publicity required for this step. However, as the commission noted, 'unfortunately no catalogue was published, and this considerably limited the reach of the publicity'. Most of the works were thus dispersed in the museums of Paris and the provinces. After 1954, no further publicity was given to this matter. The announced inventory was never published. The museum curators were advised to be discreet and no efforts were made to actively trace the owners.

After an inquiry at the museums (all of which replied except for the Cluny Museum), the number of such art works and objects was as follows (according to *Le Monde* of 28 January 1997): 1878 items at the Louvre Museum, 969 paintings, 619 works of art, 685 sculptures, 163 drawings, 33 antiques and 85 very important paintings now at the Orsay Museum (Courbet, Puvis de Chavannes, Monet, Sisley, Revon, Gauguin, Rodin, Mailleul). Among others, the Orsay Museum has Courbet's famous painting *The Cliffs of Etretat after the Storm*. A number of items could not be identified in certain museums. In October 1992, the Minister of Justice declared that the museums are only provisional holders of these works, which cannot be integrated in their collections, and they must restore them to their legitimate owners where these are known (even though it is considered in certain milieux that they are now ownerless). This is also the position of Françoise Cachin, director of the French museums.

III Restitution and the fate of despoiled property

A large part of the Jewish assets remained in the state's possession after the war. Seventy-six-thousand Jews had died in deportation and many were too young to make any claim whatsoever.

The legal framework of restitution

Between 1941 and 1942, the Resistance expressed its opposition to the looting on several occasions. In 1944, the provisional government of the French Republic recognized, from Algiers, the principle of restitution of the property despoiled by the Vichy regime. An edict issued on 21 April 1945 defined the buyers of Jewish property as being 'of bad faith' unless they had intervened at the request of the government (administrative immunity being obligatory!) or the Jewish owner. The edict of 9 August 1944, which consecrated the restoration of Republican law, established the invalidity of the measures taken subsequent to the end of the last Republican government (on 16 June 1940). On 16 October 1944, the French authorities were enjoined to restore certain impounded property.

The two edicts of 14 November 1944 authorized the despoiled Jews to recover the property which had not been sold and to demand their apartments. The administrators were obliged to return this property or to make themselves known to the Ministry of Finance. This edict was a disappointment for the Jewish organizations in that it authorized disaster victims – evacuees, or refugees, dependants of mobilized soldiers, war prisoners, political deportees or internees in forced labour camps – to keep the apartments taken from the Jews. The edict of 11 April 1945 ordered the restitution of the impounded property which had been the object of a forced sale and annulled the acts carried out without the consent of the interested party. The Ministry of Finance was enjoined to investigate the despoilment dossiers through the Service of Restitution of Property of the Victims of the Spoliation Laws and Measures.

Steps taken by Jewish institutions after the war

From 1943 onwards, Jewish institutions in the Resistance manifested concern about spoliation and included this issue in the constituent charter of the CRIF in 1944. From the end of the war, the Contemporary Jewish Documentation Centre (CDJC), directed by Isaac Schneershon, tried to establish a 'spoliation file' from the official documents of Vichy. In April 1946, the government authorized Schneershon to examine the archives of the Commissariat Général aux Questions Juives, and this enabled him to draw up a file of 65,000 despoiled Jewish properties, to trace the path of property ownership and the characteristics of their original Jewish owners. The CDJC thus drew up a directory of despoiled properties and a directory of provisional administrators (over 7000 names).

On 2 June 1947, the head of the Restitution Service sought the aid of the CDJC, and the latter sent a team of researchers to carry out fresh inquiries in the archives of the Commissariat Général aux Questions Juives. A list of 27,000 unclaimed or assumed to be unclaimed properties was drawn up. Many properties were thus still in the hands of the provisional administrators. In 1948, the inquiries came to a stop when the activities of the Restitution Service were suspended.

The CDJC called for the Jewish community to appoint an institution to be responsible for confiscated properties so that the future income would go to communal reconstruction. The CRIF and the *Consistoire* (the umbrella organization for religions affairs) were opposed for legal reasons and also out of fear that the Jewish community would stand out too much in the nation. When the Jews reached an agreement on the selection of a responsible official, Justin Godard, the government failed to agree.

In 1951 the CDJC, supported by the Alliance Israélite Universelle and the CRIF, was authorized to check the forementioned 27,000 files of confiscated property and was again given access to the archives. However, it was able to control only 10,000 files. Of the 2500 buildings not claimed in 1947, 850 remained unclaimed (out of the 143 remaining in Paris, the CDJC asserted after an investigation that 80 had been recovered, while the Deposit and Consignment Office held over 23 million francs from the transfer of the sold buildings. As regards the enterprises and small businesses, the CDJC examined 13,000 files but was unable to identify the unclaimed accounts, since the interested parties did not have to apply to the Restitution Service in order to reopen blocked current accounts after the Liberation. When the CDJC attempted to conduct an inquiry in the banks in 1952, the Ministry of Finance objected by maintaining that this was impossible due to banking confidentiality.

In 1953, a former internee of Drancy brought to the CDJC 18,000 stumps of search/receipt books from Drancy, which proved that money confiscated was from the internees in this camp. The CDJC attempted to take further steps to allow the despoiled Jews and the beneficiaries to recover these amounts, but the Ministry of Finance granted an extension of only three months. Despite the CDJC's activism, the spoliation dossier was gradually abandoned by the state and by the Jewish community. Activism was thenceforth directed towards compensations negotiated nationally and internationally with the Claims Conference.

IV The Matteoli Commission

In July 1995, immediately prior to the ceremony commemorating the Vélodrome d'Hiver round-up, Serge Klarsfeld, the Nazi hunter and Holocaust researcher, gave an account of a 1944 report by Maurice Kiffer, an employee of the Police Prefecture and 'liquidator' of Drancy's accounts, which pointed out that 12 million francs and a large chest of items confiscated from the internees had been deposited in the Deposit and Consignment Office. This information was prominently treated by the press and led premier Alain Juppé's government to appoint a commission of inquiry. Headed by Jean Matteoli, chairman of the Economic and Social Committee and himself a deported Resistance fighter, the commission was asked to study the question of the spoliation 'of the persons considered Jewish by the occupying forces or the Vichy authorities'. In January 1998 his commission delivered a preliminary report to Prime Minister Lionel Jospin.[1] What emerges from this inquiry?

Firstly, Matteoli acknowledged the absence of any inquiry into this question other than the work by Joseph Billig[2] and the dispersion and the vast size of the archives; the Commissariat Général aux Questions Juives alone has 62,460 files of enterprises or buildings. An inventory was made of this source, to be indexed and published in the near future. A guide of available sources and the collection of texts relative to the reparation of the spoliations will also be published by the Commission. In order to progress with study of the sources, the Commission decided to concentrate above all on the Aryanization of the properties, the billion franc fine, the thefts in the camps and the looting of the art works.

What was most easily tackled was the billion franc fine. The Commission reconstructed the way this sum was collected and paid in four instalments in the course of 1942. At the time of the liberation, the Deposit and Consignment Office restored certain shares which had served for the payment of the fine and which were still in its possession. A report of the entire operation was released in February 1999.

On the other hand, the Aryanization study is more complex. Realizing the impossibility of analysing the 62,460 dossiers, the Commission chose a representative sample. It emerges that the dossiers concern about 90,000 persons of whom the enterprises of 23,000 were liquidated or sold. It is not yet possible to quantify the properties despoiled.

In the case of the thefts carried out at Drancy, information on which led to the creation of the Commission, considerable progress has been made. All the camp accounts for the period August 1941 to July 1943, before the camp administration was taken over by the Nazis, have been conserved in the Police Prefecture archives. These accounts do not include the thefts of Jewish property by the inspectors, indicated officially by the person in charge of the deposits. At the end of a bureaucratic process, the amounts from the liquidation of Jewish property were paid into the Deposit and Consignment Office, 90 percent into an account opened in the name of the internee and 10 percent into an account opened in the name of the Commissariat Général aux Questions Juives. Thus an inventory was taken of 7000 dossiers of individual deposits from June 1942 to August 1944. Only 200 deposits were refunded by the Deposit and Consignment Office to escaped internees or their beneficiaries after the war. According to its regulations, the Deposit and Consignment Office is bound to pay to the state the consignments and deposits which it holds and which are not reclaimed within thirty years of their deposit. When the amounts concerned do not exceed 1000 francs, no official publication reports this (publication in the Official Gazette). In 1958 the French franc was devalued (1000 francs of 1940 were now worth 10 francs). Thus 7192 confiscated deposits, together with interest, were paid in the 1970s to the Public Revenue Department under the greatest official silence. Yet these amounts concern only the period until July 1943, when Drancy became a concentration camp. On 8 December 1947 the safe of these deposits, located in the Bank of France, was officially opened. The inventory drawn up at this time has 116 pages. On the basis of this inventory, two case files were lodged with the Police Prefecture, containing the information on the identity of the person concerned, the date of his deportation, the case file number, and what became of the individual after the war. Certain records have no name. The Commission was unable to determine whether certain objects were returned, but it is clear that other objects were sold although the sum of these sales is unknown until the present day.

In short, the *Matteoli Commission* has done the groundwork for the clarification of the history of the spoliation and the restitution.

Appendix: Findings of the Matteoli Commission

(Major points from the second interim report, February 1999)

- $2.9 million taken from deportees to Nazi death camps were never claimed and remained in a government bank.

- At least two-thirds of the roughly $1 billion of Jewish property that was seized in France was reclaimed after the war.

- The thousands of seized paintings and other art works in French museums and French embassies and government buildings should be assembled and publicly exhibited, in order to let rightful owners and heirs to make claims.

- French financial institutions (particularly banks) were over-enthusiastic in implementing anti-Jewish decrees of confiscation, even before requested to do so by the Germans under the Vichy laws.

- The 1 billion franc fine which was imposed on French Jews by the occupation forces reflected the failure of antisemitic stereotypes and expectations on Jewish wealth.

- Serge Klarsfeld, a member of the Matteoli Commission, said in a separate opinion that the cost of professional limitations resulting from the Vichy anti-Jewish discriminatory laws amounts to 5 billion francs at the current rate.

Notes

1 *Study Mission on the Spoliation of French Jewry, Stage Report*, April–December 1997, 31 December 1997; this can be consulted on the internet: /http://www/ladocfrancaise.gouv.Fr.
2 *Le Commissariat Général aux questions juives, 1941–1944*, 3 vols (Paris: Editions du Centre, 1955–60).

11
Quiet Collusion: Sweden's Financial Links to Nazi Germany

Sven Fredrik Hedin and Göran Elgemyr

How much stolen gold did the Swedish Central Bank accept from Nazi Germany? Sweden's trade policy dealings with Nazi Germany have been written into the history books, together with the political concessions. The Swedish Central Bank's gold transactions with the Third Reich, however, have scarcely been touched upon by Swedish historians. During the postwar decade, Sweden was forced to hand back 13,000 kilograms of gold bullion to Belgium and The Netherlands. But, according to newly discovered documents, well before the end of the war the Central Bank judged that 20,000 kilograms of gold purchased from the Nazis could be 'contaminated'. The key question is whether the Central Bank acted in good faith during the war – or was it aware that it was buying looted gold?

This study focuses on one aspect of Sweden's response to war and genocide which indicates a shameful willingness to avoid moral responsibilities when material benefits can be reaped. It is a chapter of Swedish history which must be told, but its shadows should not cause one to forget other Swedish responses from which we derive moral pride: the rescue of the Danish Jewish community and the efforts of the indefatigable diplomat Raoul Wallenberg are episodes which should be recalled in this context.

To buy or not to buy?

Before the war, neither Sweden nor Switzerland had dealt in German gold. Because of the Allied blockades, both countries became dependent on imports from Germany, and Germany became even more dependent on supplies from the neutral countries. This included products of vital importance for the war effort, such as tungsten, chromium, manganese, crude oil, iron ore, ball-bearings, precision instruments and industrial diamonds. Of thirty-four kinds of raw materials essential for modern warfare, Germany was entirely self-sufficient in only four, and totally dependent on outside supplies for twenty-three. This alone shows what a crucial role the gold played for the Third Reich: bullion became the means of payment when the clearing balance went into the red. It was also necessary for the Germans to sell gold to gain access to convertible currencies. Sweden and Switzerland represented golden points of access for Nazi Germany. Both countries bought much more gold than was needed to level out the balance of payments.

When the original transactions were facilitated, what did the Swedish officials know of the origins of this gold? A document in the Central Bank archives, a memo dated 19 February 1943 from Ivar Rooth, the bank's governor at the time, provides an answer to this question. It was typed in five copies and stamped 'secret'. A worried Rooth recorded a conversation he had had with trade minister Herman Eriksson about the gold deals:

> At the beginning of February, I notified the trade minister of the following. In view of the declaration from the British and other Allied governments that claims may be forthcoming on property deriving from the occupied countries, the Central Bank faced the risk that gold it had bought or might buy in the future from the Reichsbank could be placed in this category. As it seemed likely that the Reichsbank, having sold gold to the Central Bank for a total of SEK 70 million under a previous agreement, would apply to sell further quantities, the risk faced by the Central Bank was likely to grow.
>
> I therefore asked whether the issue of possible further gold transaction should be raised either by myself in a letter to Puhl [Emil Puhl, deputy-governor of the Reichsbank]...the reason being that I wanted to bring the British declaration to Puhl's attention and to request – in order to avoid any unpleasantness or losses for the Central Bank – that the Reichsbank should in confidence declare its readiness to supply only such gold as did not fall into the category described in the British declaration.[1]

Ivar Rooth had been seized with misgivings. What if it was looted gold that the Central Bank had purchased or would be purchasing? The Central Bank had clearly not posed this question before, and the time had now come to seek guarantees before buying further consignments.

Otherwise, the Central Bank might incur losses. Trade minister Eriksson provided Rooth with a reply that the bank should not ask for any formal assurances – but the minister added that there was 'nothing to prevent [Rooth] from raising it in passing during a personal conversation with Puhl'. Thus, the Swedish coalition government urged the Central Bank to continue buying what might be stolen property.

Hardly had the Allied warnings been filed away when the German Reichsbank once again sought to sell gold to the Swedes. This time for SEK 35 million. This caused Rooth to raise the matter once again, both with Eriksson and with finance minister Ernst Wigforss. Neither the trade minister nor the coalition government, it turned out, had had any change of heart:

> I pointed out that a matter of this nature was not something I alone could take responsibility for and said I would bring it before a meeting of the [Central Bank] executive board. The trade minister then authorized me to record in the minutes of the meeting that the government wished the Central Bank to agree to the Reichsbank request for further gold transactions but that the Central Bank should not make this conditional on a declaration from the Reichsbank regarding the nature of the affair.

Once again, the tenor of the government's directive is that the bank should not ask whether the gold is stolen, but should keep buying. The Central Bank executive board, too, was worried about the possibility of buying stolen property when Rooth brought the matter to its attention. One of those present commented that the government had 'dismissed the risks rather too hastily'. At the same time, the board members expressed the hope that the government would either give them a written explanation of its position or send a representative to a board meeting who would read into the minutes the government's view of the matter. The meeting decided to call on His Majesty the King to appoint a representative who could negotiate with the bank's executive board.

Rooth's memo reveals a number of peculiar circumstances. He claims that the matter was brought before the executive board on 18 February 1943. When we checked the minutes of that meeting, we found no record of the matter at all, either in the normal records (for routine matters) or the special records (for secret matters). This was clearly a very sensitive issue. Not even the board's decision to take the unusual step of calling on the Swedish monarch to appoint someone to 'negotiate' with the members has been included in the minutes of the meeting. Neither is there any mention of the Allies' warnings. There is, however, a minute referring to the board's approval of gold transactions with the Reichsbank: the Central Bank could not 'to any reasonable extent' refuse to take delivery of gold as the German gold sales were to be used to regulate the clearing balance between the two countries.

Another document shows that the executive bankers were more perturbed than Rooth's memo indicated. Rooth's archives contained notes from an 18 February 1943 executive meeting (attended by, amongst others, Ivar Andersson MP and chief editor of the *Svenska Dagbladet*, J. E. Bjornsson, MP, Petrus Gränebo MP, Dag Hammarskjöld, chairman and state secretary in the finance ministry, and Rooth). The committee was perturbed by the government's dismissiveness, worried about how to identify recast gold, but agreed that the appropriate policy should be to continue the purchases if an assurance as to the commodity's bona fide status was furnished.

Only a few days after this meeting was held, Rooth and the executive board were able to relax. Gunnar Hägglöf of the foreign ministry disclosed that during Sweden's trade negotiations with Germany he had met Emil Puhl, who had given him assurances that all the gold Germany had sold to the Central Bank had its origins in the prewar period. A memo from Hägglöf to this effect was filed, dated 22 February 1943. Both Rooth and Hammarskjöld were to refer to it time and again to justify Sweden's gold dealings. The strategically important Hägglöf assurance assumed an intriguing character when we discovered that the intervention with Puhl had involved the banker and industrialist Jacob Wallenberg. He was part of a trade policy delegation negotiating with Germany. In a memo dated 16 May 1946, Rooth wrote:

> With Hägglöf's approval, Wallenberg called on Puhl on 18 February 1943 and requested that no gold bullion from occupied territories should be included in the consignments. Puhl was grateful that this had been conveyed to him in person rather than through official channels. If the latter course had been chosen, it would not have been possible to solve the problem. Puhl expressed his readiness to ensure that gold from occupied countries would not be included in future deliveries to Sweden.

This was a cryptic exchange. Puhl probably felt that a direct petition from the Swedish Central Bank or via diplomatic channels would be likely to complicate matters. A request by Hägglöf would doubtless have been considered an official one. According to another memo, it was

Puhl's deputy that dissuadel the bank executive board from demanding a special meeting with a Swedish government representative.

Thus, there was a certain inclination among the Swedes to buy gold, even if they had become more cautious with time. Despite this wariness, Emil Puhl was invited to Stockholm (incidentally, in 1941 he had been made a Knight Commander First Class of the Royal Order of the Polar Star, a prestigious Swedish decoration). Puhl's visit took place a couple of weeks after D-Day, by which time it was clear that Germany would lose the war. Nevertheless, Puhl was given a magnificent reception. Meetings were arranged with ministers, top public finance officials, the heads of the leading commercial banks, Enskilda Banken, Skandinaviska Banken and Handelsbanken.

Could it have been the imminent German collapse that prompted the invitation? Were the government, the Central Bank and the commercial banks anxious to ensure that Puhl would protect Swedish financial interests in – or complicity with – Germany? This can only be a matter for conjecture. One thing is certain: the visit cannot have escaped the attention of Allied intelligence.

What could the Swedes have known indirectly?

In 1946, Rooth was to declare to the Swiss National Bank that Puhl had provided an assurance that looted gold had never been sent to Sweden. Puhl did not, however, appear to have given assurances about future consignments which, as it transpired, were to involve large quantities – altogether about 10,000 kilograms during the remainder of 1943. The final consignment was acquired at the beginning of 1944, by which time the Swedish Central Bank had bought a total of 34,564 kilograms since the trading began in 1939. When the Germans surrendered in May 1945, the Swedish Central Bank owned 22,466 kilograms of gold, deposited at the Swiss National Bank in Bern.

It was not until March 1944 that the Central Bank executive finally decided not to take delivery of any more gold from the Reichsbank. It could no longer be viewed as 'internationally saleable'. The reason was that the Allies had issued a fresh warning about the gold. Could the Central Bank have known – from indirect sources – that Germany's gold assets were largely looted?

Rooth's network of contacts might give us a clue. He had excellent channels of information so as to be able to keep an eye on other countries' gold holdings and on major gold deals on the European continent. As Swedish Central Bank governor, he was on the board of the Bank for International Settlements (BIS) in Basle. This bank, which was supposed to promote cooperation between the various states' central banks and also facilitate international payments, continued its operations throughout the war years. The BIS board of directors was drawn from countries on different sides of the war and their representatives in fact continued to work together throughout the war years. The senior economist at the BIS was a Swede, Per Jacobsson, with whom Rooth maintained a regular correspondence (the Eizenstat Report notes that Jacobsson was actively informing the Allies of the activities of Emil Puhl![2]). Rooth also had excellent relations with the Swiss National Bank, which traded extensively in gold with Nazi Germany. This broad network of contacts must have given Rooth an insight into the Germans' gold dealings, which were on a scale that far exceeded the country's holdings of prewar gold. The alarm bells should have rung. Rooth knew at first hand that Germany had seized gold from the reserves of Austria and Czechoslovakia, Belgium, France and other countries. Much of it was remoulded in Berlin into new ingots that were given false prewar stamps and certificates of authenticity.

A study of Swedish links to German industry and to the Nazi regime's efforts to sell a variety of valuable looted items was produced by Dutch historians Gerard Aalders and Cees Wiebes. In *The Art of Cloaking Ownership: the secret collaboration and protection of the German war industry by the neutrals: the case of Sweden,*[3] an array of dealings with Germany are documented, many of which centre on the Wallenberg family. A considerable number of Swedish business people were willing to help Germany liquidate the valuables it had stolen from the governments and citizens of occupied countries. The fencing network spread broadly throughout Swedish business and financial circles: one did not need to be particularly well connected or influential to be aware of the number of transactions which were cloaked or of the looted property that was being sold off. It is difficult to believe that top bankers and public finance officials could have been oblivious to these activities. It is no less difficult to believe that these officials would not have recognized their own complicity, even it if was not documented.

An internal move, aimed at investigating the origin of the gold that was taken by the Central Bank in 1944, suggests cold feet. How much of the gold could be classed as stolen – or 'contaminated', as they preferred to call it. An estimate was made. Over 14,000 kilograms were considered 'free of risk', while 20,000 kilograms were considered 'at maximum risk'. At the time this was worth about SEK 95 million. In order to assess the 'risks' as early as the beginning of 1944, the Central Bank must have been very well informed about the Reichsbank's peculiar gold transactions. A reasonable conclusion is that in 1943 the Swedish Central Bank already knew or suspected that a share of the gold could have been stolen from other countries' central banks.

A report from Switzerland suggests that even while the gold trading was in progress, the Swedish Central Bank had something to hide. The Swiss foreign ministry reported to its Washington delegation in May 1944 that the Swiss National Bank (SNB) in Bern had equipped German gold ingots with Swedish identity markings – outright falsification. Despite a thorough scrutiny of the national and central bank archives in Bern, we have been unable to find clear confirmation of this, only certain indications suggesting it to be true.

In 1946, the Western Allies began to apply pressure on the neutral states to force them to account for having dealt in Hitler's looted gold. Switzerland was the first, then it was Sweden's turn. In the negotiation with the Swiss, it emerged that Emil Puhl had told his interrogators that the Swiss National Bank knew that not all the gold it had taken delivery of was German prewar property. This caused Ivar Rooth to dispatch the following instructions to his staff: 'NB – R. wants everything about Puhl's promise to be struck from the memo as the Swiss letter shows that the promise was not kept'.

A parallel example: the Swiss

It is interesting to note that the Swedish and Swiss central banks reacted in almost the same way to the first warning from official Allied quarters in January 1943. As previously mentioned, Ivar Rooth raised these concerns with the Swedish coalition government in 1943. For its part, the Swiss National Bank initially contented itself with noting that the Swedish Central Bank, according to Rooth, planned to continue buying gold from Germany. But in the autumn of 1943, the Swiss National Bank was beginning to get cold feet. Governor of the Swiss National Bank, Ernst Weber, who realized that the gold transactions could have political implications, wrote a letter to the Swiss Minister of Finance, Ernst Wetter. Weber carefully detailed the warnings and the guidelines that the Swiss National Bank had followed. A refusal to buy gold, he wrote, could be interpreted as a breach of neutrality.

Bearing in mind the fact that most of Europe had been occupied by Germany, Weber's line of argument makes remarkable reading. He maintained that the Swiss National Bank would have to assume that gold offered by any central bank must be bona fide. This applied even where it was reasonable to assume that the gold in part came from occupied countries. Weber did suggest one precaution, however: as far as possible, future procedure should involve direct delivery of gold from Germany to the payee. This was not to imply, however, that the SNB would not continue buying gold from Berlin in the future. Weber failed to inform his finance minister that Rooth, a month earlier, had begun to grow wary. In a letter to Weber, Rooth had said that he was not sure how the Swedish Central Bank's gold policy would develop. 'Personally, I recommend the utmost caution', wrote Rooth.

Weber offered no moral considerations but referred to the fact that the Swedish Central Bank, too, intended to buy gold from the Reichsbank and had recently taken delivery of a consignment in Bern. The Swiss Federal Council accepted the Swiss National Bank's policy without reservation, although it did advise a degree of restraint. Thus the governments of both Sweden and Switzerland took the same approach. They completely ignored the Allies' warnings and the claims that the gold might be stolen.

The reactions of both the Swiss National Bank and the Swedish Central Bank to the Allied warnings show that they were aware that the gold might have been stolen. Nevertheless, all the banks did was ask Puhl if they had, by chance, been sent gold that was not prewar bullion. The banks demanded no guarantees that future consignments would be legitimate. Source material from that time shows clearly and unequivocally that their repeated declarations that they bought the gold in good faith do not hold water. On the contrary, the hunt for profit triumphed over morals. Sweden and Switzerland went hand in hand.

Examination of the archives reveals that much that is related to the Swedish Central Bank's monetary gold has never been documented on paper. Otherwise, the archives have been 'tidied up'. Thus we have been unable to find any explanation for the 'Gentleman's Agreement of 4 February 1944', to which the Swedish Central Bank sometimes refers in its correspondence with the Reichsbank at the time. Another important piece of the puzzle is also missing. The BIS archives are hermetically sealed. The bank has been accused of considerable acquiescence towards the Germans both during and after the Second World War. Its purchase of Belgian gold was rapidly repaid. But Ernst Weber refused to put his name to the bank's decision – that the gold had been bought in good faith!

Postwar post-mortem: the truth begins to emerge

The assurances to which the Swedish bankers had referred in support of their claim came from Emil Puhl. He is said to have told them that the gold was prewar German property and nothing else. After the war it emerged that this was a barefaced lie. Puhl told the American authorities that the Swiss National Bank had indeed been aware that not all the gold it bought had come from prewar sources. Moreover, at the Nuremberg Trials, Puhl admitted that the Reichsbank had accepted gold from the extermination camps – gold teeth, wedding rings, spectacle rims, jewellery and so forth. This gold had then been recast as ingots.

The central banks in the neutral countries cannot be expected to have known about the gold from the concentration camps, although it cannot be said with certitude that they did not. This also applies to Portugal and Spain. But the gullibility of which they claim to have been guilty can also be viewed in the light of what the central bank governors knew about Puhl and the Reichsbank's gold stocks.

Emil Puhl was a member of the Nazi Party, a loyal tool of the regime. An event that occurred in 1939 should have made Ivar Rooth and Ernst Weber more cautious. In that year, Hitler fired Hjalmar Schacht, who had had the temerity to point out that the enormous rearmament effort was placing a great burden on the national economy. Five of the bank's executive board members were fired at the same time. Of the two who were retained, Puhl was one. In practice, he became the leading official at the bank and thereby Hitler's financial henchman.

Ivar Rooth met Puhl on his regular visits to Switzerland – as well as in Berlin – and the two became good friends. After the capitulation, Rooth saw to it that the Puhl family was not left wanting when the German banker himself was in custody. When Puhl was in prison, he requested personal testimonials from both the Swedish envoy in Berlin, Arvid Richert, and from Ivar Rooth. Richert provided him with a testimonial, but Rooth hesitated. In a personal letter to Puhl dated July 1947, however, he writes of the German's criticism of Hitler and the Nazi party during the war. In December 1947, Rooth was given permission by the foreign ministry to make a personal statement on behalf of Puhl. As yet, this document has not been brought to light. Emil Puhl was sentenced in the aftermath of the Nuremberg trials, in what were known as the Wilhelmstrasse proceedings, to five years in jail for crimes against humanity. The court cited the fact that he had known the Reichsbank had taken over and recast gold from the concentration camps. He was conditionally released after six months and is said to have been employed thereafter at the Dresdener Bank in Hamburg.

The strange thing, bearing in mind the claim of ignorance and gullibility, is that neither Rooth nor Weber – nor the members of their executive boards – felt deceived by Emil Puhl. After the war, the Swiss National Bank and the Swedish Central Bank discussed the gold transactions in general and Puhl in particular. This was presumably to enable them to present similar stories to the Allies, who had pledged to investigate things and bring the guilty to account. In 1946, the Swiss National Bank interviewed Rooth and he defended all of the bank's decisions – and his faith in Puhl's assurances. In doing so, Rooth did not mention that in 1943 he had been concerned about buying stolen gold, nor that he had taken the precaution of contacting the Swedish coalition government because of this. Moreover, he failed to inform the Swiss National Bank that at the beginning of 1944 his bank had calculated how much gold was 'at maximum risk'. It was clearly important for Rooth to give the impression that the Swedish Central Bank had acted in good faith.

Why was there so much Swedish interest in the imprisoned Puhl a couple of years after the capitulation when the Holocaust had long been revealed and documented? Was the intention to accommodate Puhl so that he would not let slip any strange and unfavourable information about Swedish financial dealings with Germany? The Swedish commission has quite a few riddles to solve.

Repayments

On the Allied side, the negotiations in Washington for the return of the looted gold were conducted by the Tripartite Commission on the Restitution of Monetary Gold. Within this commission, Britain, France and the US also acted on behalf of the other Allied countries. Switzerland refused to the very last to accept that it had done anything wrong, but finally agreed to award 'symbolic damages' of 250 million Swiss francs, which was only a small part of what the Allies had demanded.

Compared with the Swiss, the Swedish government was relatively accommodating in negotiations about identifying looted gold. After six weeks of tough negotiations, during which the commission presented overwhelming evidence, Sweden was forced to return 7152 kilograms of gold to the Belgian national bank. Among the evidence were notes kept with typical thoroughness by the German authorities detailing the origins of the gold that was melted down, recast and given prewar insignia. The Dutch central bank also presented claims to Sweden in 1946, but these were rejected. The Dutch persisted, however, and by 1954 had scraped together enough evidence to have Sweden recalled to the negotiating table in Washington.

In Berlin, documents had been found clearly showing that Germany had seized about 32,000 kilograms of Dutch gold florins. These had been recast as gold ingots and had naturally been stamped as prewar bullion. The end result was that Sweden had to repay 6000 kilogram of gold to the Netherlands, worth SEK 35 million at the time and almost 500 million today.

Finally, the question has to be asked whether Sweden has really paid its debt in full? Compromises were reached with Sweden and Switzerland on the return of the gold loot, as outlined in the first Eizenstat Report (pages 121–7). Yet a remarkable discrepancy remains. Sweden has paid back just over 13,000 kilograms of gold. But the quantity of gold 'at maximum risk', according to the Swedish Central Bank in 1944, was over 20,000 kilograms. Because of the masked nature of related transactions, identification could be extremely difficult. Who today can lay claim to the 7000 kilogram difference?

Postscript: the 1996 Swedish Commission

In late 1996, the Secretary-General of the World Jewish Congress, Israel Singer, visited Stockholm to meet with Swedish Foreign Minister Lena Hjelm-Wallén. He asked her to appoint a state commission to look into the fate of Jewish assets that may have been deposited in Sweden during the war, and had since been forgotten. In principle, the foreign minister accepted the proposal, but she thought that a working group under the guidance of the chief legal adviser of her ministry, with the participation of other ministries, government agencies, the Bankers' Association and the Jewish community, would fulfil the same purpose. The group started its work quickly, but was soon overtaken by events.

The first article on Sweden and the Nazi gold, which was written by the present authors, was published in *Dagens Nyheter* on 21 January 1997. The subject had not been touched upon by any professional Swedish historian and consequently it suddenly became newsworthy. The media coverage was considerable. In leading articles some newspapers asked for the immediate establishment of a state commission. It took only three days for the prime minister to announce that such a commission would be appointed, to be called the 'Commission on Jewish Assets in Sweden at the Time of the Second World War'.

The tasks of the Commission include the investigation of the fate of Jewish property in Sweden and of Jewish property from other parts of Europe that may have come into Swedish hands. The Riksbank's gold acquisitions were an area for particular attention, as were previous instances of communal restitution – such as the 1960s decision by the Swedish Bankers' Association to donate money to the Red Cross, following an internal audit addressing precisely these questions.

The Commission's chairperson is a former cabinet minister and retired county governor, Rolf Wirtén. He is assisted by six full members, of which two have been selected by the Jewish community in Stockholm, twelve advisers and two experts. All in all, a wide array of inputs: historians, lawyers, judges, accountants, diplomats, economists, bankers, civil servants.

Media reports in late 1997 suggested how broad the investigations may have become. Searches for documents and information volunteered by members of the public revealed that: some Swedish companies purged Jews from their ranks of employees to curry favour with German clients; certain commodities traders agreed to stop trading with Allied countries to guarantee links with Nazi Germany; and significant diamond smuggling was facilitated by Swedish purchasers.

The Commission's interim report on one part of its work, 'The Nazi Gold and the Swedish Riksbank', released in mid 1998, agreed that the Reichsbank had disguised the origin of the gold it was selling, part of which was originally the property of the Nazi regime's victims. A total of 37.4 tons of gold was received by the Swedish National Bank from the Reichsbank; most transactions took place in Switzerland and most of the gold remained in Bern. Of this, some 20.9 tons had been stolen by Germany from the central banks of Belgium and the Netherlands, leaving 16.4 tons to be accounted for. The Commission did not find evidence that some of this gold may have been non-monetary gold – but explicitly did not exclude the possibility, because available information is too fragmentary.

The Commission's conclusions about the implications of these gold transactions, in light of the contemporaneous awareness of the economic and material liquidation of European Jews, are critical of the bankers' and politicians' choice to look away from the moral implications of purchasing gold from Germany – and the expedient use of the cover of neutrality to materially benefit from the war for as long as possible: 'Seen through present-day eyes, however, there is reason to query whether the special gold agreement attached to the trade agreement was really necessary for the entire duration of the war.' The commission concluded that because of the awareness that gold being traded was very likely to have originated from theft from monetary and non-monetary sources, 'Sweden is implicated in the history of that gold.' The Commission affirmed that Swedish officials were aware of the economic persecution of the Jews from the 1930s onwards, and that 'from 1942 it was known in Sweden that the plan for the Holocaust had been put into effect'. Regarding gold transactions in particular, the Commission agrees with the narrative described in this study:

> By the beginning of 1941 at the latest, it was clear to the Swedish policy-makers that the Reichsbank was using central bank gold from occupied countries for Nazi Germany's international trade and that gold of this kind was not fully viable internationally. This led the Governor of the Riksbank, Ivar Rooth, to contemplate sorting the gold by origin. After a warning had been received from the Allies early in 1943, the Swedish government gave the Reichsbank informally to understand that gold confiscated from central banks could not be accepted as payment. After a verbal pledge had been given not to deliver gold of this kind, the gold transactions continued as before. It was only after a repeated warning from the Allies, at the beginning of 1944, that the Riksbank informed the Reichsbank that no further gold could be accepted, in spite of the Riksbank previously having committed itself to purchasing more.

> There is only one single proof of any Swedish policy-maker having ever perceived the risk of gold on offer having been confiscated from Jews or other persecuted individuals, namely in the summer of 1944, when the Governor of the Riksbank considered whether the Riksbank should accept a proposal from the Reichsbank to deliver 1.5 tons of gold coins. That proposal was prompted by the Riksbank, as the Reichsbank saw it, having committed itself to buying the corresponding amount of gold. Sweden was no longer accepting gold in bar form. The Reichsbank objected to paying in Swiss francs instead. The proposed payment in gold coins was accepted, following consultations with the Government, after Emil Puhl, Vice President of the Reichsbank, had given a verbal assurance that there was not question of coins taken from Jews or suchlike being involved.

At this stage of the inquiry, the Commission saw fit to affirm that 'moral and political responsibility for ensuring today that the requisite measures are taken should be assumed by the Government'. Today's Swedish government, which initiated a country-wide project for Holocaust education in schools, is indicating its willingness to hear and act upon such conclusions.

Appendix: The Commission on Jewish Assets in Sweden at the Time of the Second World War

(Final Report, March 1999)

Some excerpts:

- The economic dimension of the Holocaust 'has long remained relatively uninvestigated'.

- 'Recently' the accepted Swedish view of Sweden's role during the Second World War has been questioned . . .
  'One finds that Sweden's policy towards the belligerent great powers for most of the war was based on power politics. Moral issues were excessively disregarded and actions were taken with the overriding purpose of keeping Sweden out of the war and maintaining essential supplies. Today, of course, such an attitude can seem deplorable.'

- 'Looking back' one finds it doubtful whether Sweden can be said in a formal sense 'to have honoured its commitment and the Washington agreement (1946) in the matter of heirless property.'

- 'Germany was Sweden's most important trading partner both before and during the Second World War. Accordingly, there was a wide interface between Swedish and German business interests . . . During the war, the Swedish government assured progressively stronger control of foreign trade . . . [and] came to control the volume and emphasis of trade with Nazi Germany.'

- The Commission adheres to its previous criticism that the moral aspects of Sweden's attitude to gold confiscated and plundered from individuals were not openly, broadly and seriously considered in connection, at the latest, with purchase of gold coins in the summer of 1944. Similarly, the Commission maintains that, so far, there is no clear indication of the Riksbank's acquisitions having included gold from the death camps, while on the other hand the possibility cannot be excluded of certain shipments of gold – more specifically, 16.4 tonnes – having contained a minor proportion of gold which had been confiscated or plundered from Jews in other connections.

- Stockholm's Enskilda Bank, headed by the Wallenberg brothers, also acquired securities from abroad during the war...and the possibility...of being of Jewish origin cannot be discounted.

- It cannot be excluded that a certain amount of the gold [received as commission by the Enskilda Bank] has been confiscated or plundered from individuals.

- There may have been cases of one or more [Swedish] subsidiaries in Nazi-dominated territories taking over real estate which Jews were forced to surrender.

- The issue of Aryanisation did not prompt any general debate or political discussion of principles (even before the war).

- Knowledge of the Holocaust did not affect trade policy [even] when it was increasingly clear that Germany was probably going to lose the war, the government then chose to continue trade relations. . . .

The moral question of the attitude to be taken to business relations with Nazi Germany in view of the ongoing persecution of the Jews, was never asked in parliamentary or governmental discussion of Swedish–German trade...Retrospectively, the Commission finds it deplorable.

- Needless to say, the difficulties of elucidating any of the looted assets in Sweden are compounded by more than fifty years having passed before the question of the plundering of Holocaust victims came in for serious attention. In the meantime, for instance, archives have been destroyed. Added to this, most of the dealers and enterprises mentioned in the report of the Allies are no longer active, with the result that archives have been lost.

- It is necessary that this work should continue on the basis of all the historical documentation which has now been uncovered. A number of important questions have been raised in the course of the Commission's work. Some of these have been answered completely, others only partly and others again not at all.

- In addition, the Commission wishes to draw attention to a number of general fields, which deserve to be researched in greater depth.

- The importance of Sweden's trade with Nazi Germany as regards the ability of the latter to continue its persecution of Jews and others until as late as 1945. This research field is made relevant not least by the latter-day debate on whether Sweden's trade with Germany prolonged the war and with it the sufferings of the Jewish people.

Notes

1 For full references and sources see the interim report of the Commission on Jewish Assets in Sweden at the time of the Second World War, 'The Nazi Gold and the Swedish Riksbank' (English translation, Stockholm, August 1998).
2 'US and Allied Efforts to Recover and Restore Gold and Other Assets Stolen or Hidden by Germany During World War II', May 1997, p. 39.
3 Amsterdam University Press, Netherlands State Institute for War Documentation, 1996.

12

'Ex-Enemy Jews': the Fate of the Assets of Holocaust Victims and Survivors in Britain

Stephen Ward and Ian Locke

The flow of money to Britain in the 1930s

Britain was a very appealing destination for flying capital, arguably the most attractive in Europe in the 1930s.[1] The City of London and New York were the undisputed financial centres of the world. The pound, along with the dollar, was the international currency, and the stability of the British banking system went unquestioned. Despite the devaluation of the pound in 1931, foreign capital flowed massively into Britain from 1931 onwards, reaching some $4 billion between 1931 and 1937, more than ten times the amount flowing to Switzerland.

The channels by which Jewish funds were transferred to Britain were varied and numerous, hence the complexity of tracing such funds. A major difficulty was to get round exchange controls, that is, the ban placed by governments on the buying of foreign currencies. The most common method of dealing with this difficulty was to use a counterpart in Britain, effectively swapping assets. This could also be done through commercial transactions, as long as controls were limited to capital account transactions – that is, the conversion of domestic currency into foreign exchange for the purpose of foreign investment.

Money could also be physically transported, though the method was dangerous – people could more easily smuggle jewellery or other valuables such as stamps. Another common channel was for a British citizen to open an account on behalf of foreign friends. This most likely took place within networks of family, business or social relationships, to which most Jewish families belonged. Assets transferred to Britain did not necessarily take the form of bank accounts: the purchase of securities, life policies and works of art was common practice.

Where money was deposited in a bank, it was not necessarily in one of the best-known clearing banks. The type and number of financial institutes receptive to Jewish flight capital was much greater than today. One of the main characteristics of British banking was the diversity of specialist banking institutions operating in the London capital market.

The clearing banks were engaged in deposit banking, an activity dominated since 1918 by the 'Big Five' (Barclays, Lloyds, Midland, Westminster and National Provincial). They controlled some 80 per cent of the domestic market and were fairly insular in outlook. The merchant banks, by contrast, had specialization in financing foreign trade by accepting bills of exchange. Merchant banks took deposits, largely from companies, foreign states and very wealthy individuals. There were some fifty-eight merchant banking firms in 1930, and forty-five in 1940, several having gone out of business during the depression of the 1930s. There also existed discount houses, specializing in dealing with bills of exchange, which they usually sold to the clearing banks. There were more than twenty discount houses in the early 1930s, several of them still family partnerships.

As a leading financial centre, the City of London had attracted, since the mid-nineteenth century, all the major foreign banks. The Deutsche Bank, for example, opened a branch as early as 1870, the Swiss Bank Corporation in 1898. In addition there were the Anglo-colonial and Anglo-foreign banks which operated in foreign countries, including continental Europe, and in the British Empire. Some twenty-five of them were based in London in the 1930s, among them Barclays Bank DCO, Lloyds and the National Provincial Foreign Bank. Many financiers operated in the City of London in all types of activities, including foreign exchanges. A number were of Central European Jewish origins, belonging to the second or even the first generation in Britain.

Wartime: freezing enemy assets

With the outbreak of war Britain moved quickly to make sure the huge volumes of foreign capital in London stayed there. A Trading with the Enemy Act from the First World War was reenacted in 1939, to put under British government control all enemy assets in Britain. As more countries were invaded, so the assets of those countries were added to the frozen pool. The Trading with the Enemy Department came under the Board of Trade and had close liaison with the independent Bank of England, the Treasury and other government departments.

Each territory was assigned to a specific administrator. Five categories of 'enemy' were defined, including corporations, partnerships and individuals resident in enemy territory.[2] An enemy did not include necessarily a person who happened to be an enemy subject. Head offices of banks circulated their branches with instructions about enemy accounts. Many enemy accounts were, it seems, consolidated in a single office. In the Midland's case, this was in the Enemy Debts Department.[3] It is evident that private banks continued much as before.

Banks, including British branches of 'enemy' banks such as the Deutsche Bank, and neutral banks like Credit Suisse, were required to give the Custodian details of enemy assets, including name, address, property, details of securities, life polices, other articles, credit balances and any liabilities (or indebtedness).[4] These lists were forwarded by the banks to the appropriate custodian. Enemy debts were registered with the Assistant Secretary for Finance. Details of the terms of the account, standing orders, and copies of any special licenses granted by the Treasury to the account holder were also required.

Penalties for non-compliance included a fine of up to £50 and prison terms for non-disclosure or non-compliance and a fine of up to £10 a day for failing to produce documents. The onus was on the banks to produce documents and declare any balance or asset considered enemy.

The economic position of the Britain which decided how to distribute the hundreds of millions of pounds in frozen Trading with the Enemy accounts was markedly different from the Britain which had passed legislation to freeze it. During the war Britain had spent 50 per cent more than its income, and faced an external debt of £3500 million. The crisis over Britain's economic prospects was brought to a head by President Truman's cancellation of the Lend-Lease assistance in August 1945. Though 'Britain was treated as a would Truman's be creditor with dubious references'[5] by defaulting on its loans from the US after the First World War, a $3750 million conditional US loan and a further £1250 million Canadian loan were secured. In consequence, Britain was desperate for foreign exchange to bolster the value of the pound.

British negotiators had high hopes of reparations, which also conveniently fulfilled a desire that Germany should be punished. It was seen that 'the only notable compensation we can hope to receive from her [Germany] for all the evils she has inflicted on us is to export her export markets'.[6] The reparation policy underpinned attitudes towards the frozen assets. Under the Paris Treaty of January 1946, Britain was to receive a total of just over $105 million (at 1938 prices) from repara-tions.[7] The Americans were suspicious of British claims.

Bankrupt Britain

In 1945, the new Labour government in Britain, with its bankrupt economy at home and an unrecognizable political landscape in Europe, began negotiations for a series of monetary and financial agreements which sought to establish renewed trading relations.

This was the context in which it decided how to deal with almost £400million of frozen assets held by the Custodian of Enemy Property. The politician in charge of the department was the President of the Board of Trade, Sir Stafford Cripps. The junior minister with respons-ibility as Minister of Overseas Trade was Harold Wilson, just 31 and newly elected as an MP. In 1947 it was Wilson who took over from Cripps, with Arthur Bottomley replacing Wilson as his junior.

It was a huge department. 'The Board of Trade reigned over the vast and complex empire of controls, constructed piecemeal during the war now affecting almost all public and private consumption . . . Alto-gether it employed more than 14,000 civil servants and received more than a million letters a month. No department generated more paper, spawned more statistics, was governed by more intricate and detailed legislation.'[8]

The economic plight of the country and the ethos of the department meant that they saw their preeminent task to build up British exports.[9] Wilson 'pursued this goal with a single-mindedness which alarmed some of his colleagues who believed that higher priority should be given to developing industries at home.'[10] He was a passionate fighter for the British interest, happy to make deals with anybody if the price was right,[11] and a fervent believer in reintegrating the Eastern bloc into world trade.

Britain wanted to use as much money as possible to satisfy British creditors.[12] But it also wanted to be seen as a continuing bastion of financial rectitude, so as not to scare away foreign investors, and bolster the pound. Thirdly, led by the Board of Trade and Wilson, it wanted to regenerate export markets for British goods, and obtain timber and other scarce supplies as cheaply as possible.

The agreements had to try to settle claims by prewar and wartime commercial and government creditors against each country, using in part the seized and frozen assets (private and commercial) held by the Custodian of Enemy Property. The settlements created two types of 'enemy', the occupied territories being 'technical enemies' and Germany and its satellites 'belligerent enemies'. They were defined partly according to their role in the war, but their treatment owed much to their anticipated role in the future of the continent.

The treatment of Germany was unambiguous. It had been agreed in 1945 between the leaders of Britain, the USA and the Soviet Union[13] that German assets should be used to pay for the war – the principle of reparations. The detail of this policy was confirmed at the Paris Reparations Conference in 1946, which set up a world body, the Inter-Allied Reparations Agency, to oversee claims on German assets.[14]

This dictated the British postwar treatment of Germany. Britain had frozen some £15–£20million of German assets, and it kept them. They were used to go as far as possible to repay British traders who had been left with unpaid debts from German counterparts at the start of the war. Among these was the British government itself, in the form of the Export Credits Guarantee Department, along with Exchequer expenses.[15] The claims of the original account holders were a low priority. By the time the closing date was reached, British trade creditors of Germany had received almost three shillings in the pound, totalling £19.5 million and German 'victims' had been paid £125,000.[16]

In the decade following the war, Western Germany was rehabilitated by a series of agreements – the Bonn Convention (1952), the Final Act of London (1954) and the Paris Agreement (1954).

Britain chose to deal with Germany's satellites – Hungary, Bulgaria and Romania – as 'belligerent' enemies – effectively in the same way as Germany itself, although there was no international sanction for the policy. The Emergency Laws Bill (1953) removed any legal right of challenge by creditors by allowing Britain to define any country as enemy. The crucial difference from Germany – on paper at least – is that peace treaties were signed with each of these countries. But in reality the frozen assets of these countries were retained by Britain in the same way as if they had been part of Germany. 'Victims' were compensated in the same way as German victims, on the same criteria. Again, this was a unilateral decision by Britain, the natural corollary of its arbitrary decision to retain the assets.[17] By the time the agreements were wound up in 1956–7, creditors had been paid dividends of approximately £8 million, and victims had received approximately £1.5 million.[18]

All other countries, the 'technical' enemies, came to be referred to interchangeably as 'Allies'. Money and property agreements were negotiated with each country. The common settlement with all these countries was that prewar debts and future trade deals were tied together in often unpublished treaties. The frozen assets became a sterling credit to allow the foreign country to buy British goods. The account holders were repaid by their own governments in local currency. Not only 'victims', but *all* account holders in these countries, were entitled to reclaim their money.

The agreements were not the same, and contained anomalies. For example, Austria was treated as an ally. By the Moscow Declaration of 1943, the Allies agreed to treat Austria as a liberated area and forego any reparations. In the protocol at Potsdam of 1 August, Prime Minister Attlee sought and received confirmation of this status. In 1944 the Controller-General of the frozen Austrian assets 'did not see how it [Austria] could hope to survive if it started with a burden of old debt'.[19] International agreement would allow the country to assert its independence from Germany and make a new start,[20] so that active Nazis were as entitled as their victims to reclaim assets in England. But Austria's international weakness allowed British diplomats to insert into the Money and Property Agreement of 1952 a caveat that only those assets which were not in sterling were returned to Austria. The sterling was used 'in the settlement of pre-war debts to the UK'.[21]

Another example was Poland, which became Communist midway through negotiations (1946), and had already extracted from Britain a unique concession that all the money should be handed over *en bloc* to the Polish government.

For 'technical enemies', lists of the bank accounts and claimants were forwarded by the Custodian to the corresponding authorities. Nationals and their heirs could now reclaim their assets. The burden of administration lay with the foreign government, while control stayed with the British.

All account holders from Italy, victim or not, were entitled to reclaim their money. Britain was probably inclined to be generous with Italy for being on the right side of the Iron Curtain. British creditors did not lose since Italian government assets in London happened to be more than adequate to settle all prewar accounts.[22]

Nazi victims: the policy

The seizing of 'enemy' assets in London was sanctioned by peace treaties signed with each belligerent enemy. To give the policy an air of equity, the *ex gratia* payment system was extended from Germans to include Hungarian, Bulgarian and Romanian victims of Nazi persecution. The extension was described ten years later as an 'act of grace' by the Board of Trade.[23] The administrators of the Trading with the Enemy Department were therefore left with the task of trying to stretch the funds, already inadequate to satisfy the trade creditors, to another group as well. The British trade creditors were a vocal and powerful lobby group.[24] The Nazi victims were not.[25]

An official history of the department reveals in detail how the civil servants approached their dilemma, favouring the creditors over the claimants. (Written in 1965, by A. W. Mackenzie, principal of the Enemy Property Branch in 1965, the history was unpublished, but released under the thirty year rule on 1 January 1996. It was internal, marked 'confidential'.) Officials were given a strong predisposition to be harsh by the policy laid down by successive Ministers at the Board of Trade.

Arthur Bottomley, the overseas trade junior minister to Harold Wilson, wrote to J. L. Edwards, Economic Secretary at the Treasury on 17 November 1950: 'The property here of Jews who have died heirless in belligerent enemy countries (except in the case of Italy) will normally come into the hands of one of the Administrators of Enemy Property; and will eventually be used along with other assets owned by non-Jews in belligerent enemy territories to satisfy as far as gross value will go, the claims of British creditors on those countries.'[26] A letter from P. J. Mantle at the Board of Trade to I. K. Matthews at the Foreign Office on 17 March 1954[27] said that 'to release the property of all ex-enemy Jews – including those who are not qualified as victims of racial or religious persecution' would be 'logically impossible'... 'It would mean an extension of our policy beyond the limits of anything ever contemplated and might well deplete catastrophically the amount available to divide among the pre-war (British) creditors of Romania, Hungary and Bulgaria.'

On Christmas Eve 1948, the Board of Trade issued the rules claimants would have to satisfy to receive *ex gratia* payments. Initially applicants were given just six months to apply. (The date was progressively extended to 1956 for Germany, and 1957 for Romania, Hungary and Bulgaria.) Four points had to be satisfied, with supporting documentation. A British consul had to certify documents were correct. The correct forms should be used and if a document was in a foreign language a certified translation in English was necessary.[28]

To be a 'victim of laws discriminating against race or religion' claimants had to demonstrate all of the following: that they had been deprived of liberty; that they had left 'enemy' territory; that they did not act against the Allies and that they did not enjoy full rights of citizenship. Heirs could claim if the victim had died 'before the end of hostilities' (this was later extended to August 1947).

Nazi victims: the results

For twenty years the policy was deliberately not enshrined by statute, because government lawyers advised that if it was kept ad hoc, there could be no challenge to interpretation in English courts.[29] The Board of Trade solicitor made clear the official view in a minute of October 1951: 'We are not bound either morally or legally to test the propriety of our interpretation of the policy by making reference to an interpretation of the Rules furnished by someone else . . . we decide whether certain property shall or shall not be released. . . .'[30] None the less, claimants' files came to be regarded as the departmental 'case law' of the policy.

The officials applied a tight and literal interpretation of 'deprivation of liberty'. John Foster, a Conservative MP and QC, an expert in international law, reviewed the policy at the time and said that it was to 'restrict the application of the *ex gratia* release to the few persons hardy enough to survive lengthy confinement in an actual death camp.'[31] Claims from inmates of labour camps were not allowed, 'even though (the camp) was intended solely for Jews, political opponents of the regime etc.', if the conditions of the camp were not known to have been extremely harsh.[32]

One woman, Bertha H., who was refused her money on the same grounds, had been subjected to frequent long interrogations by the Romanian Iron Guards in her home at night early in the war. She had survived until the end of hostilities by living with non-Jewish families, and had then been persecuted as a capitalist by the new Communist government.[33] One man, according to the officials' own summary, 'lost 13 members of his family in concentration camps, and all his family property was confiscated. He only saved his own life by going underground and thus lost his own property. When he got back, the property was nationalized without compensation.' He escaped from Communism, but he was turned down because he had not been deprived of his liberty.[34]

Explaining the thinking behind this interpretation, a junior minister, Toby Low (later Lord Aldington, deputy chairman of the Conservative Party), told the Commons, 'As regards hiding cases, it was not only persecuted Jews who went underground, but sometimes criminals.'[35] Low explained that the evidence of 'hiding' often only came from the victim himself, with no corroboration. The department decided that the fact that Jews could still be 'enemies' even though they had been deprived of rights of citizenship.[36]

An extremely high burden of proof was demanded before claims would be accepted. A 60-year-old who had left Bulgaria in 1948 for Israel was refused his £500 from England because he could not prove he had been deported from Sofia to the suburb of Pleven with his wife and two children in 1943. In any case, according to the British legation in Sofia, Pleven was 'not a prison, camp or ghetto to their knowledge, simply a place to which Sofia undesirables were banished.'[37]

Others were turned away because they had not left enemy territory, which for the purposes of the definition continued to include Romania, Hungary and Bulgaria long after peace treaties had been signed, and Germany even after it joined NATO. One man, a Mr Kostelitz, who was refused, had been in the Bergen-Belsen concentration camp and was one of only 1700 who reached Switzerland.[38] After the war he had returned to Hungary before it became Communist, had not left again by the qualifying date of 1947, and was therefore an enemy.

The department did not allow claims through a nominee in a 'friendly' country, on the grounds that the money might end up in the 'enemy' country.[39]

The biggest section turned away were those out of time, the ones who escaped from Communism after 1956. Even Harold Macmillan, the prime minister, recognized that this was an injustice. The fund had already been closed. He came up with a very political solution; to continue to pay claimants using any 'enemy' assets which continued to be discovered in the 1960s. Civil servants decided not to publicize the continued right to claim, so that numbers were kept small.

After the cut-off date, claimants were expected to claim from the 'enemy' government. Imre Breuer, who had escaped to Israel, then England, dropped the claim for his Hungarian father's money when he heard this, believing it would endanger the lives of his family still trapped under Communism.[40] In any case, officials recognized there was practically no possibility of Communist countries paying out.[41]

Where victims had died too late from the effects of the war (that is, after the cut-off date of 15 September 1947), no allowances were made to pay their heirs. One man had been sent to the Moghilev camp in Romania where he contracted typhoid, having endured 'other horrors of the camp. He survived to be released in a completely broken-down condition, and eventually died 21.5.48.' His heirs had still not been paid in 1956, although the case had remained 'under review' because the cause of death was so clearly the camp.[42]

Officials would sometimes wait for one objection to be defeated before erecting another. The relatives of the joint owners of a company who had both been killed in camps tried to reclaim its assets from London. The company had been confiscated by the Nazis, along with all other Jewish businesses, under the 1938 Ordinance for the Elimination of the Jews from the Economic Life of Germany, but the London assets had been left. For several years, until 1954, officials argued that the Wolffs must have continued to run the business under the Nazis until 1941, because that was when official notice of the confiscation was published in a newspaper. Eventually they gave way on that point, but now requested hard evidence that Ida Wolff had actually died. A certified hand-written judgement of death, confirming that she was transported to Poland and had died in a concentration camp on or about 1 August 1942 was finally produced, and some of the assets paid out, ten years after the war. According to the papers, the family had been in dire need of the money for the whole of that period.[43]

For German victims, there was no transfer to the new German government of the obligation to pay all victims whose assets had been taken by the British government to pay trade creditors. The Bonn Conventions[44] specifically gave the Federal Republic responsibility to compensate refugees who had been persecuted under Nazi race and religious laws, and to repay pensions and some securities to claimants who had been rejected by Britain for *ex gratia* payments. There was no provision for any payments to be made on the assets of deceased victims.

By June 1964, *ex gratia* releases to German victims totalled £125,153 from assets of £19.5 million; £754,745 to Romanians from assets of £7.5 million; £753,436 to Hungarians from assets of £3 million; and £5,140 to Bulgarians from assets of £380,000.

A gesture to victims

In the five years following the end of the war, the debate within the government had been whether any heirless money among the frozen deposits in Britain should go to the foreign governments of its former owners, to the British Exchequer, or back into the banks where it would stay indefinitely. Now a new claim arose; for the money of dead Jewish people to be used to help living ones.

By the early 1950s Jewish organizations were able to look more carefully at the consequences of the Trading with the Enemy Act for Holocaust Victims, and they began to claim for compensation for Jews generally rather than for restitution for individuals.

On 7 November 1950, Barnett Janner MP and A. G. Brottman, Secretary-General of the Board of Deputies of British Jews, made the new claim in a meeting with Arthur Bottomley, Minister at the Board of Trade.[45] Janner later set out the arguments in writing to Bottomley, concerning 'the disposal of heirless and unclaimed bank balances in this country which belonged to Jews who perished as a result of the Hitler persecution in Continental camps.'[46] Understandably, the Board did not appreciate exactly how the 'unfreezing' had taken place, and where these dormant accounts now lay. They did understand the nature of the victims, however.

> Property of this kind which belonged to Jews living in enemy countries is presumably under the control of the Custodian of Enemy Property. There is however property in this country, including bank balances, which belonged to Jews who were nationals of, or residents in, countries allied to the United Kingdom, and who perished under Nazi oppression when these countries were overrun by the enemy.
>
> The great majority of these victims had no opportunity of making any disposition of their property in Britain before death, and because of the ruthlessness of the Nazi campaign against Jews, involving in many instances the annihilation of whole families, such property has for the most part remained unclaimed and heirless.

It went on with a straightforward demand that the government force banks to disclose 'all deposits which have not been claimed since the beginning of the war'.[47] The Department acknowledged that large numbers of the seized 'enemy' accounts were Jewish: 'It was recognized that a disproportionate share of the accounts in London would belong to Jews because much of the foreign trade of those countries passed through Jewish hands.'[48]

But, predictably, the Board of Trade rejected the suggestion because it would reduce the funds available to British creditors. Publicly, the Treasury rejected the notion of dormant bank accounts from invaded countries being used in this way because it would 'prejudice the question of Dormant Funds, which was then under consideration'. The Board of Trade knew it was in the process of losing control of this money when restrictions on the banks were lifted, but did not apparently tell the Jewish delegation.[49] The issue was not pursued by the Board of Deputies nor by the prominent politician Lord Samuel.

Demands by Jewish organizations for a share of enemy funds persisted. In 1954 the United States passed a law permitting the President to devote $3 million from heirless accounts in that country to be given to Jewish charities. This set the agenda for future demands in Britain, for a charitable fund, and for its source to be from ex-enemy country funds.

The minds of Board of Trade officials were, however, firmly set. Their task to distribute the money to British creditors, and a small number of '*ex gratia* victims' was clearly defined. Attempts by Jewish groups to alter the terms of distribution were 'attacks'.[50] These officials were given a lead by the senior politicians of both parties. In 1949 the Chancellor of the Exchequer, Sir Stafford Cripps, argued: 'To hand over part of these assets to a body not accountable to H.M. Government is not feasible, even if it were established there was indeed property in this country of victims of Nazi persecution who had died without leaving heirs.'[51]

A Conservative, Donald Kaberry, parliamentary secretary to the Board of Trade, told the Board of Deputies that the difficulty in identifying exactly which accounts were heirless meant it was not possible to set up a charitable fund. He wrote in May 1955: 'It remains impossible either to define, identify or estimate the extent of Jewish property in the hands of the custodian or to say what part of any property he holds is "heirless".'[52]

By 1956 the political considerations had changed, and the idea of a victims' trust came to be seen as increasingly attractive. The President of the Board of Trade, Peter Thorneycroft, now realized that 'the setting up of such a fund would provide some sort of an answer to further representations about the alleged shortcomings of the victims' concessions'.[53] In particular, the new stream of refugees from Hungary was threatening to excite public sympathy for those deprived of funds by Britain. The Trust proved a convenient way to pay off these cases without having to reopen the deadline for Hungarian victims' *ex gratia* payments.

The objections to such a fund had by now largely evaporated. By now, assets had nearly all been distributed to British creditors, so the amount left, some £250,000, could well be paid as a lump sum to a charity. It was realized that it would be politically unacceptable for the government to be seen to be appropriating individuals' assets. Giving them to victims could be defended. Payments through the Trust would be made to people who 'had been persecuted before 1945 on racial, religious or political grounds in European countries at war with the UK' and 'were in fact suffering'.[54]

The Board had correctly anticipated there would be difficulties over who got the money. They stipulated four Jewish trustees with a non-Jewish chairman, and took a year to persuade the right people to serve.[55]

Sir David Eccles became the new president in 1957. As it was, there were complaints from one MP that 'an undue proportion' of the trust's money would go to Jews because most of the trustees were Jewish. The Nazi Victims Relief Trust's maximum award was £1500. Most were for £500. Any later award given to the claimant under *ex gratia* arrangements had the sum deducted. Any award was subject to income tax, and, in German cases, to double taxation.[56] If politicians had hoped this final gesture would close the Jewish victims question, they were disappointed.[57] One victim in particular, Dr Marco R. Cohin, an eminent Romanian jurist, victim of the Nazis and the Communists, had only just escaped from Romania in 1957. He had missed the final date to reclaim his money in Britain, but persuaded the new prime minister Harold Macmillan that he was a deserving case. The questions over time-out cases were to occupy officials through much of 1958.[58]

The government made further payments out of reserve funds, but limited the number of applicants by keeping the policy secret.

Dormant accounts in British banks

During the war, banks apparently regarded Trading with the Enemy Legislation as a *force majeure*. The mechanics of compliance caused them more concern than the principle of giving over clients' money.[59] The onus was on the financial institutions to find 'enemy' accounts, and, although there are suggestions of oversights, there is no evidence that any of them deliberately tried to hide any assets from official scrutiny. As institutions whose whole business ethic was based on trust and probity, they obeyed.

After the war, the banks became proprietorial once more about their clients' money, at least in Allied countries. During Anglo-Dutch negotiations, it became clear to the British government that 'the banks felt that the direction to pay the Netherlands Embassy money... in respect of individuals... disregarded the principle of secrecy with regard to bank accounts.'[60] The banks' position was strong because British banking practice is clear – that an account remains with the bank in perpetuity in case an heir ever turns up to claim it.[61]

Various government departments appeared to toy, from time to time, with the idea of trying to keep this money for the Exchequer. The Treasury wrote to Sir David Whaley at the Bank of England in 1946: 'It seems attractive to consider some procedure which would turn unclaimed bank deposits, etc., in for the benefit of the taxpayer... we ought not to release from the Custodian ban in a hurry. Once they are gone we shall never get them back.'[62]

But after detailed considerations of the legal implications, the Board of Trade decided the British would have a weaker case than the foreign governments to this 'hard core' of dormant accounts, and decided to let them stay with the banks in preference to letting them go abroad.[63] Mantle (in the same memorandum) explained that lifting the Trading with the Enemy restrictions: 'resulted in the return to the banks' [control] of a number of balances which will inevitably go to swell that mysterious reserve of the Banks known as unclaimed balances.[64]

After five years the initial arrangements for 'Allied' claimants were concluded. Any unclaimed assets returned to normal bank control. The relevant Section 6 of the Trading with the Enemy Act was thereby 'lifted', country by country, through the early 1950s.

The value of the residue from each country is not recorded by the Trading with the Enemy Department, but the totals paid out before controls were lifted were: France, £149 million; Belgium, £54.3 million; Greece, £14.4 million; Norway, £4 million; Denmark, £13 million; Netherlands, £55 million; Luxembourg, £11.5 million.

A departmental estimate from 1950 suggests that, depending on the country, between 1 per cent and 10 per cent of accounts were still unclaimed in Allied countries.[65] In the West, it was unlikely that these balances would ever be reclaimed by account holders. Unless they were dead or unaware of the account, owners and heirs would already have claimed before 1950. It was reasonable to assume that remaining Eastern bloc accounts would not be reclaimed for the foreseeable future for the same reasons. In addition, even living claimants who knew about their accounts would not be expected to make claims, because the Iron Curtain would remain solid.

At the end of the process, the banks had lost the money from the Polish account holders, never recovered the money from the four 'enemy' countries, but apparently regained control of accounts from all other former enemy countries.

Other assets of victims may still exist in British financial institutions. Any accounts opened by Europeans before the war in the name of a nominee, such as a solicitor, would not have been recognized as 'enemy by the banks'.[66] The Board of Deputies acknowledged, in a 1955 memo, that many of these would be dormant too.[67]

In later years, when the original account holders came to seek their funds, the banks were not always as helpful as they might have been. According to H. Chaimoff, they asked him for a fee, and told him how difficult it would be to trace an account, because there were no centralized records.[68] The absence of centralized records suggests that the banks did not anticipate such applications in any numbers in future. There is no evidence that, like the Swiss banks, the British refused legitimate claims backed by account details. But, as with the Swiss banks, the burden of proof was on the applicant.

Returning to the issue

The issue of Britain's postwar handling of enemy assets began to resurface in 1997. The previous year, in 1996, a reexamination of postwar restitution of gold and other valuables looted by the Nazis was accelerated by government and official initiatives on both sides of the Atlantic.

In the United States, the Senate Banking Committee held a series of widely publicized hearings into Swiss bank accounts which had not been returned to Holocaust victims or their families.

Primarily using newly-uncovered documents emerging from the National Archive in Washington, the Holocaust Educational Trust began to release research findings showing how much the British government had known abut the flow of gold from Germany to Switzerland during the war.

The British Foreign Secretary, Malcolm Rifkind, agreed to try to answer the Trust's questions by researching the official archives, and, in, September 1996, published a report which demonstrated how the Swiss had accepted large quantities of gold which they must have known to have been stolen and which they then, in 1946, refused to repay more than a small fraction of. Mr Rifkind raised the issues at meetings with the Swiss government.[69]

The Trust then began to research the fate of bank accounts in Britain which had belonged to Holocaust victims. Many of the files of the Trading with the Enemy Department had been closed in the early and mid-1960s, which meant, under the British Thirty year rule, they had newly become open at the Public Record Office. At the same time, account holders had seen the furore surrounding unpaid Swiss accounts, and were moved to try to reopen the issue in Britain.

When the first edition of this report was published in September 1997, the British government stalled, saying it needed to search the files itself.[70]

In spring 1997, Lord Janner, chairman of the Trust, had suggested to British Foreign Secretary Robin Cook that he should consider hosting an international conference into looted gold. Mr Cook took up the idea, and in December representatives of forty states attended the conference in London, and agreed to meet again in a year's time in Washington.

In April 1998, the government published its own research into British bank accounts, confirming the Trust's findings, and 'accepted the general principle that confiscated assets placed in the UK by victims of Nazi persecution after the war should be returned to them by the UK'. The president of the Board of Trade, Margaret Beckett, apologized publicly for the insensitive handling of the issue after the war.[71] Lord Archer of Sandwell was appointed in June 1998 to draw up the machinery for repayment of these assets.

Conclusion

Britain undoubtedly retained money of Holocaust victims in Germany, Hungary and Romania. It treated many victims of the Nazis and of Communism harshly and insensitively, at a time when they were most in need of help. There may have been some genuine expectation that the victims' own governments would reimburse them. By the time it became clear that they would not, the British government had already disposed of the funds, and finding money from the Exchequer was never contemplated. That policy was consistent through both Labour and Conservative administrations.

The policy was shaped initially by the overwhelming economic pressures on the postwar Labour government. The policy did not derive from antisemitism. Insensitivity to victims stemmed at least in part from ignorance of the Holocaust and the realities of life under Communism, in part from unquestioning bureaucratic rule-following. It is therefore the duty of the financial institutions and government agencies to rectify a long-standing inhumane treatment of Holocaust survivors.

It was completely understandable in the context of the 1940s that victims could be overlooked and misunderstood. The policy became less defensible as the decades passed. It must have been difficult for individuals who put their money in English banks for safekeeping from the Nazis to understand why it was not waiting for them when they eventually escaped from Communism.

The policy of the banks then and now has been rigid compliance with the laws. With the so-called 'technical enemy' accounts, Holocaust victims' assets have been treated like any other. In doing so, financial institutions have profited to an extent from the assets of victims of the Nazis.

Notes

1 For a recent analysis of European finance during this period, see Charles Feinstein (ed.), *Banking, Currency and Finance in Europe between the Wars* (Oxford, 1996).
2 Trading with the Enemy Bill, Clause 2, Bank of England, C40/1000, 1938.
3 Midland Bank Overseas Department, Circular no. 15, 1940.
4 Trading with the Enemy (Custodian) Order 1939 (SR&O), no. 1198, II, p. 3202, 16 September 1939.
5 Lord Shinwell, *I've Lived Through It All* (London: Gollancz, 1973)
6 Donald MacDougall, *Don and Mandarin: Memoirs of an Economist* (London, 1987) p. 49.
7 Final Report to Member Governments, Inter-Allied Reparations Agency, September 1961, p. 69.
8 Philip Ziegler, *Wilson: The Authorised Life of Lord Wilson of Rievaulx* (London, 1993), p. 63.
9 Simon James, *British Cabinet Government* (London, 1992) p. 63.
10 Ziegler, *Wilson*, p. 63.
11 Ibid., pp. 63–5.
12 This was particularly the case for British creditors of Romania (see James F. Byrnes, *Speaking Frankly*, New York, 1947, p. 148).
13 Yalta Treaty, February 1945; Potsdam Treaty, July–August 1945.
14 Inter-Allied Reparations Agency, Final Report, September 1961.
15 BT [Board of Trade] 215/25, pp. 1448–9.
16 Ibid., BT 216/32, p. 1764; 1948 Release of Asset, BT 271/135
17 Ibid., BT 216/26, pp. 1496–7.
18 Bank of England, Eastern Europe, OV 111/36.
19 Ibid., BT 216/27, p. 1582.
20 Ibid.
21 Official History, FO [Foreign Office] 466/8, p. 1764.
22 CAB [Cabinet Papers] 128/6, July 1946.
23 AEP [Administration of Enemy Property] History, Representations for the release of assets, AEP to Foreign Office, BT 271/506.
24 AEP History, Distribution of German Enemy Property, BT 216/21, p. 1011.
25 Board of Deputies, Minutes of All Party Meeting, House of commons, 10 July 1956, point 5, B6/CL/21.
26 BT 271/417
27 PRO [Public Record Office] BT 271/506
28 AEP History, General Summary 2446, BT 271/119.
29 AEP History, Victims, BT 216/23, p. 1241.
30 Board of Trade solicitor to Campbell, 1951, Elias Wolff Case, BT 271/582.
31 Memo from John Foster QC MP to Trading with the Enemy Department, 1950, BT 271/1369.
32 Ibid.
33 AEPD Memo to Home Affairs Committee, Nazi Victims Relief Trust, 5 June 1956, BT 271/597.
34 Ibid.
35 Hansard, 29 March 1956, cols 2408/19.

36   H. N. Edwards, TWE Depot to R. Brash, Foreign Office, Status of Jews in Romania, 29 November 1950, BT 271/326.
37   E. P. Assa (Bulgaria), Claim, 1949–59, BT 271/759.
38   BT 271/629.
39   BT 216/23, p. 1191.
40   Interview with HET [Holocaust Educational Trust] 20 August 1997.
41   Minute of Controller General, AEP Official History, BT 216/11.
42   AEPD Memo for Home Affairs Committee, Nazi Victims Relief Trust, 5 June 1956, BT 271/597.
43   Elias Wolff case, BT 271/582.
44   26 May 1952, CMD 8563.
45   BT 271/417.
46   26 February 1951, BT 271/417.
47   Ibid.
48   P. J. Mantle to I. Mathews, 15 March 1954, BT 271/506.
49   AEP History, Victims, BT 216/23, p. 1206.
50   Ibid., p. 1210.
51   Ibid., pp. 1193–4.
52   BD, C11/8/7/1.
53   BT 216/23, p. 1227.
54   Ibid., p. 1225.
55   Ibid., p. 1226.
56   May 1960, BD B6/2/12.
57   BT 216/23, p. 1230.
58   Ibid., p. 1231.
59   On 24 May 1944, the Midland was worrying about the administrative burden of working out interest on the accounts: '[this] will clearly entail an amount of clerical labour...we propose to charge our Interest Account with a "deficit" of £24,500...' (Chief Foreign Manager Midland Bank Overseas to C. T. Sadd, Vice-Chairman, Midland Bank Archives).
60   BT 216/2, p. 52.
61   Ibid., p. 51. See also *Tournier v. National Provincial and Union Bank of England Ltd.*, All England Law Reports 1923, p. 550.
62   T 236/390.
63   P. J. Mantle to Mr Howard, internal minute, 10 August 1954, BT 271/236, p. 3.
64   Ibid.
65   Memorandum on Cessation of Allied Release Arrangements, Closure of Money and Property Agreements 1950, BT 271/292.
66   BT 271/292.
67   Edwin Green, Archivist, Midland Bank to HET, 27 August 1997.
68   B6/3/9
69   Chaimoff to HET, 16 September 1996. 'Nazi Gold – Information from the British Archiever'.
70   DTI press notice, 8 September 1997.
71   DTI press notice, 3 April 1998.

13

The Norwegian Moral and Material Statement

Historical and moral settlement for the treatment in Norway of the economic liquidation of the Jewish minority during World War II: White Paper No. 82 to the Storting (1997–98) (*extracts*)

(Recommendations by the Ministry of Justice and the Police of 26 June 1998, approved by The King in Council on the same day)

1 Main contents of the White Paper

The Ministry of Justice hereby submits a White Paper to the Storting on historical and moral settlement for the treatment in Norway of the economic liquidation of the Jewish minority during the Second World War. The economic liquidation of the group as a whole was unique, and the organized arrest, deportation and physical destruction of the Jews was genocide. Since the aim was to completely destroy the Jewish group in Norway, the economic and physical liquidation must be regarded as two parts of the same crime. The proposition is based among other things on the work of the Skarpnes Committee, which was published in Official Norwegian Report (NOU) 1997:22, 'Confiscation of Jewish Assets in Norway during World War II'. The report made clear what economic consequences it had for the surviving Jews that the rules for reparation applied after the war did not take sufficient account of the Holocaust, i.e. the Nazis' genocide against the Jews.

In the White Paper the Ministry of Justice proposes that the historic and moral settlement is given economic expression by making collective and individual settlements. The collective settlement is proposed to consist of three parts. The first is the allocation of a sum to ensure the preservation of Jewish culture and the future of the Jewish community in Norway. Secondly, it is proposed to support efforts outside Norway to commemorate and develop the traditions and culture that the Nazis sought to eradicate. Finally, it is proposed to set up a resource centre on the Holocaust and on religious minorities' position and history in general. It is proposed that the individual compensation should take the form of an *ex gratia* payment to persons in Norway who were affected by the anti-Jewish measures during the war.

This White Paper has been drawn up in close collaboration with representatives of the Jewish community in Norway.

The Ministry of Justice wishes by these means to make a worthy final settlement.

2   Background

A number of individuals had their property seized by the Nazi occupation authorities and the Quisling regime during the Second World War, but of these it was the Jews who were by far the most seriously affected as a group. The seizure of property belonging to the Jewish community was an integral part of the Nazis' attempt to eradicate the entire Jewish community in Norway.

The first measures against the Jewish population in Norway were initiated in May 1940, when radios belonging to Jews were confiscated. This was followed by the registration of real estate owned by Jews, special stamps on Jewish identity documents, economic liquidation and arrests, culminating in the period of November 1942 to March 1943 in the deportation of Jews from Norway to Auschwitz.

The general rules governing seizures made during the period 1940 to 1943 were directed at members of the Norwegian government-in-exile in London and their administration-in-exile, members of the Resistance movement and people who had left the country illegally since the invasion in 1940.

In addition to these general rules, in October 1942 the Quisling regime adopted certain special provisions concerning the seizure of property belonging to Jews in Norway. The law laid down that property of any kind belonging to Jews in Norway should be seized by the state, including property belonging to the spouses and children of Jews.

It is estimated that the number of Jews in Norway before the war and up to the arrests in 1942 amounted to about 2200. Seven hundred and sixty-seven Jews were deported from Norway, mainly to Auschwitz, and of these only thirty survived. Two hundred and thirty families were completely eradicated. Those who were not deported fled the country, mainly to Sweden. There were also about fifty Jews imprisoned in Norway and about ten who remained in the country in hiding. Every person who was defined as a Jew by the Nazi authorities had his or her property seized. In accordance with special rules for Jews, which were introduced by agreement between the Quisling regime and the German occupation authorities, the seized gold, silver and jewellery belonging to Jews was taken out of the country without being registered. Other valuable goods were also not registered, and some property was plundered and thus not officially seized. Property was also given to Nazi organizations and individuals.

A special institution was set up to administer the seized property, called the Liquidation Board for Confiscated Jewish Property, but this also began administering property seized from other Norwegians as the war went on. The Jewish estates were liquidated while they continued to exist as legal persons even when the physical persons had been killed. This meant that taxes and other costs continued to accrue right up until the estates were finally settled after the war. In this way 163 Jewish estates were in debit, since they owed money to the Reparations Office, and the survivors were made liable for these sums, cf. NOU 1997: 22, p. 97. At the end of the occupation the archives of the Liquidation Board contained information on about 11,500 to 12,000 estates whose property had been partly or entirely taken over by the Nazi regime. Of these 1053 were Jewish and involved about 2000 people. Between 7000 and 8000 estates were registered as no-assets estates, i.e., funds had not been transferred either into or out of the Liquidation Board's accounts, and these were, with a few exceptions, non-Jewish estates.

There were several reasons for the no-assets estates of the non-Jewish. These were, in the main, (a) that the seizure was only pro forma, so that the property was registered but not expropriated or sold, (b) that the owners had no assets or had managed to hide them, or (c) that the estate had been plundered before being registered. The reasons for the 118 Jewish no-assets estates were either (a) that in accordance with the rules of the Quisling regime the property was to be kept out of the registration and therefore of the common fund, or (b) that the estates had been plundered before registration.

The operation of the Liquidation Board was financed by the seized assets. Much of the property was sold as soon as possible after the seizure, often at public auction. The money obtained by the realization of the seized property was put into the Liquidation Board's account and constituted a common fund.

After the war three institutions were established to ensure the return or replacement of the confiscated property:

- the Reparations Office for Confiscated Assets (the Reparations Office),
- the Offices for War Damage to Buildings and Movable Property,
- the Settlements Division of the Ministry of Justice.

The Settlements Division took care of all the cases that did not come under the sphere of the other institutions. One of its major activities was dealing with *ex gratia* compensation pursuant to Provisional Act No. 4 of 25 April 1947 relating to compensation for certain damages and losses resulting from the war in 1940–5, etc.

The Reparations Office took over all the archives of the Liquidation Board and used this information in addition to claims registered after the war to carry out its tasks. These tasks consisted mainly of returning property that had been traced to the rightful owners or of providing compensation for objects that had disappeared. This was done on condition that the property had been registered by the Liquidation Board during the war.

The rules laid down by the occupation authorities were invalid under civil law, and everything that had been seized could in theory be claimed by the rightful owner irrespective of whether or not the new owner had acquired it in good faith. The extent and value of the seized assets that were returned to their rightful owners after the war are not known, but there was a considerable amount of property that was returned in kind. The bulk of real estate, for example, was returned. Here, however, there was a difference between the Jews and other Norwegians. Since so many Jews had been killed, sometimes whole families, a considerable number of objects could not be returned to their rightful owners. . .

The regulations for the settlement of estates after the war that were enforced by the Office for War Damage to Movable Property were based on two main principles: reconstruction and an even social distribution. Insurance principles were to a large extent ignored and instead account was taken of the victim's economic position and needs, the extent of the damage and what had been damaged. Movable property used for professional purposes was as a rule compensated for according to the valuation, whereas the loss of personal movable property was compensated for according to a sliding scale. The principle of even social distribution meant that the greater the loss the smaller the percentage of compensation. Compensation was also calculated for households as a whole, which sometimes led to substantial discrepancies for households with extensive property and correspondingly large losses. These principles affected the Jews particularly seriously because of the extent of the liquidation. Because the Jewish community, with its institutions and religious centres, had suffered total economic liquidation, it received as a whole considerably reduced compensation in relation to its actual losses. The principle of reconstruction also led to reduced compensation in cases where the authorities regarded the compensation as having no importance for reconstruction.

In short, these rules meant that the Jews as a group were more seriously affected than others, since this group consisted of people of all ages, in contrast to that of other Norwegians, which was dominated by young men.

What characterized the Jewish group after the war was that so many of its members had been killed. Thus they were in a different situation, especially emotionally, from other Norwegian refugees who returned home after fleeing the country because of their resistance to the Nazi regime. The leaders and heads of families in the Jewish group had in many cases been killed, which weakened the ability of these families to safeguard their interests. In some cases whole families had been wiped out, and because of the close family ties within the group, all of the survivors had lost relations, either close or distant.

In section 16, subsection 5, Provisional Act No. 3 of 25 April 1947 relating to war damage to movable property laid down a general provision that the amount of compensation could be reduced or in the case of partial damage completely rejected 'when this is found to be reasonable with regard to the claimants' financial status and needs'. This had direct economic consequences in cases where many members of a family had been killed. Reduced compensation was paid because, as it was put, the heirs could otherwise have profited from the war, since under normal circumstances they would not have inherited from so many people at once. In addition the payments were regulated by establishing an order of inheritance. On account of the differentiated inheritance tax, which was lower for direct heirs than for more distant relatives, the percentage paid out varied according to whether the heir was direct or indirect. The order of inheritance was established on the basis of assumptions of who had died first in a family that entered the gas chamber together. There are examples in the available evidence where the result of this supposed order of inheritance was very unfavourable for the survivors, cf. NOU 1997: 22, pp. 100–2 and pp. 110–11.

Since death certificates were not issued in Auschwitz, those who died there were classified as missing persons, not as dead. The survivors were not given assets from their estates since the assets were transferred to the public guardian's office. This applied to half of the group of survivors. From the public guardian's office the assets were transferred to the probate and bankruptcy court to be dealt with there. This process took many years, during which new orders of inheritance were also established. During the administration of estate proceedings, amounts charged to the estates included mortgage debt, taxes and inheritance tax. It is probable that such deductions in connection with public and private administration of estates were almost equivalent to the total payments to the Jewish group from the reparations agencies, cf. NOU 1997: 22, pp. 110–11. It was also difficult for the survivors to find out what their rights were, partly because no separate office was set up for Jewish matters, in contrast to the situation for other groups with a common fate, cf. NOU 1997: 22, p. 88.

In the spring of 1995 new information about the Jewish property seized by the Quisling regime was published in the media, and the Norwegian Government decided to have the facts clarified as far as possible. Thus in March 1996 a committee was appointed to survey and evaluate the facts of the case. The Government stressed that it wished to have all the facts so as to be able to evaluate suitable follow-up measures.

3   NOU 1997: 22 'Confiscation of Jewish Assets in Norway during the Second World War '

The committee to investigate what happened to the property of Jews in Norway during the Second World War was appointed on 29 March 1996 by the Norwegian Ministry of Justice. The committee had the following composition:

- Country Governor Oluf Skarpnes (Chairman)
- Professor of Law Thor Falkanger, University of Oslo
- Professor of History Ole Kristian Grimnes, University of Oslo
- Judge Guri Sunde, Nedre Telemark District Court
- Assistant Director Anne Hals, National Archives
- Psychologist Berit Reisel, Oslo
- Historian Bjarte Bruland, Bergen

Berit Reisel and Bjarte Bruland were appointed to the committee on the recommendation of the Jewish community. Anne Hals asked to be excused from duty as a member of the committee and, on 11 June 1996, the Ministry approved her replacement by Miss Eli Fure of the National Archives. Executive Officer Torfinn Vollan from the office of the County Governor of Vest-Agder was the committee's secretary.

The committee received the following terms of reference:

'(1) The committee is entrusted with the task of surveying what happened to Jewish property in Norway during the Second World War. The report of the survey shall *inter alia* provide a description of:

- The laws and regulations of the Quisling regime concerning the confiscation of Jewish property.
- The way in which the confiscation was carried out, and the names of the agencies involved.
- The extent of the confiscations, including:
- the number of persons and enterprises whose property was confiscated;
- the type of property that was confiscated and its estimated value;
- how and by whom confiscated property was handled (sold, transferred, etc.).
- The actual and legal difference between the confiscation of Jewish property in Norway,
- Confiscation by the Quisling regime of property belonging to other Norwegians.

....

(9) The committee shall survey how and to what extent confiscated property was returned to the Jews after the war. This survey shall include a description of:

- Laws and regulations that applied to the restitution.
- How the restitution was organized.
- Measures that were taken to ensure that the property was returned.
- Property that was returned and the value of this property.
- What happened to the property of Jewish families that were annihilated during the war and,
- Where possible, a summary of the total value of the confiscated property of these Jewish families. . .'

The committee submitted its report to the Minister of Justice on 23 June 1997. The report is divided into two parts, a majority report and a minority report. The majority consisted of the Chairman of the Committee, County Governor Oluf Skarpnes, Professor Thor Falkanger, archivist Eli Fure, Professor Ole Kristian Grimnes and District Recorder Guri Sunde. The minority consisted of psychologist Berit Reisel and historian Bjarte Bruland.

The report was published as NOU 1997: 22 'Confiscation of Jewish Assets in Norway during World War II'.

4　The Government's fundamental views concerning the settlement

The Government has chosen to base its views on those of the minority of the Skarpnes Committee.

The injustice done to the Jewish people can never be undone, but the Government considers that the historical and moral debts with regard to the economic liquidation of Jewish assets must be settled, and that this settlement should also be expressed in economic terms.

The Government wishes to emphasize that the Nazis' attempts during the war to eradicate the Jews as a people have played a central role in the development of international rules concerning genocide. This genocide aspect has placed the Jews in a unique position among the many victims of the German occupation of Norway.

The settlement must primarily be based on a broad moral approach, which must be given a form and a content that take account of the special nature of the case. The Government has proceeded on the assumption that the settlement should be limited to economic considerations.

The collective settlement must emphasize that compensation is being made to the Jewish community in Norway as a whole, especially because the economic and physical liquidation was directed at the Jews in Norway as a group. In addition there is the fact that many of the Jews who were killed did not leave surviving family members. In this context it is natural to have an economic settlement in the form of an allocation for common Jewish purposes at both national and international levels. At the same time, by offering payments *ex gratia*, the Government wishes to support the individuals who were adversely affected by the persecutions in Norway during the Second World War.

The Government is also preparing to set up a monument at Vippetangen in Oslo in memory of the Norwegian Jews who were deported to Germany during the war.

5 Economic implementation

5.1 Collective compensation

Collective compensation will emphasize that a debt is being settled in relation to the Jewish community because the economic and physical liquidation was directed at the Jewish community in Norway as a whole. Not only was privately owned Jewish property confiscated, but Jewish institutions and religious centres in Norway were economically liquidated. In its evaluation of the total sum to be allocated in the collective compensation, the Government has taken account of the fact that some Jewish families were totally eradicated and thus received no individual compensation.

It is proposed that the collective compensation should amount to NOK 250 million, and it is proposed that the money should be divided as follows:

(1) An amount of NOK 150 million to the Jewish communities in Norway. The money is to be spent on ensuring the preservation of Jewish culture and the future of the Jewish community in Norway.

(2) An amount of NOK 60 million for support outside Norway's borders for commemorating and developing the traditions and culture that the Nazis tried to eradicate. The money is to be allocated through a fund to be administered by a board with representatives appointed by the Storting, the Government, the registered Jewish communities in Norway and the World Jewish Congress/World Jewish Restitution Organization.

(3) An amount of NOK 40 million to be used to set up and run a resource centre for studies of the Holocaust and religious minorities in Norway.

5.1.1 Ensuring the preservation of Jewish culture and the future of the Jewish community in Norway

An amount of NOK 150 million is to be allocated to the Jewish communities in Norway. The money is to be spent on ensuring the preservation of Jewish culture and the future of the Jewish community in Norway.

There are at present two Jewish congregations registered in Norway, one in Oslo and one in Trondheim. All Jewish organizations and institutions in Norway are represented through these two congregations and they also safeguard the interests of Jews who are not registered as members. The County Governor's offices in Oslo and Akershus and in Sør-Trøndelag advise that these congregations have about 1050 registered members as of 1 January 1998, 920 in Oslo and 127 in Trondheim. The Jewish community estimates that there are almost 1600 Jews living in Norway today.

In 1939 there were just over 2000 Jews in Norway, almost all of whom were registered as members of the congregations. Religious and cultural life flourished, and there were several synagogues, children's and old people's homes and a holiday home. After the war only 750 members remained. Many of the leaders were no longer there and the institutions had been abandoned. Everything had to be totally rebuilt. Of the three synagogues, only one of the two in Oslo could be used. The other one was not restored, and the synagogue in Trondheim had to be reconstructed. In 1960 a Jewish community centre was built in Oslo, with economic help from Jewish organizations abroad. According to the Jewish community they have been dependent on economic support from Jewish institutions abroad to keep up their cultural and religious activity. The membership and level of activity began to rise again at the beginning of the 1980s.

The Jewish community is one of the oldest minorities in the country and is well integrated into Norwegian society. In the light of this and of the tragic history of the war there is a great need for information from this minority group. Such information will make a substantial contribution to greater pluralism and tolerance.

In order to ensure the future of the Jewish minority in Norway, the community needs funds for premises, equipment and above all qualified leaders and other workers in the fields of religion, culture, teaching, information, social work and administration.

An estimated NOK 50 million of the NOK 150 million is intended to be used for repayment of debts and investment such as the rehabilitation of buildings and property, including the purchase of a graveyard and day-care facilities and the establishment of a Jewish museum and library. The income from the remaining NOK 100 million is intended to be used for the operation and development of organizations and institutions that will ensure the future of the Jewish community in Norway.

It is proposed that a fund be set up consisting of the collective allocation to the Jewish communities in Norway. The fund will be administered by a board consisting of three representatives of the Jewish community in Oslo and two from the Jewish community in Trondheim. The members are to be appointed by the boards of the two communities, and they will also be responsible for drawing up guidelines for the board of the fund. The transfer of money will be made when the board has been appointed. It is proposed that the amount will be transferred to the Jewish congregation in Oslo on behalf of the whole Jewish community in Norway.

The Ministry of Justice is to receive an annual report on the use of the funds, including accounts audited by a chartered accountant.

5.1.2 Support outside Norway's borders for commemorating and developing the traditions and culture that the Nazis tried to eradicate

NOK 60 million is being given in support of Jewish institutions or projects outside Norway. The funds (capital and any income) are to be allotted to institutions or projects whose aim is to commemorate, reconstruct or develop Jewish culture or traditions that the Nazis almost succeeded in totally eradicating. The funds are preferably to be used for teaching, research or information purposes. They may be either allotted to existing institutions or to new institutions established for this purpose. The institutions or projects must be politically neutral.

It is proposed that the money is placed in a fund with a board consisting of one representative appointed by the Storting, one by the Government, one by the Jewish communities in Norway and one by the World Jewish Congress/World Jewish Restitution Organization, and Nobel Laureate Eli Wiesel is proposed as chairman of the board. In cooperation with the registered Jewish communities in Norway, the Ministry of Justice will lay down the statutes and instructions for the work of the board in accordance with the general guidelines that have been proposed. Any administrative costs are to be covered by the allocation.

5.1.3 Establishment of a resource centre for studies of the Holocaust and religious minorities in Norway

One of the most important lessons learned from the Second World War and the Holocaust was how vulnerable minorities are to prejudice, hatred and persecution, which taken to extremes led to the most systematic and gruesome genocide in history. The best means of combating prejudice is through unbiased information, which relies on knowledge of the minorities in our society. Thus the sum of NOK 40 million is proposed for the establishment and operation of a documentation and resource centre for promoting expertise in Norway on the Holocaust in general and more specifically on the Norwegian chapter of the history of the Holocaust.

A resource centre for the religious minorities in Norway is proposed as part of this centre. It should create a foundation for broad knowledge in Norwegian society of the minorities' history, philosophy of life, traditions, culture and position in Norwegian society. It should develop educational material in these areas, support research on the different minorities and minority issues in general, and serve as a place to hold meetings, seminars and dialogues between the minorities and between the minorities and other groups in Norwegian society. The resource centre is to be politically and ideologically neutral.

The intention is to establish the centre in cooperation with one of the universities in Norway. The issue has been raised with the Ministry of Education, Research and Church Affairs and the University of Oslo. It has been proposed that the ministry should establish links with one of the faculties or departments of the University of Oslo. The issue must, however, also be dealt with in the usual way by the appropriate bodies of the university.

A separate board is proposed for the centre, and the academic freedom of the institution must be ensured. The members of the board must include people with interdisciplinary expertise. The Holocaust part of the centre will be set up after a dialogue with the Jewish communities in Norway and other Jewish expertise, for example from Yad Vashem in Jerusalem, and the centre for religious minorities will be set up in collaboration with the relevant minority groups. This will ensure that these groups have an influence on the profile and work of the centre. The Ministry of Education, Research and Church Affairs will set up the centre. The budgetary responsibility will be transferred to the Ministry by agreement.

5.2   Individual compensation

The Government proposes a compensation in the form of a standard amount of NOK 200,000 to those persons in Norway who suffered from the anti-Jewish measures, for example who had their property and assets confiscated by the occupation authorities during the war. Many of these are now dead, and spouses and direct heirs will take their place and inherit according to the provisions concerning distribution laid down in the Inheritance Act . . .

It is important for the dignified conduct of the moral settlement that there are clear rules as to who is entitled to payments and how they should be made. It is important to avoid harrowing processes being triggered by the settlement.

5.2.1 Who are entitled to payments?

Payments will be made on application to those persons in Norway who suffered from the anti-Jewish measures, for example by having property and assets confiscated by the occupation authorities during the Second World War.

There is no definite information as to who would be included in the individual settlement but, in connection with the work of the Skarpnes Committee, the minority of the committee drew up a list of the Jews who were deported or fled from Norway between 1941 and 1942. The list contains 2173 names and is expected to be useful in finding the people who may be entitled to the settlement.

Payments will be made subject to the following conditions:

(1) A payment will be given to persons who were born before the end of 1942 and who suffered in Norway from the anti-Jewish measures, for example who had their property and assets confiscated by the occupation authorities during the Second World War. The payment will amount to a standard sum of NOK 200,000.

(2) If the person concerned is no longer alive, the money will be paid to the heirs according to the provisions concerning distribution laid down in the Inheritance Act, but limited to spouses and direct heirs.

(3) The payment to each individual is limited to NOK 200,000.

One of the conditions is that the persecution must have taken place in Norway. This affiliation criterion is intended to emphasize that the settlement is primarily aimed at Jews living in Norway before and during the war. In addition to Norwegian nationals, this includes foreign nationals and stateless Jews. Jewish refugees from other countries are eligible if they were temporarily staying in Norway during the war and suffered from anti-Jewish measures in this country.

Thus compensation will be made to all Jewish families and individuals who either had their property confiscated or were subject to confiscation orders and Jewish families and individuals who did not own assets that could be seized and who therefore had no economic losses after the liquidation, but who suffered in other ways from the persecution or who lost their lives, for example in concentration camps or prison.

The standard payment is set at NOK 200,000. If the person entitled to the payment has died, the sum is distributed between the bereaved in accordance with the distribution provisions in the Inheritance Act, except that only the surviving spouse and direct heirs are entitled to it. The rule concerning the minimum amount for a spouse (section 6 of the Inheritance Act) does not apply, and a surviving spouse may not retain an undistributed estate with regard to the payment . . .

5.2.2   Procedure for applying for compensation

The Ministry of Justice aims to announce the arrangement in the Norwegian and international press. A time limit of six months is proposed. Applications must be received by the Ministry of Justice by this deadline, so that the matter can be dealt with within a reasonable time.

In collaboration with the Jewish communities in Norway, the ministry will inform all those members of the communities for whom this is relevant. The ministry assumes that the Jewish communities in Norway will inform their sister organizations in Sweden and other relevant countries. The World Jewish Congress/World Jewish Restitution Organization will also be informed.

5.2.3   Documentation requirements

The application should include name (and any previous names), address, date of birth, period of stay in Norway and address during the stay in Norway.

Applications on behalf of deceased persons should contain an explanation of the relationship with the deceased and this should as far as possible be documented. The existence of any other heirs should also be indicated.

However, the special nature of the case means that documentation may be difficult to obtain, for example there may be a lack of written documents and information may be unreliable. This must be taken into consideration when the cases are being dealt with and when decisions must be based on information that cannot be documented. It is further assumed that the Jewish communities in Norway on request will assist with the clarification of questions of identity in this work. The Skarpnes Committee went through the material in the National Archives and a new review is not planned . . .

6   Economic and administrative consequences

NOK 250 million is being set aside for collective settlement. The Ministry of Justice has the task of providing assistance in the transfer and use of the funds in collaboration with the Jewish communities in Norway. The Ministry of Education, Research and Church Affairs will set up the centre for the study of the Holocaust and of religious minorities in Norway.

With reference to the calculations mentioned under subsection 5.2.1, about 2200 Jews are in principle entitled to individual compensation. Many of these are now deceased, and it is assumed that spouses and direct heirs will receive compensation in their place. A total of 767 Jews, including whole families, were deported and killed. Many of these did not leave spouses or children and since other heirs are not included there will not be anyone entitled to seek compensation on behalf of the deceased. Given that payment is to be made only following application, there may be some individuals who, for some reason, will not apply. Hence it is very difficult to predict the number of applications. The ministry estimates, however, that payments will be made to or on behalf of 500 to 1000 of the original 2200 Jews. Thus the individual compensation will amount to NOK 100 to 200 million. If the individual payments amount to substantially less than NOK 200 million, the Government will consider increasing the amount of the collective settlement. The recipients of the individual compensation payment will not be liable to income or inheritance tax on the amount.

The costs of publicizing individual compensation and the necessary legal advice in connection with the establishment of the fund, cetera are estimated to amount to NOK 1.25 million.

It is proposed that the applications for the individual compensations are dealt with in the first instance by the Ministry of Justice, which will need three executive officer years in addition to the necessary secretarial assistance. Expenses will also be incurred in connection with the handling of appeals and other administrative functions. The Ministry of Education, Research and Church Affairs will encounter expenses in connection with the establishment of the Centre for the study of the Holocaust and the religious minorities in Norway. These expenses are estimated to amount to a total of NOK 3.25 million.

The ministry estimates that the establishment and administration of the scheme and its publication will amount to NOK 4.5 million, and that up to NOK 3 million of this, including part of the expenses for the three executive officer years in the Ministry of Justice, will be incurred in 1998 . . .

With respect to the allocations for 1999, the ministry will take these up with the Storting in connection with the ordinary work on the budget.

The Ministry of Justice and the Police hereby recommends:

that Your Majesty approves and signs the submitted proposal for a White Paper to the Storting on historical and moral settlement for the treatment in Norway of the economic liquidation of the Jewish minority during the Second World War.

We Harald, King of Norway, hereby confirm:

that the Storting is requested to make a decision on the historical and moral settlement for the treatment in Norway of the economic liquidation of the Jewish minority during the Second World War in accordance with the submitted proposal.

The recommendation by the Ministry of Justice and the Police is enclosed.

Proposal
for the decision on changes in the budget term for 1998

I

Expenses

Chapter	Purpose	
478	Historical and moral settlement for the treatment in Norway of the economic liquidation of the Jewish minority during the Second World War	
(New Item) 01	Allocation for operational costs, can be transferred	3,000,000
(New Item) 70	Allocation for ensuring the preservation of Jewish culture and the future of the Jewish community in Norway	150,000,000
(New Item) 71	Allocation for support outside Norway's borders for commemorating and developing the traditions and culture that the Nazis tried to eradicate	60,000,000
(New Item) 72	Allocation for *ex gratia* payment, estimated amount	10,000,000

II

Authorization

In accordance with the guidelines in the White Paper, the Storting consents to the proposal that a commitment can be given in 1998 concerning the payment in 1999 of individual compensation to persons who were affected by the anti-Jewish measures during the Second World War up to the amount of NOK 200 million, including the allocations for 1998.

14
Austria: the Evasion of Responsibility

Itamar Levine

The *Anschluss* and Aryanization of Jewish property

Since the end of the Second World War, Austrian leaders have consistently reiterated the same position *vis-à-vis* the conflict: Austria was the first victim of Nazi Germany and is therefore under no obligation to compensate anyone. The fact is that in perpetrating and perpetuating this lie, they were aided and abetted by the Allies. The Austrians draw attention to the Allied statement of October 1943 (the so-called Moscow Declaration), which – in an attempt to spark domestic resistance against the Nazis – recognized Austria as an occupied country. However, the Austrians recoil from another sentence in the same declaration which reminds them of their responsibility for willingly serving on the German side during the war.

The truth is that most Austrians greeted the Nazi *Anschluss* with great enthusiasm. Newsreels from March 1938 depict throngs of people standing in the streets of Vienna cheering on the tanks emblazoned with the swastika. As discussed below, when formulating the postwar balance of powers, the Allies pragmatically decided that Austria would be viewed as a liberated country, thereby granting it the opportunity to reinterpret the 'guilt clause' of the Moscow Declaration. One of the outcomes of this historical blurring of Austria's wartime role was that Austrian Jews were obliged to embrace former enemies as friends and fellow victims. Such is the context of the Jewish community's efforts to reconstruct their existence, an ambiguous fiction which benefited the Austrian state to the detriment of the Jews.

One of the first steps taken by the Germans was to organize the appropriation of Austrian Jews' property. Already in April 1938 the Property Exchange (*Vermögensverkehrsstelle*) was founded to assume responsibility for the Aryanization of Jewish property: the confiscation of property, in exchange for paltry sums (if anything was paid at all), and its transfer into the hands of so-called Aryans – mostly members of the Nazi party. In sum, this bureau handled some 25,500 cases of Aryanization, approximately 80 per cent of the businesses that were owned by Jews.

An anonymous document kept among the testimonies of witnesses, housed at the Wiener Library at the University of Tel Aviv, recounts in detail the process by which Austrian Jews were robbed. From the content of this document, it is clear that its author held a central position in the Jewish community of Austria, for it reads as an eyewitness account. It is likely that it was Dr Josef Loewenherz, the head of the community from May 1938, who took the opportunity to leave behind him a detailed report about developments in Vienna in the wake of the *Anschluss*. The document describes the methods by which properties were stolen:

> The law said that factories, businesses and shops must be sold by the owner within a reasonable time. In practice, however, all the Jewish manufacturers and also the Christian Social manufacturers were simply imprisoned, and were only set free after signing a contract selling their establishments to a Nazi loyalist for a nominal amount. This amount, as a rule, came to between 5% to 15% of the real value according to the balance figure, this having been carefully established beforehand.
>
> The business establishment, including cash balances and stocks, had to be handed over at once to a sort of official receiver, a *kommissar*, so that nothing could be removed by the real proprietors. Only in cases where the special knowledge of the proprietor or their business routine had to be used (the *kommissar* as a rule having no idea of the business they had to take charge of), could the proprietor work as an adviser in exchange for a small payment.
>
> In small shops the *kommissar's* charges were so high that nothing remained for the proprietor, and the stock had to be sold off to cover expenses. By these simple means alone, thousands had to give up their businesses without actual force being exercised.
>
> It was stated by the law that the purchase price should not be handed to the Jew but to the Property Exchange. This government office should only pay the Jews the cost for subsiding on a modest income or the cost of immigration. But as a rule nothing or next to nothing was paid, and the Jewish proprietors, fearing imprisonment, had to leave things as they were.

Another section of this document speaks of the disposal of real estate owned by Austrian Jews. According to the anonymous author, owners of the best properties were the most likely to be arrested, and their property was stolen by means of draconian taxes. At first, a 25 per cent tax was levied on all assets valued above 50,000 Reichsmarks, even if the property was mortgaged. In addition, a 20 per cent tax was levied on all land holdings owned by Jews. It should be noted that such tax rates, even in normal circumstances, generally forced the owners to sell the property in question; clearly, under the conditions of Nazi Austria, the Jewish owners could not realize much more than the amount necessary to pay the tax.

This appropriation was followed by persecution and, eventually, murder. On the eve of the *Anschluss*, 185,000 Jews lived in Austria, 170,000 of whom were in Vienna. Of these 126,000 emigrated prior to the outbreak of war, and 2000 more emigrated after September 1939. Fifteen thousand of those who emigrated were trapped in their countries of refuge, and were later murdered. More than 65,000 Austrian Jews perished in the German death and concentration camps. Only 1747 deportees survived the Shoah.

Property declarations: mute witnesses to a theft of enormous proportions

On 27 April 1938, only six weeks after the *Anschluss*, Austrian Jews were ordered to declare any property worth more than 5000 Reichsmarks. Detailed forms were provided for furnishing such details, which bore a heading stating the punishment for those who did not submit the report before 10 July: 'monetary fine, prison for serious criminals, confiscation of property', etc. In 1940 the Germans evaluated the value of private property (to differentiate between communal property and real estate) of Austrian Jewry at $1.5 billion in nominal value; in current terms, the figure surpassed $15 billion. This was a realistic estimate, considering that there were over 70,000 Jewish households in Austria, and many Austrian Jews were well-off or even wealthy.

The Jews were ordered to list their agricultural property, forest holdings, immovables, business and industrial property, professional practices, securities, uncollected debts, savings, bank deposits, life insurance policies, pensions, annuities, jewellery, art works, precious metals and stones, copyrights, etc. In any case of doubt, the form's text affirmed, details of every item should be provided. Most importantly, Jews were asked to estimate the value of the property and to deduct only the loans regarding the property as held at 27 April 1938. This detailed documentation allows us to calculate today, with great precision, the value of the property that was stolen from these Jews. The forms are all housed in the National Archives in Vienna, where they are freely accessible. To the property declarations were later added additional documents updating the original listings. Most of these related to subsequent purchases of property – either voluntarily or within the framework of Aryanization. In some cases, for which the files became themselves heavy volumes, the plundered property is known with certainty and the exact financial damage can be assessed.

A few examples from the declaration files: A woman born in 1873 reported that her café was closed by the authorities, and that the sum she received for its sale was insufficient to pay any amount of money to her two partners. This woman was left with only 900 Reichsmarks, the value of which was eroded due to the devaluation of the currency. On the back of this declaration form was affixed a stamp with a clear meaning: nach Polen – deportation to Poland. A man born in 1874 declared his carpentry workshop in Vienna, adding that 'the business is presently in the process of being Aryanized'. Another woman, born in 1891, listed the securities that she owned, and was forced to sell those which were held abroad to the local branch of the Reichsbank. It is reasonable to assume that this sale was carried out based on an arbitrary valuation of the Reichsbank's clerks. The same woman also recorded her 'brooch, ring, necklace, silver cup, bracelet, carpet, etc., of a total value of 350 Reichsmarks.'

A woman born in 1889 owned one-third of a rental apartment block in Vienna. She reported the sale of the building for 37,000 Reichsmarks, of which only 10,000 remained in her hands after expenses. The same woman purchased a 'boat ticket for the purpose of emigration', passed a course for professional accreditation, and bought equipment for the voyage. In order to subsist, she sold two carpets, keeping a ring, necklace and two old and damaged carpets. The value of the property that remained in her possession was 5,850.92 Reichsmarks.

As noted above, almost all of the property was stolen in one way or another. Those that succeeded in emigrating afterwards were forced to sell their assets privately. The belongings of those murdered in the Shoah were stolen either while they were still in their countries of origin or when they arrived at concentration and death camps. What is remarkable about the Austrian case is that, unlike most countries, there is evidence of exactly what was taken from each Jew in the form of property declarations.

The proof contained in document form is supported by personal testimonies. Gideon Eckhaus, the chairperson of the Association of Austrian Immigrants in Israel, recalls his family's experience:

> My late father was a partner in two shops which sold a wide variety of clothes and haberdashery. By chance, my father was on a business trip to Italy five days before the *Anschluss*, and could not return. After the *Anschluss* prices plunged, and from the small living that could be made through the business, my uncle gave us money with which we could subsist. The Nazis placed two *kommissars* in charge of our two stores; one of them, whose name was Miller, asked me to work in the store without payment. He was there mostly in the evening in order to close the cashbox and take most of the turnover. That was how they operated in many cases. Today, Austria is the 11th wealthiest economy in the world, a figure which speaks for itself. Go and research the chronicles of the Austrians' diligence, your conclusions will explain the origins of Austria's wealth.

Dr Ron Zweig of Tel Aviv University, an expert on the subject of the restitution of stolen Jewish wealth, recalls that in 1962, as a child, he accompanied his parents on the first visit of members of his family to Austria since the Shoah:

> My grandfather had a small bank account in Vienna, of which my father had all the details. The bank said while they would be happy to return the money, it would first be necessary to pay account fees – which added up to more than what remained in the account. If this isn't theft then I don't know what is. My family had a medium-scale factory in Vienna which was confiscated in 1938 and transferred to members of the Nazi party. Those who received the factory paid tax to the party, and the money was sent to Germany. My grandfather absolutely forbade us to speak with Austrians, and only after he passed away was it decided that the family would claim compensation. The Austrian response was that the money was transferred to Germany, and what remained was stolen by the Russians in 1945.

Years of unsuccessful negotiations

Many different methods were used in Austria to strip Jews of their assets. Ordinances, coercion, and outright theft quickly impoverished the

185,000-strong community. After the war, survivors struggled to regain possession of their former assets, and barely managed to receive any form of compensation for years of persecution and imprisonment in Nazi camps. Indeed, due to the strategic pressures of the nascent Cold War, the Allies were anxious to coopt the postwar Austrian state into the Western fold. For this reason, they made many concessions to Austria – including absolving Austria from paying reparations at the Potsdam Conference of mid 1945.

In the early postwar years, the harried, traumatized, and divided Jewish community had been forced to deal with the government as it defined itself – as a victim of Nazism: 'Jewish organizations had to accept the fiction of dealing with the innocent victims and not with the perpetrators of Nazi war crimes. It was difficult to claim reparations from a "victim" and impossible to get Allied support for such claims. All the Jews could do was to appeal to Austrian goodwill and decency, hoping that Austria would not enrich herself with the property of Jewish victims of Nazi persecution', writes Thomas Albrich. For those who did not return, the Austrian state hampered heirs' efforts for property to be reinstated or, in the cases where there were no heirs, to be handed over to the Jewish people.

These aspects of the story of Austrian Jewish property are buried in the files of the Israeli State Archives in Jerusalem. Here one can find testimonies of efforts, for the most part unsuccessful, to receive some form of compensation from Austria during the 1950s. Various financial evaluations of the scope of looted property have been made over the years. In 1953, the American Jewish Committee estimated that the aggregate material losses of Austrian Jews were some $1.25 billion ($10 billion in current values). The Israeli State Archives house a file which actually details claims made with considerable precision: a summary of the claims made by Austrian Jewish organizations is found in a Foreign Ministry memo from January 1954:

(A) Personal reparations for incarceration or due to damage to health; compensation and pension payments to former government clerks and to former employees of regional administrations; compensation for serious damage to professionals and to employees of private institutions; social security payments; claims for accommodation for Austrian Jews who are yet to find suitable lodgings. According to the organizations' appraisal, the aggregate of these claims is 665 million schillings.

(B) Compensation for confiscated movable property is as high as 660 million schillings. However, for negotiations reasons, the organizations reduced the amount to 300 million schillings.

(C) Compensation for uninherited property amounted to 1000 million schillings. In 1938 the value of registered Jewish property rose, according to a report of the Property Exchange, to over 2 billion Reichsmarks. The organizations also reduced this claim to 300 million schillings.

As already noted, the Austrian stance remained that it was not obliged to compensate anyone, for it had been a victim of Nazi Germany. 'Since all Austrians were victims of National Socialism, there was no reason for a privileged treatment of Austrian Jews. In fact, the remaining Austrian Jews thus suffered from "double victimization",' claims Albrich. While serving as Austrian Ambassador to Israel, Herbert Kroell said in late 1995:

> although we do not recognize collective guilt, we do accept responsibility for the acts of the many Austrians who collaborated in perpetrating the Nazi crimes, and hope that we can aid the victims. Austria returned all of the communal property to Jewish organizations. After the war a committee was established to take care of claims regarding private property and, in my opinion, this is not a subject which is on today's agenda. Since 1945, seven laws have been passed concerning the return of property, and 42,000 cases have been settled. In principle, Jewish victims received more generous compensation than other victims, although there certainly may be cases which have not been resolved due to technical complications.

This official Austrian position was not only inconsistent with the historical truth, but it contradicted detailed agreements signed by Austria with Germany and with the victorious Allies. According to the agreement signed between Austria and Germany in 1955, Austria assumed ownership of all the German property which remained on Austrian land, and relinquished claims for compensation from Germany. In this way, Germany refused to pay any form of compensation to Austrian Jews, and redirected their claims to the government in Vienna which had effectively received compensation *in their name*.

As such, according to the analysis of Paul Grosz, then the president of the Austrian Jewish community, a trap was created: 'Austria claimed that she was the first victim of the Nazis, and thus is not responsible for the Third Reich's crimes. Germany claimed that she is not responsible for what took place in Austria, because the worst Nazi criminals came from Austria.' Eckhaus adds, 'It is absolutely clear that the money that Germany paid to Austria should have been earmarked, above all else, to the Nazis' victims. It is difficult to determine what the Austrians have actually done with that money. There were rumors that they used the money to pay soldiers who returned from the front, where they fought alongside the Germans; I have not verified these rumors.'

In 1955 the Allies granted Austria its independence. In Section 26 of the agreement with the Allies, the subject of compensation to victims of Nazis for their property losses is stated. Austria recognized the principle of returning property plundered after the *Anschluss*, and also its obligation to compensate the former owners when the property was not returnable. As such, Austria committed itself to transferring heirless property of deceased Nazi victims to organizations which deal with the welfare of survivors.

In practice, the Austrian strategy was to slow the negotiations with Jewish groups by demanding intricate bureaucratic requirements. One of the tactics employed by the Austrian government in negotiation with Jewish organizations was to suggest that if the Jews were more demanding than pleased the government, the 'spectre of Austrian antisemitism' was brandished: when negotiating various treaties in London in 1947, Austrian Foreign Minister Gruber commented that Jewish demands might spark 'afresh the embers of antisemitism in Austria'. Since the war, the negotiations have been conducted by the local community together with a number of international Jewish organizations (the World Jewish Congress, the American Jewish Joint Distribution Committee, the American Jewish Congress), which were frequently divided over strategies and goals.

The Conference on Jewish Material Claims took a leading role in negotiations, and its Executive Vice-President, Saul Kagan, has dealt with the Austrians for over forty years. Kagan wholly rejects the central claim distancing Austria from the obligation to compensate the Reich's victims, noting that 'every western European country which was then occupied, such as France and the Netherlands, passed laws to compensate the victims of the war. Today we know from recent research that the Austrians wanted to do their utmost to rid themselves of our claims.' Noach Flug, Secretary-General of the Center of Holocaust Survivors Organization in Israel, adds: 'One of the Austrian ministers of finance said that it is imperative to defer the subject for as long as possible so that the problem will be solved biologically.'

The state appropriates cultural treasures

During the early postwar years, Austria was in control of other valuable Jewish property – thousands of books which were stolen from Shoah victims. In 1952, Dr Shlomo Shunami, a senior librarian in the Jewish National Library in Jerusalem who dedicated many years to locating stolen books throughout Europe, learnt that between 100,000 and 150,000 volumes which had been owned by Jews were located in the cellars of a Habsburg palace in Vienna. Similarly, 120,000 books that were stolen from Dutch Jews had been distributed amongst Austrian libraries.

In January 1952, the Austrians had already begun appropriating books for themselves. Shunami came across a 1951 memorandum written by Dr Essinger, Director of the Austrian Library in Vienna, and sent to the Bureau of Regional Education. The subject of the note: the distribution of books from the basements of the Habsburgs. With considerable precision, Essinger detailed the books' subjects, quantities and destination. The date of the letter is significant, for the Austrian law determined that December 1951 was the last opportunity for registering claims for stolen property; Austria did not even wait until this brief claims period had expired.

The Essinger document recorded that the National Library in Vienna and the University Library were sent 128,000 items, almost all of which were books which were categorized 'unable to return to their owners'. In addition, the two libraries received some 4500 books stolen by the Gestapo in Vienna. Other books were transferred to the library of the parliament, the library of the chancellor, to the Albertine Museum in Vienna, to schools, to Catholic libraries, and other destinations. In total, more than 186,000 books were redistributed.

If one considers that in almost every instance the Nazis' victims were those who were left heirless, it is almost certain that these books were the property of Jews. The Austrians did not take this fact into consideration. However, the Minister of Education, whose office received Essinger's report, did not bother to inform Israel about this matter. He promised representatives of Israel in January 1952 – one year after the Essinger report was circulated – that he would look into the subject, while he indicated that it is obvious that 'Austria is not to be considered as heir to this property.' In 1955 Dr Kurt Werner, the director of Israel's

National Library, reached an agreement in Vienna for the return of about 40 per cent of the books to Israel. Although there are no details of the agreement, and since its implementation was not fully documented, based on the work of Shunami and others, some 80,000 books were shipped to Israel. About 100,000 books remained in Austria, most of them having belonged to Holocaust victims.

Another case of cultural property theft with a happier ending is the fate of what became known as the Mauerbach collection. Towards the end of the Second World War, thousands of stolen art works were hidden in a salt mine in Althusa, near Salzburg, so that they would be sheltered from the Allies' aerial bombings. The American army occupied the region and returned some 10,000 works of art to their owners. The pieces whose owners could not be located were dispatched to a monastery in Mauerbach, near Vienna. The collection included pictures, sculptures, furniture, antique weapons and coins.

In 1955, in the agreement with Germany, Austria gave an assurance that within eighteen months it would return property stolen during the war to its rightful owners. However, fourteen years passed until the Austrians passed a law which affirmed the indisputable right of property owners or their heirs to repossess stolen art works. The Austrian government printed in 1969 the first (albeit partial) listing of property whose owners were unknown, and provided for property return claims to be submitted until the end of 1972.

The list was printed only in a semi-official newspaper which is not read abroad; almost all of the survivors and their heirs live outside of Austria. Of the 1200 claims made, only seventy-one were granted. The remaining art works were transferred – subsequent to the orderly passage of legislation – to the Austrian state. Selected items decorate the walls of Austrian government offices and its embassies across the globe. The remainder was left in storage in the cellars of the Mauerbach monastery.

The situation began to change only when the media entered the picture. *Art News*, the most widely distributed art journal in the United States, exposed the story in 1984. After pressure was applied by the World Jewish Congress and members of the American Congress, Austria eventually permitted claims to be submitted for a renewed nine-month period. This time, the complete list of items was published, but the Austrians were still inflexible and exceedingly meticulous. One survivor recalls that the official who took care of his claim asked to know what kind of frame bordered the painting for which he claimed ownership – and which he had last seen decades before. Some 3000 claims were lodged, of which 350 articles were returned to 190 survivors and heirs.

In 1994, *Art World* once again took up the matter, and the Austrians realized that they needed to solve the problem decisively. In July 1995, the parliament decided to return the Mauerbach collection to Jewish communal organizations. It was decided to sell the collection and to give 88 per cent of the proceeds to the community in order for it to be distributed to needy survivors of the Shoah. The remainder was earmarked for other organizations of survivors of Nazi persecution, as some of the pieces with Christian themes may not have come from the collections of Jews. It is important to recall that the Nazis also persecuted some non-Jews, mainly on political grounds, and that the property of such political persecutees was also seized.

The auction was held in Vienna at the end of October 1996, under the hammer of Christie's. The original evaluation of the auction's 8000 items was $3.5 million. In fact, the sales raised $14.4 million – apparently because many buyers, aware that the money was going to charity, were willing to pay significantly more than the genuine value of the items. The treasurer of the World Jewish Congress, Ronald Lauder, who chaired the public committee overseeing the auction, purchased tens of items and donated them to the art museum at Yad Vashem. In March 1998 a new commission was established by the Ministry of Education of Austria to deal with looted art.

Restitution and reparations: too little, too late

In fairness to the Austrians, as Paul Grosz notes, all Jewish communal property was returned, and compensation was paid in the cases of destroyed buildings. Also, real estate was mostly returned to its owners or their heirs, although in a number of cases of Aryanization, the Jewish owners were required to return the sum originally exchanged for the Aryanization transaction. The outstanding problem is the refusal to restitute the property which was unclaimed – because the owners and heirs had perished. Thomas Albrich summarizes that 'recovery under Austrian restitution laws was secured only to the extent of approximately 250–280 million dollars, meaning that at least 720 million dollars worth of property and several hundred million dollars worth of non-property damages remained un-recovered.'

Meanwhile, almost nothing was done in the field of individual compensation. The original source of this compensation was a Fund for the Aid of Victims of 550 million schillings which was created in 1956. According to Saul Kagan, Executive Director of the Conference of Jewish Material Claims Against Germany, this fund provided very small one-time grants; the largest payment given was 30,000 schillings. Gideon Eckhaus says that the fund did not fulfill its task, because 'the money ran out in the middle; in my estimation, this happened because the money was firstly made available to army veterans.' Long years of negotiations finally convinced the Austrians to also pay pensions to those persecuted by the Nazis. Kagan had to visit Vienna repeatedly, gradually accumulating concessions: payments to more Jews, broadening of pension rights, and more. He stresses that there was not a single Austrian initiative to call the payments 'reparations'; Vienna was consistently careful to speak of 'assistance', 'social security', and so on.

In recent years Austrian governments' perspectives towards the country's role during the Nazi period has changed, but this development is yet to be translated into substantive progress in compensating victims of the Nazis. The change was first expressed by the immediate past chancellor, Franz Vranitzky, who, during a visit to Israel in June 1993, acknowledged for the first time the part played by Austrians in the Shoah, and requested forgiveness from the survivors and the descendants of the murdered. Subsequently, in November 1994, Austrian President Thomas Klestil, when addressing the Knesset, said that his government had not sufficiently alleviated the suffering of the survivors.

These declarations paved the way for the first reparations provided by the Austrian government to survivors of the Shoah. In June 1995 the Austrian parliament authorized an allocation of $50 million to survivors (Jewish and Gentile); each survivor received 70,000 schillings ($7000). The fund is managed by Hana Lessing, a young and dynamic Jew. Lessing emphasizes the importance of running an efficient operation, for a large number of the survivors are eighty, ninety, and even 100 years old. The legislation says that the right to receive compensation cannot be bequeathed, hence the need to work quickly.

The fund employs a large staff. When work began, it sent out 500 questionnaires a day to survivors around the world. Two months after commencing, the fund had already provided money to the first 250 survivors, and Lessing estimates that if the present pace of work is maintained some 23,000 survivors will receive financial support by the end of 1998. As of the end of November 1996, the fund had paid an aggregate of $6.7 million to more than 9500 survivors, the clear majority of whom are Jews. Until then the fund had received 22,000 responses to the surveys sent to 25,800 known survivors. Of those who had already received payments, at November 1996 more than 4000 live in the United States, 1700 live in Austria, 1200 are in Great Britain, and some 1000 are Israelis. Close to 10,000 of the responses came from the USA, 4200 from Israel, 4100 from Austria, and 3200 from the UK.

The amount provided by the 1995 fund does not come close to the reparations provided by Germany, and Gideon Eckhaus says that if they had wanted to provide even symbolic compensation it would have been preferable to give 100,000 schillings (about $10,000), because 'that amount is written better and sounds better'. There is also a second major problem: the inability to bequeath the right to compensation. Some 250 people who completed the questionnaires passed away before the compensation reached them. In any case, the Austrian state has promised that it will not keep the funds that are not distributed to those who have a right to be compensated. This money will be used for projects memorializing the Shoah – in Austria itself, this is principally in educational institutions. This does not rule out the possibility that part of this money will be donated to Yad Vashem, to building a monument in Israel, or to an old-age home in Israel. In October 1998 the government of Austria announced the establishment of a committee on property from the Holocaust. The body includes representatives of the government, the local Jewish community, the World Jewish Restitution Organization and historians. The committee, which was agreed between the two major political parties in Austria, will examine the historic background of the confiscation of Jewish property and possible ways of providing compensation.

But until the question of Austrian responsibility for participating in the persecution and destruction of European Jewry is raised openly, Austria's relationship with Jews will remain under a dark cloud. By failing to acknowledge the nation's role in committing a grave injustice, Austrians preclude the attainment of justice. The issues of reparations and property restitution represent the tangible aspects of the concerns surrounding Austria, Jews, and a reconciliation of histories. 'All that the Austrians paid until now in compensation for the loss of property', says Eckhaus angrily, 'represents an act of deception *par excellence*.' An Austrian involved in the issue agrees: 'If we are talking about genuine compensation – this would need to be on a scale of billions.' And Dr Ron Zweig simply says: 'Forget the question as to whether the Austrians were guilty or not. Why haven't they returned the property?'

Bibliography

Primary

Archives of the State of Israel, Jerusalem.
Property forms of Austrian Jews in the National Archives in Vienna: Division 06-R001/1 – *Vermœgensverkehrsstelle*, 1938–45.
'Treasures of the Exile', files at the National Library, Hebrew University of Jerusalem.
Zionist Central Archives, Jerusalem.

Secondary

Albrich, Thomas, 'Jewish Interests and the Austrian State Treaty', *Austria in the New Europe, Contemporary Austria Studies*, vol. I (1993).
'Law and Practice under National Socialism – An Austrian View', Wiener Library (Tel Aviv University), Survivors' Testimonies Division, no. 100, p. iii I (A-E).
The Trial of Adolf Eichmann, vols 7–8 (Jerusalem, 1995), pp. 2493–2522, 2680–2874.

Interviews

Gideon Eckhaus, Chairman of the Association of Austrian Immigrants in Israel (January 1998).
Noach Flug, Secretary-General of the Centre for Holocaust Survivors in Israel (June 1997).
Paul Gross, President of the Austrian Jewish Community (January 1996).
Saul Kagan, Executive Vice-President of the Conference on Jewish Material Claims against Germany and Austria (April 1996).
Herbert Kroell, Austrian Ambassador to Israel (December 1995).
Hana Lessing, Director, Austrian Fund for Survivors (May 1997).
Dr Ron Zweig, Historian at Tel-Aviv University (February 1996).

15
Franco's Spain: Willing, Unwanted Ally of Nazi Germany

Cesar Vidal

The Republic (1931–9)

If one studies earlier references to Spain in *Mein Kampf*, there can be no doubt that the country is marginal to Adolph Hitler's global outlook. Spain was viewed as an irrelevant political entity whose imperial opportunities were over, guilty of racial sin, and in which anticlericalism would be a logical outcome. Nazi Germany's ties to Spain were overwhelmingly shaped by a projection of German needs onto the Iberian Peninsula. Most devastatingly, in the 1930s Germany exploited the Spanish rebels' admiration for Nazism and the chaos of the civil war to give German soldiers practical experience and to experiment with military technology and strategies.

Nazi agents upgraded their presence in Spain with the triumph of the 1933 elections. The Spanish Right were undoubtedly more interested in contacting the Nazi authorities in Germany than vice versa. Leaders from the CEDA (Confederation Espanola Derechos Autonomos) and the Falange pursued contacts with the NSDAP (National Sozialistische Deutsche Arbeiter Partei – the Nazi Party). In 1934,[1] Count Welczeck, the German ambassador in Madrid, contacted his superiors in order to describe the various fascist groups existing in Spain, and also explained the supportive role of the Catholic Church.

The situation changed radically with the outbreak of the Spanish civil war.[2] The initial results of the military insurgents' efforts to overthrow the Popular Front government were mixed, and the country was divided into two zones. What was intended to be a rapidly victorious coup turned into an extraordinarily cruel civil war.[3]

Franco tried, almost simultaneously, to obtain help from Italy's Mussolini and from Nazi Germany. He used a German businessman,

Johannes Bernhardt, to try to reach Hitler directly and to try to convince him that supporting the Spanish cause was a way of countering the Communist advance in the Mediterranean. In mid 1936, the envoys were rebuffed by German ministries who wanted anything but to intervene in the civil war that had just broken out in Spain.[4] However, an interview with Rudolf Hess led to a direct meeting with the Führer, who was asked for a shipment of light weapons, anti-aircraft artillery and planes, in the name of the battle against anarchy and Communism. Although Hitler's initial remark about Franco was scathing – 'He lost!' – he ordered the ministers of war and the airforce to intervene in Spain to help the rebels. Germany provided Franco's rebels with airplanes, pilots and military advisers, whose active involvement had a decisive impact on the insurgents' struggle. A fascist military alliance between Spain, Germany and Italy was forged on the peninsula.

Around this time, beginning on 14 September 1936, the republican government began to transfer the Bank of Spain's gold reserves to the Soviet Union. The gold was transported in 10,000 crates, weighing at least 559 tons, at the value of approximately 1,734,166,767 gold pesetas.[5] This is a crucial factor in our analysis, since it shows that, on the eve of the Second World War, Spain had practically no gold reserves.

Before the end of September 1936, Franco became the head of the government of the Spanish state. In October a 'national government' was formed which both Hitler and Mussolini were prepared to recognize as soon as Madrid fell.

The Nazi aid furnished to Franco was escalated in mid October 1936. It would be linked to a name that symbolized German intervention in Spain – the Condor Legion – and was to have a very special importance for Franco, but an even greater one for Hitler. Eager to know the effects of certain types of action on civilian populations, the Germans convinced Franco to begin a series of bombardments over Madrid.[6] In a number of the bombing raids on the stubbornly resistant capital, the targets were not military but civilian. On 18 October 1936, the day after the vast bombing of Madrid, Italy and Germany nevertheless announced their diplomatic recognition of the Franco regime as the legitimate Spanish government. Even though this measure did not make up for his defeat in the capital, it was enthusiastically received by Franco. He declared that Germany, Italy, Spain and Portugal were the bastions of culture, civilization and Christianity in Europe.

German plunder of Spanish products was not limited to its interest in mineral ores, which were indispensable for the maintenance of the

German steel industry.[7] The Germans also wanted Spain to be transformed into a lucrative business venue for the present and the future. In June 1937 Franco signed an economic agreement with Germany which obliged Spain to supply raw materials and to acquire German manufactured products.[8] Spain also agreed to pay its war debt in marks – amounting at the time to 50 million Reichmarks – with 4 per cent annual interest.

The Second World War

Spain repeatedly indicated its willingness to enter the war in alliance with Germany and Italy – only to be met with German discouragement. The Spanish leadership identified with the ideological drive of the Axis powers, and expected to be rewarded with broadened territorial authority in the Nazis' envisaged postwar order; the Nazis leaders, however, refused to even promise Spain territorial rewards for supporting the Axis.

Franco and his ministers repeated similar errors of judgement. In September 1940, the Spanish dictator showed that he firmly believed that Great Britain would shortly capitulate as a result of the German bombardment and indirectly advised the British ambassador that the best thing that his compatriots could do was to concede defeat. According to Franco, if the British did not give up, it was because of Hitler's 'humane and realistic' attitude, which clouded their outlook. Insofar as peace was concerned, Great Britain should not fear accepting it, since Mussolini and Franco would guarantee it.[9]

Mismatched Spanish–German expectations were epitomized by the long-awaited encounter between Hitler and Franco, which took place in Hendaya in October 1940. Franco expressed his pleasure at meeting personally with the Führer, who had furnished him with so much aid during the Spanish civil war. Hitler responded with courtesy toward the Spaniards who, under the Caudillo's leadership, had confronted Communism, and emphasized the importance of their meeting at a time when France was defeated.

The protocol of Hendaya, signed on 23 October 1940, brought Spain into the Steel Pact, the political–military pact that Germany and Italy signed in March 1939. The agreement meant strong cooperation between Spanish police, OVRA, and the Gestapo and wide collaboration in the military and diplomatic field. It was British pressure and Spanish dependence on economic supply from Western countries that prevented Spain from entering into further involvement with the Axis military effort.

On several occasions Franco expressed his willingness to fight on Hitler's side and in a few months after the beginning of the war Spain moved from 'neutral' to 'non-belligerent' status. Franco had territorial wishes which he planned to gain in his alliance with the Nazis: mainly Gibraltar but also territories in North Africa. Following his meeting with Hitler he instructed his brother-in-law and Minister of Foreign Affairs, Ramon Serrano Suner, in this direction. He also signed a secret protocol committing himself to entering the war on the side of the Third Reich. Following the Nazi assault on the Soviet Union, the Franco government decided to dispatch a military unit to aid the Germans. After some internal discussion, and because of the fear of the Allies' reaction, the unit was made up of volunteers as well as conscripts from the Spanish army.

Franco's ideological affiliation to the German government also embraced Nazi antisemitism. In late 1942 – and contrary to Franco's postwar propaganda – Jewish refugees arriving in Spanish territory were interned in concentration camps (such as that of Miranda de Ebro), and later delivered to German authorities. The widespread nature of these actions explains the suicide of Walter Benjamin (who was a prominent philosopher and literary critic in Germany), who preferred death at his own hands to being captured by Spanish police at the border. Furthermore, the Falange had begun to draw up lists of Jews in the Balearic Isles, with a view to deporting them towards Nazi camps in the future. From 1943, Franco authorized Jewish refugees to cross Spanish territory, but not to remain in Spain. Before the end of the year some Spanish legations abroad offered refuge to Jewish refugees.

The economic relations between Nazi Germany and Spain were outstanding. The Germans penetrated deeply into the Spanish economy with a network of German enterprises which controlled the management of critical raw materials and exports in Spain. The Steel Pact brought a sharp rise (ten times) in Spanish exports to Germany (fifteen times in food products). There were tensions between Spain and Germany because of the huge credit balance of the Germans, who could not pay for all Spanish exports. The traffic of gold and other methods of payment enriched many people from the Franco regime, and would later help to cover up many of the details involved. The Safehaven documents reveal the protest of the Allies and the growing use of Spain as a haven for many Germans and their assets. According to one British document, from June 1945 there were some 20,000 Germans in Spain, living mostly free and maintaining large amounts of property.[10] The Eizenstat Report estimates that private German assets in Spain stood at $95 million.

Beginning in the spring of 1942, the OSS (Office of Strategic Services) in Madrid started to collect data on Franco's relations with the Third Reich, which left no doubt as to the good relations between them. The use of Spanish airports by the Nazi air force, the cover given to German submarines in Spanish ports (Operation Moro), and the assistance in espionage accorded to the Third Reich, were all well known.[11] At the beginning of 1944, the OSS managed to identify 3000 enemy agents in Spain and more than 400 members of clandestine enemy services.[12]

Actually, the Fletcher report estimates that $138 million were laundered through the National Swiss Bank and reexported to Spain and Portugal. In the case of Spain, the figure arrived at was $30 million in gold and another quantity, between $30 and $39 million in other German assets. In fact, in January 1948, a group of researchers established that Spain had acquired at least 26.8 tons of gold (about $30.3 million) originating from the Swiss National Bank, the Bank of Portugal and the German Transatlanic Bank. The importance of the sum can be appreciated if one bears in mind the fact that Spain did not have gold reserves in 1939, as a result of the republican government's shipments to the USSR, and that, indisputably, at the end of the war, the Bank of Spain possessed no less than 67 tons. Of these, 38.6 tons were acquired between March 1942 and February 1946, with almost two-thirds coming from Switzerland.

The end of the Second World War placed the Franco regime in a delicate international situation. Not only did it owe its existence to Hitler's direct intervention, but in addition it had collaborated closely, militarily and economically with the Third Reich. In spite of everything, even the end of the war did not signify the disappearance of the good relations that have always existed between the Nazis and the Franco regime.

After the war, the Allies' plans to liquidate German enterprises in Spain and to expel German nationals were only partially implemented. Many Germans were well briefed by Spanish friends, and Gestapo members enjoyed special police passports until March 1946.

The outbreak of the Cold War undoubtedly not only consolidated Franco's regime, as a US ally, it also made it possible for it not to be held responsible for these matters. In effect, in an exchange of notes in May 1948, the Allies reached an agreement with Franco's regime, by virtue of which the Tripartite Commission was to receive only the sum of $114,329 (101.6 kilograms). Insofar as the German assets are concerned, the discussions continued until 1958 – when Spain was already part of the US defence system in Western Europe – and no payment was ever made. These assets presumably included valuables plundered by the Nazis, including works of art belonging to Jews, such as the paintings which were transferred through Spain thanks to the intervention of Manuel Aznarm (grandfather of the current Spanish prime minister), who was ambassador of Spain in Argentina at that time. In August 1958, by virtue of the signing of a protocol – which came into effect on 2 July 1959 – the question was settled. Franco's regime emerged elegantly from a compromising complicity. A thorough investigation of Spain's behaviour during the war and sincere acknowledgement of responsibility is still needed.

Appendix: Allied Relations and Negotiations with Spain[*]

Although Spanish General Franciso Franco declared Spain neutral in 1939, he was openly sympathetic to the Axis powers, which helped bring him to power, and only gradually abandoned his inclination to join the Axis. Spain supplied Germany with critical commodities, intelligence, and even some troops – the Blue Division – for the Eastern Front. By 1943, however, Spain had gradually adopted a more honestly neutral policy, largely in response to Allied economic warfare, the growing strength of Allied armed forces especially in North Africa and the Mediterranean, and the reversals experienced by Germany from 1942 onward. Nonetheless, Spain's strategic location and its supply routes to North Africa and South America gave Germany a conduit for important wartime materials, which Franco continued to supply. Private Spanish merchants were also Germany's principal source of vital commodities smuggled from Latin America and Africa, including industrial diamonds and platinum.

Wolfram was a major component of Spanish exports to Germany. As the second largest producer of this critical commodity (after Portugal), Spain sold Germany over 1100 metric tons annually between 1941 and 1943, providing more than 30 per cent of Germany's industrial requirements, and which, when combined with Portuguese sales to Germany, accounted for at least 90 per cent of Germany's wartime wolfram needs,

---

[*] Extract from the summary of 'US and Allied Wartime and Postwar Relations and Negotiations with Argentina, Portugal, Spain, Sweden, and Turkey on Looted Gold and German External Assets and US Concerns about the Fate of the Wartime Ustasha Treasury', the June 1998 supplement to 'Preliminary Study on US and Allied Efforts to Recover and Restore Gold and other Assets Stolen or Hidden by Germany during World War II', US State Department.

which the Allies estimated to be 3500 tons annually. Allied economic warfare efforts against Spain were generally unsuccessful in the early years of the war. The Allied objective was to purchase enough of the ore to satisfy Spain's export demands and prevent it from increasing its trade with the enemy. The Franco regime combined desultory trade negotiations with the Allies and secret agreements with Germany to ensure the continued delivery of critical war supplies. In January 1944 the Spanish Minister for Industry and Commerce defended Spain's agreements with Germany, noting that Spain felt it 'impossible' to deny Germany a commodity which 'had a very high value in wartime.' The Allies hesitated to act decisively against Spain for fear of driving Franco more fully into the Axis camp, but in January 1944 the Allies imposed an oil embargo on Spain.

In negotiations with Spain during the embargo, Britain favoured a compromise that would allow Spain to resume wolfram exports to Germany at the 1943 level, but the United States continued to demand a complete ban. Finally in May 1944, as Germany's defeat became inevitable, Spain agreed to limit exports of wolfram to Germany. Secretary of State Cordell Hull believed that if he had had wholehearted British support, he would have achieved the objective of a complete ban on Portuguese wolfram exports to Germany. The Allies soon learned that senior members of Franco's Cabinet cooperated with Germany in smuggling more than 800 tons through July 1944 in violation of the agreement. Spain's exports of wolfram to Nazi Germany ended with the closing of the Franco-Spanish border in August 1944.

The American-led Safehaven programme encountered resistance in the US Embassy in Madrid. Intelligence operations to gain information about Spain's wartime support for Germany were undermined as US Ambassador Carlton Hayes preferred a less aggressive attitude towards Franco and his government. Britain was less interested in the postwar political goals of Safehaven than in negotiating a trade agreement with Spain and ensuring the flow of Spanish goods to Britain in the postwar period.

In May 1945, just before VE Day, in response to an Allied request, Spain issued a decree freezing all assets with Axis interests. The Allies estimated German external assets in Spain at the end of the war at about $95 million. American experts, using some captured German documents, conservatively estimated in 1946 that between February 1942 and May 1945 Spain acquired about 123 tons of gold worth nearly $140 million (over $1.2 billion in today's values): 11 tons directly from Germany and German-occupied territories, 74 tons from the German account at the Swiss National Bank, and about 38 tons directly from the Swiss National Bank, which the Allies believed included some looted gold (about $376 million in today's values). US estimates indicated that 72 per cent of the gold, worth approximately $100 million, acquired by Spain had been looted by Germany from the nations it occupied. Other reports of Spanish gold acquisitions included an SSU intelligence report that trucking gold from Switzerland to Spain became necessary by late 1942 because Germany could not pay for Spanish goods in any other manner; a War Department report that 203 tons of German gold were trucked from Switzerland to the Spanish Foreign Exchange Institute between January 1942 and February 1944; and a German diplomatic report that SOFINDUS, a large German state-owned enterprise in Spain, acquired about 83 tons of gold bars from Switzerland in 1943.

Protracted postwar Allied negotiations with Spain over the restitution of monetary gold and the application of external German assets for reparations began in Madrid in September 1946. The Allied–Spanish negotiations were more intermittent and lengthier than the Allied–Swiss and Allied – Swedish negotiations which had preceded them. In October 1946 Spain agreed to turn over to the Allies an estimated $25 million in official and semiofficial German assets. In January 1948 Spain insisted on separating the negotiations over assets and gold, declaring that it would restitute any looted gold but would not sign an agreement that did not include a reciprocal claim for Spain's lost Civil War gold. The two sides agreed in May to a complex formula for liquidating private German assets (then estimated at $20–23 million), in which Spain would get about 24 per cent and the Inter-Allied Reparations Agency about 76 per cent of the proceeds. None of the proceeds was slated for the $25 million fund for non-repatriable victims of Nazism, as envisioned in the January 1946 Allied Reparations Agreement, because the Allied negotiators believed the fund would be fully subscribed by the amounts obtained from Switzerland, Sweden, and Portugal.

The two sides signed a separate agreement in May 1948 that Spain would return $114,329 (101.6 kilograms) out of about $30 million in looted Dutch gold that the Allies had identified at the Spanish Foreign Exchange Institute and be allowed to keep the remainder. This portion was the only gold that Spain had purchased directly from the Banco Aleman Transatlantico, a German institution, and the Allies claimed that under the terms of Bretton Woods Resolution VI only the original purchaser of the gold from Germany was liable for its return. The Allies publicly acknowledged that Spain had not been aware at the time it acquired the gold that it had been looted. In addition to the

101.6 kilograms of looted gold, Spain turned over to the Allies $1.3 million in gold bars and coins it had seized from German state properties at the end of the war.

The Allied–Spanish negotiations coincided with Allied efforts to ostracize the Franco regime. The Allies explored ways short of direct intervention to end the Franco regime and allow the Spanish people to choose freely a new government. During these years Spain was excluded from the United Nations, pending a UN review of wartime Spanish support for the Axis, as well as from the emerging Western alliance, and most governments around the world downgraded their diplomatic relations with the Franco regime. Economic sanctions against Spain were under consideration but were ultimately excluded by the Allies for fear of exacerbating tensions that could bring about another civil war or allow Communism to gain a foothold in Spain. By 1948 the United States had concluded that these attempts at isolating Spain were counterproductive and were detrimental to the Spanish economy. As a result, with the signing of the May 1948 agreements, the United States released over $64 million in assets frozen since the war and informed Spain that it would allow it to use its remaining gold as collateral for private loans.

In 1950 the Federal Reserve Bank of New York held $50 million worth of gold as collateral for loans by Chase National Bank of New York (now Chase Manhattan) and National City Bank (now Citibank) to the Spanish Foreign Exchange Institute. Part of the collateral consisted of looted gold Spain had purchased from Switzerland and Portugal during the war. Both the State Department and the Treasury Department ruled that, pursuant to postwar Allied restitution policy, the gold was considered 'tainted only in the hands of the first purchaser'. Thus Switzerland (not Spain) was held legally responsible for providing this quantity of gold to the Tripartite Gold Commission. At the request of Citibank, the looted gold Spain used to collateralize its loan was resmelted into 'good delivery' bars by the US Assay Office. In 1951 Spain collateralized a $10 million extension of one of the loans using gold, including $2.6 million in looted gold that it had bought directly from the German account at the Swiss National Bank and had never revealed to the Allies. Both Treasury and State allowed the Federal Reserve to accept the looted bars, arguing that since Spain had negotiated the May 1948 Allied–Spanish accord on looted gold 'in good faith' they would not consider them looted.

In 1951 Spain halted the distribution of German assets in an effort to garner a larger percentage and gain West Germany's assurance that it would not hold Spain responsible for compensating German owners of liquidated property. Intermittent negotiations continued until 1957, when Spain agreed to turn unliquidated assets over to Germany and Germany agreed not to hold Spain liable for compensation. This opened the way for an Allied–Spanish agreement in which Spain turned over the money it had blocked since 1951 in exchange for $1 million liquidated after that date. The total value of funds derived from German assets in Spain and disbursed by the Inter-Allied Reparations Agency amounted to about $32.8 million, taking into consideration the fluctuation of the value of the peseta in the 1950s as a result of Spain's severe economic problems, stemming from the devastation of the Spanish Civil War and the Second World War. Altogether Spain received at least $5.3 million in liquidation proceeds.

By 1950 the Allies joined the US effort to normalize relations with Spain, and the assets negotiations were subordinated to efforts to integrate Spain into the Western economic and military framework and provide Spain with substantial economic and military assistance – even though it was to remain formally outside the Western Alliance until its accession to NATO and the European Community in the post-Franco 1980s.

Notes

1   Welczeck to the Ministry of Foreign Affairs, number 395/34. Report: Fascism in Spain.
2   The most complete work from the military point of view is C. Vidal, *La Guerra de Franco: historia militar de la guerra civil espanola* (Barcelona, 1996). For a general study of the Spanish civil war, see P. Broue and E. Temime, *La revolucion y la guerra de Espana* (Madrid, 1974); G. Cabanellas, *La guerra de los mil dias* (Buenos Aires, 1975); R. Carr, *La tragedia espanola* (Madrid, 1986); G. Esenwein and A. Shubert, *Spain at War* (London and New York, 1995); J. Zugazagoitia, *Guerra y vicisitudes de los espanoles* (Barcelona, 1977); C. Vidal, *Recuerdo, 1936: Una historia oral de la guerra civil espanola* (Madrid, 1995).
3   On this subject, see M. Anso, *Yo fui ministro de Negrin* (Barcelona, 1976) p. 134, and, especially, D. Martinez Barrios, *Memorias* (Barcelona, 1983), pp. 365ff.
4   Hans Heinrich Dieckhoff (the last prewar German ambassador to America) points out in his memorandum dated 5 July that both the German foreign ministry and the war ministry agreed that the Spanish emissary should not be received by any military authority and that there should be no thought even of sending them weapons.
5   A. Vinas, *El oro de Moscu* (Barcelona, 1979), pp.129ff.
6   Oral testimony on this topic in C. Vidal, *La Guerra de Franco*.
7   In 1937 Germany had to import from Spain 1,620,000 tons of iron; 956,000 tons of pyrite; and another 2000 of other minerals.

8   GD (German Documents), p. 417.
9   Text of the letter in C. Vidal, *Intrepidos*, p.141.
10   PRO, FO 3712/49610, 2593.
11   Charles Burdick, 'Moro: the Resupply of German Submarines in Spain, 1939–42', in *Central European History* (1970).
12   Murphy to Mowinckel, 4 June 1945, 'X-2 Case Materials Illustrating German Safehaven Practices', RG 226, Entry 116, Oficina del Director, Microfilm Publications 1642, Reel 108.

16
Portugal's Double Game: Between the Nazis and the Allies

Antonio Luca

In recent years it has become almost commonplace to say that Salazar, Portugal's dictator for nearly four decades, was just a conservative and authoritarian leader, cooperative with the Allies and mistrusting towards Nazi Germany. Not only Portuguese historic revisionists trying to sell this image of their idol, but even an official American report – despite a few sharp criticisms regarding the Salazar dictatorship – leaves the taste of a positive comparison between Portugal and the other neutral countries of Europe.[1] This rewriting of history does not lead to a balanced view of what really happened. The fallacy about the Salazar regime stems from a misinterpretation of its ties with Britain.

The ties between Lisbon and London were very strong and date back several centuries. Portugal fully depended on England to maintain its connection with the overseas colonies that constituted the Portuguese Empire. Moreover, it depended on England for vital supplies such as coal and later on the United States for fuel. His Majesty's government felt it could reach a much better arrangement with the ascendant fascist dictatorship than with parliamentary democracy which was too weak to control the burgeoning workers' movement.[2]

At the time of the Second World War, the prevailing conditions caused a paradox: the fascist dictatorship in Portugal had to comply a lot more with Allied than with Axis demands and had to behave as an Allied-friendly neutral, while the Swiss and the Swedish democracies were acting as Axis-friendly neutrals.

Portuguese fascism and its attitudes towards human rights should under no circumstances be mistaken for this economic dependence and geo-strategic alignment. Portugal's relations with Nazi Germany cannot be regarded as an honourable chapter in its history.

Salazar's refugee policy

Despite the positive memories of many refugees who stayed in Portugal, it is important to note that Salazar's decisions in this field never reached a point of conflict with the Nazi strategy. In the 1930s, Jewish refugees were still accepted into Portugal in a relatively liberal way. Immigrants with advanced technical skills could be of use in a country like Portugal despite some opposition from some trade unions. Only a few hundred refugees wished to take advantage of this open-door policy. Until *Kristallnacht* in November 1938 many German Jews still contemplated remaining in Germany.[3] At this stage the Nazis were ready to allow Jews to immigrate to Britain, the United States and other Western countries which closed their doors. Even Adolf Eichmann tried to push the Austrian Jews to go abroad. The first stage of Nazi policy was one of pressures and expulsions.

After November 1938 increasing numbers of Jews began looking for a way out. In November 1939, Salazar ordered that the visas for a selected list of refugees be issued centrally in Lisbon. In February 1940, in reaction to the request of a group of refugees who intended to go to Brazil, the Portuguese legation in The Hague was ordered to issue transit visas only in those cases in which the refugees were Catholic.[4] Salazar always listened to the warnings of Captain Agostinho Lourenço, the director of the police PVDE with whom he conferred weekly. His chiefspy expressed his concerns as to the consequences of welcoming too many Jewish refugees into Portugal. The instructions to the Portuguese consul in The Netherlands were to verify case by case and to let in Jewish refugees only with a special permit.[5]

After the French capitulation to Nazi Germany, the Portuguese restrictive policy suddenly faced hundreds of thousands fleeing from the Nazis without their belongings. Salazar and the PVDE (Policia Defesa Vigilancia Do Estado) had reason to fear that those refugees could quickly destabilize his dictatorship. Some thousands of refugees continued on to overseas destinations after transit through Portugal. This estimate includes both legal and illegal transits (without visas). The Portuguese regime granted visas but only on very stringent terms. The refugees were not allowed to remain in Portugal. They could receive only a Portuguese transit visa, and that, on condition that they could present at least three additional documents: a visa to leave France, a visa to enter some third country such as the USA, and a ticket on a steamship to their next destination. At this stage, if they were lucky enough to obtain the Portuguese visa, they would still have to request a visa to cross Spain.

This was a complex and costly process, and whenever a stage was missed, one had to begin the process again from square one.[6]

It was not to the Portuguese–Spanish border guards that Salazar assigned the role of turning back refugees, but rather to his consular bureaucrats abroad. Most of them followed his orders. Aristides de Sousa Mendes, the consul in Bordeaux, is the one famous exception to that rule, and he was recognized by Yad Vashem as a Righteous Among the Nations. The persecution which he suffered for the rest of his lifetime is testimony to Portugal's restrictive policy. Many personal tragedies resulted from this policy. Desperate people queued for hours, days and weeks in front of the consulates. Some of them committed suicide. Others took the chance and travelled without the Portuguese visa. The 512 Luxembourg Jews who had been expelled by the Gestapo, arrived at the Portuguese border without visas and were sent back. Many of them ended up in Treblinka.[7] Many others succeeded in crossing the border into Portugal without visas and owed their survival to a fortunate circumstances. Some were helped by local aid organizations and others were welcomed because they brought in some money and paid part of the housing bills.[8] The serious question remains: how many people tried but failed to transit Portugal?

Shortly after the German attack on the Soviet Union, the Portuguese regime forbade the issuing of any visas for refugees from Eastern Europe.[9]

After the German invasion of Hungary in March 1944 the Portuguese Minister to Budapest, Sampayo Garrido, was dismissed for his liberal policy of granting protection to a few Hungarian Jews whom he knew personally. Another diplomat, Carlos Branquinho, replaced him with strict instructions from Salazar. However, during his stay the destruction of Hungarian Jewry became a dramatic reality which could no longer be ignored. The Allies warned the dictator Horthy by radio that every Hungarian official involved in the deportations would be indicted after the war. The neutral legations to Budapest met together to discuss a common policy. Carl Lutz from the Swiss Legation and Raoul Wallenberg from the Swedish Legation strongly influenced the mood of other neutrals by at least confronting them with the practical example of how they could react to the deportations. The Vatican, who had taken over the formal call to the neutrals' meetings, still made a clear-cut distinction between those Jews who adhered to their faith and those who had converted to Christianity. The Catholic Church and the Spanish and Portuguese governments knew that the Nazis were losing the war and that any steps to protect a few Hungarian Jews might be politically wise.

Even Himmler's SS started playing the card of Jewish hostages, sometimes suspending or accepting the suspension of deportations, in the hope that this might bring the Allies to the negotiating table and eventually to a separate peace. In this framework, it is not surprising that the Portuguese chargé d'affaires Branquinho would witness the shift in Salazar's policy and would issue about 700 'protective passports', which in some cases saved Jews from the death camps.

Salazar and the Nazi plundering

Since early in the 1930s, Salazar knew very well the nature of his trade partners in Nazi Germany. The head of his legation in Berlin, Alberto da Veiga Simões – a conservative diplomat and fairly hostile to the Nazi – regularly sent him shocking reports on the despoliation of the Jews. The director of his censorship services, Salvação Barreto, reported to him on the plundering of the Jews in Danzig.[10] After the invasion of Poland, there was little concern in the censored Portuguese press about the violence perpetrated against Polish Jews, but some reports on the plight of Polish Catholics were published and left no doubt as to the methods used by the Nazis wherever they arrived.[11]

It is clear that Portuguese officials knew how gold reserves were seized by the Nazis in Czechoslovakia, Danzig or The Netherlands.[12] In November 1940 the British House of Commons specifically discussed the suspicion that Portugal might be shipping gold stolen by the Germans from occupied countries to the United States. For the first time, Salazar had to give specific instructions to his ambassador in London in order to deny the charges.[13] It was obvious that the Nazis were financing their purchases abroad with looted assets, as it was impossible to ignore that the Jews and the citizens of the occupied countries were among the victims of the Nazi robbery.

Salazar represented the interests of Portuguese industrialists and bankers who grabbed this opportunity to make profits from both belligerent sides. They sold to Germany tinned sardines, cork, wool, textile products and above all wolfram – all of them at very inflated prices.[14] As the usual Portuguese trade deficit with Germany was replaced by a German deficit, Salazar allowed the Banco de Portugal to take Swiss francs from Germany and to buy Nazi gold from the Swiss National Bank (SNB). In 1941–2, this laundering circle was most active: some 120 tons of gold came into the possession of the Portuguese central bank, the main purchaser of SNB gold during the war.[15] In October 1942 the Secretary-General of the Banco de Portugal, Cabral Pessoa, made clear to his Swiss colleague Victor Gautier that the Portuguese central bank had been buying gold from Switzerland and not from Germany, partly because of political and legal reasons. The Portuguese reservations – clearly understood by Gautier – evaporated, as long as the gold from the Reichsbank passed through Swiss hands.[16]

The Reichsbank had been delivering Dutch gold ingots through Switzerland in their original form. At some point it started worrying about effects that the disclosure of such deficiencies might have on relations with the Portuguese bankers. By December 1942 the Reichsbank directors asked their Swiss colleagues whether they could get back some of what they had already delivered to the Portuguese and resmelt them. The Swiss bankers declined the request and advised the Germans that the Portuguese were now showing less concern about the origin of the gold bars.[17]

It is known that, at least after January 1943, the Prussian mint smelted the Belgian gold reserves.[18] Some of them ended up in the vaults of the SNB, some in the Banco de Portugal, a smaller part in the Swedish Riksbank. Salazar and his bankers only reduced their use of the Swiss laundering circle when the Prussian mint started resmelting looted gold in a systematic way. Nineteen forty-three was no longer a year of intensive laundering, but one of intensive resmelting: in Germany and, according to many reports of British spies, also in several Portuguese banks, following the advice of the Banco de Portugal.[19] Mainly in 1943 and in the first half of 1944, Portugal had a net balance of some 44 tons acquired from the Reichsbank, which made it the second largest purchaser of 'German' gold during the war, next to Switzerland.[20]

In certain cases, the Portuguese government not only had a general knowledge about the payments being made with looted assets, sometimes it even knew very well from whom those assets had been stolen and who were the victims. According to a decree of the German occupation forces in The Netherlands, every Dutch Jew had to deliver his or her assets to the Bank Lippmann-Rosenthal (LiRo). Among these items, Portuguese bonds were a very substantial portion of the booty taken over by the Nazis: they could possibly be exchanged against a credit in escudos, deposited in an account in Lisbon and remain disposable for German expenses in Portugal. A Nazi official, Alfred Flesche, commissioner at the LiRo and president of the German Trade Chamber in Amsterdam, travelled to Lisbon in December 1942 with Jan Voetelink, a consul of Portugal in The Netherlands, and a high-placed official in the same bank. They wanted the Portuguese government to take over the bonds and to credit the Nazi-controlled LiRo with their value in escudos.

The Portuguese finance ministry had fears about eventual claims from the former owners and was therefore assured by the visitors about the precautions taken in the expropriating procedure.[21] These negotiations apparently brought few results, but the fact that they were conducted highlights the readiness of the Portuguese dictatorship to trade belongings of Jewish victims.

Business and politics

Nobody could seriously expect the Portuguese dictatorship to sell on credit to Germany and, given its lack of prewar gold and currency, it was obvious that Germany paid with looted property. In May 1942 the Portuguese central banker Álvaro Pedro de Sousa, following Salazar's instructions, accepted the proposal that the German deficit could be paid in gold. This represented a most satisfactory agreement for the Nazis.[22]

At this stage of the war Britain and America were less worried about the looted gold and more concerned about the nature of the goods sold to the Germans. The Allies kept the pressure on Portugal through the Navy certificates ('navicerts' – certificates which allowed movement of ships), which since the summer of 1940 were issued only in a restrictive and selective fashion. At the same time, the Allies made the war much more expensive for the German – and in some ways even rewarded the Portuguese double-dealing – through preemptive purchases which helped to inflate the prices, for instance, of wolfram by up to 3500 per cent.[23]

For obvious reasons the wolfram issue became the most important source of conflict between Salazar and the Allies in the late phase of the war. The British Ministry for Economic Warfare and the US Treasury Department were especially active against a Portuguese policy that they believed was outrageously pro-German after the wolfram agreement of January 1943. During the six months previous to the landing in France, tension between the Portuguese dictatorship and the Western Allies was stronger than ever. For the first time since 1926, the British considered the possibility of overthrowing Salazar and moved in the shadows to prepare a *coup d'état* that might be necessary and, in that case, had good prospects of success.

In early June 1944, precisely as the Allied troops were landing on the beaches of Normandy, Salazar was capitulating under Anglo-American pressure and forbade any further exports of wolfram.[24] But he was not yet giving up his most stubborn political goal: paving the way for the Nazis to negotiate a separate peace with the Western Allies. His opposition to the policy of the Casablanca summit (which called for the unconditional surrender of Germany) could no longer take the form of legal wolfram supplies, but it could mean collaboration with the Nazi efforts to find communication channels to the West. This can explain why the Portuguese government reversed its policy and agreed to receive in Lisbon the famous Chorin family – Hungarian-Jewish industrialists and bankers, who owned the enormous Manfred Weiss works that had been left behind in the trusteeship of the SS.

At that time, Heinrich Himmler was secretly trying to talk with the West through the neutral countries. These efforts were not authorized by Hitler, who would have viewed them as high treason. The SS had some important cards to play: it was still operating the death camps and could try to blackmail the Allies with the fate of millions of hostages. Among these hostages were over forty members of the Chorin family. The SS officer Kurt Becher was trying to exploit their fate in his negotiations. There is no document explaining why Salazar made an exception and allowed the Chorin family into Portugal with a forged visa. A logical explanation is probably related to his wish to advance the SS goal of a separate peace by showing its good will. The cautious Portuguese dictator would not expose himself by helping the SS strategy actively.[25]

The appeasing face of the Cold Warriors

The strong line of the American Secretary of the Treasury, Henry Morgenthau, against the neutrals and the Bank for International Settlement (BIS) lost its appeal when Cold War considerations took over. After the war the neutral countries managed to negotiate a cheap political and financial bill. The Swiss, the Swedes and later the Spanish concluded very favourable agreements for themselves.

The Portuguese case followed a totally different pattern. The negotiations were much longer (until 1953), the agreement took even longer to be signed (1958) and the amount of returned gold was far below the proportions paid by the other three countries; it involved 4 tons, to be handed over only when the Federal Republic of Germany restored their entire value to Portugal.[26] As early as 1946 the Portuguese negotiators and their counterparts of the TGC (Tripartite Gold Commission) agreed to organize a subcommittee that would investigate the amounts of Reichsbank gold acquired by the Banco de Portugal. This subcommittee soon pointed out the above-mentioned amount of 44 tons. In other words, it concentrated on the gold that came directly from

Germany thus ignoring the bulk of the looted gold accepted in Portugal. According to OSS (Office of Strategic Services) reports, 70 per cent of the gold received through Switzerland was looted. It seems unlikely that the TGC delegation was unaware of the OSS reports, particularly if we take into account that the American vice-consul to Lisbon, Theodor Zanthaky, often acting as a member of the delegation, had close ties with the OSS. The TGC not only feigned a very improbable ignorance at the 120 'Swiss' tons, but also hurried to reduce their demands for Portuguese restitution. The original 44 tons demand went down to 38 tons in November 1947,[27] to 21 tons one week later,[28] to 10 tons and then to 7 by May 1948.[29] In 1953 they finally signed for the above-mentioned 4 tons and still had to wait a long time before the Portuguese were willing to deliver any gold at all.

The Portuguese delegation effectively exploited the Cold War environment. First they claimed that traded gold from Austria and Czechoslovakia was not relevant because their invasions were accepted by the international community.[30] As for the Belgian gold, the Portuguese said, this could not be spoken of as loot because the Banque de France was acting as trustee of the Belgian bankers and gave the ingots to the Germans in accordance with the agreement of the Vichy government.[31] Caeiro da Mata, the new Minister for Foreign Affairs, and also a member of the Board of Directors of the Banco de Portugal and the former ambassador to Vichy, reminded the Americans that they still recognized Pétain as legitimate head of the French state when he was delivering Belgian gold to the Nazis.[32] Surprisingly enough, the British tried to justify Pétain in the discussion, blaming only the Nazis who confiscated Belgian gold. The Portuguese went one step further, claiming that the Germans were allegedly exerting their right to war booty.[33]

The first Eizenstat Report explains that the Allies softened their position because of the pending renewal agreement on the Azores (against the view of the Treasury Department).[34] The fact that these demands disappeared in the following rounds of the negotiations demonstrates that the Atlantic partners had good reason to help the Salazar regime to stay in power. Unlike Switzerland or Sweden, Portugal was a country in which the peasants and the working class lived in extreme poverty. The fortunes acquired by some Portuguese industrialists during the war did not change this picture. Money earned in wartime remained in very few hands. In 1945, the danger of real hunger was still there, in spite of the Allied controls having been dropped – the country looked like 'a man with full pockets and an empty stomach', in the words of the concerned British ambassador.

The best way to prevent new mass unrest after the war was to financially support food imports. This is precisely what Salazar did through his minister Daniel Barbosa.[35]

Getting rid of evidence

While the TGC negotiators were forgetting the 'Swiss' gold and were kept busy with the 'German' gold, the Portuguese government was getting rid of tainted ingots. Three trails have been mentioned thus far: the Far East, Switzerland and Poland. The latter two may be connected with each other. Beginning in the immediate postwar period and continuing at least until the late 1950s, Portugal insisted on buying Polish coal,[36] the price of which was at that time far above the average and the quality of which was far below the average available on the international market.[37] The State Department suspected Portugal of paying for those imports directly to Poland with looted gold and warned Warsaw about the danger of weakening its own claims at the TGC.[38] The answer from Warsaw is unknown, but the Polish government appears to have been unmoved by Washington's threats. Shortly thereafter the Polish government was to sign the 1949 agreement with Bern. It would get the dormant accounts of Polish citizens in Switzerland against the guarantee of indemnifying the property of Swiss capitalists whose holdings were expropriated in Poland.[39] Given the circumstances of increasing East–West tension, it may be assumed that whoever went into such a bilateral deal with a major war profiteer must have already given up any expectations as to the equanimity of the TGC.

On the other hand, the French government suspected Portugal of paying for the Polish coal through Switzerland. There could very well be some gold for Poland included among the gold sent from Portugal to Switzerland in the second half of the 1940s.[40] The French Ministry of External Affairs sent a letter to the SNB, mentioning a Portugal-based firm, which was supposed to import Polish coal from a Switzerland-based one. The Banco de Portugal was supposed to be selling gold to the SNB, which was to pay the respective amount in Swiss francs to the Swiss firm. Confronted with this version by SNB director Paul Rossy, the Portuguese central bank denied having sold any ingots with the purpose of buying Polish coal. In the meantime, the SNB dropped the case, because it got hold of some new information and believed that the currency used in the Polish–Portuguese deals was the US dollar.[41]

The Far East trail focuses on Macao, the Portuguese colony on the Chinese border. The public's attention was drawn to the Macao connection early in 1998 by a navy officer, Fernando Brito, who, for a period of six months, had weekly witnessed an average entry of half a ton of gold ingots into the colony.[42] He saw the Reichsbank imprint on many of the ingots. Brito's statement is especially important because, in the second half of 1966, he was a member of a committee organized by the Portuguese colonial authorities to control those entries.

The press officer of the Banco de Portugal, Nuno Jonet, has repeatedly stated that there are no more Nazi gold bars in its vaults, with just three or four exceptions – some kind of museum pieces. It is understandable that, after the war, the state and the bank wanted to get rid of most of the compromising gold. The historian who worked on behalf of the Banco de Portugal, Joaquim da Costa Leite, vehemently denied any connection between the bank and the Nazi ingots detected in Macao.[43] Assuming that Costa Leite's denial is right and that the Nazi ingots flowing through the colony did not belong to the Banco de Portugal, another question must be raised: whose gold was the Portuguese government helping to launder?

Epilogue

The public discussion about looted gold started in the Portuguese press in late October 1996 and put both the government of the Socialist Party and the Banco de Portugal under fire. Although Salazar's personal archives and the documents of the Ministry of Foreign Affairs have been accessible for some time, an essential piece of the puzzle is still missing: the archives of the central bank remain closed. On 19 December 1996, the bank announced it would hire the historian Costa Leite to organize its archives and to open them without undue delay. The definition of 'undue delay' was left unspecified. But on 22 March 1997 the vice-president of the SNB, Jean-Pierre Roth, brought additional pressure on the Portuguese political and monetary authorities by reminding them that the Banco de Portugal had indeed been the main purchaser of Reichsbank gold through the SNB during the war.[44] It was not long before the Portuguese government reacted. On the following day, then Prime Minister António Guterres announced that all archives of the Portuguese state would be opened immediately. The central bank was supposed to have similar plans and to have shared them with the prime minister. In April 1997, Guterres went to Washington, where he emphatically repeated his commitment to full transparency before the world press.

The Portuguese commission which supervises the research by Costa Leite is chaired by former president Mario Soares, himself a political opponent of Salazar. However, Soares dismissed publicly the allegations against Portuguese conduct during the war and declared that all archives will be opened to the public. The international commission under Soares, which included Mr Israel Singer of the World Jewish Congress, was never called to meet and discuss the findings. In a statement by another official of the World Jewish Congress, Dr Avi Beker, in April 1998 some reservations were made on the working methods of the Soares commission. It remains to be seen when and what will be opened for independent research. In the meantime, many questions remain open.

Notes

1   *US and Allied Efforts to Recover and Restore Gold and Other Assets Stolen or Hidden by Germany During World War II: Preliminary Study* (US Department of State, Washington, DC, 1997), pp. 24, 43.
2   Fernando Rosas, *Portugal entre a Paz e a Guerra, 1939–1945* (Lisbon: Estampa, 1990).
3   António Louçã, 'O regime salazarista e os refugiados', *Política Internacional*, no. 9, October 1994.
4   Arquivo Histórico–Diplomático, Ministério dos Negócios Estrangeiros (hereafter AHD–MNE), Telegramas expedidos para a Legação em Haia, no. 4, 9.2.40.
5   Patrick von zur Muhlen, *Fluchtweg Spanien-Portugal. Die deutsche Emigration und der Exodus aus Europa, 1933–1945* (Bonn: Dietz, 1992), p. 155. See also Ansgar Schafer, 'Hindernisse auf dem Weg in die Freiheit. Der portugiesische Staat und die deutsche Emigration', *Exil*, no. 1/93.
6   Muhlen, *Fluchtweg*, p. 157.
7   Ibid., pp. 161.
8   Ibid., p. 159.
9   Eva Ban and Antonio Louca, 'Dois diplomatas portugueses face ao Holocausto, Budapeste, 1944', in *Historia*, no. 15, December 1995.
10 *A Voz*, 6 April 1940.
11 Gian Trepp, *Bankgeschafte mit dem Feind. Die Bank fur Internationale Zahlungsausgleich: von Hitlers Europa-Bank zum Instrument des Marshallplans* (Zurich: Rotpunktverlag, 1993), p. 29ff.
12 David Marsh, *Die Bundesbank: Geschafte mit der Macht* (German translation, Munich: Bertelsmann 1992), p. 156.
13 *Dez Anos de Política Externa: A Nação Portuguesa e a Segunda Guerra Mundial*, vol. XIV (Lisbon, 1993), Documents 353, 373 and 388.
14 Rosas, *Portugal entre a Paz e a Guerra*, p. 147.
15 Michel Fior, *Die Schweiz und das Gold der Reichsbank: Was wusste die Schweizerische Nationalbank?* (Zurich: Chronos Verlag, 1997), p. 140ff. The author gives the corresponding values of the purchases in Swiss francs.

16 Gautier's Report on his travel to Madrid and Lisbon, 12–26 October 1942. Archives of the Swiss National Bank (from now on ASNB), Gebundene Zahlungsverkehr, Portugal-Berichte, Korrespondez, 1941–1943.

17 Fior, *Die Schweiz und des Gold de Richsbank*, p. 52.

18 *Informações acerca do ouro belga apreendido pela Alemanha*, Processo verbal de 14 June 1946, AHD-MNE, Repartião das Questões Económicas (RQE), P3-A25-M16.

19 *Gold Imports into Portugal*, 9 October 1944, National Archives, USA *External Assets and Looted* Gold, RG 43, Box 48 and Memorandum on Looted Gold, 9 September 1946. AHD-MNE (RQE), P2-A7-M626.

20 Memorandum on Looted Gold, 9 September 1946, AHD-MNE (RQE), P2-A7-M626.

21 Microfilms E694708-E694714, Bundesarchive, Berlin. See especially A. Flesche's report to the German legation in Lisbon, 12 December 1942, E94710 and F11.

22 Willi Boelcke. *Die Kosten von Hitlers Krieg: Kriegsfinanzierung und Kriegserbe in Deutschland, 1933–1948* (Padeborn: Ferdinand Schöningh, 1985), p. 120.

23 Rosas, *Portugal entre a Paz e a Guerra*, p. 147.

24 Ibid., p. 83.

25 António Louçã, 'As SS em demanda duma paz separada. O caso da família Weiss-Chorin e seu exílio em Portugal', in *História* (Maio, 1995).

26 Note from the Portuguese Ministry of Foreign Affairs to the Portuguese Legation to Bonn, June 1953. AHD-MNE PEA-M123.

27 Proposal delivered by the Allied Delegations at the meeting on 18 November 1947. AHD-MNE (RQE), P2-A7-M626.

28 Tomás Fernandes' Notes on the unofficial meeting of 25 November 1947. AHD-MNE (RQE) P3-A25-M16.

29 Tomás Fernandes' Notes on a conversation with António de Faria, 28 May 1948. AHD-MNE (RQE), P3-A25-M16.

30 *Memorandum da Delegação Portuguesa sobre ouro adquirido pelo Banco de Portugal à Alemanha*, 24 September 1946. See also *The Allied Delegation's Reply to the Memo dated September the 24ᵗʰ, 1946, of the Portuguese Delegation.* AHD-MNE (RQE), P2-A7-M626.

31 From the Portuguese Ministry of Foreign Affairs to the Embassy of the USA, 8 July 1948. AHD-MNE (RQE), P2-A7-M626.

32 *Apontamento de conversa com o Ministro*, 19 May 1948. AHD-MNE (RQE), P2-A7-M626.

33 Note from the British Embassy to the Portuguese Ministry of Foreign Affairs, 2 February 1949. AHD-MNE (RQE), P2-A7-M626.

34 *U.S. and Allied Efforts*, p. 106.

35 Rosas, *Portugal entre a Paz e a Guerra*, p. 187.

36 Letter from the Portuguese Ministry of Economy to the Portuguese Ministry for Foreign Affairs, 17 October 1952. AHD-MNE, P2-A52-M36.

37 *Comércio Externo*, ed. Instituto Nacional de Estatística, vols 1946–1956.

38 AHD-MNE (RQE), P3-A25-M14.

39 Peter Hug and Marck Perrenoud, *Assets in Switzerland of Victims of Nazism and the Compensation Agreements with East Bloc Countries* (Task Force: Bern, October 1996), pp. 96ff.

40 See interview by the truck driver José Resina de Almeida to Ana Gomes Ferreira, *Público*, 1 November 1996.

41 *Aide-mémoire* from the French Embassy in Bern to the Swiss Federal Political Department, 14 April 1947. ASNB. *Auszug aus dem Protokoll des Direktoriums*, Swiss National Bank, 17 April 1947. ASNB. Letter from Paul Rossy to the Banco de Portugal, 21 April 1947. ASNB. Answer from the Banco de Portugal, 23 April 1947. ASNB. Final answer of the 30 April 1947. ASNB.

42 *Historia*, No. 34, August/September 1997.

43 Joaquim da Costa Leite interviewed by the daily *Público*, 22 January 1998.

44 Quoted in *Público*, 22 March 1997.

17

The Robbery of Dutch Jews and Postwar Restitution

Gerard Aalders

Introduction

During the Second World War, of the approximately 107,000 people deported to the death camps from The Netherlands, only some 5200 returned. The possessions of 135,000 Dutch Jews were robbed in a systematic fashion. It was generally based on ordinances *(Verordnungen)* that had the force of statute law, and sometimes on 'measures', 'decrees' or 'orders' issued by the *Sicherheitsdienst* (SD) (see, for example, Plate 8). The SD's orders usually sanctioned the theft of bicycles, radios and household effects. It also sold stamps, with which deportation temporarily could be postponed, as we will see later. The National Socialist occupying forces went to remarkable lengths to give the theft (often euphemistically referred to as 'surrender') a semblance of legality. The ordinances governed non-commercial associations and foundations, companies, and individuals.

Unlike most of the occupied countries in Europe, which had a military government, The Netherlands had a civilian one headed by Dr A. Seyss-Inquart. The Austrian-born commissioner derived his power from an *Erlass des Führers* (Führer Decree) of 18 May 1940, and in all his ordinances he referred consistently to Hitler's Decree. This Decree, in its turn, was written with the Hague Convention on Land Warfare (1907) in mind – again this semblance to legality – of which Article 43 reads:

> The authority of the legitimate power having in fact passed into the hands of the occupant, the latter shall take all the measures in his power to restore, and ensure, as far as possible, public order and safety, while respecting, unless absolutely prevented, the laws in force in the country.

If we place the limiting provision in the Führer Decree ('as far as it is compatible with the occupation') against 'unless absolutely prevented' in Article 43, it is evident that Hitler gave himself more than ample room for manoeuvring within the range of this article. It was the first step on the road to the total expropriation of Dutch Jewry. The next phase was the definition of the term 'Jew' in Ordinance 189/1940, 22 October 1940 (article 4) as:

(1) [. . .] a person with at least three grandparents who are full-blooded Jews by race.

(2) A Jew is also a person with at least two grandparents who are full-blooded Jews and who (1) was either a member of the Jewish religious community on 9 May 1940 or who subsequently became a member, or (2) was married to a Jew on 9 May 1940 or subsequently married a Jew,

(3) A grandparent shall be a full-blooded Jew if he or she was a member of the Jewish religious community.

The definition may seem precise, but article 4 of Ordinance 189/1940 allowed many borderline cases. Mixed marriages (*Mischehen*), in particular, caused the National Socialistic looting organization many administrative problems, which could only be resolved by a deluge of provisions, exemptions and individual measures. This may have delayed the theft slightly, but it certainly did not prevent it.[1]

On 3 February 1941 the Jews were ordered to have themselves registered and on 1 July 1941 a list with Jewish family names was published. In the same year the report 'Statistics of the Jewish population in The Netherlands' was completed, containing many details about persons of Jewish origin; a distinction was made between Dutch Jews and immigrants. Finally, in the same year, 'Statistical data on Jews in The Netherlands' became available.[2]

So by then the Germans knew who was a Jew, where the Jews lived and furthermore many details about their private lives. What they needed next was an organization to carry out the looting. In fact, two plunder institutions were established in the summer of 1941: the *Vermögensverwaltung und Rentenanstalt* (VVRA) and *Lippmann, Rosenthal & Co.* (LiRo).

The VVRA (Administration of Formation of Interest Institution), established on 31 May 1941 on the order of Seyss-Inquart, with a founding capital of just 100 guilders, played a central role, and a large proportion of all the loot stolen in The Netherlands flowed into its coffers. Lippmann, Rosenthal & Co., was a well-known Jewish bank in

Amsterdam with an outstanding domestic and international reputation. On 28 July 1941 the Germans established a new 'branch'. From that date onwards there were two banking institutions in Amsterdam with the name Lippmann, Rosenthal. In order to distinguish one from the other, the name of the street where the respective banks were established was added: LiRo Nieuwe Spiegelstraat and LiRo Sarphatistraat.

The LiRo bank on Sarphatistraat was to acquire the dismal reputation as 'robbery bank'. The ('adopted') name of the new 'bank' was chosen intentionally and was no coincidence: the good name of this banking institution was used to allay as far as possible the disquiet and possible panic resulting from the forced registrations and transfers by means of the issue of *Verordnungen*. As noted above, the Germans were at pains to present this expropriation as a legally responsible affair.

The Dutch Jews were forced to surrender their personal property, ranging from household effects to art collections, to LiRo Sarphatistraat while Jewish companies and non-commercial associations and foundations had to hand their property to the VVRA. In addition, part of the loot, which originally had been surrendered to LiRo, was transferred to the VVRA.

Anti-Jewish property ordinances

On 24 June 1940, Ordinance 26/40 on Enemy Property was issued, concerning the businesses and possessions of Dutch people who had fled the country in May after the German invasion. Many Jews had left the country, but so had citizens of other states with which Germany was at war.

Enemy property had to be registered with the *Deutsche Revisions- und Treuhand AG* in The Hague and then surrendered to the *Generalkommissar für Finanz und Wirtschaft*. Ordinance 26/40 related to all property, both movable and immovable, Jewish and non-Jewish. Non-Jewish property was sold only in exceptional cases, probably out of fear that German possessions on enemy territory would undergo the same treatment.[3]

Non-commercial associations and foundations (both Jewish and non-Jewish) had to be registered under Ordinance 145/40 (20 September 1940), and Jewish companies about a month later (Ordinance 189/40).

Ordinance 145/40 did not apply exclusively to Jewish institutions. Trade unions, for instance, were also affected by this measure. The occupier regarded unions and clubs where members gathered on a regular basis and where they could exchange thoughts as a potential hotbed for resistance. On the other hand these institutions could be used for the spreading of National Socialistic propaganda. In both cases direct control was considered to be desirable.[4] Here, as well as in the case of Enemy Property, the Jews suffered the highest losses, as all their associations and foundations, contrary to the non-Jewish ones, were liquidated.[5] The 'legal' basis was provided with Ordinance 41/41 (28 February 1941). Within eight months after the forced registration, about 7700 organizations were liquidated.[6]

Administration of Jewish businesses was taken over from 12 March 1941, on the basis of Ordinance 48/41. The Ordinance made use of the information which was received through the forced registration in the autumn of the preceding year. Jewish companies were 'Aryanized' to 'purify' the Dutch economy of Jewish elements. Small firms (shops, retailers, ragpickers, etc.), which were the only source of income for many Jewish families but not of any interest to the Germans from an economic point of view, were liquidated, usually by Omnia Treuhand.[7]

Most of them, along with the smaller, prosperous Jewish companies, continued to operate under an administrator (*Verwalter*). The sale of companies was carried out through the mediation of the Niederländische Aktiengesellscheft für die Abwicklung von Unternehmungen (NAGU).[8] NAGU was a German accounting firm that dealt with interested buyers on behalf of the German authorities.

The proceeds of the sales were deposited in full with one of the banking connections of the *Vermögensverwaltung und Rentenanstalt*. The VVRA was responsible for repaying the original Jewish owners in 100 quarterly instalments, that is, over 25 years, or at 4 per cent per annum without interest. In practice, the length of the repayment term was immaterial because when Seyss-Inquart established the VVRA in May 1941, plans already existed to deport the Dutch Jews. The repayment was farcical but entirely in keeping with the Germans' desire for a veneer of legality. And again, they also wished to avoid panic and confusion among their victims.

Jewish agricultural property, real estate and mortgage loans were also expropriated by means of Ordinances and sold to German and Dutch people (usually black marketeers and Dutch National Socialist collaborators).

The so-called LiRo Ordinances (named after Lippmann, Rosenthal & Co., Sarphatistraat), were particularly notorious and nearly every Jew came into contact with LiRo. The First LiRo Ordinance (Ordinance 148/41, 8 August 1941) forced 'delivery bound' Jews to open an account with LiRo. There was, however, a 'free maximum' of 1000 guilders per person and some other, rather complicated rules under which Jews could be exempted from delivery.[9] Under this First LiRo Ordinance, governing private financial assets, 'delivery bound' Jews had to surrender their cash, cheques, bank balances and securities to LiRo. Bank and giro services were compelled to transfer the balances in the accounts of their Jewish customers to LiRo. Whether a customer was Jewish was determined by means of a questionnaire that was sent to every account holder. The Jews lost virtually all control of their bank balances at LiRo. It would be beyond the scope of this brief history to consider the many special provisions.[10]

The Second LiRo Ordinance (Ordinance 58/42, 21 May 1942) was the definitive *coup de grâce* to private Jewish ownership. 'Collections of whatever sort', gold, silver, platinum, works of art, precious stones, 'rights of patent, copyrights and concessions': all of these had to be surrendered.

Article 12 stipulated that wedding rings and 'dental fillings made of precious metals in personal use' were exempted from the order. 'Until further notice' would have been a fitting addition, because in January 1942 (at the Wannsee Conference) it had already been decided to exterminate the entire Jewish population and culture of Europe. It was thus only a question of time before golden fillings, crowns and wedding rings, in short the *Totengold*, would also fall into the hands of the Nazis. Moreover, all amounts receivable (including insurance benefits), rights of trade marks and inheritance were sequestered and amounts receivable from third parties (including international claims) had to be registered. The 'free maximum' of 1000 guilders per person was cut back to 250 guilders per family. Horses, vehicles and vessels had to be registered with the *Zentralstelle für jüdische Auswanderung* (Central Office for the Emigration of Jews).

The Nazis were concerned that the Jews might conceal such valuables as foreign currency (pounds, dollars, etc.), precious metals and precious stones – 'illegal' property in their eyes – and so a special method was devised to rob them of these 'illegal' possessions as well. In exchange for the surrender of gold, silver and precious stones they received a stamp which exempted them from deportation until further notice (*bis auf Weiteres*). It seems that the *Reichssicherheitshauptamt*, RSHA (the Central Security Department of the Reich) in Berlin had worked out this plan for delay of deportation in exchange for payment in valuables during the months of July and August 1942. In fact, it was only an extension of the possibility, created a few months earlier, to obtain an emigration permit for hard currency. This period of delay was fairly short, ranging from half a day to three months. Each stamp was issued at a price between 20,000 guilders (until 10 June 1943) and fl. 30,000 (after 10 June 1943) and had to be paid in precious stones, precious metals or in British pounds, American dollars or Swiss francs. The Germans were able to acquire a total of about 10 million guilders of additional possessions in this way. The *Befehlshaber der Sicherheitspolizei und des SD* (BdS) in The Hague carried out the 'stamp scheme' from August 1942 onwards on orders of the RSHA. During the last round-up of 29 September 1943, the last holders with a stamp that gave protection against deportation 'until further notice' were arrested, and in the course of 1944 were deported to *Vorzugslager* Bergen-Belsen, where most of them perished.[11]

The deportations to the death camps in the East began in the summer of 1942. When the Jews, already stripped of practically all their possessions, arrived in the Westerbork transit camp they were put through the Lippmann-Rosenthal rigmarole one more time; the bank also had a 'branch' in this camp in the province of Drenthe in the eastern Netherlands. Jewellery which deportees had smuggled in with them, and which belonged to the German Reich, according to the LiRo decrees, were taken from them in this antechamber of death. Directly after the deportation of Jews to Westerbork, the vehicles of the *Hausraterfassung* (Domestic Property Registration) drove up to empty their houses from top to bottom. This work was conducted by the firm Puls, which is why the plundering in Amsterdam was known in Amsterdam as 'pulsing'. Crockery sets, household goods, furniture, carpets and ornaments, literally everything was loaded up and removed. Tables, chairs and suchlike were mostly shipped to Germany to replace furniture which had been destroyed in Allied bombing.

The looting of art

Already before the issue of the Second LiRo Ordinance the Germans had been after the Dutch art collections. Hitler had created a special unit for this type of theft, the *Einsatzstab Reichsleiter Rosenberg*, ERR, (Reich Leader Rosenberg's Special Task Force). The ERR looted libraries, art collections, religious objects and archives under a special Decree issued in June 1940. The Decree was directed at Jews as well as Freemasons and other 'enemies of the Nazi-ideology'. This specialized looting unit was particularly active in France, where famous collections such as that of the Rothschilds were confiscated. The ERR in The Netherlands was mainly active in the plundering of libraries and furniture.[12]

The art booty in The Netherlands was more modest in scale and in practically all cases the looting was carried out by a special taskforce, the *Dienststelle Mühlmann*, named after its leader Dr Kajetan Mühlmann, a friend of Seyss-Inquart. Both the ERR and the *Dienststelle* were active before the LiRo Ordinances took effect. Many thousands of paintings and other types of art from Holland found their way to Germany through the offices of the *Dienststelle*. The 'regular customers' included Adolf Hitler and Hermann Goering, but Seyss-Inquart always made sure that Hitler had the first choice. Both top Nazis employed a special 'art agent' who bought art on behalf of their respective masters.[13]

These Dutch collections were not stolen 'at gunpoint': the Germans paid for them in guilders. But they did not pay a real price and most of the purchases were made under duress: it is obvious that an 'offer' is hard to refuse if Hitler's or Goering's representative is on your doorstep. Out of fear of the consequences if they should not accept the offer, Jews (and also non-Jews) agreed to sell for prices far below market value. Such sales were known as 'technical' – in contrast to 'direct' – looting. The sale of the Goudstikker art firm, 'bought' by Hermann Goering, was a typical case of technical looting.[14] Quite remarkable was the great hurry in which Goering bought the collection: even before Seyss-Inquart managed to issue the Ordinance on Enemy Property, which certainly would have been applicable to the proprietor of the firm, the Jew Jacques Goudstikker fled to England after the invasion. The motivation for Goering's fast proceeding was undoubtedly that he was afraid that under the rules of the Enemy Property Ordinance he would only have had second choice, after Hitler.

The famous Mannheimer collection was 'bought' by Seyss-Inquart and shipped to Germany with destination Linz, the place of Hitler's youth where he planned to build the largest museum of the Reich (*Sonderauftrag Linz*). Both the Mannheimer and the Goudstikker collections were bought for far less than the real market value and both cases must be qualified as 'technical looting'.

From May 1942, art was bound to be delivered to LiRo, on the basis of the Second LiRo Ordinance. The Netherlands had only a few Jewish art collections of international significance and the best (Mannheimer and Goudstikker) had already been removed at the beginning of the war. It would seem that wealthy Dutch Jews preferred to invest their money in shares, or in houses, companies or real estate.

Disposal of assets

LiRo disposed of practically all its stolen assets. The property stolen from Dutch Jewry amounted to at least 1 billion guilders. About a third of that sum consisted of securities in the form of shares and bonds. Listed securities were mainly sold at the Amsterdam Stock Exchange for an amount of approximately 110 to 115 million guilders.[15] Large portfolios were brought over to Berlin (where a part fell into Soviet hands after city's fall) and non-valuable securities were left in the vaults of LiRo. Other packets of securities found their way to Sweden, Switzerland and other neutral countries.[16] During the war the administration of VVRA and LiRo got mixed up, and in a number of cases blocks of securities were transferred from LiRo to VVRA without any collateral.

Deposits and claims were cashed and insurance policies turned in for their cash value. LiRo bought German bonds (*Reichschatzanweisungen*) or Dutch bonds for the bank and giro balances and the proceeds of the sales of securities, jewellery, collections, etc., although it seems that in most of the cases real valuable personal assets were shipped to Germany. The sales channels and the recipient German organizations are known with a fair degree of precision but there appeared to be little left to recover after May 1945.

Items of lesser value were sold in the Netherlands, quite often for low prices, their proceeds deposited at LiRo's general account and used for the buying of bonds. It is an established fact that the LiRo staff conducted considerable fraud and theft on their own account. One of the LiRo directors was dismissed for this reason. It is not known how much of this booty ended up abroad.

The restitution

Postwar restitution has been a highly complicated and protracted process. For the Jews it was often a painful process, as their claims were often met with counter-claims in cases where their possessions had been sold more than once. There was no problem, for instance, when a house passed into the hands of a German or Dutch collaborator. The collaborator had to leave immediately – they got arrested in any case – and the Jewish family could move in again. But in the case of securities and bonds which had been sold and resold several times, the case was more complex. The dweller had taken up residence clearly in bad faith, but what about the twentieth owner of shares in Royal Dutch? Because the situation was unique in Dutch history and there was lack of jurisprudence, special legislation was required.

Restitution, particularly of securities, took more than a quarter of a century, and the Securities Registration Division was not closed until 1 October 1971.

The restoration of legal property rights was entrusted to the Council for the Restitution of Legal Rights, appointed under the London Restoration of Legal Rights Decree. This Decree, referred to shortly as E 100, aimed at 'cancelling the numerous civil law acts performed under the pretence of justice otherwise and executed under direct or indirect compulsion' of the Germans during the occupation.[17]

The Dutch government in London was already informed at an early stage about the looting practices of the Germans and 'Radio Oranje', the mouthpiece of the government in exile, had broadcast warnings to the Dutch not to buy securities and goods that had supposedly been robbed by the occupiers. In order to product the individual interests of the Dutch citizens the London government issued Royal Decree A1 an 24 May 1940, only ten days after the capitulation. It gave the government the right to act fiduciary owner in order to safeguard its citizens, rights to claims and possessions. It ws a preventive measure, like Royal Decree A 6 of 7 June 1940, which prohibited transactions with the occupiers without prior special permission from a commission.[18]

The Allies had recognized the German looting practices and on 5 January 1943 they issued the 'Inter-Allied Declaration against Acts of Dispossession committed in Territories under Enemy Occupation or Control'.[19] The Netherlands government in London belonged to the signatories of the Allied Declaration and her own measures against acts of dispossessions would materialize, as we have observed, in the Decree of Restoration of Legal Rights.[20]

Another Decree which should be mentioned is E 93 (September 1994). E 93 determined that all measures (with a few exceptions) taken by the Germans were considered never to have been valid. Under this authority one of the first acts of the LiRo custodians was to instruct the Netherlands banks to wipe out the paper transfer of title to LiRo of foreign securities held by Jews abroad, and to restore full title to the original owner.

Looted property was not automatically restored to the robbed Jews. There were third parties who had bought property in good faith. In such cases the dispossessed Jew received compensation from the person or agency that had obtained the property in bad faith. In many cases that was LiRo or VVRA.[21] The Council for the Restoration of Legal Rights was the legal body that judged in cases where questions with regard to property rights arose. The Council was an umbrella organization that met on only one occasion, namely on the day of its inauguration, 20 August 1945.

The LVVS (Liquidation Vermogen Verwaltung Sarphatistraat) was immediately faced with an enormous problem. Rather than keep separate accounts for 'full-blooded Jews', since 1 January 1943 LiRo had deposited everything in a single collective account (*Sammelkonto*). When the LVVS commenced its work in May 1945 only 2000 account holders were known; by the time the *Sammelkonto* had been unravelled, four years later, there were 70,000 accounts. A second problem was that the administration of both looting institutions had been destroyed or disappeared. Moreover, during the war large packages of shares and large sums of money had been transferred from LiRo to VVRA. But nobody knew precisely how and it was evident that the book-keeping of both looting organizations had to be disentangled and reconstructed before the authorities could even begin restitution. In short, in 1945 it was absolutely unclear what belonged to whom in the estate of LiRo and VVRA.

A third serious restitution problem was caused by the great number of deaths in the concentration camps. Complete families had been exterminated and that created an enormous heritage puzzle: who was entitled to inherit what and from whom?

Unclaimed property

If the rightful owners were not known, natural persons (lawyers, notaries) were initially appointed to administrator unclaimed property: later, foundations established by the Netherlands Property Custodian were also appointed as administrators. If it was established that the rightful owners were no longer missing, which in practice usually meant that they were dead, the administration was considered resolved. Notification was often a question of chance. Anyone who had information about unclaimed property, most of them relatives, was expected to notify the authorities. Heirs were traced by the Registrar of Births, marriages and Deaths or by means of notices published in national newspapers. When an heir was found, the case was usually handed over to a notary, who attended to its further settlement. A recurrent problem was that no death certificates were issued for Jews murdered in concentration camps. I 1949 this problem was resolved by the Death Certificates (Missing Persons) Act.[22] Administration was nonetheless continued in many cases, sometimes by the notary concerned and sometimes by the Foundation for the Administration of Missing Persons and Unclaimed Property (BAON[23]) in Amsterdam. If administration was wound up, many estates were managed for a given period in accordance with the Civil Code, particularly if there was uncertainty regarding the fate of the heirs, their place of residence, identity or the primacy of their right of succession. Because of the Dutch law of succession it was important to know who had died first, the husband or his wife.

By Royal Decree of October 1959 it was decided that Joods Maatschappelijk Werk, JMW (Jewish Social Service Foundation), should benefit from claims to LVVS of persons who were missing or could not be found (and who were assumed to be dead), on the condition that JMW would disburse the amount to the rightful claimant if he should report after all.

The balance of the estate of unclaimed property that was not subject to the Royal Decree regarding LVVS was transferred to the State Consignation Fund.[24] No exceptions in a legal sense were made for Jewish estates from the period 1940–45 and they, too, were subject to the provisions of the Consignation of Monies Act. At the end of the given period, the estates devolved to the state. Such estates were published in the *Staatscourant* (Government Gazette).

Cash, giro balances, bank balances and securities[25]

Cash, giro balances and bank balances were, as we have noted, deposited with LiRo and the most important sales channel for securities was the Amsterdam Stock Exchange. At the time of the liberation, securities that had not been sold were lying in LiRo's vaults or had been deposited with banks in Amsterdam or Germany.

It is important to note, however, that the 'dispossessed' accepted 90 per cent compensation from the Securities Restitution Guarantee Fund and other bodies. Partial compensation for foreign securities was provided by the former Federal Republic of Germany under the German *Bundesrückerstattungsgesetz*, Brüg (the so-called *Wiedergutmachung*) of 1957.[26] Where the rightful owners could not be found, the securities devolved to the state. Part of the capital surrendered to LiRo, in the form of cash, bank and girobalances and cheques (with a total value of 26–55 million guilders),[27] was used to maintain and enlarge the camps at Vught and Westerbork, to cover the running expenses of the *Hausraterfassungsstelle* (which stripped Jews' houses after the occupants had been deported) and to pay 'bounties' to people who betrayed Jews. In addition it went to cover the costs of the extensive LiRo staff, while the Jewish Council and the *Jüdische Unterstützungstelle* were paid from LiRo's resources.

Insurance policies

Insurance policies numbering 22, 368, with a value of about 25 million guilders, were registered with LiRo. The insurance companies were forced to surrender all the policies of their Jewish customers and deposit the cash value with LiRo. After the war, a number of test cases were held which generally led to the restoration of the policy-holders' rights. It is unclear how many of those entitled to do so actually sought legal redress.

Companies

About 2000 companies were 'Aryanized' and a further 13,000-plus were liquidated. It is virtually impossible to put a real figure on their value. The purchase prices were usually far lower than their true value and no account was taken of goodwill. Jews suffered the greatest financial losses in this area because they received virtually no compensation for their companies and absolutely none under the War Damage Act. If the premises were owned (that is, not rented), the rights of the original owners were restored in that they recovered possession of the premises. The proceeds of the 13,000 liquidated small businesses, about 6.5 million, had been transferred to VVRA. The Aryanized companies had generated approximately 75 million guildgers. That sum had also been transferred to VVRA. As noted, these sums are much too low. It seems reasonable to assume that the real losses that the Jews suffered were between 150 and 300 million guilders.[28] In general, immovable property (worth about 150 million guilders and agricultural land (about 17 million guilders were restored. With regard to mortgages (about 22 million guilders), claims were granted against the Niederländische Grundstücksverwaltung (in liquidation). The exacts outcome of the last category is unknown.

Art and other collections

Not all works of art were seized under the Second LiRo Ordinance. In many cases the *Dienststelle Mühlmann*, the special art agents of Hitler (Dr Hans Posse) or Goering (Andreas Hofer) and sometimes the Einstazstab

Reichsleiter Rosengberg (ERR) had already struck. The Germans confiscated about 6 million guilders worth of art works, various collections and gold and silver. This amount is much too low, due to the German habit of underestimating. The real value must have been many times higher. The reason for these (almost permanent) underestimations was that the items were sold to friendly relations and in that light the sales must be regarded as a kind turn. The 'sale' of the Mannheimer collection by the custodians of the bankrupt Mannheimer estate (Fritz Mannheimer died in 1939) to Seyss-Inquart is a good example of technical looting: the custodians had two choices, either to confiscate or sell far below (about 3 million guilders the real market value. It is evident that the last option-sale under duress–was preferable to the first.[29]

The *Stichting Nederlands Kunstbezit*, SNK (Netherlands Officer for Fine Arts) was responsible for the recovery of art after the war. A great deal has never been recovered: about 20 per cent of the first-class works and about 80 per cent of works of the second rank. It can be assumed that these are now scattered throughout the world. Already during the war many works of art and precious stones had been shipped by diplomatic pouch.[30] Many of them are in Russia.[31] Recently the work of the SNK has been heavily criticized. The staff of the bureau consisted mainly of art historians, who appeared to be more interested in the extension of the national art treasures in The Netherlands museums ('Mobilier National') than in the restitution to the rightful owners. The director of the SNK was sacked but the scandal itself was hushed up.[32]

Most criticism of the functioning of the Restoration of Rights was directed against its very slow start and the long extended period of the execution process which lasted until 1971. Bureaucratic and legal problems partially account for the long delay. There was also an emotional component which made the Jews feel that the Restoration of Legal Rights Decree malfunctioned. Many Jews felt lost and deserted when they came back from the concentration camps or out of hiding. They experienced the atmosphere in The Netherlands after their return as cold and chilly. Care was practically non-existent, they were left to themselves and they blamed the authorities for the fact that no special legal arrangement has been made for them. The attitude of the Netherlands government was felt as too legalistic towards this group of Dutch citizens who had suffered most from the war.

Notes

1   Archives of the Rijksinstituut voor Oorlogsdocmentatie (Netherlands State Institute for War Documentation – hereafter RvO), Doc. II, LiRo.

2   *Statistiek der Bevolking van joodschen bloede in Nederland* and *Statische gegevens van de joden in Nederland.* From these sources we learn that the Germans had an overwhelming amount of information on the Dutch Jews: names, dates and places of birth, sex, address, marital status, profession, religious or not religious, their spread over the country, etc. It was believed that only a few Jews had chosen not to have themselves registered.

3   Stephan H. Lindner, 'Das Reichskommissariat für die Behandlung feindlichen Vermögens im Zweiten Weltkrieg', in *Zeitschrift für Unternehmengeschichte,* Hans Pohl und Wilhelm Treue (ed.), Beiheft 67, 1991, pp. 161–7.

4   L. de Jong, *Het Koninkrijk der Nederlanden in de Tweede Wereldoorlog,* vol. 5, part 1, pp. 418–23.

5   RvO, Bregstein archive, Box 20, folder 1075, Rechtsherstel, 'De liquidatie van het joodsch onroerend goederenbezit.'

6   RvO, Doc. II, Verenigingen-opheffing and de Jong, *Koninkrijk,* vol. 5, part 1, pp. 420–1.

7   See: Gerard Aalders, 'Three Ways of German Economic Penetration in the Netherlands: Cloaking, Capital Interlocking and "Aryanization"', in *Die 'Neuordnung' Europas. NS-Wirtschaftspolitik in den besetzten Gebieten,* Richard J. Overy, Gerhard Otto and Johannes Houwink ten Cate (eds). Omnia Treuhandgesellschaft G.m.b.H. was a German accounting firm with a branch in The Hague since the autumn of 1941.

8   The NAGU (*Netherlands Company for the Liquidation of Enterprises*) stood under the supervision of the *Wirtschaftsprüfstelle* (German Economic Control Office), which in its turn came under the *Generalkommissar für Finanz und Wirtschaft* (Reich Commissioner for Finance and Economic Affairs).

9   RvO, Doc II, Lippmann, Rosenthal & Co., Sarphatistraat, Box 217, Folder D, 'Op wie de Verordening van toepassing is'.

10   See for these provisions: RvO, Doc. II, Lippmann, Rosenthal & Co. Sarphatistraat. Box 215, Afdeling Inspectie II, Interne circulaires.

11   B. Karlsberg, *Beschleuniging durch Besondere Verfahren, Sammelverfahren Belgien, Frankreich, Niederlande* (Muich, 1981); also de Jong, *Koninkrijk,* vol. 6, part 1, pp. 279–80; Presser, *Ondergang,* pp. 99–101; RvO, Collectie 281, Box 37, 43, 44, 45 ('S-actie') and idem, 'Notities voor het Geschiedwerk', no. 112: *Der Entziehungsvorgang bei der Sog. Sperrdiamanten-Aktion und die im Individualfall vorliegenden Beweisunterlagen.* Today's worth of 10 million guilders is roughly 114 million guilders (57 million US dollars).

12   In practice the looting of furniture ('M-aktion') was carried out by the *Hausraterfassung* (Domestic Property Registrations) on order of the ERR.

13   RvO, Notities voor get Geschiedwerk, no. 118. *Entziehung offentlicher und privater Bibliotheken in den besetzten Westgebieten und Ihre Verbringung nach Deutschland.*

14   See, for instance, the *New York Times,* 12 January 1998: 'Heirs Claim Art Collections Lost to Nazis in Amsterdam'.

15   Joh De Vries, *Een Eeuw Vol Effecten. Historische schets van de Vereniging voor de Effectenhandel en de Amsterdamse Effectenbeurs 1876–1976,* p. 203.

16 See for an extensive treatment of a Swedish case: Gerard Aalder and Cees Wiebers, *The Art of Cloaking Ownership: The Secret Collaboration and the Protection of the German War Industry by the Neutrals. The Case of Sweden* (Amsterdam, 1996), pp. 93–104.

17 Quoted from Hennie van Schie, 'Rostoration of Economics Rights after 1945', *Dutch Jewish History* (Jerusalem: Institute for Research on Dutch Jewry, 1984), p. 404.

18 These Decrees were published in: *Staatsblad van het Koninkrijk der Nederlanden uitgegeven te Londen (Jaargangen 1940) t/m 1943 Serie A t/m D.*(Bulletin of Acts and Decrees).

19 See for the complete text of the *Inter-Allied Declaration: Foreign Relations of the United States* (FRUS), vol. 1 (1943), *General* (Washington, 1968), pp. 443–444.

20 Published in: *Staatsblad van het Koninkrijk der Nederlanden uitgegeven te Londen,* January 1944, Serie E.

21 Initially the name of LiRo was kept but when the the original LiRo bank came back in business, it became too confusing and the name was attend to LVVS.

22 See: *Staatsblad van het Koninkrijk der Nederlanden,* NO, J 227 Wet van 2 Juni 1949, houdende voorzieningen betreffende het opmaken van akten van onverlijden van vermisten.

23 Bureau Afwezigen en Onbeheerde Nalatenschappen, BAON.

24 R. A. Kiek, 'Vermogens verdwenen joden vloeien in de staatskas' in *Nieue Israelisch Weekblad,* 3 August 1985.

25 Ciphers for securities bank and giro balances and cash are derived from: Ministry of Finance, Archief Bewindvoering, rubriek 1450 LVVS, Eindverslag van Beheerders-Vereffenaars Betreffende Liquidatie van Verwaltung Sarphatistraat (LVVS.) ann het Nederlandse Beheersinstituut te's-Gravenhage, 24 April 1958 (Final Report LVVS) and ibid., Eindverslag van Beheerders-Vereffenaars Betreffende Vermügensverwaltungs-und Rentenanstalt (VVRA). aan het Nederlandse Beheersinstituut te's-Gravenhage, 24 April 1958 (Final Report VVRA).

26 B Karlsberg., *Beschleuniging durch besondere Verfahren, Sammelverfahren (Belgien, Frankreich, Niederlande)* (Munich, 1981). The German Democratic Republic never did participate in any form of Wiedergutmachung reparation.

27 All the amounts are in the values of the time. In 1945 1 US dollar was fl. 2.65.

28 RvO, Doc II, 'De behandeling van aan joden toebehorende vermogensvoorwaarden tijdens en na de oorlog'.

29 Adriaan Venema, *Kunsthandel in Nederland 1940–1945,* pp. 172–185 and pp. 489–493.

30 Gerard Aalders, 'By Diplomatic Pouch: Art Smuggling by the Nazis', *Spoils of War: International Newsletter,* no. 3 (December 1996).

31 Konstantin Akinsha, and Grigorii Kozlov, *Stolen Tresure: The Hunt for the World's lost Masterpieces* (London, 1995).

32 Lien Heyting, 'Kunstroof en Recuperatie' (Art looting and Restitution series) in *NRC-Handelsblad,* 10 October 7, 14 and 21 November 1997; idem, 'De dubbele agenda van A.B. de Vries. Fraudes bij de Stichting Nederlands Kunstbezit, in *NRC-Handelsblad,* 27 March 1998.

18
Italy: Aspects of the Unbeautiful Life

Furio Moroni

Belated confrontation

The film *'La Vita è Bella'* [Life Is Beautiful], released in the winter of 1997–8, is a symptomatic example of the Italians' belated confrontation with the Holocaust. Directed, co-written by, and starring the comic actor Roberto Benigni, it is about an assimilated Italian Jew who dies in Auschwitz, but not before saving his 5-year-old son. Combining the horrors of Auschwitz with gentle humour, the film makes one weep and laugh at the same time. It became a box office hit in Italy but it also sparked heated debate on the legitimacy and wisdom of making a film about the Shoah which is also humorous.

The film deliberately shows Italian Jewry as they indeed were before the Second World War, highly assimilated and some even members of the Fascist Party. During the first half of the film there is scant mention that the major character is a Jew, until antisemitic slogans suddenly and shockingly appear. Benigni explained that he was attempting to portray 'a Jew who was not recognized by precise signs, but who was the same as I am'. Most of the Italian Jewish community received the movie warmly and even sponsored its screenings.[1]

La Vita é Bella is just one example of the recent Italian fixation on the Holocaust, as well as other Jewish matters, which appear anew almost on a daily basis. Publishers compete to acquire titles on Jewish history and manuscripts of Israeli writers, and scholars and intellectuals hold discussions on the Holocaust. Only recently, several conferences in Rome, Milan, Genoa, Venice, Sienna and Naples have examined the moral significance of the Holocaust and European antisemitic persecutions.[2]

Like other nations in Europe, the Italians did not confront the Holocaust directly. Even the work of Primo Levi, the internationally known writer, which describes his experiences in Auschwitz, became recognized only thirty years after the war, and that without significant self-examination of the Italian role in the atrocities. For many Italians the Holocaust was viewed as just one part of the bloody panorama that characterized the Germans' occupation of 1943–5. The role of Benito Mussolini and the special form of fascist Italian antisemitism in executing the Nazi 'final solution' of the Jewish problem was not confronted as an issue. It was known that the Nazis had fascist sympathizers but the Holocaust was not studied as an Italian experience. Official historiography and textbooks in universities or schools did not treat the Holocaust nor its ramifications in Italy as a distinct topic.

The postwar rulers of Italy failed to recognize the uniqueness of the Holocaust. As explained by Meir Michaelis, 'they equated the Jewish victims of racial persecution with the Gentile victims of political persecution, and the Jewish survivors of Auschwitz with the Gentile survivors of German prisoner-of-war camps'.[3] There was a clear effort by the government to minimize Italy's share of the blame for the Holocaust.

It is true that after Denmark, Italy has the distinction of having saved the highest percentage of Jews, and almost four-fifths of them survived Hitler's Final Solution. None the less, the death of 7860 Jews was a unique tragedy and affected almost every Italian Jewish family. Until 1936 Italy faced less antisemitism than any other country among the Western democracies, and the terrible shock of fascist antisemitism and the extermination of their brethren dealt a major blow to Italian Jewry.

The Italian Jewish community is the oldest continuous settlement in Europe and its emancipation in the nineteenth century was a unique achievement. Jews were fully integrated and embedded in Italian society and politics. They were remarkably secular in their culture, living in a progressive stage of assimilation. In 1938, 43.7 per cent of all married Jews had Gentile spouses.[4]

The Jewish response after the Holocaust was also limited and restrained regarding Italian responsibility to the Jewish victims. Jewish leaders tended to emphasize the rescue of their brethren by Italians and claimed that the Italian people had a high resistance to antisemitism. The general tendency was to emphasize the 'good hearts of the Italians' compared to the cruelty of the Germans.[5]

In addition to Primo Levi, who became a symbol of humanism and survival, writings by other Italian survivors have won fame throughout the Western world. These include Silvano Arieti's work *The Parnas* and the work of Giorgio Bassani, *The Garden of the Finzi Continis*, which became a successful film. This novel portrays the persecution and deportation of a prominent Jewish family of Ferrara, which refused to believe in its own imminent destruction. Though these works did not create public debate over the Italians' role in the Holocaust, it maintained the issue in the public interest for several years.

Typically, a study initiated by the Union of Italian Jewish Communities was published in 1961 but did not focus on the crimes of Italian fascism – but rather on the anti-fascist opposition. The attitude towards Mussolini is reflected in the claim that Mussolini's antisemitism was in a sense more shameful than its German model, since Mussolini, unlike Hitler, did not believe in the 'guilt' of his Jewish victims.[6] This fact, which is historically correct, also explains the ease with which Italians, including some of Jewish leaders, escape serious debate on (what is termed by the literature) Mussolini's antisemitism of political opportunism, unlike the German racist, biological, religious antisemitism. The general desire of the Italian intelligentsia to forget their Holocaust experience was reflected in the negative response to the NBC *Holocaust* mini-series in 1979. Many reviewers dismissed it as an American soap opera.[7]

Serious debates among the Italian public appeared in the late 1980s after the screening of a three-part television programme in Italy about rescue activities in Italy and Italian-occupied territories. The producer, Nicola Caracciolo, claimed that, in addition to Italian public resistance to implementing Hitler's policy of genocide, Mussolini himself helped the Jews, albeit in an 'ambiguous and contradictory manner'. Jewish activists opposed this view and demonstrated that Mussolini himself, and not Hitler, imposed antisemitism in Italy, and that, until July 1943, Italian Jewry had been persecuted and humiliated by Italian fascists, not by the German SS. This ugly aspect, the collaboration and betrayal that led to the deaths of thousands, is widely discussed in the memorial book published in 1991 by Liliana Picciotto Fargion of the Jewish Documentation Centre in Milan.[8]

The atrocities of political opportunism

The brutality of Mussolini's political opportunism is well reflected in the policies of his fascist regime towards the Italian Jewish community. Benito Mussolini began his relations with the Jews in a very positive fashion and, until 1936, fourteen years after seizing power, antisemitism was a marginal phenomenon in Italy. During this period Mussolini publicly condemned racism and antisemitism and had cordial talks with Jewish and Zionist leaders such as Dr Chaim Weizman, the President of the World Zionist Organization and Dr Nahum Goldmann, from the planning committee of the World Jewish Congress.[9] In 1930–31 the Union of Italian Jewish Communities was established by a special fascist legislation, providing it with a legal status and financial base. Against this background it is understood why Mussolini's declaration of war on the Jews took most observers of fascism by surprise. This sudden break led to the debate over the origins and nature of fascist racialism and antisemitism and to the special terminology of Mussolini's cynical opportunism. This notion of opportunism can explain how it is that Mussolini both attacked and defended the Jews throughout his career. As early as 1917 he spoke on the links between Bolshevism and international Jewry, while as late as 1944 he insisted that he was not an antisemite.[10]

From 1936 Mussolini launched an antisemitic campaign which, unlike previous anti-Jewish polemics, was explicitly directed against Italian Jews. The racial laws waited until 1938 because Mussolini needed time to prepare the Italian public. The adoption of the discriminatory laws in the autumn of 1938 therefore marked the racist antisemitism of Mussolini as well as his full commitment to the Rome–Berlin Axis.

There are, indeed, some differences between the Nazi racist antisemitism and what Mussolini adopted. Many Italians regarded 'biological' racism as a Nordic import which ran against their values and Catholic teachings. Nicola Caracciolo tries hard to highlight the differences between Nazi antisemitism and its Italian expressions. Caracciolo concludes that, because of public opposition, the racial laws were not applied in Italy until 1943, during the final period of German domination.[11]

Susan Zucotti, however, emphasizes that Mussolini initiated the racial legislation, which marks the change in fascist policy toward the Jews, without any concrete demands from Hitler. Zucotti also rejects the attempt to describe Italian racial laws in only spiritual and cultural terms. She explains that racial laws were clearly based on biological principles and that they were applied to mixed marriages. Zucotti, however, also claims that Italian antisemitism did not have an ideological base, but was the product of mindless and cynical opportunism.[12]

In sum, Mussolini did not share the same degree of racial antisemitic hatred of the Jews as Hitler's Nazism. In his opportunistic process of moral bankruptcy, he began as Hitler's admirer and ended up as his captive puppet. Only then was he prepared to get involved in persecuting Jews, though not in their systematic murder.

Box 1 **Italian Racial Laws**

On 20 July 1943 the World Jewish Congress published a review and evaluation of the racial laws passed by royal decree and their effect on the Jewish community in Italy:

The Racial Laws

The racial legislation was a series of anti-Jewish royal decrees and laws:

(a) Decree-Law No. 1381 (7 September 1938), forbidding foreign Jews from living in Italy, Libya and the Aegean Islands, ordering their expulsion within six months, and cancelling the citizenship granted to foreign Jews naturalized after 1 January 1919.

(b) Decree-Law No. 1779 (15 November 1938), later altered to law no. 98 (5 January 1939) dealt with the position of Italian Jews in education. All Jewish professors and teachers were dismissed from office and were forbidden to teach anyone other than Jewish pupils. Jewish pupils and students were expelled from all schools and colleges. The Jewish communities were permitted to set up elementary and high schools of their own.

(c) Royal Decree-Law No. 1728 (17 November 1938), later changed to law no. 274 (5 January 1939) dealt with the overall status of the Jews:

Marriage between Jews and Gentiles was forbidden.

A special census of all the Jews was ordered and a special notation of their status had to appear in all their official papers.

They were barred from military service.

They were barred from office as guardians or trustees for non-Jewish minors.

They were not allowed to own, manage or act as directors or auditors to firms concerned with national defence or employing over 100 workers.

They were not permitted to own land having an official estimated annual income of over 5000 Liras ($250 at the time), or buildings in populated areas having an estimated annual income in excess of 20,000 (about $1000).

They could not employ Gentile servants.

> They were not allowed to hold positions of any kind with the government, the Fascist party, provinces, towns, or any other organizations controlled by them or connected to them, public associations or organizations, banks and insurance companies.
>
> (d) Royal Decree-Law No. 126 (9 February 1939) gave detailed instructions for the carrying out of the confiscation of the estates which fell under the previously mentioned provisions and the compensation paid by the government in the form of a special 4 per cent Treasury Certificate redeemable after 30 years. This decree also gave all the relevant instructions for the liquidation or transfer of firms or business falling under the above definitions.
>
> (e) Royal Decree-Law of 22 September 1938 established the provisions concerning the dismissal of all Jewish officers, non-commissioned officers and men from service in the army. Regular soldiers and NCOs were given 'honorable discharge' whilst all officers were placed on the retired list.
>
> (f) Royal Decree-Law of 21 November 1938 determined that Jews were not permitted to be members of the Fascist Party.
>
> (g) Law No. 1054 (20 June 1939) barred Jews from all professions such as lawyers, notaries, accountants, doctors, dentists, nurses, chemists, pharmacists, architects, journalists, industrial consultants, auditors, etc.
>
> (h) Law No. 1024 (13 July 1939) gave authority to a special committee appointed by the Department of Interior, to establish the 'Aryan' status of Jews who could prove that actual facts were not in accordance with what appeared on birth records. This law was intended to permit the Aryanization of those who asked for the privilege of proving their mother's misconduct.
>
> (i) Law No. 1055 (13 July 1939) set the rules in connection with the use of Jewish names by Aryan families, and of Aryan names by Jewish families.

The racial laws passed by Mussolini's regime also served as the basis for the anti-Jewish economic laws which led to the confiscation of Jewish property (see Box 1). The process of the dehumanization of the Jews by stripping them of their basic human rights was the prelude to their physical liquidation.

When Italy entered the war on 10 June 1940, new anti-Jewish measures were decreed and the antisemitic campaign in the press was intensified. However, fascist Jewish policy differed from Hitler's practices and Mussolini did not yet join Hitler in the deportation of the Jews to the East. The same was the case in the Italian-occupied territories in France, Yugoslavia and Greece, which became havens of refuge for persecuted Jews. Following the Italian armistice in September 1943, however, all Jews of Italian nationality under German control were to be included and the Final Solution was applied. From September 1943 thousands of Jews were deported from Italy to Auschwitz and to other concentration and death camps, including 1800 from Rhodes. While many Jews were saved by Italians, it is also clear that the transports of Jews could not have been carried out without active Italian collaborators.

Mass arrests of Jews had started in the spring of 1940, when those of foreign nationality, men, women and children, were thrown into jail with no charges against them. From September 1940 thousands of Jews were brought to concentration camps, along with other enemy aliens and suspected Italians. These concentration camps were far better than those established by the Nazis. Families lived together and there were social and cultural programme and schools for the children. Even at this stage, representatives of Italian Jewry emphasized that 'antisemitism as a popular feeling' is not rooted in Italian society. In their memorandum to the World Jewish Congress in New York, on 20 July 1943, Dr Angiolo Treves (chairman) and Dr Harry Bernstein (secretary) explain:

> Even now, after five years of propaganda, information reaching the Italian immigrant groups here indicates that the feelings of the Italian people have not been changed substantially in this respect, at least as far as the older generations and really responsible groups are concerned.[13]

With the instalment of the fascist satellite and puppet regime under Mussolini in September 1943, the camps were used for the deportation of the Jews. The south of Italy fell into the Allies' hands while the north, including Rome and the majority of the Jews, became the Italian Socialist Republic (RSI), headed by Mussolini. At this stage the confiscation of Jewish property became part and parcel of the liquidation process. The Germans concentrated on what is termed by Professor Daniel Carpi as the 'manhunts for Jews' – the imprisonment of the Jews before deportation to the death camps.[14]

The fate of Jewish property under Mussolini

Although no comprehensive investigations have as yet been conducted concerning the fate of Jewish property plundered in Italy during the years of racial persecution, it is apparent that what occurred there was similar to what has already been revealed in other occupied countries. Almost all the studies conducted on the issue of Jews, property were mostly devoted to the perverse judicial mechanisms which made it possible for the state to plunder Jewish assets, rather than to the actual quantification of the looting. In practice, the fascist regime, through its racial legislation, entrusted itself with the right to dispossess the Jews of their property, defined as assets 'in excess' to the limitations stated in the racial laws. The mechanism by which this process took place was through the establishment of the special agency for the disposition of 'excess' Jewish property, the Ente di Gestione e Liquidazione Immobiliare (EGELI) which was set up in Rome. It was empowered by the ministry of finance to 'supervise the purchase, the transactions and the selling of the excess Jewish assets'. According to the Official Gazette of 27 March, this agency soon became 'the secular arm of Fascism for implementing within the framework of the antisemitic campaign, its economic and financial directives.'

The EGELI, according to its statute, was not authorized to deal with confiscation or assessment of property – a task assigned respectively to the Ministry of Interior and the District Tax Bureau. Its primary function was to receive 'from the technical offices of the public treasury the documents relevant to assessments of Jewish real estates exceeding the allowed limits and informing the Finance superintendency about the data resulting from these same documents in order to issue the decree to transfer the exceeding assets to the EGELI'.

The EGELI statute also provided that payment for real estate property transferred to the Agency was to be made by means of 'special bonds' payable in thirty years and at a 4 per cent annual interest. The properties thus confiscated by the EGELI would be sold later 'according to a gradual plan of sales and based on annual projects to be approved by the Minister of Finance'. The amounts raised by these transactions, would at the end be 'deposited in a special account at the central Treasury'.

By noting that 'the approved form of expropriation' was probably based on a pre-existent principle asserting 'the coercive transfers for public benefit', historian Fabio Levi, in his essay 'Application of the Laws against Jewish Properties' (published in 1995), observed that 'it was a real legal monster inconsistent with the norms regulating the property rights... ; a legal monster with very little precedent even in the Fascist time.'[15]

The extent of the plunder and how much (which after 8 September 1943 included all personal assets) was confiscated and resold by the EGELI between 1939 and 1945, is still a mystery. Answers probably lie buried in the EGELI archives, which, as is known, have not yet been thoroughly explored. An estimation of the amount of assets managed during those years by the EGELI can be deduced from a summary of its activities, contained in a 66-page report written by the EGELI directors who, at the beginning of June 1945, handed over their offices to two new managers appointed by the Comitato di Liberazione Nazionale (the National Liberation Committee) that organized the Italian Resistance Movement.

Based on this report, and also cited by Adolfo Scalpelli,

> accounting the value of the Jewish assets (lands and buildings) exceeding the authorized quota at around 726,000,000 Italian lire, for all of 1943, EGELI was allotted assets for the amount of around 55,600,000 lire, namely hardly 7.6 per cent of the total of the exceeding assets. Of these 55,600,000 lire, coming from the transfer of almost 265 firms, the EGELI sold, during 1943, 9,794,122,80 lire gaining a net profit of 29,537,371.15 lire. Considering arisen variations, the EGELI remained in charge, for all of 1943, of Jewish assets exceeding the quota for a comprehensive value of 45,938,094.64 lire: an absolutely modest sum compared to the calculated amount of 726,000,000.

The sum of 726 million Italian lire in 1943, multiplied by the revaluation coefficient 415 calculated by ISTAT (the Italian National Statistics Office) is worth today more than 301 billion lire ($180.6 million).

At this point, a question immediately arises. If only around 46 million lire, out of the 726 million which represented the total of the exceeding Jewish assets, reached the EGELI, where did the remaining 680 million lire end up? This amount, if recalculated by the above-mentioned ISTAT coefficient, today runs into about 282 billion Italian lire ($169 million). According to Scalpelli, 'these assets were directly managed by 19 banks invested with their duties by a special proxy on 9 June 1939'. Although Scalpelli lists all those nineteen banks, he does acknowledge that – concerning the fate of those 680 million lire – 'only they who had experts able to find out the whereabouts of their assets can give an answer'.[16]

Since the war, the whereabouts and fate of the Jewish assets confiscated by the fascists have not be determined. It is still not known what happened to property whose owners perished – did it reach their heirs, what was the fate of the heirless property and what was the extent of success in retrieving property without the aid of experts? At this stage in history, the major bulk of Jewish property confiscated by the fascists has never been recovered, and the whereabouts is still an unsolved mystery. What happened to the assets of those who did not have the experts able to get back their real estates? Among the owners of those assets, how many were Jews deported to concentration camps, who never returned? Did their heirs succeed in recovering the assets entrusted to the banks and managed by them? What happened when there were no heirs to claim the confiscated assets?

After fifty years, many of these questions remain without clear and definitive answers. Lacking relevant information, it is possible to raise the hypothesis (which must be proven) that at least some of these nineteen banks, after having managed the assets entrusted to them, have for different reasons kept them in their vaults.

Another point for inquiry is, why, in their report of June 1945, did the former administrators of EGELI prepare a balance only for 1943? After 8 September of that year, EGELI, whose headquarters had in the meantime moved to San Pellegrino in northern Italy, began taking possession, on behalf of the RSI, not only the exceeding real estate assets but also all the Jewish personal assets which were transferred to its holdings. Thus the property administered by EGELI was considerably increased.

The situation came to a head after the so-called 'Declaration of Verona', the programmatic document in which the government of RSI declared, on 14 November 1943, the Jews as 'foreigners' and, therefore, belonging to 'an enemy nationality'. On 30 November, the Minister of Interior, Guido Buffarini-Guidi, issued an ordinance which not only ordered the arrest and the internment of the Jews but also the immediate seizure of their real estate property, assets of all kinds and personal belongings, to be requisitioned by the fascist government. Besides the overt and absurd exaggeration of declaring the Italian Jews 'enemy foreigners', this measure was a flagrant violation of the same war legislation already enforced in Italy, according to which enemy assets could only be seized (as a temporary acquisition) and not requisitioned (as a definitive appropriation).

In the wake of the institutional foray started by Buffarini-Guidi, the following 1 December the Ministry of National Education ordered 'the seizure of all pieces of art belonging to the Jews and the Jewish organizations'. On 4 January 1944, a law was passed which provided new rules regarding Jewish property, in practice giving sanction to the total plundering of the Jews of Italy. In order to provide at least a shadow of legality to this state-conducted robbery, article 15 of this law by decree asserted that profits resulting from the sale of confiscated Jewish property would serve to cover the cost of 'assistance, subsidies and compensation for war damages to those who suffered from enemy air raids' and who resided in the RSI territory.

At first, it seems incomprehensible why the Jews should pay for damages caused by a conflict declared by Mussolini. According to Fabio Levi, this legislation was possible 'because in the Fascist propaganda the Jews were always depicted as those who had the main responsibility for the war, and therefore it was lawful for them to be deprived of their assets.'

As historian Renzo De Felice stressed in his book *History of Italian Jews Under Fascism*, 'these measures adopted by the Fascists against the Jews at the end of 1943 and during the first months of 1944 were for sure caused not only by the need of satisfying on this issue the Germans . . . but also by the very precarious economic and financial situation of the RSI.'[17]

On 12 March 1945, the RSI's Ministry of Finance sent Mussolini a 'note' with the balance for the first year in which the confiscation of Jewish property was carried out. That document informed the Duce that up to 31 December 1944, 5768 writs of seizure were sent to the EGELI. The Agency reported that it had confiscated land worth more than 855 million lire and real estate assets worth more than 198 million. These values were calculated on the basis of the average market prices of 1940, but in the note it was stressed that 'if one wanted to get the real and updated value of the real estate, the above mentioned amounts would have been notably higher'.

Added to these millions were more than 731 million Italian lire in industrial and other varied shares, state bonds worth more than 36 million and 75 million in cash. To all this – the note said – there should be added 'many other shares whose quotations had not been possible to evaluate', more than 182 business and shops whose value had not been estimated yet and other seized assets (furniture, jewellery, linen, various goods) whose value could be assessed only when sold. It is quite obvious that the scope of confiscated property held by EGELI far exceeded the partial value of the properties which were possible to estimate, which ran to more than one billion and 895 millions lire.

The plunder of Jewish property continued from September 1943 until December 1944. From one year to the next, the Italian lira was greatly devalued and the coefficient 415 calculated by ISTAT for 1943 slumped to 93 the next year, that is, less than one quarter. If one multiplies only those 1895 million lire by 93 (without taking into account the non-assessed assets and more than 2000 writs of seizure issued up to 25 April 1945) the total amount reaches the astounding figure of 176 billion and 235 million lire ($105.6 million). This estimate the previous year, before devaluation, was equivalent to almost 786 billion and 500 million lire ($471.9 million).

It must be borne in mind that in many cases the EGELI did not succeed (or succeeded only partially) in receiving the confiscated property, due to the interference and sectorial motives and interests of other public bodies.

Proof of this inefficiency on the part of the EGELI, as well as the extent of state looting by the RSI in northern Italy, is evident from an article published in Rome by a daily newspaper, *Il Messaggero*, on 11 February 1954. The article reports the finding of a remarkable quantity of gold coins, jewellery, valuable paper currencies, banker's drafts and money orders worth almost one billion Italian lire in the vaults of the Vicenza branch of the Banca d'Italia. This treasure, the paper wrote, had been left there in deposit by 'authorities of the RSI'.

It is not surprising that such a fortune, worth today close to 19 billion Italian lire as per ISTAT revaluation ($11.4 million), was 'found' in a branch of Banca d'Italia nine years after the end of the war. It raises the suspicion that someone had hidden the money there, waiting to get it back in quieter days. However, this assumption raises other disturbing questions: most probably this was not an isolated case, and the question is, how many more assets were thus quietly stashed away by the RSI authorities?

It is reasonable to presume that a large amount of assets, if not all, were stolen from the Jews and as such, were they ever returned to their legitimate owners? And, if not, where did they end up?

Abortive efforts

In the south of Italy, which was under the Allies' influence, some formal measures regarding confiscated property were already taken in January 1944. In this area, to which King Victor Emanuel and Prime Minister Pietro Badoglio fled after the fall of the fascist regime in July 1943, the imprisoned Jews were liberated. (Most of the camps were in the south.)

Reacting to the manhunt for the Jews in the north, where most of them lived, and to the confiscation of their property, the government in the south issued a special decree on 20 January 1944, three days before the landing of the Allied forces there. This decree, in which King Emanuel repealed the racial laws of Mussolini, was the first of ninety decrees and regulations dealing with the return of Jewish property which were enacted up until 1997.

Despite this impressive record of government regulations, little was achieved in the area of restitution. On 11 May 1944, law no. 364 designated the Jewish community as the successor of heirless Jewish property. It took fifty-three years before the government of Italy began to implement this law. Italian bureaucracy blocked progress, and not necessarily as a result of antisemitic feelings.

At the end of 1946 the legal adviser of the World Jewish Congress, P. R. Binenfeld, reported on the negotiations of the peace treaty between Italy and the Allies. The agreement, signed in February 1947, contains stipulations (in article 77) to return property taken by force to Germany after 1943. The Allies did not care much about compensation to Italian Jews but rather concerned themselves with taking over Italian property in areas under their control (Germany, Austria and Italy). Further legislation, in March 1947, charged the Jewish community with the responsibility of managing heirless Jewish property. No real effort was made to return property which was bought cheaply following its confiscation by Mussolini's forces. The government did not provide proper laws for these cases and did not compensate those Italian Jews who submitted documents of their original ownership.

World Jewish Congress documents highlight the complexities of the fate of Jewish property in the city of Trieste. Trieste was an Italian city from 1920 until the end of the Second World War but, because of conflict with Yugoslavia, the United Nations established autonomy there in 1947, though control remained in the hands of the Allies, the US and Great Britain. Only in 1954 were most of the city and its territories returned to Italy, and some parts to Yugoslavia. Members of the Jewish community of Trieste, many of whom arrived from Central and Eastern Europe with their belongings, could not retrieve their property, which had been looted by the German army. According to WJC documents, some of the property which belonged to Jewish refugees was seized by the American army and was held in the vaults of the Bank of Italy in Rome. When the WJC's Binenfeld investigated the matter, he revealed, once more, the negative role of Great Britain, which demanded that the money be transferred to the international organization of refugees and opposed its return to the Jewish people. This was a consistent British position against financial aid to Jewish survivors of the Holocaust who could immigrate to Palestine. This policy also continued after the establishment of the State of Israel.[18] In 1954 the WJC negotiated directly with the Italian government on compensation for the property which was stored in Trieste, but without success. In the Central Zionist Archives in Jerusalem there are files containing the bi-weekly reports of the Italian Jewish community to the WJC on the restitution efforts since 1946. In November 1957 the Jewish community of Italy wrote a memo to the WJC about personal compensation from Germany. Several European countries opposed this, including Great Britain, France and Norway, but the Italian Jewish community continued to put on pressure and in July, 1961 an agreement between West Germany and Italy was signed for between 30 and 40 million Deutschmarks.

Documents revealed in 1997 showed how the Central Bank of Italy tried to hide its gold in 1943 before the Germans seized control of the country. Also, declassified documents demonstrated how, in 1944, Switzerland demanded looted gold from Nazi Germany which the Nazis had taken over from the Central Bank of Rome. After the war, Emil Puhl, the Vice-President of the German Reichsbank, told his American investigators that the transfer of the looted gold to Switzerland was done in order to persuade the Swiss government to continue to maintain commercial relations with Germany and to provide Germany with a credit line.[19]

Only in 1997 did the government of Italy make a gesture of restitution to its Jews. Too little too late. In July, 1997 the Italian parliament approved a government bill allocating 3 billion lire ($1.7 million). The bill specified that the money given to the Jewish community is compensation for 'looted assets of Jews, who were racially persecuted, or for heirless assets whose owners cannot be identified'.

In August 1997 the Italian ministry of finance returned five bags of jewellery which were seized after the war. In September 1998 the Italian minister of finance, Carlo Azeglio Ciampi, announced the establishment of a commission of ten people to investigate the issue of stolen Jewish property from the Second World War. The commission will work under a special presidential decree empowering them to gain access to public and private archives. The candidate to head the commission is former parliamentarian Tina Anselmi.

The estimates of looted Jewish property in Italy are far higher in their value. The Italians have confronted their ugly past very late and have shown how little was done for more than fifty years. It is clear that, in this respect, Italian life was not so beautiful.

Notes

1 'An Unusual Holocaust Film is a Controversial Hit in Italy', *International Herald Tribune*, 21 January 1998.

2 '*Ossessione*: a Comic Film about Auschwitz and a Provocative Book are Just Two Examples of Italy's New Preoccupation with the Jews', *The Jerusalem Report*, 2 April 1998.

3 Meir Michaelis, 'Italy', in David S. Wyman (ed.), *The World Reacts to the Holocaust* (Baltimore: The Johns Hopkins University Press, 1996), p. 519.

4 Ibid.

5 See the chapter on Italy in the *American Jewish Yearbook* of 1998.

6 Michaelis, 'Italy', pp. 541–2.

7 Ibid., p. 552, fn. 76.

8 Ibid., pp. 542–3.

9 For an extensive review and analysis of the evolution of Mussolini's anti-semitism see: Meir Michaelis, *Mussolini and the Jews: German–Italian Relations and the Jewish Question in Italy, 1922–1945* (Oxford, 1978).

10 Ibid., pp. 407–11.

11 Nicola Caracciolo, *Uncertain Refuge: Italy and the Jews During the Holocaust* (University of Illinois Press, 1995). See, in particular, the foreword by Renzo De Felice.

12 Susan Zuccotti, *The Italians and the Holocaust: Persecution, Rescue and Survival* (New York: 1987), p. 40.

13 'War and Post-War Problems', Memorandum on the Jews in Italy and Libya, presented by the Italian Jewish Representative Committee affiliated with the World Jewish Congress, 20 July 1943, World Jewish Congress, New York.

14 Daniel Carpi in the *Holocaust Encyclopedia*, pp. 726–9.

15 Fabio Levi, 'L' Applicatzione delle leggi contro le proprieta degli ebrei (1938–1946)' ('The application of laws against Jewish property, 1938–46'); Saggio in *Studi Storici*, September 1995.

16 The following are the nineteen Italian banks, each one for a specific territorial area, which dealt directly with the administration of Jewish real estate seized from the fascist authorities and assigned to EGELI. The banks were assigned this by special proxy issued on 9 June 1939, according to the provisions of article no. 12 of the law by decree no. 126 on 9 February 1939, regarding the limits imposed by the fascist racial laws on real estate property owned by Italian Jews. Piedmont and Liguria: Credito fondiario dell'Istituto San Paolo di Torino. Lombardy: Credito fondario della Cassa di Risparmio delle Provincie Lombarde (in Milan). Euganean Venezia: Istituto di credito fondiario delle Venezie (in Verona). Provinces of Trento and Bolzano: Istituto di credito fondiario della Regione tridentina. Province of Gorizia: Credito fondiario della Cassa di Risparmio di Gorizia. Emilia: Credito fondiario della Cassa di Risparmio di Bologna. Tuscany: Credito fondiario del Monte dei Paschi di Siena. Marche, Umbria, Abruzzi and Latium: Credito fondiario della Banca Nazionale del Lavoro. Campania, Puglie, Lucania and Calabria: Credito fondiario del Banco di Napoli. Sicily: Credito fondiario del Banco di Sicilia. Sardinia: Credito fondiario sardo. For the cities of Rome and Zara: Istituto italiano di credito fondiario. Moreover, for the respective provinces: Banca popolare di Cremona, Banca agricola mantovana, Cassa di

Risparmio di Parma, Cassa di Risparmio di Reggio Emilia, Cassa di Risparmio di Modena, Monte di Bologna, Cassa di Risparmio di Forli. (Source: *L'Ente di Gestione e Liquidazione Immobiliare: note sulle conseguenze economiche della persecuzione razziale*, Essay by Adolfo Scalpelli in *Gli ebrei in Italia durante il fascismo, Quaderni del Centro di Documentazione Ebraica Contemporanea di Milano, 1962, n.2.*)

17   Renzo De Felice, *Storia degli ebrei italiani sotto il fascismo* (Rome: Einaudi, 1993).

18   Based on study of WJC documents in the Central Zionist Archives by Itamar Levine, 'Italy and Compensation for Holocaust Victims' (special investigative report) *Globus* (Israeli financial daily), 23 April 1998, pp. 57–67.

19   'Tales of Hiding Gold from the Nazis' (on the Central Bank of Italy) in *International Herald Tribune*, 10 February 1998; Itamar Levine, ibid., p. 67; and *The New York Times*, 23 May 1998.

19
The Vatican and the Shoah: Unanswered Questions of Material Complicity

Arieh Doobov

The Second World War in retrospect

The Roman Catholic Church, which directs from the Vatican City the activities of a network of spiritual, educational, charitable and diplomatic institutions across the globe, had a unique status during the Second World War. The Holy See was neutral, yet like any institution it had its own list of prioritized interests. Despite the centralized hierarchy which is such a dominant characteristic of Roman Catholicism, Catholics reacted in various ways to the moral challenges of the war.

In certain countries, in cases where Catholic leaders rallied against Nazi Germany and its collaborators, Catholics were targeted by the Nazis as enemies of the regime. Courageous voices in pulpits berated National Socialism for its brutality and hatred, as for its passionate secularism and idolatry. The fate suffered by thousands of such daring, outspoken individuals was often horrific: many were incarcerated and murdered for their defiance. Others, an inestimable number, endangered their very lives in a deliberately understated manner in quietly sheltering the persecuted. A number were motivated by Christian teachings to aid the targets of hatred and brutality, knowing the risk that hung over their deeds. Some Catholic institutions, in a similar manner, opened their doors to Jews and others escaping the black fate which awaited them at the hands of the Nazis and their collaborators.

Yet the reaction of other Catholics was diametrically opposed. Some Catholic figures, both clerical and lay, enthusiastically rallied to the Nazi cause in the German heartland and beyond. Some Catholic clerics themselves took leadership positions in affiliated regimes, others spoke in favour of the Nazis when they taught and preached. Some who saved Jews' lives by hiding them in homes, schools, monasteries or convents, baptized orphaned Jewish children and later refused to allow them to return to a Jewish home after the war. They, too, found the source of their motivation in their Catholic faith.

The most ambivalent – and most hotly debated – Catholic reaction emanated from the Vatican City itself. The spiritual and temporal guide of the wartime Roman Catholic Church, Pope Pius XII, is himself the focus of controversy: to what extent did he encourage Catholic succour for the persecuted and how did he balance the interests of Roman Catholics with those of others trapped in the mire of the conflict? What became known as an infamous 'silence', his failure to name the Jews as victims of Nazi Germany, is today a vacuum filled only with conflicting interpretations.

In the context of this ambivalent record, this essay addresses questions which arose in the present wave of interest in the war's moral and material implications. Claims that the Vatican played a role in the disappearance of property stolen from Jews and other victims of the war – and ultimately became the beneficiary of the loot gathered by Nazis and their collaborators – are outlined. The question of the Vatican's complicity in such a matter must be raised despite sensitivities arising from the period in question, and with full recognition of the progress that has been made in developing mutually respectful relations between Jews and Catholics through postwar initiatives. Yet troubling concerns that are being addressed with relative openness in countries across Europe must also be raised by the Vatican. It is not only a matter of rendering accurate the historical record, but the fact that such questions bear upon present-day issues.

It is broadly acknowledged that full awareness of the Vatican's possible links with stolen property can only be achieved when the Holy See's own archives are opened for independent study. Jewish organizations have long appealed for such openness, but the Vatican remains unwilling to permit unguided eyes to peruse the documents from the Church's past. The debate over the acts of the Holy See during the pontificate of Pius XII – whichever side is argued – will retain the label of 'polemical' until all that can be disclosed is disclosed, all documents which shed light are brought to light. Furthermore, the historical stature of Pius XII will remain tarnished in the eyes of Jews, many Catholics and other interested parties, until his role is fully revealed and explained. At a Yad Vashem symposium on the Vatican and the Holocaust in June 1998, historian Yehuda Bauer noted that the Vatican's 'lack of openness causes a lack of faith' in the institution's goodwill. The beatification of Pius XII, the mechanisms of which are presently underway, will remain controversial until a complete historical accounting is made.

This paper is not an attack on Catholics or on the clerical leaders who in recent years have taken monumental steps in facilitating conciliation between Catholics and Jews. The process of conciliation has enabled Catholics to undertake a brave confrontation with the lamentable history of Jewish–Catholic relations, and has enabled a theological rethinking to gave birth to a new and respectful Catholic teaching about Judaism and Jews. The process continues, both sides approaching an historical narrative about common concerns that is mutually compatible. Conciliation depends upon the momentum of this historical reckoning.

The Vatican's wartime perspective: an undeclared balancing of priorities

A discussion of the Holy See's response to the war must take note of the preoccupations of the Catholic Church leadership. The temporal priorities of the Church are often not as apparent as those of a state, whose interests are chiefly determined by the protection of a defined territory, a clearly identifiable citizenry, and material strategic sustenance. This is not to say that a government's ideology is not complex or prone to moral complications, but that the Church's agenda is shaped by such factors as a large but dispersed community of believers and a plethora of domestic church–state relationships, and is guided by a universal spiritual mission. While the Church to this day considers itself the government of the Catholic people – parallel to states' governments – its nexus with its public is unique.

The modern political era began with the incremental replacement of traditional regimes, headed by divinely approved monarchies, with states legitimized by the people or nation. The Roman Catholic Church struggled to redefine itself as a spiritual entity without realms over which it ruled or where it benefited from established influence. On all fronts, the philosophical partners of modernity were ideas dominated by rationalism, manifested in a secularism which threatened the Church's hold on its public. By the twentieth century, the secular threat had many faces, but in the eyes of Church leaders its most dire incarnation was Soviet-based Communism. The Bolshevik leadership, which determinedly suppressed religious activity, made secularism a core element of Soviet identity, and encouraged 'anti-God' movements. While Catholicism was not the leading denomination in much of the prewar Soviet Union, the papacy viewed – not incorrectly – Communist sympathy throughout Europe as being a harbinger of anti-religious regimes across the continent. In addition, the commonly-perceived, if mythical, conspiracy between international Jewry and Communism, which occupied the public imagination, did not engender sympathy towards Jews in the hearts of anti-Communists. Eugenio Pacelli, from 1939 Pope Pius XII, spent many of the interwar years as a papal diplomat in Germany. He is widely viewed as having regarded the destruction of Communism as one of his own life missions.

Another concern for the Church in those decades of uncertainty was the fear that Vatican condemnation of Nazi and other extremism would cause a break between the Catholic establishment and its own public. In Germany, where the population was overwhelmingly supportive of Nazism once the National Socialist party assumed office, the Church avoided forcing the faithful from having to choose between their traditional faith and the ideology that ruled their political lives. Not only might this undermine the Church, but they also feared the development of a 'liberal, pluralistic society that would threaten their fundamentally conservative social outlook. In their minds the church's well-being was inescapably tied to the preservation of the old social order in Germany and elsewhere in Europe.'[1]

Not only did the twentieth century witness the Roman Catholic Church's normalizing its ties with democratic modern states, but it also saw the gradual process of conciliation with an age-old target of Christian hostility, Judaism and the Jews. Until this process was launched in the *postwar* years, Christian theology viewed Jews as responsible for the murder of Jesus, cursed for all generations to suffer from a vulnerable present and an uncertain destiny. Indeed, for centuries Christian rulers defined Jews as official 'outsiders', required them to live in ghettos restricting their movement and interaction with wider society, steered them to taking on professions (such as usury) deemed immoral by Christian teachings, and obliged them to wear humiliating clothes distinguishing them from non-Jews. In other cases, Jews were banished entirely from Christian lands – or were allowed to stay if they renounced their faith. Well into the twentieth century, traditionalist Catholics were among the most adamant opponents of the legal and social acceptance of Jews and other minorities delivered by emancipation. Theologically-based anti-Judaism established a pattern that profoundly influenced modern antisemitism, both agreeing that Jews were distinct from the rest of humanity. Modern antisemitism's thorough dehumanization of the Jews, which facilitated their mass murder, drew upon centuries of theologically encouraged disdain.

A new understanding was reached in the 1960s when the Second Vatican Council, convened by Pope John XXIII, carried out a fundamental re-engineering of Roman Catholicism. Prior to these reforms, Catholicism's traditional antagonism towards Jews and Judaism remained.

These ideological and theological factors were components of the Church's wartime policy compass: tacit support for the enemies of Communism was a guiding principle for the Church leadership, a precept which, where necessary, overrode consideration for the welfare of persecuted peoples such as the Jews. Historian Michael Marrus, in his *The Holocaust in History*, provides a summary of the Vatican leadership's approach to the extremism-cum-barbarism of the age prior to the war and during the war years:

> As fascism extended its influence in Europe during the 1930s the Vatican remained aloof, occasionally challenging fascist ideology when it touched on important matters of Catholic doctrine or theological position of the church, but unwilling to interfere with what it considered to be purely secular concerns. Beyond this, the Vatican found most aspects of right-wing regimes congenial, appreciating their patronage of the church, the challenge to Marxism, and their frequent championing of a conservative social vision.[2]

Regardless of the authoritarian character of the Church, it is essential to recall that the Vatican's policy agenda did not prevent individual Catholics from spontaneously coming to the aid of Nazism's human targets. As noted above, some Catholics and Catholic institutions were extremely brave protectors of Jews and others. The Holy See also sheltered hundreds of Jews in Rome. But without detracting from the virtue of these deeds, such admirable responses cannot be used to obviate the fact that other arms of the Catholic church were supporters of Nazi Germany's agenda, or to obscure the fact that the Church's leadership's reticence in the Jews' hour of need is a valid target for criticism. Both sets of responses transpired, both must be reckoned with.

Unanswered questions of material complicity

Since the war years, a number of allegations have arisen regarding the Vatican's ties to properties seized by Nazis and their collaborators from their victims. The chaotic immediate postwar years and the perplexing establishment of new alliances between governments and intelligence services serve as the backdrop for these developments. As noted above, Roman Catholic clergy and lay leaders had been guided by different priorities during the war years. For those who supported the Nazi or affiliated regimes, such liaisons did not cease with the war's end. Indeed, the Third Reich failed to overpower the Communist threat with striking consequences: the defeated and retreating German armies left a political vacuum in much of Central and Eastern Europe – which the conquering Red Army filled with Soviet-friendly governments. Anti-Communists had suffered precisely the fate they had dreaded. Catholic leadership now faced an emboldened and enlarged enemy.

While the link between the horrors of Croatia and the Vatican's leadership can only be speculated upon, it is known that the postwar years saw anti-Communist networks emanating from Roman Catholic institutions. Catholic figures who had been instrumental supporters of regimes in Central and Eastern Europe now became critical operative links for escape routes for war criminals, for handling finances for escape and anti-Communist resistance, and for forging Cold War alliances between Western intelligence and knowledgeable opponents to newly-installed Communist regimes. The Cold War's realignment of friends and foes resulted in a new coincidence of enemies: many Nazis and their collaborators became partners of the West's anti-Communist agenda. In many cases such fugitives were directly recruited by Western intelligence; in other cases, where Catholic networks did the groundwork, the West was willing to overlook criminal pasts to permit recruitment into the anti-Communist network.

A number of the fugitives benefited from the treasures they had amassed – through theft, appropriation, counterfeiting – from countless categories of victims. When Jews, Romanies, political opponents and others lost their lives, their material possessions were absorbed into the revenue of a government or filled the pockets of politicians and soldiers. Already during the war such assets were being stored for an anticipated future need, in secret caverns or even in bank accounts and vaults. Such funds were used to finance the material well-being of many fugitives and to back anti-Communist subversion.

Recent revelations regarding stolen properties establish the links between the Holy See and the Ustasha-led Croatian regime. The Croatian wartime state's policies of forced conversions of Serbian Orthodox to Catholicism, the mass murder of Serbs, Jews and Gypsies in death camps such as Jasenovac, cast shame on the Catholic Church. Yet in the postwar years, the Vatican's link to the perpetrators of such acts remained operative: a number of Ustasha leaders were assisted by Catholic clergy, operating in close connection to the Vatican, to flee Europe. Intelligence reports submitted by Office of Strategic Services (OSS) operatives, and released decades after the fact from the US National Archives, state that the Americans had been made aware that Vatican officials were pivotal in using illicit funds or the Church's own monies to facilitate Nazis escaping Europe.[3] The Americans, British and French knew of this operation and tacitly assented.[4]

More recently, the US National Archives have permitted the wider release of previously classified intelligence reports and various documents; previously, documents from this period were accessible only through freedom of information procedures. These declassified papers have turned international attention to, among other episodes, the details of services provided by Swiss financial institutions to Nazi Germany during the war, information about other 'neutral' countries' trade with the German regime, and other incidents of wartime profiteering. Among the documents found in the National Archives by researchers are a number of papers discussing the Vatican's link to covert operations, in particular dealing with the Vatican's ties to Croatia.

In 1997, the research team for an American television documentary came across a document discussing a transport of loot with parallels to the fore-mentioned shipment. The memorandum was authored by Emerson Bigelow, an expert in illicit funds who followed intelligence reports gathered by officers in the field concerning stolen valuables. Again, the connection between Ustasha gold and the British army's intelligence is present. Yet instead of referring to unidentified 'priests', Bigelow states that gold was divided into two destinations: the British gold pool, and the Vatican, as follows:

> The Ustascha [sic] organization (a Croatian fascist organization, headed by Ante Pavelic) removed funds from Jugoslavia [sic] to total 350 million Swiss francs. The funds were largely in the form of gold coins.
>
> Of the funds brought from the former Independent Croat state where Jews and Serbs were plundered to support the Ustascha organization in exile, an estimated 150 million Swiss francs were impounded by British authorities at the Austro-Swiss frontier; the balance of approximately 200 million Swiss francs was originally held in the Vatican for safe-keeping. According to rumor, a considerable portion of this latter amount has been sent to Spain and Argentina through the Vatican's 'pipeline', but it is quite possible this is merely a smokescreen to cover the fact that the treasure remains in its original repository.[5]

In today's values, 350 million Swiss francs is worth approximately US $295 million, meaning that assets to the value of US $180 million may have been absorbed into the Vatican's financial holdings. The 1997 release of this document prompted American President Bill Clinton to promise an internal inquiry into the fate of the property. An exhaustive study is still awaited. Elan Steinberg, of the World Jewish Congress, responded that the revelation of the Bigelow letter 'is an extremely significant development that fits into the pattern of the Nazi gold question. It is a pattern that involved not only Switzerland and other neutral countries, but, according to US intelligence documents, went to the heart of the Holy See.[6]

The June 1998 US State Department report on stolen wartime assets and trade with Nazi Germany reported, inconclusively, on the fate of the Ustasha war chest:

> The Ustasha regime in Croatia accumulated a treasury that apparently included valuables stolen from the dispossessed and deported Jewish and Sinti-Roman victims of the ethnic cleansing campaign. A variety of wartime and postwar US Intelligence reports confirm Ustasha regime treasury of some size, but no authoritative quantification proved possible. Nor was it ever clear how much came from Croatian Jewish victims – although one US intelligence report speculated that it might be as much as $80 million in gold, mostly coins. Official and postwar information does confirm that the Croatian regime transferred gold to Switzerland toward the end of the War . . .[7]

As noted above, the postwar fate of the Ustasha booty was linked to the common anti-Communist interests of the Allies and the surviving Ustasha affiliates. The June 1998 State Department report agrees with many of the conclusions of *Ratlines* by Mark Aarons and John Loftus, a 1991 study branded as polemical by the Catholic establishment. The report affirms that Ante Pavelic was in control of an uncertain quantity of stolen assets which he used to protect himself in postwar Europe and finance his escape. By early 1946 Pavelic had arrived in Rome from where his subsequent flight to Latin America was arranged. This escape was probably directed by Father Krunoslaw Dragonovic from the College of San Girolamo, a centre for Croatian clerics – and for Ustasha operations.

Dragonovic is perhaps the key to understanding these secretive machinations: he had long been an Ustasha supporter, had many contacts with international aid organizations such as the International

Committee of the Red Cross, and was well connected to intelligence circles. Dragonovic was also a seasoned member of the Vatican milieu. He was the pivot around which secreted fugitives, stolen money, complicity with intelligence agencies, and escape routes revolved. In an interview with the authors of *Ratlines*, the foremost defender of the Vatican's wartime actions, Father Robert Graham, commented as follows: 'I've no doubt that Draganovic was extremely active in siphoning off his Croatian Ustashi friends. . . Just because he's a priest doesn't mean he represents the Vatican. It was his own operation. He's not the Vatican.'[8]

This distancing does not tally with the Vatican's official recognition of the San Girolamo operation as the Croatian Committee of the Pontifical Welfare Commission,[9] nor with the fact that the deputy director of San Girolamo was the Vatican's official representative to the institution.[10] This status helped Dragonovic and his peers benefit from the Vatican's diplomatic immunity. *Ratlines* details many cases of direct Vatican intervention on behalf of Croatian refugees, a number of whom were also war criminals.[11]

The US report confirms the framework in which postwar Ustasha activities took place, but stops short of confirming details. Further information is certainly present in the US National Archives, British archives, Swiss banking records, Croatian archives, and unquestionably in the Vatican City itself. The foreign policy arms of the Holy See are numerous, comprising both formal Secretariat of State operations and scores of particular channels between the Church and abroad. San Girolamo's personnel were far from being strangers to the Vatican, and the question of whether its highest offices tacitly acquiesced to the institution's operations or were more deeply involved is still unresolved.

In December 1997, the London Conference on Nazi Gold gathered representatives of over forty countries primarily to exchange information as to the fate of stolen Jewish and other victims' property. Although the Holy See initially declined the British Foreign Office's invitation to participate in the conference, this decision was amended some weeks before the meeting and two official observers were sent from the Vatican City. The Jewish and Romany delegations both raised the issue of stolen assets eventually being placed in the hands of the Vatican. A number of delegations joined these voices to demand that the Vatican open their archives to independent researchers. Lord Mackay of Clashfern, who chaired the conference, summarized the scene:

> There were a number of calls for the Holy See to open its wartime and postwar archives, which, it was suggested, might contain relevant

information. The Holy See delegation, which had made it clear from the outset that they were attending only as observers, did not respond.[12]

The Holy See's silent presence is perplexing. The Roman Catholic Church repeatedly issued blanket statements denying any allegations linking the Holy See to acts of impropriety in such matters. Yet the delegation to London – comprising an archivist and a diplomat – was seemingly dispatched to gauge the intensity of allegations and to study the response strategies of other delegations. One week after the conference closed, the Holy See's authoritative spokesman to the media, Joaquim Navarro-Valls, stated: 'Regarding the gold looted by the Nazis in Croatia, searches done in the Vatican archives confirms the inexistence [*sic*] of documents related to the subject and thus refute any kind of supposed transaction attributed to the Holy See.'[13] He added with certainty that the internal investigation, of which no written report was released, authorizes the Holy See to 'look to the past with serenity'.[14]

At the June 1998 Washington seminar on assets looted during the war years,[15] thirty-nine countries participated and agreed to cooperate in resolving contentious ownership questions. Germany and its allies were estimated to have seized hundreds of thousands of art works during the war, many of which were not restored to their owners or heirs subsequent to the war. The Holy See, which owns one of the largest art collections in the world, did not respond to the US State Department's invitation to attend the Washington meeting. Its expertise in this field has, therefore, been denied to this international effort to restore property to its owners.

While evidence about the fate of stolen property often consists of assessments of intelligence experts and historians, concrete evidence exists of another form of improper actions by the Vatican: banking transactions with financial institutions blacklisted by the Allies. As part of the total warfare strategy used by the Allies, which saw the British innovation of an Office of Economic Warfare, the Axis' enemies endeavoured to cripple the German war effort by economically isolating Germany and her strategic partners. Intelligence officers carefully dissected the German state's structure and identified non-German financial institutions which served as a critical conduit for foreign exchange and other tradables – such as gold. It is this intelligence work that bequeathed a wealth of reports about Germany's financial institutions which, upon their declassification in the 1990s, are the source of many present-day charges of wartime profiteering and financial collaboration with the Axis powers. During the war, the Allies published a blacklist of Germany's intermediaries, with whom dealings by Allies and neutrals were declared illegal.

Intelligence reports declassified in 1997 by the US National Archives indicate that the Vatican's financial agencies illegally dealt with German banks. The Institute for Religious Works was found to have conducted transactions – often via Switzerland – with the German Reichsbank in 1944 and 1945. The wires link the Vatican's bank to the Reichsbank through Credit Suisse, and to the blacklisted Swiss – Italian Bank of Lugano via the Union Bank of Switzerland. The reports, of which three have been located in the Archives, cite instructions wired between banks which were intercepted by field officers. As such, the substance of these reports is not informed assessments but documented facts.

Another link in the illicit chain was recorded in a 1956 US Federal Reserve Bank memorandum about the presence in the American bank of 2500 gold bars minted in Prussia during the war. The dark origins of this gold were obscured by a false date – the year 1937 – which ostensibly permitted the bullion to be traded without fear of transgressing wartime prohibitions. Furthermore, postwar agreements about returning stolen monetary gold, negotiated by the Allies with wartime neutrals and non-belligerents, permitted these bars to be bought and sold without inhibition. Of these 2500 bars, most were the property of Swiss banks who traded the gold for third parties including the International Monetary Fund, Canada, the United Kingdom, The Netherlands, and the Vatican. Such questions of material complicity with the Nazi regime and its collaborators overshadow the wartime history of the Church, and demand clarification.

Conclusion

While the Holy See's spokesman says reassuringly that the Roman Catholic Church can 'look to the past with serenity', such calm historical reflection eludes many whose study of the Vatican's past produces a host of unanswered questions. The Holy See remains the last of the institutions controlling knowledge to guide followers towards a desired truth, not just in the spiritual realm but also in the many temporal fields the hand of the papacy touches. Steering a sturdy course through modernity, the period characterized by the granting of choice to the individual as to which truth is to be upheld, the Vatican's hand was exposed in London in December 1997. At the London Conference on Nazi gold, delegation after delegation, with varying degrees of willingness, acceded to the consensus demand that light must be brought to national histories even when they are shameful. Only the Vatican declined.

This resistance recalls the official refusal to examine critically the Vatican's wartime role for decades after the conclusion of the Second World War. Pope John XXIII's convening of the Second Vatican Council took landmark steps in altering the theological 'contempt' for Judaism, but a substantive treatment of the war years was not issued until 1998. The delay reflects either the hierarchy's indifference towards what Jews and many Catholics regard as a highly problematic and sorrowful historical episode in Jewish–Catholic relations, or perhaps the depths of the challenge the period poses to Catholic thought and institutions of spiritual and temporal authority. The soul-searching that is taking place has clearly divided the Roman Catholic Church on how to understand its role during the Shoah.

Time and again, scholars who have devoted time and energy to understanding the relation between the Church hierarchy and issues concerning Jews – and their fate during the Shoah – are confronted by a familiar brick wall: historians arrive at a point at which they can only speculate, wondering what picture complete access to historical information would permit them to paint. At such a point, a narrative is guided by a combination of knowledge and professional instinct. The report issued by the US State Department in June 1998, which summarized intelligence gathered during the war about illicit flows of assets, was summarized *vis-à-vis* the Vatican by Under-Secretary Stuart Eizenstat:

> The troubling questions raised by the case of the Croatian Ustasha treasury require answers, including an accounting of the gold and valuables of the victims of Ustasha terror and the escape from postwar trial and punishment of its leadership. But what we learned is troubling. The Ustasha puppet regime of the Nazis in Croatia systematically murdered and looted its Serb, Gypsy and Jewish citizens of perhaps $80 million in gold. After the war, leaders of this fascist regime found refuge in the pontifical College of San Girolamo in Rome, which, with the aid of looted gold, helped finance the escape of Croatian fascists to South America. This pontifical College also cooperated with the 'ratline' created by the US Army's Counterintelligence Corps which got such infamous war criminals – but anti-communists – as Klaus Barbi to South America. It will be critical for Croatia, Serbia and the Vatican to open their archives to obtain the full picture of this sordid story.[16]

The Roman Catholic Church has affirmed that it stands shoulder to shoulder with the Jewish people in countering Holocaust revisionism. Cardinal Edward I. Cassidy, speaking at the World Jewish Congress's conference 'My Brother's Keeper: Antisemitism and Prejudice in a Changing World', in Brussels in 1992, said that any attempt to 'falsify history to deny the dreadful crimes committed against the Jews' must be refuted. As noted above, recent years have broadened the understanding of these crimes, so that profiteering as well as indifference to the fate of 'the other' are viewed as reprehensible. The truth about these crimes deserves to be illuminated. The Church is uniquely positioned to allow many facts, however unpleasant, to find their place in history books. Until that time, discussion of the Vatican's response to the Shoah will remain in the realm of debate and denial.

It is telling that, while scholars produce scores of books on the 'darker' aspects of the histories of states, nations and organizations, to date the scholarly output on the Holy See's ties with Nazi Germany and its stance on the Holocaust consists of only a few volumes. Only a handful of studies have been authored, as have been cited above, and few have been written in recent years. Scholars have been able to sketch particular faces of the Church hierarchy during the war but an all-embracing study is elusive precisely because the only avenue towards such a sorely needed work is via the inaccessible Vatican archives. Because so much information remains stored silently in archives, innumerable details about the Holocaust are unknown; in Israel Singer's words, 'our own history is not yet known to us.'

The Church may produce or authorize the works which conform to a conservative, non-critical view of history, but such scholars are unlikely to be forthcoming with frank analyses. In the meanwhile, the Church will label any works questioning or refuting its preferred view of history as polemical or prejudiced. The Church's own narrative is itself an example of such bias. The more one listens to Catholics educated in modern, culturally diverse environments, the more distant one is from the clear-cut vision of the Holy See, the clearer this concern becomes: an independent accounting must be undertaken.

Notes

1   John T. Pawlikowski, 'The Vatican and the Holocaust: Unresolved Issues', in Marvin Perry and Frederick M. Schweitzer (eds), *Jewish–Christian Encounters over the Centuries: Symbiosis, Prejudice, Holocaust, Dialogue* (New York: Peter Lang, 1994), p. 305.

2   Michael Marrus, *The Holocaust in History* (Manover University Press, 1987), p. 179.

3   Communication between Parsons and Dowling, 29 August 1947, USNA, Myron Taylor Papers, Box 17.

4   See, for example, 'US and Allied Wartime and Postwar Relations and Negotiations with Argentina, Portugal, Spain, Sweden, and Turkey on Looted Gold and German External Assets and US Concerns about the Fate of the Wartime Ustasha Treasury', US State Department, June 1998.

5   Emerson Bigelow to Harold Glasser, US Treasury Director of Monetary Research, 21 October 1946.

6   Quoted by Tyler Marshall, 'US Document Links Vatican and Nazi Gold', *Los Angeles Times*, 23 July 1997.

7   'Report Summary' from 'US and Allied Wartime and Postwar Relations and Negotiations with Argentina, Portugal, Spain, Sweden, and Turkey on Looted Gold and German External Assets and US Concerns about the Fate of the Wartime Ustasha Treasury', US State Department, June 1998, p. 10 (internet edition).

8   Mark Aarons and John Loftus, *Ratlines* (London: Mandarin, 1991), p. 89.

9   Ibid., p. 90.

10 'US and Allied Wartime and Postwar Relations and Negotiations with Argentina, Portugal, Spain, Sweden, and Turkey on Looted Gold and German External Assets and US Concerns about the Fate of the Wartime Ustasha Treasury', US State Department, June 1998, p. 147 (footnote 25).

11 See, for example, Aarons and Loftus, *Ratlines*, p. 117.

12 London Conference on Nazi Gold, 2–4 December 1997, Chairman's Conclusions.

13 Frances D'Emilio, 'Vatican–Nazi Gold', Associated Press, 9 December 1997.

14 Ibid.

15 Washington Conference on Holocaust Era Assets, Organizing Seminar, US State Department, 29–30 June 1998.

16 From 'Remarks by Ambassador Stuart E. Eizenstat, US Under Secretary of State for Economic, Business and Agricultural Affairs, to the Israel Council on Foreign Relations', Jerusalem, 15 June 1998.

20
Confiscation in Belgium: Diamonds and other Jewish Properties

Viviane Teitelbaum-Hirsch

When the Second World War broke out in Belgium on 10 May 1940, approximately 65,000 Jews[1] were living there. Only 7 per cent of the Jewish population were Belgian born. Most Jews in Belgium were of Polish origin, and spoke Yiddish as their mother tongue. They were concentrated mainly in Antwerp and Brussels, but also in Liège and Charleroi. This immigration had occurred primarily during the interwar period, although an earlier wave had taken place at the beginning of the century. Many were craftsmen, merchants or workers and lived very modestly. In Antwerp the majority worked in the diamond business, whereas in Brussels they were mainly active in textiles and leather or trades related to such fields. In 1941 only 55,000 Jews were present in Belgium.

Between the occupation and the beginning of deportation in the late summer of 1942, the Germans gradually suppressed all Jewish life in Belgium by different police regulations, orders, laws and enactments. From October of 1940, when the first decrees[2] against the Jews were published, until June of 1942 when they were obliged to wear the yellow star and observe a curfew, the Nazis slowly plundered the Jewish population of Belgium, stealing all its belongings and forbidding all its activities; Jews were unable to earn a living. Thus, when deportations began in Antwerp in August 1942, and two weeks later in Brussels, Jews had already been deprived of everything they owned.

During the German invasion in May 1940, many Jews tried to escape to France and Britain. Some succeeded in making their way to souther France or even to Spain, while others reached Brazil, Cuba, the United States and Britain. After weeks of wandering, many others elected to return to their homes in Belgium. Many families discovered upon their return that they had already lost everything. Their apartments were occupied, and their belongings had been stolen. Still, in the early months of the occupation, when no visible and open anti-Jewish measures had been taken, the Jews tried to reconstruct their lives within the community. In Brussels and Antwerp, aid committees were formed.

In October 1940, a Belgian government-in-exile was established in London. Inside Belgium, however, the administration continued to function and government representatives and *secretaires generaux* led successive cabinets and forwarded the German orders to their respective administrations. Actively or passively, many Belgians, as well as governmental authorities in Belgium, helped the Germans to set up a structure that planned and organized the plunder of the Jews. Worse still, they also helped in the arrest and deportation to Auschwitz of 25,000[3] Jews. At the same time, the other half of the Jewish population that did escape the Final Solution, was, to some degree, saved with the help of Belgian citizens who helped them to hide.

During the occupation Belgium was under Military Administration, the *Militarverwaltung* (MV), led by the General Alexander Von Falkenhausen and headed by Eggert Reeder. That administration adopted anti-Jewish policies with the ultimate aim of eradicating the Jewish presence in Belgium. They eliminated Jews from all positions in public and professional life, confiscated their possessions, and finally sent them to the death camps. These actions were implemented progressively, so that at the beginning of the occupation, the Jews did not feel especially threatened, although they were the victims of certain restrictive economic measures. Many Jews were deceived by the fact that anti-Jewish regulations were declared as 'anti-immigrant' to obscure their meaning.

Anti-Jewish regulations

On 28 October 1940 the first regulations were published. They would eventually total eighteen. First of all, the Nazis defined who was to be considered a Jew and obliged all such people to declare themselves. They then established a registry of the Jews, the Registre des Juifs, and eliminated those on the list from public administration, legal and teaching positions and from the media.

In November of 1940 the OberKommando des Heeres (OKH, Supreme Command of the Armed Forces) ordered the Aryanization of the Belgian economy.[4] This meant the rapid and total eviction of the Jews from the national economy. Gradually all Jewish merchandise was to be seized for the benefit of the Reich or occupation forces. Next, economic measures were taken against the Jewish community, and Jews had to declare their enterprises. On 31 May 1941 Jews were obliged to mark their enterprises so that they could be identified as Jewish. Signs had to be posted in the windows written in three languages: '*Judisches unternehmen – Entreprise juive – Joodsche onderneming*'. Jews also had to declare their capital, real estate and other assets. At the end of 1941, the Association des Juifs en Belgique (AJB) was created by decree and all Jews were ordered to become members. Later, in July of 1942, the AJB would send out the 'labour drafts' which were, in fact, letters of invitation to deportation. Therefore, it became the first target of the Jewish Resistance.

Jewish children were forbidden to continue to attend schools and the AJB set up its own educational institutions. This decree was applied in April 1942. Other decrees followed until, in June of 1942, every Jew was ordered to wear the yellow star. This measure aroused some indignation among the non-Jewish population and awakened the feeling of solidarity that the Nazis had striven to avoid. A movement was launched that aided those Jews who sought safety in hiding.

By the summer of 1942 Jews had been identified, marked, isolated, forced to live in particular quarters, robbed and also deprived of most means of existence. As E. Reeder,[5] head of the Military Administration, mentioned in a report to Berlin,[6] the Jewish community of Belgium was in effect ready for deportation. In fact, 45 per cent of them would be murdered. According to the final report of the Group XII[7] of the MV that dealt with Jewish and enemy assets in Belgium, the total sum of the Jewish plunder was about 225 million Rentenmark[8] (about 2812 billion Belgian francs of 1940).

Obligatory registration for Jews was conducted simultaneously with the registration of Jewish enterprises. This procedure facilitated the identification of 43,193 Jews (16,437 families). Twenty-eight thousand declarations will be the object of a report.[9] Divided as such, 7700 enterprises and around 3000 properties were registered in the Registre des Juifs.[10]

From the beginning of the occupation, the MV sent *verwalters*[11] (trustees) to organize the liquidation of private companies and estates belonging to Jews (*feindvermogen*), or to manage those enterprises worthwhile keeping. Since the work was quite important, the MV decided to replace the trustees by the Brusseler Treuhandgesellschaft, a Belgian limited liability company created by the Germans on 12 October 1940 to act as general trustee.

Aryanisation of the Belgian economy and liquidation of enterprises

As noted above, a total of 28,000 declarations were the object of a report; 7700 Jewish enterprises were declared. Half of those were commercial and small-scale production enterprises and the other half, industrial ones. Of the 7700, the Germans estimated that 300 were of real national interest for the German economy and for the needs of the Reich.

The German Military Administration tried to initiate a 'voluntary' Aryanization process and therefore systematically pushed all owners of small enterprises to sell their companies. Only those enterprises which could prove that on 1 May 1940 they neither belonged to Jews nor had any Jewish financial participation could escape this procedure. But in most cases the Jews had already fled the country, had gone into hiding somewhere in Belgium, or had been arrested and a *verwalter* was asked to do the job. Many German and Belgian enterprises showed interest in acquiring Jewish businesses. 'Aryanization' was launched in late 1941 and the rate was accelerated in March and April of 1942 with the systematic liquidation of Jewish businesses in the textile, leather and diamond industries. By 12 May of that year a total of 6057 firms[12] had received liquidation orders.

From 1 July 1942 the Brusseler Treuhandgesellschaft dealt with the liquidation of the still existing Jewish enterprises. Therefore it created a special section called the *Sammelverwaltungen* (collective administrations).

The Germans benefited from the help of the Belgian authorities in the textile and leather industries through the Offices de Marchandises Belges (Belgian Merchandise Bureau), the Office Central du Cuir,(Central Bureau for the Leather Industry), the Centrale belge des Textiles (Belgian Textile Bureau), and in the diamond industry's Diamantcentrale. Those organizations were, in fact, part of government offices. Belgian companies also benefited from this period. For instance, in the fur business, two well-known enterprises profited from the situation by keeping an important stock for themselves and transferring only part of the merchandise that was to be utilized for the German army.[13]

All money from the sales of Jewish enterprises and merchandise was deposited in the Devizenbanken and later concentrated in one bank: the Société Française de Banque et de Depots in a Sperrkonto (blocked account), allegedly in favour of the Jews, but never handed over. Jewish enterprises were crossed off the Belgian Register of Commerce (Registre de Commerce).

The diamond business

In 1938, 60 per cent[14] of the world production of rough diamonds were polished in Antwerp. It was in that city that the first diamond exchange centre was built in 1893.[15] Before the invasion in May 1940 Antwerp counted over 6000 manufacturers and salesmen in the diamond business, and 25,000 workers. As soon as the war broke out some diamond dealers found their way to the United States, Portugal and Britain, where over 500 of them gathered in one office: the Correspondence Office for the Diamond Industry (COFDI). There they registered and kept the diamonds sent to England and then restored them to their owners after the war.

In order to control the market the Germans set up the Diamantkontrollstelle in August of 1940 under the leadership of the German diamond dealer William Frensel.[16] Regulations of 5 and 31 July obliged dealers to declare all merchandise to the Devisenschutzkommando. In November of 1940 the Diamantkontrolle was replaced by the Diamant-controle of the Belgian Ministry of Economic Affairs, and in February 1941 the Diamantcentrale[17] began to supervise the whole market under the direction of the ministry, just as was the case for industries such as textiles and leather. All diamond dealers had to register their stock of rough and polished goods. If diamonds belonging to Jews were sold, the proceeds from the sales were deposited in a Sperrkonto at the Westbank, whereas the stolen gold was immediately sent to the Reichskreditkasse in Berlin on the account 'Frensel Juden and Feindvermogen'. Jewellery was often sold to German officers.

In July of 1941 the Nazis organized raids on the diamond centres and confiscated thousands of carats of diamonds. On 15 November all Jews had to deposit all their polished goods. On 14 March 1942 the same applied to rough diamonds (see Plate 9).

Before the war there were 400 brokers in the city of Antwerp, amongst whom at least 350 were Jews. In the beginning of autumn 1941, only seven were permitted to continue working. On 8 April 1942 they were also obliged to leave.

In May 1942 Frensel was designated as *verwalter* for all Jewish diamond dealers. All Jewish firms had to disappear. In total 1271 firms were liquidated, to which the 700 firms of absent Jews must be added, and from whom all diamonds, jewels, gold and money had also been confiscated. When the Devisenschutzkommando opened the 700 safes of those absent diamond dealers, on the spot they collected 8 million Belgian francs worth of gold and diamonds.[18] Again all deposits at the

Westbank were to be transferred to the Société Française de Banque et de Depots in Brussels in March of 1944. When Frensel died in May 1944 the Brusseler Treuhandgesellschaft took over as trustee.

By January of 1944 it appeared that 9,400,000 carats of industrial diamonds had been handed over by Belgium to Germany. In 1948 a memorandum written in Karlsruhe by Lt. Colonel Chief S. Buquenne of the Belgian mission of the US Army stated that the value of the plunder of those 1271 diamond firms was estimated at $25 million ($222 million today).

Mobelaktion

On 31 January 1942 a document marked 'secret' was addressed by the Oberkommando des Heeres (OKH) to the Einsatzstab Rosenberg[19] (Operational Staff Rosenberg). It dealt with the confiscation of the contents of Jewish apartments to be sent to Germany 'for the good of the German people'. This confiscation was to be organized by the Reichsministerium für die Besetzten Ostgebiete (RMfdbO, Reich Ministry for the Occupied Eastern Territories), and by the German Military Administration in Belgium.

On 7 April 1942 Alfred Rosenberg was officially placed in charge of the plunder of art collections, libraries and Jewish religious objects.[20] Mader was placed in charge of the Mobelaktion in Belgium.

Nearly 6000 homes were plundered and the confiscated furniture totalled about 100,000 cubic metres or the equivalent of 15 tons of furniture transported on forty train shipments that added up to 1800 wagons.[21] The apartments made available to the Quartierambt of the different cities were emptied with the help of Belgian moving companies, who made an enormous profit between 1941 and September 1944.[22] Many households were also emptied by Belgian citizens who knew of the escape of Jewish neighbours before the Germans did, or who were entrusted with belongings which they never returned.[23]

In Belgium about 7000 pieces of real estate were declared as owned or partially owned by Jews or Jewish enterprises. On 31 December 1943, 2853 real estate properties[24] were under German Administration with an estimated value of 56 million Rentenmarks.[25] They were located as follows: 1070 properties in Brussels, 1395 in Antwerp and 379 in other cities. Those figures included single apartments, although they were primarily one-family houses or apartment buildings.

The German administration – under the direct control of the MV – had not benefited from the support of the Belgian judiciary system in this context, although many notaries collaborated with the enemy. The Attorney-General forbade Belgian notaries to endorse and ratify the sales titles. But the Germans circumvented the Belgian law and declared sales in the presence of a German notary as valid. Many homes were sold under questionable circumstances. Banks started selling the houses of Jews who had fled in the early days of war, had been arrested or were in hiding, since they could no longer pay the monthly mortgage payments. With the help of notaries, those houses were sold at good prices to friends and business relations.

Between 1942 and 1944, rental income of the confiscated properties produced a profit of 28 million Belgian francs.[26] In addition, until the end of 1943, another 12 million BF were deposited in Sperrkontos. Nevertheless German authorities in Belgium complained to Berlin[27] that 'profits could have been much higher if some of the households would have been evacuated sooner and left in better condition by the Jews who fled or were arrested.'

Banks

From 24 October 1942 the Brusseler Treuhandgesellschaft 'administrated' all Jewish accounts and assets in banks and savings banks. Although Jews already had to deposit all their assets in Devizenbanken, German authorities decided to concentrate them in one bank, the Société Française de Banque et de Depots, in order to control all deposits and withdrawals easily. A *verwalter* was sent there by the Brusseler Treuhandgesellschaft. The Belgian banking association, the Association des Banques Belges, asked all banks to comply in a friendly manner with the German demand in order to facilitate the transactions that could then be executed rapidly.

Both the Brusseler Treuhandgesellschaft (BT) and the Devisenschutzkommando had been active in forcing the safes to be opened. To conform to those requirements, the banks opened the safes in the presence of witnesses. They could then carry out an inventory of the contents that were sent to the Société Française de Banque et de Depots in a collective account. The total value of stocks, shares and other assets added up to 216 million Belgian francs as of 31 July 1944.[28]

To determine if an account had a Jewish owner, the Germans based their investigations on the declarations of the Jews who completed them, or asked the banks who would give the information to the BT.

In other instances, a special indication from Belgian or foreign authorities was necessary. In March of 1941 the Association Belge des Banques
also had to hand over information concerning 'enemy assets'.[29] Immediately after the occupation of Belgium, 'enemy' banks[30] had been put
under the control of Group VIII.

Foreign currencies as well as gold had to be deposited at the bank of
issue. Jews had to give up all their gold: coins, fine gold, pure gold, and
that blended with jewels. Other metals had to be declared at the compensation office in Brussels. A report from the Devisenschutzkommando[31] indicated that 797,832 kilograms of gold[32] coins and bars
had already been confiscated in 1941. A document from the Belgian
National Bank pointed out that between 7 August 1940 and 22 February
1941, 14.5 million RM worth of gold and 6.3 million RM worth of
foreign currencies had already been transferred to the Reichsbank.

Deportation

The decision to deport the Jews of Belgium had been taken in Berlin at
the RSHA (Reichssicherheitszhauptant – the central Security Department of the Reich). SS Lieutenant Kurt Asche, in charge of Jewish Affairs
in Brussels, set an initial goal of 10,000 – later raised to 20,000, by Adolf
Eichmann. Deportation of Jews from Belgium was executed in two
phases. Between 4 August and 31 October 1942, within less than three
months, two-thirds of the Jews arrested in Belgium were sent to Auschwitz. The last third was sent to death between the end of autumn 1942
and the end of summer 1944. The last convoy, number XXVI, left
Mechelen on 31 July of that year, transporting 563 persons including
47 children. Seventeen transports left Belgium in 1942, six followed in
1943 and five in 1944. From among those, a train leaving Mechelen on
31 January 1944 transported 351 gypsies. Although no one from that
transport was gassed upon their arrival, and even the children were
admitted to the camp, only thirteen survived.

In June 1942 Belgian Jews were drafted for forced labour and most of
them were sent to work in northern France, to build fortifications along
the coastline for the Todt Organization.

In September of 1943, during 'Operation Itlis', 829 Jews of Belgian
nationality were arrested and 794 were sent to Auschwitz on transport
XXII B, despite pressures from the Belgian government and particularly the director-general of the Ministry of Justice who complained
orally to the Military Administration. From this transport, very few Jews
survived.

In total 25,257[33] Jews were deported from Mechelen to Auschwitz in twenty-eight transports. Only 1205 survived. One hundred and forty-six were sent to Buchenwald, Ravensbruck and Bergen-Belsen. Seven survived. In total 5430 children were sent to the death camps.

The deportation procedure facilitated another stage in the theft of the Jews. At the transit camp of Mechelen, they were stripped of all valuables still in their possession such as watches and jewellery. The Brusseler Treuhandgesellschaft organized a permanent representation of their office to remain in the camp. About 5000 watches taken in the camp were left by the Germans in the safe of the Société Française de Banque et de Depots. The rest were sent to Germany.

In Mechelen the Jews also had to declare any bank account that was left and they were obliged to hand over the keys of their apartment. If they had been arrested in the street they also had to report their address. As the Resistance organized itself in Mechelen, incorrect addresses were written down as the keys were delivered.

Resistance

On 15 July 1942, the AJB was ordered to set up a special bureau in order to organize the mailing of the 'labour draft' (*Arbeitseinsatz*) to the Jews. This created a violent reaction within the Jewish community. In reaction to the collaboration of the AJB, and because the situation of the Jews was deteriorating by the day, an underground Jewish defence organization was created the same month. This group was called the Jewish Defense Committee (Comité de Defense des Juifs, CDJ). Later the CDJ even attacked a transport of Jews to Auschwitz.[34]

The first action that was undertaken by the CDJ was the destruction of the card index of the AJB in order to stop the mailing of the draft letters. The operation was successful but led the SS to immediately begin raids in order to arrest the number of Jews required for their transports. Next, the CDJ, which was in regular contact with the general resistance organizations (as well as with the AJB, through some activists working there), organized the rescue of adults and children by finding hiding places. Over 4000[35] Jewish children went into hiding with new identities. This was organized by the 'Children section' of the CDJ and done with the active support of Catholic, Protestant and lay movements. With the help of the local population, Communists and churches, 25,000 adult Jews spent the war underground.

Liberation and restitution

On 4 September 1944, Brussels was liberated. One month later, the CDJ became the Aide aux Israelites victimes de la Guerre, the AIVG (Aid to Jewish War Victims). Their aid focused on the elderly and the poor, with the help of the Joint Distribution Committee, but they were mainly concerned with the hidden children who now became war orphans. The old orphanages of the AJB were reclaimed by the AIVG and new homes were created to fulfill the need. All told there were fourteen homes.

Many of the survivors who had placed their children with Gentiles sought to retrieve them from convents and families all over the country. There were many dramatic moments when children realized that their parents would never return, or when they did not recognize the parents who came to retrieve them.

During the occupation, the Pierlot government-in-exile had issued a statement on 10 January 1941,[36] declaring that all the decrees of the German Military Administration were null and void, and committing itself to the restoration of stolen property to its rightful owners. It also declared that it would punish Belgians who had collaborated with the Germans. The Pierlot government returned from London in September 1944 and immediately launched the Gutt operation, named after the Minister of Finance, to fight inflation.

Already at that time Jews realized that not only the Germans had profited in the plunder of the Jewish community of Belgium, but also Belgian banks, insurance companies, notaries, process servers and many other individuals. Upon their return, most Jews discovered that their furniture and all of their possessions had been stolen by the Nazis. They also learned that their houses had been sold by the bank as soon as they had been deported or gone into hiding.

Immediately after the liberation some of the Jews who survived the war and returned to recover their belongings were very disappointed. Mostly they received only a 'no' or a 'I do not know' for an answer and did not dare fight the system. In cases when they attempted to pursue the matter, they generally lost.

Institutions and individuals suffered severe amnesia. Banks simply replied that they had turned the money over to the Nazis and could not answer the demands of claimants. Notaries argued that houses were sold and that investigations were not advisable since taxes on their properties for such a long period would be higher than any benefit they could expect![37] Neighbours did not recognize them and pretended that they could not understand why former Jewish neighbours were now claiming the furniture they were living with.[38]

The United Restitution Organization, with the help of the AIVG and some Jewish lawyers, tried to file some claims. However, only the Germans paid some restitution – a lump sum – to some of the Jews through the Bundesruckerstattung[39] for the apartments that were emptied. Stolen valuables, bonds and shares, businesses, bank accounts, real estate, art objects and libraries were not returned. Following the war, the Jewish community was occupied with recovery efforts and did not have the political clout to press for investigation.

The Office de Récupération Economique (ORE),[40] a branch of the Ministry of Economic Affairs, tried to evaluate the damage and to compensate for stolen goods. In fact it worked actively in the field of the works of art. Although some art works have been returned to their legal owners – not all Jewish – many paintings or sculptures which the Belgian government recovered were donated to Belgian museums or auctioned of, since no appropriate publicity was made concerning those objects.

In 1946 nine crates containing mostly freemason materials,[41] and Jewish libraries from Antwerp and Brussels returned from the American Collecting Point in Offenbach, Germany. In 1949 another four were restituted to Belgium. Many masonic art works are still unaccounted for, most Jewish art and libraries are still missing. In fact, concerning recuperation of art works, Belgium has based itself juridically on the Interallied Declaration against Acts of Disposession Committed in Territories under Enemy Occupation or Control, the Joint Declaration (1943) and on the decisions of the Paris Conference in 1945 concerning reparations.

In 1993 Belgium decided to resume research on stolen art and to that effect a catalogue was published soon after to try to identify missing paintings.[42] From 1994 onwards an annual meeting has been held at the General Secretariat of the Benelux Economic Union, enlarged on historical grounds with a French delegation. A symposium took place in Brussels in October 1996 on 'Cultural Goods Spoiled during the Second World War'.

That same year Germany and The Netherlands restituted archives and books to Belgium. These were the first cultural objects to be returned to Belgian ownership.[43] The Belgian books originated from the Algemeene Diamond Workers' Association of Antwerp, the private collections of the Socialist ministers Camille Huysmans and Arthur Wauters, and the Jewish family Andriesse.

In 1966 state clerk Dumonceau De Bergendael made some inquiries[44] for the Ministry of War Victims concerning bank accounts and values confiscated from Jews. It was very difficult for him to get any information from banks even then and no archive was to be found that could be shown to him. Finally, he found out that different amounts were effectively transferred by the DSK to the Société française de Banque et de Depots in the form of money, but also diamonds, gold and jewellery. It seems that some of those transfers remained there and after the war they were put in an account called 'Malines'.[45] A few weeks later he also discovered that one safe still contained many sealed envelopes deposited there by the Brusseler Treuhandgesellschaft in the name of Jews, and other envelopes deposited there in August 1944.[46] No survivors or heirs having been found for these values, they were transferred to the Ministry of Finances[47] in 1959 and 1965 in an account called 'bien sans maître' (goods without owner). It seems that at the Société Française de Banque et de Depots few envelopes remained; they were kept under the name 'Clients Israël'.

As the Germans were extremely scrupulous in their methods, many things are indeed traceable even today. All Nazi documents and notes are still available in different archives in Belgium. However, the Belgian government has not initiated a serious investigation nor conducted research in this matter.

Only in 1996, as a result of the international campaign for restitution, did Belgian Jewry establish its own investigation team in the form of the Belgian section of the WJRO. In addition to establishing claims on property, the Belgian WJRO aims to reassess the history of the plundering of Jewish property and to determine which sectors of the government and the society collaborated with the Nazi anti-Jewish activities. This is an aspect of Belgian history that has not been confronted seriously. Belgians always preferred to contemplate the memory of rescue and resistance, which is reflected in its relatively high number (1000) of Righteous Amongst the Nations recognized by Yad Vashem. The Belgian government, however, had never considered examining its own responsibility during and after the war. It did not even recognize the legal status of racial deportees, or, as in France, grant the status of internees or 'political' deportees.

In March 1997, at the insistence of the Belgian section of the WJRO, the Belgian Prime Minister Jean Luc Dehaene accepted the creation of a commission of inquiry to trace the destination of the properties 'abandoned' by the Jews in Belgium at the time of their deportation or during the war. This commission was headed by the former Governor of the

Belgian National Bank, Jean Godeaux. It is composed of twelve members, including five representatives of different ministries, two historians, one former attorney-general and four representatives of the Jewish community. The Belgian press immediately relayed all information on Belgian banks or stolen gold to the WJC or the WJRO – and its Belgian section released it. The press in Belgium played a positive role in exposing collaboration, and highlighting the role of the administration and private institutions during the war.

The commission was installed during the summer of 1997 and started work soon after. It was asked by the government to present a preliminary report underlining the aspects of the research to be done. This report was scheduled to be presented to the prime minister by the beginning of 1998. It was delayed repeatedly and a few months later, at the beginning of April, Godeaux resigned, expressing concern that international influence, as in the case of Switzerland, might prejudice his work. Lucien Buysse, former marshal of the royal household, was appointed to replace Godeaux as the president of the commission.

Buysse submitted his preliminary report – consisting mainly of lists of sources and archives to consult – during the summer and has been allocated a financial budget from the government in September of 1998 to be able to start the research. The commission also has started investigating banks and insurance companies' representatives [48] and it seems that some limited new elements are starting to show up, but very slowly in this sector.

Meanwhile at the WJRO, Belgian section, over 800 persons have filled in forms to testify to the plunder they or their family have suffered.

Nearly fifty years after the liberation of Belgium, steps are being taken for the recovery of property, recognition of suffering and education of the youth. School programmes, exhibits, ceremonies and political activities will hopefully lead to a better understanding of this history. However, banks and insurance companies have not participated in this effort. To this day they seem to ignore most demands, give evasive answers and suffer from severe amnesia.

In the Flemish part of the country the support of this type of confrontation and remembrance is weaker than the sentiment more broadly found in Brussels or in the French part of the country. Recently Flanders asked its Parliament to vote in favour of amnesty for Nazi collaborators, and recently they even asked for financial compensation for them.[49] In Northern Belgium, no real effort is being made to contribute to the investigation of those dark chapters in Belgian history.

Notes

1 Maxime Steinberg, *L'étoile et le fusil, la question juive, 1940–1942*, Vie ouvrière, collection 'Condition humaine' (1983).
2 *Verordnungsblatt*, October 1940; the military command official decrees.
3 *Memorial de la déportation des Juifs de Belgique*, presented by S. Klarsfeld and M. Steinberg, edited by the *Union des Déportés Juifs de Belgique, filles et fils de la déportation*, the Beate Klarsfeld Foundation.
4 Decree O.K.II Gen. Q.K. Verw. (W) II/21.33/40 of 11 November 1940.
5 Member of the Nazi Party since 1933, he received the SS grade.
6 Ministry of War Victims, *Ministère des Victimes de la Guerre*, Tr. 148.282/R.123.
7 Final Report of the Military Administration in Belgium and North of France, written after the war. Economic Department, Group XII; Chapter 16, German records microfilmed at Alexandria (GRMA)T.501/107.
8 This represented one-tenth of 'enemy properties' (Final Report, op. cit.)
9 Final Report (op. cit.).
10 Ibid., chapter on Jewish properties. This refers to the Jews that declared their belongings, and all went through Mechelen, including the 900 former Germans.
11 The *Verwalters* were placed under the control of Group XII, except for banks and insurance companies, controlled by Group VIII. Administration of houses was placed under direct control of the F.K. and indirect control of Group XII.
12 Final Report, op. cit.
13 Ministry of War victims, *Ministère des Victimes de la Guerre*, inquiry of state clerk Dumonceau de Bergendael, 6-23-25/1/1965, in Brussels and Gent, R.497/Tr.193987.
14 Which means 11,755, 243 carats.
15 '*Le diamant, mythe, magie et réalité*', ed. J. Legrand (Flammarion, 1979).
16 Married to a Belgian woman, Frensel was a member of NSAPD since 1935. Arrested in May 1940 by the Belgian police but released soon after by the German Administration.
17 This office would be led by A. Michielsen, member of the fascist Belgian party, VNV, and was attached to the Ministry of Economic affairs under the responsibility of the secretary-general, V. Leemans.
18 Final Report, op. cit.
19 *Ministère des Victimes de la Guerre*, Tr. 148.282/R.123.
20 Masonic lodges were among the first targets of the 'Sicherheitsdienst', followed by 'Einsatzstab Reichleiter Rosenberg'. The lodges of Antwerp and Brussels were even used during the war as depots of spoiled cultural objects or as national socialist administrative centres.
21 Steinberg, *L'étoile et le fusil*.
22 For instance the firm Arthur Pierre received 4,585,239 BF from 1942 to 1944 for moving Jewish furniture. The numbers of hired movers doubled between 1941 and 1944. Put an trial and condemned to five years of prison for collaboration with the enemy, the firm Arthur Pierre was rehabilitated by the Court in 1971. Source: Israel Shirman,'*La politique allemande à l'égard des Juifs de Belgique, 1940–1944, mémoire de philosophie et lettres* (ULB, 1971).
23 Viviane Teitelbaum-Hirsch, *Comptes d'une mort annoncée, les spoliations des Juifs en Belgique* (1997).

24 Final Report, op. cit.
25 Ibid., which meant 700 million BF by value of May 1940, but their real value is at least 100 per cent higher, according to German reports, and even higher than that.
26 Final Report, op.cit.
27 Ibid.
28 Based on the rate of 12 December 1943. Final Report, op. cit.
29 Eight decrees would be published concerning enemy assets which included those assets of persons who had English, French, Egyptian, Sudani and Iraqi nationality. Later they would also include Monaco, USSR and the USA.
30 The Following banks were considered as enemies: the Banque de Paris et des Pays-Bas, la Société Française de Banque et de Depots, the Banque Lambert, the Credit Lyonnais, the Credit du Nord belge, the Société belge de credit industriel et commercial et de depots, the Banque Jules Joire, the Westminster Foreign Bank Ltd, the Guaranty Trust Company of New York.
31 01729/*Erfolgsubericht* from 20 May 1940 to 30 April 1941.
32 This refers to non-monetary gold only.
33 *Memorial de la déportation des Juifs de Belgique.*
34 Convoy xx in April 1943.
35 Viviane Teitelbaum-Hirsch, *Enfants Cachs, Les larmes sous le masque,* ed. Labor (1993).
36 *Loi, relatif aux mesures de dépossession effectuxes par l'ennemi, Londres, Moniteur,* 25 février (decree concerning stolen goods, published in London in February).
37 Teitelbaum-Hirsch, *Comptes d'une mort annoncée, les spoliations des Juifs en Belgique.*
38 Ibid.
39 Germans have paid in Belgium a compensation for the stolen furniture according to paragraph 44 of the Bundesruckerstattung 1957. The percentage has been defined differently for each country. In Belgium this was negotiated with the ORE (l'office de Recuperation économique).
40 And later by the OBEA (Office Belge de l'Economie et de l' Agriculture), which continued the work of the ORE affect 1967.
41 Transports of freemasonic ritualia and work of arts from 1941 have been easy to trace, see *Spoils of War, International Newsletter,* no. 3, 1996.
42 *Missing Art Works of Belgium,* Part II, Belgian State, Ministry of Economic Affairs, 1994.
43 *Spoils of War, International Newsletter,* no. 3, December 1996.
44 Inquiries from 15-25-26-31/5 & 1/6/1966 in Brussels, *Ministère des Victimes de la guerre,* R497/Tr. 208040.
45 Also the name of the city Mechelen in French.
46 Inquiries of 25-27/7/1966, *Ministère des victimes de la guerre,* R 497/Tr. 209202.
47 At the Caisse de Depot et de consignation.
48 The work of the commission in this area is not made available to the public.
49 Through the '*Decret Suykerbuyk*', but violent reaction has been opposed to this law proposition.

Index

Aalders, Gerard, 198
Aarons, Mark, 320
Acheson, Dean, 40, 117
Adenauer, Konrad, 3
Africa, 144
transfers of gold, 112–13
Albania, 118
Albrich, Thomas, 249, 250, 254
Algemeene Diamond Workers'
    Association of Antwerp, 337
Allies,
    Cold War and restitution, 4–5
    and German assets at end of
        World War II, 125–6, 129,
        132, 139
    and Hungarian deportations,
        271
    Italy, 308–10
    and looted gold and assets,
        16–17, 112, 116, 118, 119,
        144, 147–60, 202–3, 265,
        276, 290
    Portugal's relations with, 269–78
    reparation and restitution,
        33–47; Austria, 244, 249,
        250, 251; Eastern Europe,
        99, 105
    and Spain, 261, 262, 263–7
    and Swiss complicity, 147–60,
        199
    and Vatican, 319
American Jewish Committee, 249,
    251
American Jewish Congress, 251,
    253
American Law Institute, 74, 77
*Amoco International Finance
    Corporation v. Iran* case, 77
Andersson, Ivar, 196
Andriesse book collection, 337
Anschluss, 2, 6, 21, 67–8, 244, 250
Anselmi, Tina, 25, 310

antisemitism, 59, 261, 316
    denouncements, 1, 300
    Italian, compared with German,
        298, 299–303
    postwar, 4, 18, 21, 48
    and restitution, 9–10, 13, 70, 85,
        91, 251
    Swiss, 142, 145, 149, 154–5, 160
Antonescu, Ion, 104
Archer, Peter Kingsley, Lord Archer
    of Sandwell, 28, 224
Argentina, 22–3, 34, 36, 38, 41, 45,
    263
Arieti, Silvano, 298
Art News, 253
Art World, 254
artistic and cultural works, 29,
    164–76, 322
    Austria, 21, 23, 168, 171, 173–4,
        253–4
    Belgium, 171, 332, 337
    France, 24–5, 166–75, 184,
        186–7, 190, 191, 287
    Netherlands, 25–6, 171, 174,
        287–8, 293–4
    Spain, 263
    Switzerland and, 151, 171
Asche, Kurt, 334
Association of Art Museum
    Directors (AAMD), 174
Attlee, Clement, 214
Aubion, Roger, 119
Auschwitz, 14, 86, 114, 178, 179,
    183, 228, 232, 297–8, 303,
    328, 334, 335
Austria, 244–57, 309
    art works, 21, 23, 168, 171,
        173–4, 253–4
    Cold War and containment, 6
    commissions of inquiry, 23
    Jewish wealth, 23, 49, 50, 53,
        56–7, 61, 62, 63, 64;

property declarations, 246–8
myth of *Anschluss*, 2, 6, 21, 67–8, 244, 250
reparation and restitution, 21, 45, 68, 85, 214, 249–56
statements of responsibility and apology, 21, 30n1, 255
transfer of gold to Germany, 111, 118, 198, 276
Aznarm, Manuel, 263
Azores, 43, 276

Badoglio, Pietro, 308
Balearic Isles, 261
Baltic states,
International Research Commission, 24
Jewish wealth, 62
restitution, 9
see also Estonia; Latvia; Lithuania
Bank Enskilda *see* Enskilda Bank
Bank for International Settlements (BIS), 111, 114–15, 116–17, 119, 120, 122, 198, 200, 275
Bank of England, 111, 115, 117, 210, 221
Bank of France, 112, 184
Bank of Italy, 113, 308
Barbie, Klaus, 20, 178, 180, 324
Barbosa, Daniel, 277
Baro, Noah, 3
Barreto, Salvacão, 272
Bassani, Giorgio, 299
Bauer, Yehuda, 314
Becher, Kurt, 275
Beckett, Margaret, 28, 224
Begin, Menahem, 3
Beker, Avi, 279
Belarus,
Jewish wealth, 57, 61
restitution, 107
Belgium, 12, 327–41
art works, 171, 322, 337
Cold War and containment, 5
Commission to Study the Fate of Jewish Property, 23, 45, 338–9
gold and assets, 14, 112, 116, 151, 193, 198, 202, 204, 273, 276, 334, 335
Jewish wealth, 50
Resistance, 329, 335
restitution, 222, 336–9
Ben-Gurion, David, 3–4
Benelux Economic Union, 337
Benes, Edouard, 94, 95
Benigni, Roberto, 297
Benjamin, Walter, 261
Berenbaum, Michael, 163n32
Bergen Belsen camp, 38, 217, 287, 335
Bergendael, Dumonceau de, 338
Bergier, Jean François, 28, 145
Bernhardt, Johannes, 259
Bernheim-Jeune art gallery, 166
Bernstein, Bernard, 155
Bernstein, Harry, 303
Bigelow, Emerson, 319, 320
Billig, Joseph, 185, 190
Binenfeld, P. R., 309
Bjornsson, E., 196
Blattman-Hollweg, Heinrich, 130
Board of Deputies of British Jews, 219
Boelcke, Willi, 119
Bonn Convention (1952), 213, 218
Borer, Thomas, 143
Bormann, Martin, 168
Bottomley, Arthur, 212, 215, 219
Bousquet (war criminal), 178, 180, 183
Branquinho, Carlos, 271, 272
Brazil, 23, 45
Breton, Valentin, 170
Bretton Woods international monetary conference (1944), 116–17, 119, 151, 265
Breuer, Imre, 217
Britain, 319
Cold War, 4, 5
committees of inquiry, 28
fate of assets of Holocaust victims and survivors, 209–26
flow of money to Britain in 1930s, 209–10

Britain (*cont.*)
  Foreign Office Report (1996),
    17, 28, 45
  Franco and, 260
  freezing enemy assets in World
    War II, 210–12
  Holocaust education, 27
  refugee policy, 43
  relations with Portugal, 269,
    272, 276
  reparation and restitution, 17,
    211–24
  and restitution in Italy, 309–10
  and Switzerland, 38, 117, 148,
    323
  see also Allies; Tripartite Gold
    Commission
British Royal Institute, 58
Brito, Fernando, 278
Bronfman, Edgar M., 7, 14, 29, 35,
    99, 121
Brottman, A. G., 219
Bruland, Bjarte, 11–12, 232, 234
Buchenwald camp, 335
Buffarini-Guidi, Guido, 306
Buhrle, Emil G., 171
Bulgaria, 83
  Jewish wealth, 49, 50
  reparation and restitution, 9,
    93–4, 213–18
Buquenne, S., 332
Buysse, Lucien, 23, 339

Cachin, Françoise, 187
Canada, 38, 323
Caracciolo, Nicola, 299, 300
Cardoso, Fernando Henrique, 23
Carpi, Daniel, 303
Casablanca summit (1943), 275
Cassidy, Edward I., Cardinal, 325
Castelmur, Linus von, 134
Central Bank of Portugal, 26
Central Bank of Sweden, 27,
    193–207 *passim*
Central Europe, reparation and
    restitution, 45, 46, 83–110,
    139
Chaimoff, H., 222
Cherzow Factory case, 71, 76

Chirac, Jacques, 20, 178, 179
Chorin family, 275
Christian Socialists, Austria, 245
Christopher, Warren, 8, 92
Churchill, Winston, 4, 117
Ciampi, Carlo Azeglio, 310
Cimoszewicz (Prime Minister of
    Poland), 102
Clinton, Bill, 8, 29, 34, 35, 45, 159,
    320
Codman, Charles, 119
Cohin, Marco R., 221
Cold War, 4–6, 14, 43, 118, 120,
    156, 249, 262, 275–7, 318
  end of, 35
Collet, Charles, 170
Commerzbank AG, 132
committees of inquiry and
    historical re-evaluation, 22–9,
    121
Communism, 7, 18, 46, 48, 69,
    84–6, 88, 93, 94, 118, 122,
    139, 156, 179–80, 216, 217,
    224
  collapse of, 86, 98
  Roman Catholic opposition,
    315–16, 317, 318
  Spain and, 259, 260
Conference of Material Claims
    Against Germany, 3
Conference on Jewish Material
    Claims, 251, 254
Congress of Vienna (1815), 78
*Convention on the Prevention and
    Punishment of Genocide*, 66, 73,
    79
Cook, Robin, 223
Corporations' Commissions of
    Historians, 29
Costa Leite, Joaquim da, 26, 278
Cotti, Flavio, 15, 158–9
Couchepin, Pascal, 145
Courtois, Stéphane, 179
crimes against humanity, 66
  Papon trial, 18, 20, 68, 178,
    180–1
  principles of international law,
    71–9
Cripps, Sir Stafford, 212, 220

Croatia,
  Commission for Investigation of
    Historical Facts on the Fate
    of Property of the Victims of
    Nazis, 24
  Jewish wealth, 49
  role of Vatican, 318–22, 324
cultural plunder *see* artistic and
  cultural works
Currie, Lauchlin, 116, 154
Czechoslovakia and Czech
    Republic, 83
  art works, 174
  Jewish wealth, 49, 50, 53, 57–8,
    59, 61, 62
  restitution, 9, 24, 45, 87, 88,
    90–1, 94–7
  transfer of gold to Germany,
    111, 115, 118, 198, 272, 276

Daber, Alfred, 170
D'Amato, Alfonse, 14, 35, 121,
    149, 160
David-Weill art collection, 165,
    167, 172
De Bergendael, Dumonceau *see*
    Bergendael, Dumonceau de
de Gaulle, Charles *see* Gaulle,
    Charles de
Degas, paintings by, 169, 173, 174,
    175
Dehaene, Jean Luc, 340
Delamuraz, Jean-Pascal, 13, 155
Denmark, 193, 298
  restitution, 222
Dequoy, Roger, 170
Deutsche Bank, 29, 210, 211
diamonds, 14, 151, 204, 327,
    331–2
Dieckhoff, Hans Heinrich, 267n4
Domke, Martin, 119
Dostal, Zeno, 90
Douste-Blazy, Philippe, 24
Dragonovic, Krunoslaw, 320–1
Drancy camp, 181, 189, 190–1
Dresdener Bank, 84, 202

Eagleburger, Lawrence S., 29
Eastern Europe, 17–18, 271

alliance with Germany, 83–4
and Jewish wealth, 48, 53
myth of 'double jeopardy', 69
restitution, 4, 7–10, 44, 45, 46,
    73, 83–110, 139, 222
statements of responsibility and
    apology, 29n1
see also individual countries
Eccles, Sir David, 221
Eckhaus, Gideon, 248, 251, 255,
    256
economic reconstruction, 4–5, 41,
    43, 117, 120, 156
economy,
  Aryanization in Austria, 245
  Aryanization in Belgium, 328–32
  Aryanization in France, 184–6
  Aryanization in Netherlands,
    285, 293
  Jewish involvement in, 53–4
Eden, Anthony, 148
Edwards, J. L., 215
Eichmann, Adolf, 128, 270, 334
Einsatzstab Reichsleiters
    Rosenberg (ERR), 166, 167,
    170, 172, 287, 288, 293–4
Eizenstat, Stuart, 8, 16, 28, 92,
    155, 324
Eizenstat Reports,
  1st Report 1997, 15–16, 19, 28–9,
    124n32, 142, 145, 198, 203,
    261, 269, 276, 279n1; text of
    Foreword, 33–47
  2nd Report 1998, 29, 320, 321;
    extract on Allied relations
    and negotiations with
    Spain, 263–7
Elgemyr, Göran, 203
Enskilda Bank, 11, 27, 197, 207
Entjudung, 84
Eriksson, Herman, 194, 195
Essinger, Dr, 252
Estonia, 24
  restitution, 9, 107
*European Convention on Non-
    Applicability of Statutory
    Limitations to Crimes Against
    Humanity and War Crimes
    (Inter-European)*, 78

European states,
  committees of inquiry and
    historical re-evaluation,
    22–9
  fantasy and reality in archives,
    10–12
  myths of non-responsibility, 2,
    67–71
  and Nazism, 1–2
  reasons for conspiracy of
    silence, 19–22
  reevaluating history, 15–19
  see also individual countries
European Union, 8, 91, 92, 267

Fabianai, Martin, 170
Falkanger, Thor, 232
Falkenhausen, Alexander von, 328
Fargion, Liliana Picciotto, 299
Faust (Vice-Director of Swiss
    Banking Corporation), 131
Felice, Renzo de, 307
Final Act of London (1954), 213
Final Solution, 149, 164, 180, 298,
    303, 328
Financial Times, 150
Flesche, Alfred, 273
Fletcher Report (1945), 129, 262
Flug, Noach, 251
Forsyth, Frederick, 10
Foster, John, 216
France, 18, 19–21, 177–92, 303,
    310
  art works, 24–5, 166–75, 184,
    186–7, 190, 191, 287
  Cold War, 4, 5, 21
  committees of inquiry, 24–5, 45
  Jewish wealth, 50, 61
  Matteoli Commission, 24,
    189–91; findings, 191–2
  myth of non-responsibility, 2, 68
  public view of the Shoah,
    177–81
  and reparation and restitution,
    71–3, 187–9, 191, 222
  stages of extermination of Jews,
    181–7
  transfer of gold to and from,
    112, 198

  see also Tripartite Gold
    Commission
Franco, Francisco, 152, 258–68
Frank, Anne, 12, 68
Frank, Hans, 170
Fraser, Leon, 117
Freemasons, 165, 287, 337,
    340n20
Frensel, William, 331, 332
Funk, Walther, 150–1
Funke, M., 119
Fure, Eli, 233, 234

Gadow, Albert, 136
Garrido, Sampayo, 271
Gaulle, Charles de, 13, 177, 178
Gautier, Victor, 273
Geneva Conventions (1949), 73
genocide, 66, 75, 76, 79, 179, 227
Genocide Convention, 66, 73, 79
Gerlier, Cardinal, 183
Germany,
  and art works, 171–2
  assets in Switzerland at end of
    World War II, 39–41,
    125–41
  British treatment of frozen
    Jewish assets, 211–12, 213,
    217, 218, 224
  Holocaust education, 27
  Jewish wealth, 48–9, 50, 51, 53,
    54–6, 61, 62, 63, 64
  reparation and restitution, 2–4,
    46, 70, 85, 88, 174–5,
    211–12, 213, 217, 218,
    250–1, 292, 310, 337
  Roman Catholic Church, 316
  statements on 50th anniversary
    of end of World War II, 1,
    30n1
  Vatican's financial links, 323
  see also Nazism
Gewerkschaft Zeche Heinrich of
    Essen-Kupferdreh, 132
Glucksman, André, 21
Godard, Justin, 189
Godeaux, Jean, 23, 339
Goering, Hermann, 153, 166,
    167–8, 169, 288, 293

gold,
  looted, 111–24, 126–40
  as proportion of Jewish assets,
    64
  see also Nazism; victim gold *and*
    under individual countries
Goldhagen, Daniel, 1
Goldmann, Nahum, 3, 6, 300
Goudstikker art firm, 288
Graham, Robert, 321
Gränebo, Petrus, 196
Greece, 72, 85, 93, 303
  Jewish wealth, 50
  restitution, 222
Grimnes, Ole Kristian, 232, 234
Grossman, Ladislav, 106
Grosz, Paul, 250, 254
Gruber (Austrian Foreign
  Minister), 251
Gruninger, Paul, 13, 159
Grynberg, Henryk, 83
Gurel, Sukrm Sina, 28
Gurevitch, Beatriz, 22
Guterres, António, 278
Gutmann art collection, 174
gypsies, 36, 318, 334

Hägglöf, Gunnar, 196
Hague Convention on Land
  Warfare (1907), 282
Hals, Anne, 232
Hammarskjöld, Dag, 11, 196
Hassidic Jews, 58
Havel, Václav, 95
Hawtrey, Ralph G., 119
Hayes, Carlton, 264
Hedin, Sven Fredrik, 203
Herzog art collection, 174
Hess, Rudolf, 128, 259
Heyman, Eva, 86
Hilberg, Raoul, 55, 164
Himmler, Heinrich, 153, 272, 275
Hirs, Alfred, 151
Hitler, Adolf, 2, 143–4, 201, 258,
  259, 260, 262, 275, 282, 283,
  299, 300, 303
  and art works, 164, 165–6,
    167–8, 172, 287, 288, 293
Hjelm-Wallén, Lena, 203

Hoch (Director of Swiss Banking
  Corporation), 131
Hofer, Andreas, 293
Holocaust and History, The
  (Berenbaum and Peck), 157
Holocaust education, 27, 206, 256,
  339
  Norwegian research centre, 228,
    237–8, 241
Holocaust Educational Trust, 223
Holocaust television series, 178,
  299
Horthy regime, 59, 99, 271
Hug, Peter, 27, 155
Hull, Cordell, 264
human rights, 178, 302
  international law, 66, 71, 73, 74,
    76, 79
Hungary, 83, 144, 271
  art works, 174
  Jewish wealth, 49, 50, 57, 58,
    59–60, 62
  reparation and restitution, 9, 45,
    85, 87, 88, 93, 97–100, 213,
    214, 215, 217, 218, 220, 224
  statement of responsibility and
    apology, 29n1, 86
  Swiss agreement to transfer
    funds, 41
Huysmans, Camille, 337

IG Chemie, 136
IG Farben, 127, 136
insurance, 29, 47, 293
Inter-Allied Declaration Against
  Acts of Dispossession
  Committed in Territories
  Under Enemy Occupation or
  Control (1943), 124n29, 290,
  337
Inter-Allied Reparations Agency
  (IARA), 42, 213, 265, 267
International Association of
  Jewish Lawyers and Jurists, 89
International Bank for
  Reconstruction, 116
International Bill of Rights, 73
International Commission on
  Insurance, 29

International Committee of
Eminent Persons, 15
International Committee of Red
Cross *see* Red Cross
International Conference on Nazi
Gold, London (1997), 17, 28,
223–4, 321–2, 323–4
International Convention on the
Elimination of all Forms of
Racial Discrimination, 73
International Covenant on Civil and
Political Rights, 73
International Covenant on Economic,
Social and Cultural Rights, 73
international law, 36, 66–82, 87,
103
doctrine of state responsibility
for wrongful acts, 71
doctrine of state succession,
71–3
doctrine of unjust enrichment,
74–5
neutrality, criminality and, 78–9
non-applicability of statutes of
limitations to Nuremberg
crimes, 77–8
obligations under treaty law, 73,
87, 103–4
principle of just compensation,
76–7
principle that no one shall
profit from the commission
of an illegal act, 75
principles of international tort
liability, 74
International Monetary Fund,
116, 323
International Refugee
Organization (IRO), 42
International Steering Committee
on Restitution, 23
International Washington
Conference on Holocaust Era
Assets, (1998), 27, 29, 322
Israel, 2, 3, 6, 7, 27, 29
return of books to, 252–3
Italy, 43, 259, 260, 297–312
Commission on Holocaust
Assets, 25, 310

confiscation of property, 304–8
Jewish wealth, 49, 50, 54
reparation and restitution, 214,
308–10
transfer of gold from, 113, 118,
146

Jacobsson, Per, 198
Janner, Barnett, 219
Janner, Greville, 223
Jansen, House of, 170
Jewish community, Norway, 228,
234–8
Jewish Rehabilitation Agency,
proposed, 2
Jewish wealth, 48–65
confiscation, 48–9
estimates, 49–62
types of assets, 63–4
John XXIII, Pope, 317, 324
Joint Declaration on Recuperation
of Art Works (1943), 337
Jonet, Nuno, 278
Jospin, Lionel, 24, 190
Jost, Hans Ulrich, 151
Juppé, Alain, 24, 175, 189

Kaberry, Donald, 220
Kagan, Saul, 251, 254, 255
Kagi, Kurt, 130
Kahn, Jean, 24
Kann, Alphonse, 167
Kaufman, Henry, 28
Kemenade, J. A. van, 25
Kiffer, Maurice, 189
Klarsfeld, Serge, 24, 189, 192
Klaus, Václav, 95
Klestil, Thomas, 255
Kovacs, Laszlo, 86
Krayer, Georg F., 158
Kroell, Herbert, 250
Krupp (company), 10
Kubilius, Andrews, 109n6
Kwasniewski, Alexander, 10

Laclotte, Michael, 25
Latvia, 25, 69, 109n6
Jewish wealth, 50
restitution, 107

Lauder, Ronald, 254
Laval, Pierre, 183
Lavi, Naftali, 90, 102
Le Pen, Jean-Marie, 178, 179
legal approach to restitution,
  66–82
  national myths of non-
    responsibility, 67–71
  principles of state responsibility,
    71–9
Leguay (war criminal), 180
Lend-Lease assistance, 36, 211
Leopold, Rudolf, 173
Leprael, Amical, 170
Lessing, Hana, 255
Levi, Fabio, 304, 307
Levi, Primo, 297–8
Levin, Itamar, 158
libraries, 164, 165, 167, 170,
  252–3, 287, 332, 337
Lighthouse-Arbitration case, 72, 73
Lippmann, Rosenthal & Co.
  (LiRo), 25, 273, 283–93 *passim*
Lithuania, 69, 109n6
  Jewish wealth, 50, 57
  restitution, 87, 107
  statements of responsibility and
    apology, 30n1
Loftus, John, 320
London Conference on Nazi Gold,
  (1997) *see* International
  Conference on Nazi Gold
Lourenço, Agostinho, 270
Low, Toby, Lord Aldington, 216
Lowenherz, Josef, 245
Lublin camp, 14, 114
Lustiger, Jean-Marie, Cardinal, 178
Lutz, Carl, 159, 271
Luxembourg, 112, 222, 271
Luxembourg Indemnification
  Agreement (1952), 3

Macao, 277–8
MacCamus, J. D., 74
Mackay, Lord, of Clashfern, 321
Mackenzie, A. W., 215
McKittrick, Thomas H., 115, 117
Macmillan, Harold, 217, 221
Maddaugh, P. D., 74

Mannheimer art collection, 288,
  294
Mantle, P. J., 215, 222
Marrus, Michael, 317
Marshall Plan, 4–5, 41
Mason, Roger, 149
Mata, Caeiro da, 276
Matteoli, Jean, 24, 189
Matthews, I. K., 215
Mauerbach art collection, 253–4
media,
  and art works, 253
  Belgium, 339
  France, 179
  and looted gold, 119, 120, 278
  Norway, 12, 232
  and restitution, 10, 22, 92
  Sweden, 203, 204
  Switzerland, 13, 14, 147, 149,
    150, 155, 156
Meiescanu, Teodor, 106
Meili, Christopher, 159
Mein Kampf (Hitler), 165, 258
Menem, Carlos, 23
Messaggero, Il, 308
Metallgesellschaft, 136
Michaelis, Meier, 298
Milroy, Nicholas, 137
Mitterand, François, 19, 20, 178
modern art, Nazism and, 165,
  168–9, 173
Moghilev camp, 217
Moldova, 107
Morgenthau, Henry, 11, 117, 119,
  154, 155, 275
Moscow Declaration (1943), 67,
  214, 244
Moss, Stanley, 119
Mugica, Enrique, 26
Mühlmann, Kajetan, 288
Munich Agreement, 111, 115
Mussolini, Benito, 258, 259, 260,
  298, 299–308, 309

Nathan, Eli, 89
NATO, 6, 8, 43, 90, 267
Navarro-Valls, Joaquim, 322
Nazi Gold (British Foreign Office),
  17, 28, 45

Nazi Victims Relief Trust, 220–1
Nazism,
    confiscation of Jewish assets,
        48–9
    denouncement of, 1–2
    financing war machine, 35–9
    gold, 16–17, 28, 33, 35–6, 38,
        41–2, 43–4, 46, 111–24,
        128, 138
    plunder of art works, 164–76
    Portugal's relations with, 269–79
    Spain's relations with, 258–68
    transfers of gold to Sweden, 11,
        193–208
    Vatican and Nazi gold, 318–23,
        324
    see also Germany
Netanyahu, Binyamin, 7
Netherlands, 12, 282–96, 323
    art works, 25–6, 171, 174,
        287–8, 293–4
    Cold War and containment, 5–6
    committees of inquiry, 25, 45
    gold from, 14, 25, 116, 193, 203,
        204, 265, 272, 273
    Jewish wealth, 50, 60–1
    myth of resistance, 68–9
    restitution, 221, 222, 289–94,
        337
neutral countries, 275
    Eizenstat Report and, 15–16,
        28–9, 33–47
    fantasy and reality in archives,
        10–12
    German gold, 114–18, 119,
        151–2, 193–4
    re-evaluation of history, 15–19
    and refugees, 271
    see also individual countries
New York Times, 159
Newsweek, 13
non-responsibility, national
    myths of, 2, 67–71
Norway, 45, 157, 310
    moral and material statement
        (1997–8), 227–43
    reparation and restitution, 12,
        18, 26, 67, 71–3, 75, 160,
        222, 227–8, 230–43

Skarpness Committee, 18, 26,
    227, 232–4
Nourai, Noel Chahid, 24
Nuremberg crimes, application of
    principles of international law
    to, 66–82
Nuremberg Laws, definition of
    Jews, 52, 55, 59, 283
Nuremberg Principles, 66, 73, 74,
    78, 79
Nuremberg Trials, 22, 66, 119,
    201
Nussbaumer, Albert, 128

Odessa ring, 10
Omnia Treuhand, 285

Pacelli, Eugenio *see* Pius XII, Pope
Papon, Maurice, 18, 19–20, 68,
    180–1
Paris Agreement on Reparations
    (1945), 118
Paris Agreement rehabilitating
    Germany (1954), 213
Paris Convention on Restitution
    (1947), 5
Paris Reparations Conference
    (1946), 42, 44, 211, 213, 337
Patrascanu, Lucretiu, 105
Pavelic, Ante, 320
Peace Treaties, Paris (1947), 9, 99,
    105
Peck, Abraham J., 163n32
Pellepoix, Darquier de, 184
Perechodnik, Calel, 84
Peres, Shimon, 7
Permanent Court of International
    Justice, 71
Peron, Evita, 10
Peron, Juan, 10, 22
Perrenoud, Marc, 27, 155
Person, Groan, 27
Pessoa, Cabral, 272
Pétain, Henri Philippe Omer, 183,
    276
Picard, Jacques, 13, 149
Pilet-Golaz, Marcel, 148
Pius XII, Pope, 314, 316

Poland,
  gold transfer, 111–12, 118, 262, 272, 277
  Jewish wealth, 50, 51, 53, 57, 62
  plunder of art works, 165, 170
  restitution, 8, 9–10, 30n8, 73, 85, 87, 88, 90, 91, 100–4, 214, 222
  Swiss agreement to transfer funds (1949), 41, 45
Pompidou, Georges, 20
Portrait of Gabrielle Diot (Degas), 169, 173
Portugal, 23, 34, 36, 37, 38, 43, 45, 157, 259, 269–81
  German gold, 17, 26, 114, 152, 201, 262, 266, 272–9
  refugee policy, 270–2, 275
  reparation, 41, 43, 265, 275–6
  Soares commission of inquiry, 26, 278–9
Posse, Hans, 293
Potsdam Conference (1945), 125, 214, 225n13, 249
Puhl, Emil, 114, 133, 147, 194–202 *passim*, 205, 310

Quisling regime, 12, 26, 71, 72, 73, 157, 228, 229, 232, 233

Rabin, Yitzhak, 7
Rappard, William, 155
Ravensbruck camp, 335
Red Cross, 30n1, 149, 204, 320–1
Reeder, Eggert, 328, 329
refugees, 13, 36, 38, 42, 43, 69, 139, 142, 158, 261, 270–2, 275
  wealth of, 53, 59, 61
Reichsbank, 35, 39, 43, 111–19 *passim*, 133, 136, 137, 146, 147, 151, 169, 170, 194, 195, 196, 197, 199, 200, 205, 273, 323, 334
Reis, Jaime, 26
Reisel, Berit, 232, 234
religious minorities, research centre for study in Norway, 228, 237–8, 241
Resistance

Belgium, 329, 335
France, 178, 180, 184, 187, 188, 189
Netherlands, 68–9
Norway, 228
Restatement of the Law of Restitution (American Law Institute), 74, 77
restitution, 1, 6, 152
  effects of Cold War on, 4–6
  legal perspective, 66–82
  WJRO activities, 7
  see also Eastern Europe; Tripartite Gold Commission *and under individual countries*
Reville, Thomas, 119
Rhodes, 303
Ribbentrop, Joachim von, 166, 169
Richert, Arvid, 201
Riegner, Gerhart, 149
Riemer, Hans Michael, 27–8
Rifkind, Malcolm, 17, 121, 223
Rings, Werner, 119
Robinson, Nehemiah, 2, 6, 50, 54, 56, 57, 58, 59, 61, 88
Roman Catholic Church, 313–26
  backing for Jewish claims in Czech Republic, 95
  Belgium, 335
  France, 178–9, 183
  Poland, 101–2
  Spain, 258
Romania, 83
  Jewish wealth, 49, 50, 59, 60, 62
  restitution, 9, 85, 87, 88, 90, 91, 93, 99, 104–6, 213, 214, 215, 216, 217, 218, 221, 224, 225n12
Rongel, Irvin, 21
Roosevelt, F. D., 153, 154, 155
Rooth, Ivar, 11, 194–205
Rosen, Moses, 106
Rosenberg, Alfred, 166, 168, 186, 332
Rosenberg, Elaine, 172–3
Rosenberg art collection, 165, 166, 167, 168, 169, 172–3
Rossy, Paul, 277

Roth, Jean-Pierre, 278
Rothschild art collection, 165,
    167, 171, 172, 287
Rotopulsor, 136
Rubin, Seymour, 154
Russia, 107
    art works, 174–5, 294
Ruth, Arnie, 19
Rychetsky, Pavel, 24, 96

Safehaven programme, 41, 129,
    152, 153, 261, 264
Safran, Alexandre, 105
Salazar, Antonio de Oliveira, 152,
    269–79
Salièges, Monsignor, Archbishop
    of Toulouse, 183
Samuel, Lord, 219
Scalpelli, Adolfo, 305
Schacht, Hjalmar, 201
Schiele, Egon, paintings by, 173–4
Schloss, Adolphe, 167
Schmidt, Orvis, 162n23
Schmitz, Hermann, 136
Schneershon, Isaac, 188
Scholten, W., 25
Searle, Daniel, 174
Second Vatican Council, 317, 324
Second World War, 50th
    anniversary
    commemorations, 1, 22
Serbs, mass murder, 318
Serrano Suner, Ramon, 261
Seyss-Inquart, A., 282, 283, 285,
    288, 294
Shoah (film), 12
Shochat, Avraham, 7
Sholes, Walter, 129
Shunami, Shlomo, 252, 253
Singer, Israel, 14, 26, 35, 99, 155,
    203, 279, 325
Skarpnes, Oluf, 26, 232, 234
Slany, William, 16, 28, 34
Slovakia,
    Jewish wealth, 49, 50, 57, 58, 63,
        64
    restitution, 9, 85, 97, 99, 106–7
Smith, Arthur L., Jr, 14, 16–17, 119
Soares, Mário, 26, 278–9

Solzhenitsyn, Alexander, 178
Sousa, Álvaro Pedro de, 274
Sousa Mendes, Aristides de, 271
Southern Europe, Jewish wealth,
    53
Soviet Union, 4, 69, 118, 139, 259
    collapse, 86
    cultural plunder, 164
    Jewish wealth, 50, 61–2
    restitution, 44, 85, 107–8
    see also Cold War; Russia
Spain, 23, 34, 36, 37, 38, 45, 152,
    157, 258–68, 275
    Commission on Nazi Gold, 26–7
    German gold and assets, 14,
        26–7, 114, 152, 201, 259,
        261–7
    reparation, 41, 262–7
Steel Pact (1939), 260, 261
Steg, Ady, 24
Steiger, President von, 153
Steinberg, Elan, 35, 320
Stettinius (Swiss Secretary of
    State), 38
Stucky, Walter, 154, 155
Sunde, Guri, 232, 234
Sweden, 19, 34, 36, 37–8, 45, 152,
    157, 229, 269
    Central Bank inquiry, 27
    Commission on Jewish Assets in
        Sweden at the Time of the
        Second World War, 27,
        203–6; excerpts from Final
        Report, 206–7
    deposits and transfers of gold
        and assets, 11, 17, 114, 152,
        193–208, 273, 289
    Holocaust education, 27, 206
    reparation and restitution, 37,
        40, 41, 160, 193, 202–7,
        265, 275
Swiss Bankers' Association, 15, 27,
    41
Swiss National Bank, 36, 38,
    39–40, 114, 115, 116, 120,
    126, 128, 133, 145, 146, 150,
    151, 152, 162n19, 197–202
    passim, 262, 265, 266, 272,
    273, 277, 278

Switzerland, 142–63, 269, 275,
  289
  art works, 151, 171
  Cold War and containment, 6
  committees of inquiry, 27–8, 45
  Eizenstat Report and, 34, 36, 37,
    38–41, 42, 43, 45, 142, 145,
    155
  German gold and assets, 11, 14,
    23, 28, 34, 38, 43, 114–21
    passim, 142–4, 193, 194,
    199–200, 202, 204, 310; at
    end of World War II, 125–41
  Historic and Legal Research
    Commission (Bergier
    Commission), 28, 45, 134,
    145–6
  myth of neutrality, 2, 13–15, 69,
    78–9, 160
  Portugal's financial relations
    with, 272–3, 277
  refugee policy, 38, 142, 158
  reparation and restitution, 15,
    16, 17, 27, 28, 39–41, 42,
    45, 69, 91, 138–40, 144–61,
    202, 203, 223
  role in financing German war
    machine, 13–14, 16–17, 36,
    38–9, 142–4, 148–54
  Spain's financial relations with,
    265, 266
  Vatican transactions with
    Germany, 323
  Volcker Committee, 15, 27, 45,
    124n32

Tenenbaum-Tamaroff, Mordechai,
  84
Terezin concentration camp, 44
thefticide, 66–82
Theresienstadt camp, 38
Thomas, Albert, 114, 115
Thorneycroft, Peter, 220
Thurnten, Walther, 148
Times, The, 17
Tiso, Josef, 106
Touvier, Paul, 20, 178, 180
Treblinka camp, 271
Treves, Angiolo, 303

Tripartite Gold Commission
  (TGC), 14, 40, 43, 44, 46, 118,
  120, 122, 202–3, 262, 266,
  275–6
Truman administration, 4, 5, 16,
  43, 156, 211
Truman Doctrine, 4
Tudor, Corneliu Vadim, 91
Turkey, 34, 36, 37, 38, 41, 43, 114,
  152
  Commission on World War II
    Properties, 28

Ukraine,
  Jewish wealth, 57, 61
  restitution, 9, 107
Ulam, Adam, 5
Union Bank of Switzerland, 132,
  159
United Kingdom *see* Britain
United Nations, 79, 266, 309
  Charter, 73
  *Convention on the Non-
    Applicability of Statutory
    Limitations to War Crimes
    and Crimes Against
    Humanity*, 78
  Declaration warning neutral
    states about taking German
    gold *see* Inter-Allied
    Declaration
  General Assembly, Resolution
    (1803), 76
  Information Office, 57
United States, 11, 27, 38, 323
  calls for sanctions against
    Switzerland, 149–50
  Cold War and containment, 4–6
  committees of inquiry, 28–9; *see
    also* Eizenstat Reports
  and Eastern European
    restitution, 8, 90, 91, 92
  and German gold and assets, 14,
    41–2, 46, 115, 117, 119; Bern
    Legation, 129, 133, 135, 137
  refugees, 36, 38, 42
  and restitution, 8, 16, 22, 33–47,
    219–20, 253
  Swiss criticism of, 143, 148–9

United States (*cont.*)
   and Swiss reparation, 14–15, 16,
      125, 139, 223
   see also Allies; Tripartite Gold
      Commission
United States Holocaust Memorial
   Museum, 157
*Universal Declaration of Human
   Rights*, 66, 73, 79
'US and Allied Efforts to Recover
   Gold and Other Assets' *see*
   Eizenstat Reports, 1st Report
   (1997)
'US and Allied Wartime and
   Postwar Relations and
   Negotiations' *see* Eizenstat
   Reports, 2nd Report (1998)
Ustasha regime, Vatican and,
   318–22, 324

Vaala, Grad Liv, 18, 67
Vagts, Detley, 78
Vasilie, Radu, 106
Vatican, 271, 313–26
   statement of responsibility and
      apology, 30n1
Veiga Simões, Alberto da, 272
Vichy regime, 2, 19–20, 68, 71, 72,
   73, 112, 177–92, 276
   laws, 181, 182–3, 184, 185
victim gold, 14, 17, 33, 35–6, 43–4,
   113–14, 120–1, 146, 201–2,
   206
victims, 36
   see also restitution *and under
      individual countries*
Victor Emanuel, King of Italy, 308,
   309
Vike-Freiberga, Vaira, 109n6
Villiger, Kasper, 13
Vita è Bella, La (film), 297
Voetelink, Jan, 273
Volcker, Paul, 15, 27
Volkswagen, 10
Vollan, Torfinn, 233
Vranitsky, Franz, 21, 255

Waldheim, Kurt, 21
Wallenberg brothers, 11, 198, 207

Wallenberg, Raoul, 11, 193, 271
war crimes, 1, 66, 178
   see also crimes against humanity
war criminals, Vatican protection,
   318–19, 320–1, 324
Washington Conference and
   Agreement (1946), 14, 39–40,
   42, 125, 129, 134, 155–6,
   206
Washington Conference on
   Holocaust Era Assets (1998),
   27, 29, 322
Wauters, Arthur, 337
Weber, Ernst, 151, 199–200, 201,
   202
Weimar Republic, 126
Weizman, Chaim, 300
Welczeck, Count, 258
Werner, Kurt, 252–3
West Africa, 112–13
Westlie, Bjorn, 12
Wetter, Ernst, 199
Whaley, Sir David, 221
White, Harry Dexter, 153
Wiebes, Cees, 198
Wiesel, Elie, 79, 237
Wigforss, Ernst, 195
Wildenstein art gallery, 166
Wilhelmstrasse proceedings, 201
Wilson, Harold, 212
Wirtén, Rolf, 27, 204
WJC *see* World Jewish Congress
Wolff family, 218
wolfram, 38, 263–4, 274–5
World Federation of Polish Jews,
   103
World Jewish Congress (WJC), 14,
   27, 35, 50, 59, 86, 145, 146,
   149, 162n19, 279, 300, 301,
   303, 339
   and restitution, 2–3, 6, 7, 12, 15,
      87–8, 92, 93, 105, 121, 203,
      235, 237, 251, 253, 254,
      309–10
World Jewish Congress Institute
   for Jewish Affairs, 2, 3
World Jewish Restitution
   Organization, 7, 15, 27, 29,
      235, 237, 256, 338, 339

in Eastern Europe, 7–10, 87,
    89–91, 95, 99, 100, 102–3,
    106, 107, 108
World War II, 50th anniversary
    commemorations, 1, 22
World Zionist Organization, 300
Wyman, David S., 157

Yad Vashem Holocaust Memorial,
    159, 238, 254, 256, 271, 314,
    338
Yalta Treaty (1945), 225n13
Yeltsin, Boris, 175

Yugoslavia, 84, 303
    cultural plunder, 164
    gold, 118
    Jewish wealth, 49, 50, 59
    restitution, 88, 93

Zanthaky, Theodor, 276
Zaoui, Michel, 180
Ziegler, Jean, 143, 157, 159–60
Zionism, 2
Zucotti, Susan, 300
Zweig, Ron, 248, 256